DATE DUE

THE INTERNATIONAL COMPUTER SOFTWARE INDUSTRY

A Comparative Study of
Industry Evolution and Structure

Edited by

David C. Mowery

New York   Oxford
OXFORD UNIVERSITY PRESS
1996

Oxford University Press

Oxford   New York
Athens   Auckland   Bangkok   Bombay
Calcutta   Cape Town   Dar es Salaam   Delhi
Florence   Hong Kong   Istanbul   Karachi
Kuala Lumpur   Madras   Madrid   Melbourne
Mexico City   Nairobi   Paris   Singapore
Taipei   Tokyo   Toronto

and associated companies in
Berlin   Ibadan

Copyright © 1996 by Oxford University Press, Inc.

Published by Oxford University Press, Inc.,
198 Madison Avenue New York, New York 10016

Oxford is a registered trademark of Oxford University Press.

Library of Congress Cataloging-in-Publication Data
The international computer software industry : a comparative study of
industry evolution and structure / David C. Mowery, editor.
p.   cm.
Includes bibliographical references and index.
ISBN 0-19-509410-7
1. Computer software—Development.   2. Computer software industry.
I.Mowery, David C.
QA76.76.D471555   1996
338.4'70053'09—dc20   95-6887

9 8 7 6 5 4 3 2 1

Printed in the United States of America
on acid-free paper

Acknowledgments

This research project was supported by the Alfred P. Sloan Foundation, through grants to the Consortium on Competitiveness and Cooperation at the Center for Research in Management at the University of California at Berkeley; by the U.C. Berkeley U.S.-Japan Industry Technology Management Program, supported by a grant from the U.S. Air Force Office of Scientific Research; and by the Canadian Institute for Advanced Research. Logistical and secretarial support for meetings of the research team and preparation of this manuscript was provided by the staff of the U.C. Berkeley Institute for Management, Innovation and Organization, especially Patricia Murphy, Stephanie Tibbets, and Debbie Richerson. Professor Richard Nelson of Columbia University provided invaluable advice on project organization and structure, as well as comments on many of the chapters in this volume. Finally, Janet Mowery aided the project by copyediting the manuscript and in many other, more important ways.

Contents

Contributors

Yasunori Baba
Research into Artifacts, Center for
   Engineering (RACE)
University of Tokyo

Thomas Cottrell
Faculty of Commerce
University of Calgary

Peter Grindley
Law and Economics Consulting Group, Inc
Berkeley, California

Valery Katkalo
School of Management
St. Petersburg University

Jonathan Khazam
Intel Corporation
Santa Clara, California

Richard N. Langlois
Department of Economics
University of Connecticut, Storrs

Franco Malerba
Universita Commerciale L. Bocconi
Milan

Robert Merges
Boalt Hall School of Law
University of California, Berkeley

Yuji Mizuta
Mitsubishi Research Institute
Tokyo

David C. Mowery
Haas School of Business
University of California, Berkeley

W. Edward Steinmueller
Maastricht Economic Research Institute on
   Innovation & Technology (MERIT)
University of Limburg

Shinji Takai
School of Business Administration
Kobe University

Salvatore Torrisi
Universita Commerciale L. Bocconi
Milan

THE INTERNATIONAL
COMPUTER SOFTWARE INDUSTRY

1

Introduction

David C. Mowery

This book presents the results of a research project on the evolution of industry structure and firm strategy in the computer software industries of three leading industrial regions (the United States, Japan, and Western Europe) and one emerging market-based economy (the Russian Federation). Despite the rapid growth and economic importance of this industry (in 1985, the OECD estimated that software costs accounted for more than 80 percent of total hardware and software costs associated with new information technology applications), few scholarly studies have been published on its origins and structure in any one of these regions, and virtually no comparative analysis is available.

The chapters in this volume thus represent a pioneering effort, and many of their findings and conclusions must be treated as provisional. Among other reasons for the tentative nature of at least some of the findings of this study is the paucity of reliable, internationally comparable data on industry structure and growth. In addition, this industry has been characterized by extraordinary dynamism and fluidity in structure. These chapters analyze the situation from the perspective of late 1994, and much will have changed by the time this volume appears in print. Nevertheless, the economic importance of the software industry, which will only increase in the future, suggests that it can be overlooked no longer.

In addition to the economic significance of the software industry, several other issues motivated this study. As several of the contributors point out, the commercial fortunes of many new hardware products in the computer and microelectronics industries now depend on the availability of complementary software, much of which may be produced by independent firms. This technological complementarity has affected the strategies of firms seeking to establish their new products as "dominant designs," just as JVC and Matsushita sought to position their VHS videocassette recorder technology in a successful competition with Sony (Cusumano, Mylonadis, and Rosenbloom 1990). Many of the economic returns to advanced computing and information technologies flow from their widespread adoption in diverse applications. Would-be adopters rely on software (some of which may be self-produced) to adapt these technologies to their needs, and the availability of software for operating systems and applications influences the rate of diffusion of computer-based technologies within an economy. Realization of the productivity gains associated with computer-based hardware thus depends in part on the availability of software.

The growing importance of another type of software, "embedded" software, which is incorporated into computer printers, NMR scanners, and other laboratory and scientific instruments, also means that the product development efforts of established producers of instrumentation and computer hardware now rely heavily on software development. Indeed, one informal estimate suggests that perhaps 70 percent of the Hewlett-Packard Company's development engineering staff now are concerned mainly with software development.[1] This volume devotes little attention to embedded software, but the point is clear—in the future the competitive fortunes of hardware products will depend more and more heavily on complementary software. An interesting question concerns whether this interdependent relationship between hardware and software development can be managed across national boundaries. Is a strong national hardware industry necessary to support a strong national software industry, and vice versa?

This study also seeks to extend recent research on "national innovation systems," the network of public and private institutions that affect the creation and adoption of technologies within an economy (see Freeman 1987; Nelson 1993; Lundvall 1992). Much of this research has been concerned with comparisons of different economies, rather than individual industries in various nations. These studies have rarely considered whether the observed differences between national innovation systems reflect differences at the level of national economies or differences in the composition of industries within these economies. By comparing industry structure, government policy, and the institutional environment within a single industry across different regions, this study seeks to distinguish between industry-level and national differences and similarities. This study and other undertakings should enrich our understanding of the dynamics of national innovation systems.

The first section discusses the definition of the industry analyzed in the succeeding chapters. Following this is an overview of the computer software industry's structure. The next section discusses some of the key factors in the industry's competitive dynamics, focusing on the role of "network externalities" and technical standards. The final section describes the organization of the chapters that follow. Discussion of major issues concerning the computer software industry's future, as well as broader concerns of public policy and industry development, are in the chapter that concludes this volume.

DEFINING THE BOUNDARIES OF THE TRADED SOFTWARE INDUSTRY

Computer software is the stored, machine-readable code that instructs a computer (the central processing unit for which often consists of no more than a single microprocessor chip) to carry out specific tasks. For purposes of the discussion in this volume, three broad classes of software can be distinguished: (1) operating systems,

the basic software controls of the operations of a computer, including network controllers and compilers (referred to in the tables in this chapter as "system-level" software); (2) applications tools, which are software tools that support specific applications in software engineering or database management ("tools" in the tables), among
other areas; and (3) applications solutions, which are software instructions that enable
a computer to perform specific tasks of interest to the end user, such as accounting
and word processing ("applications" in the tables).

All three of these types of software can be provided in either "standard" or
"custom" form. Customized software frequently is sold in conjunction with broader
"computer services." There are few internationally comparable data on sales of different classes of software by region, but data from the Organization for Economic Cooperation and Development (OECD) and the International Data Corporation (IDC) suggest that "packaged" software accounted for more than 50 percent of Western
European traded software in 1985, more than 70 percent of the U.S. traded software
market, and less than 10 percent of the Japanese market. In recent years, sales of
"standard" or "packaged" software, especially operating systems and applications
software, have grown more rapidly than sales of "custom" software in all three regions.

Differences among these three regions in the importance of custom and standard
software, and in the relative importance of operating systems, applications tools, and
applications software, reflect differences in the installed base of computing technology in each region. Software for each of four different "platforms" can be distinguished: (1) mainframe computers, (2) minicomputers, (3) workstations, and (4) microcomputers. The last two of these four classes of computer hardware have
expanded dramatically since the early 1980s and account for a large share of the
standard applications and operating system software that has propelled the most rapidly growing segment of the international software industry.

Defining the boundaries and size of the software industry and tracing the evolution of the industry's structure in all of the regions discussed in this volume are
difficult tasks, for several reasons. The chapters in this volume focus on traded software—that is, software produced by one firm or enterprise for sale to another. Measured in terms of the resources devoted to creation of software of all types, however,
the "software industry" is much larger than its "traded" segment. As chapter 2 and
others point out, a great deal of software development still is carried out within
user firms.[2] Moreover, determining the boundaries between "computer services" and
"computer software," even in the traded software sector, may be virtually impossible.[3] Much of the custom operating system and applications software developed for
large mainframe computers, for example, is provided by computer service bureaus
as part of contracts that cover both computer services (such as operating a complex
mainframe or network installation) and software.

At least three groups of firms are active in the traded software industries of the
market-based regions that are the focus of this book: (1) producers of computer systems; (2) independent computer service firms; and (3) independent software vendors.
The evolution of industry structure in all of these regions has followed a broadly
similar trajectory of gradual vertical "dis-integration," albeit one that differs in important details among regions.

Computer manufacturers originally dominated the production of software, which was "bundled" with hardware. In the United States and Japan, major computer manufacturers have in varying degrees and for different reasons "unbundled" their software from hardware, enabling users to purchase these components separately. The service bureaus that originally provided users with operating services and programming solutions also have in some cases "unbundled" their services from their software solutions, providing yet another channel for entry into traded software. In addition, sophisticated users of computer systems, especially mainframe computers, developed expertise in the creation of solutions to their applications and operating system needs. In all three regions, many of the firms that have entered the traded software industry were founded by former employees of major users.

The explosion of computing power and dramatic reductions in hardware costs that have resulted from the development of the microprocessor have had interesting implications for the role of users in the development of the traded software industry. As the costs of computing technology have dropped, the array of potential applications for computers has expanded. The range of idiosyncratic applications and problems for which software could provide solutions also has exploded. This rapid expansion of market niches, especially those for standardized applications, has made it very difficult for major computer manufacturers and established producers of packaged software to maintain a presence in all of them. Rapid hardware diffusion thus has tended to erode vertical integration between hardware and software and until recently appears to have reduced the competitive significance of economies of scope among different standardized applications, limiting the tendencies toward producer concentration that might otherwise be even stronger in an industry such as this, whose costs are primarily fixed.[4]

The rapid diffusion of computing technology, primarily through workstations and microcomputers, into new applications has created enormous opportunities for entry into the creation of solutions for ever more idiosyncratic applications. The expanding installed base of ever cheaper computers has been an important source of dynamism in and entry into the traded software industry.

THE STRUCTURE OF THE INTERNATIONAL SOFTWARE MARKET: AN OVERVIEW

Detailed data on the domestic consumption of custom and packaged software, computer services, and related products and services in the United States, Western Europe, Japan, and Russia are scarce, and internationally comparable data on these markets are even more difficult to obtain. This section discusses the structure of domestic software production and consumption in the United States, Japan, and Western Europe, drawing on data from the OECD and the International Data Corporation, a leading U.S. market research firm. They should be viewed as provisional and indicative of differences in market structure rather than precise estimates of absolute magnitudes. Needless to say, they present a "snapshot" of the industry, and some elements of its structure have changed since these data were published.

The data in Table 1-1 reveal one of the most striking contrasts among these three markets, the significance of packaged software. In 1985, packaged software accounted for more than 75 percent of the traded software in the U.S. domestic

Table 1-1. Domestic consumption of software and computer services in the United States, Japan, and Western Europe, 1985, 1992, and 1994 (dollars in billions)

	Packaged software			Custom software	Processing services
	1985	1992	1994	1985	1985
United States	12.60	28.46	35.60	4.17	11.1
Japan	.27	5.96	5.95	2.74	3.77
Western Europe[a]	5.21	23.85	26.57	4.72	5.33

Source: Estimates of 1985 consumption are from OECD 1989; estimates of 1992 and 1994 consumption are from IDC 1993, 1995.

[a] Western Europe is defined as the following seventeen nations: Austria, Belgium, Denmark, Finland, France, Germany, Greece, Ireland, Italy, Netherlands, Norway, Portugal, Spain, Sweden, Switzerland, Turkey, and United Kingdom.

markct, a substantially higher share than that of Western Europe (54 percent) and far larger than its 9.4 percent share of Japan's domestic software consumption. By 1994, however, the Western European market for packaged software had increased in size from slightly more than 40 percent of the U.S. market to nearly 75 percent. The Japanese market for packaged software, while still less than one quarter the size of the U.S. market, also grew rapidly during 1985–94. The adoption of desktop computers in Western Europe and Japan has spurred more rapid growth in consumption of packaged software in these regions—as the data below indicate, the U.S. market for packaged software in the early 1990s was not much larger than that of Western Europe. But most recent studies of these markets conclude that U.S. software consumption is dominated by packaged software to a greater extent than is true of Japan or Western Europe.[5]

The large size of the U.S. packaged software market, as well as the fact that it was the first large market to experience rapid growth (reflecting the earlier appearance and rapid diffusion of mainframe and minicomputers, followed by the explosive growth of desktop computer use during the 1980s), have given the U.S. firms that pioneered in their domestic packaged market a formidable "first-mover" advantage that now is being exploited internationally. At present, links between domestic hardware and software industries may be of secondary importance in the competitive dynamics of the software industry, but U.S. software firms' presence in the first mass market for computer hardware gave them competitive advantages, most notably in tools and operating systems that are not easily overcome by prospective entrants from other nations in mass-market packaged software.

Tables 1-2, 1-3, and 1-4 contain data on market share and consumption patterns in packaged software for 1992 and 1993, using the product categories defined earlier.[6] The data in Table 1-2 display the market shares of U.S. and non-U.S. firms in the three major industrial markets in each of the three classes of packaged software in 1993. The data include packaged software produced by manufacturers of computers as well as the products of independent software vendors. These data reveal the dominance of U.S. firms in the U.S. and foreign packaged software markets. U.S. firms' market share in their home market is greater than 80 percent for all three types of packaged software and exceeds 60 percent in non-U.S. markets for tools and

Table 1-2. Market shares of U.S. and non-U.S. firms in packaged software, by region and product category, 1993 (percent)

Consuming region	Tools	Applications	System-level software
U.S. firms			
United States	83.5	87.9	94.3
Western Europe	74.6	41.3	88.7
Japan	64.7	35.3	73.7
Non-U.S. firms			
United States	16.5	12.1	5.7
Western Europe	25.3	58.7	11.3
Japan	35.3	64.7	26.3

Source: IDC 1994.

system-level software. In applications software, however, U.S. firms' market shares are considerably lower. Non-U.S. firms account for more than 58 percent of Western Europe's applications software consumption and more than 64 percent of the Japanese applications software market. These differences among the three classes of packaged software appear to reflect the importance of user-producer linkages in applications, which make much greater demands for "user-friendliness" and adaptation to local operating conditions (for example, non-English languages and characters). These linkages also account for the importance of domestic firms in supplying custom software to local firms, an industry characteristic discussed in chapters 5 and 7 in this volume.[7]

Manufacturers of computer systems remain important suppliers of both custom and packaged software in all three major markets (See chapters 2 and 5). Table 1-3 contains 1993 market share data for U.S. and non-U.S. independent software vendors (ISVs) and systems manufacturers in the packaged software markets of Japan, Western Europe, and the United States. U.S.-based ISVs account for more than 60 percent of the U.S. packaged software market; when the shares of U.S. and non-U.S. ISVs are combined, the ISV share of the U.S. software market rises to more than 69 percent. But the share of ISVs in the U.S. market is in fact slightly smaller than the market share of ISVs (both U.S. and non-U.S.) in the Western European packaged software market, which amounts to more than 70 percent. U.S. and non-U.S. ISVs account for just over 63 percent of the far smaller Japanese packaged software market.

Despite significant differences in size among these three packaged software markets, the producer structure within each is remarkably similar, with ISVs accounting for roughly two-thirds of local demand. Moreover, the market shares of non-U.S. ISVs exceed those of U.S. ISVs in both Japan and Western Europe. U.S. systems manufacturers dominate the non-ISV supply of packaged software, accounting for more than one-quarter of demand in the United States, Western Europe, and Japan. Not surprisingly, the market share of systems manufacturers is greatest in operating systems, reflecting the large markets for the standard operating systems for leading mainframe and minicomputer products supplied by multinational U.S. computer manufacturers such as IBM and Digital Equipment. ISVs accounted for less than 40 percent of packaged operating system revenues in all three markets in 1992. Their share of packaged applications software revenues, however, exceeded 85 percent in these three markets in 1992 (IDC 1993).

Table 1-4 contains data on the relative importance of various computer "platforms" in the global packaged software market for 1992, as well as projected rates of growth in the packaged software revenues associated with each platform. In 1992 mainframes accounted for more than 31 percent of global packaged software revenues, minicomputers (a category that includes the AS/400 and the DEC VAX) accounted for 19 percent, "personal computers" (which include the Macintosh and the IBM PC) accounted for almost 33 percent, and Unix-based systems (the majority of which are desktop workstations) accounted for almost 17 percent. Mainframes accounted for the largest shares of operating system and tool software revenues (respectively, 47.5 percent and 30.9 percent) in 1992, and PCs accounted for the largest share of packaged applications software revenues (46.5 percent). But the outlook for revenue growth clearly favors the desktop—projected revenue growth for the IBM PC, the Macintosh, and Unix-based systems during 1993–97 exceeds those of all other systems (with the possible exception of the IBM AS/400). Mainframe packaged software revenues are projected to grow at less than 10 percent annually during this period.

COMPETITIVE DYNAMICS IN THE INDUSTRY

Two characteristics of the economics of traded software have given rise to first-mover advantages and have affected the development of the traded software industries of Japan, the United States, and Western Europe. First, the economics of software production, like those of movies, records, television programming, and books, are dominated by the fixed costs of development. Software products that can be sold into a large market with little or no customization for specific users or market segments therefore can be extremely profitable. Because the installed base of microcomputers

Table 1-3. Share of worldwide packaged software revenues, by vendor category, 1993 (percent)

Independent software vendors by consuming region:			
U.S.	48.3	Non-U.S.	20.2
United States	61.0	United States	8.5
Western Europe	39.2	Western Europe	31.2
Japan	30.1	Japan	33.0
Systems manufacturers by consuming region:			
U.S.	26.7	Non-U.S.	4.9
United States	27.9	United States	2.6
Western Europe	24.1	Western Europe	5.6
Japan	24.0	Japan	12.9

Source: IDC 1994.

exceeds the population of mainframes or minicomputers, independent software developers face powerful incentives to serve the microcomputer market with standardized applications programs. The large markets for standardized software that have been created by the rapid diffusion of low-cost microcomputer software, the higher potential profits, and the relatively low entry barriers associated with software development have led a large number of new producers to enter the market. The diffusion of microcomputer hardware and expansion in packaged applications software markets thus reinforce one another.

The role of standards and "network externalities" in the software industry distinguish this industry from the other "software" industries noted above and may make it difficult for a new entrant to dislodge a successful and profitable first-mover. Standards affect this industry's development in several, sometimes contradictory, ways. Interoperability (the ability of programs to operate together and exchange information) is important to many users of software, especially business users. As a result, consumer choices among competing software products are influenced by the number of other adopters (a classic network externality). Once a first-mover is established, these externalities can reinforce their dominance of a particular standard application.

Table 1-4. Revenue shares and projected growth rates for packaged software by product category and platform

Platform	Share of 1992 worldwide revenues (%)	Projected annual growth rate, 1993–97 (%)
IBM AS/400		
Tools	5.1	13.7
Applications	6.2	12.5
System-level software	8.7	9.9
DEC VAX		
Tools	11.7	10.8
Applications	8.0	8.7
System-level software	2.7	7.1
IBM mainframe		
Tools	28.4	9.5
Applications	16.2	7.3
System-level software	44.6	5.8
PC		
Tools	24.5	17.9
Applications	38.9	16.7
System-level software	18.1	15.2
Apple Macintosh		
Tools	2.7	16.3
Applications	7.5	14.5
System-level software	2.4	12.0
Unix-based systems		
Tools	19.7	21.5
Applications	14.5	16.9
System-level software	16.8	16.7

Source: IDC 1993.

These first-mover advantages have given U.S. packaged software firms considerable strength vis-a-vis would-be entrants in Western Europe (see chapter 7) and Japan.

But the development of de facto standards can also support entry. Widely adopted operating systems such as DOS and Windows, for example, have provided a solid foundation for firms that provide standard applications programs (drawn by the ever-expanding array of applications associated with hardware diffusion). Indeed, applications software is an example of an industry that does not adhere to a model of technology life cycles (Utterback 1994), in which the emergence of a "dominant design" in an industry is followed by a gradual decline in entry. The creation of de facto hardware standards in microcomputers and workstations has similar effects—the IBM PC architecture's emergence as a "dominant design" propelled the supplier of its operating system, Microsoft, to a position of enormous wealth and power and attracted the attention of developers of complementary software applications. The absence of a comparably dominant hardware architecture in Japan has stunted the development of its domestic software industry, as chapter 6 points out.

This dynamic also operates in reverse—the success of a specific hardware innovation, especially in the large markets populated by less sophisticated users, depends on the creation of software to support use of the hardware. Just as the victory of JVC/Matsushita over Sony in the "Beta-VHS wars" depended on the availability of abundant software for VHS videocassette recorders, the availability of software for one or another competing hardware product affects its commercial prospects. The discussion of reduced-instruction-set computing (RISC) technologies in chapter 4 pursues this theme.

The interaction of standards and network externalities may provide a partial explanation for an enduring feature of industry structure—its high degree of segmentation. With some important exceptions (for example, Microsoft in recent years), firms in one segment of the traded software industry have not successfully entered other segments. Firms specializing in operating systems have been largely unsuccessful in extending their product lines into applications, for example. Firms that have dominated one specific segment (such as spreadsheets) have rarely proved able to enter other segments (word processing or databases). The high degree of segmentation appears to reflect the strength of first-mover advantages, which are reinforced by the investment of users in the skills and applications that complement a dominant operating system or even a dominant application in word processing or spreadsheets. In addition, as Swann and Gill (1993) point out, the user interface developed for one application historically has proven less effective or desirable in another, making it difficult for a leading firm in one market segment to establish a strong position in another.

Microsoft may prove to be an exception to this historical pattern in its ability to exploit economies of scope among its products; whether this firm's unprecedented success prefigures the future or is an anomaly remains to be seen. Regardless of Microsoft's success in spanning segments of the microcomputer software industry, it has not yet expanded significantly beyond microcomputers.[8] Firms serving one segment of the platform market—for example, mainframes—rarely have been able to move into a position of importance in other hardware platforms. The competitive significance of this limited firm mobility may decline, however, as and if the economic importance of mainframe and minicomputer platforms continues to shrink.

THE STRUCTURE OF THIS VOLUME

This volume begins with three complementary analyses of the U.S. traded software industry. Chapter 2 examines the development of the U.S. software industry's structure, discussing the origins of software in the programming efforts of both mainframe computer producers and users and describing the dramatic changes in industry structure wrought by the "unbundling" of software and hardware in the late 1960s, as well as the declines in the cost of computing power resulting from advances in microelectronics technology. Chapter 3 summarizes the federal government's role in the development of the U.S. software industry. Although this role has not been widely analyzed, it appears to have been at least as influential in the U.S. software industry as in such other postwar high-technology industries as microelectronics. Chapter 4 analyzes one example of the hardware-software interaction and "bandwagons" that are so important to firm strategy in the United States, where developers of standard software are not integrated with hardware producers. The chapter compares the strategies of competitors in the reduced-instruction-set computing (RISC) microprocessor industry, strategies whose success has rested on the creation of bandwagons among software developers.

Chapters 5 and 6 consider aspects of the Japanese software industry. Chapter 5 focuses on the changing patterns of vertical integration and "dis-integration" in the Japanese mainframe computer software industry, discussing the role of sophisticated users and mainframe computer manufacturers as sources of new firms in custom software production. Chapter 6 compares the development of the microcomputer software industries in Japan and the United States, examining the detrimental consequences for Japan's software firms of the lack of standardization in the Japanese installed base of microcomputers.

Chapters 7, 8, and 9 discuss the computer software industry in Western Europe and the Russian Federation. Chapter 7 provides an overview of industry evolution and current trends in the Western European regional software industry and focuses in detail on the differences in competitive strategy and human resource investments among firms operating in different segments of the industry. The chapter also includes a brief discussion of the strategic technology programs for the software industry that have been implemented regionally by the EU Commission. Chapter 8 examines the software industry in the United Kingdom, which was a pioneer in computer technology. The chapter describes how many of the influences that contributed to the collapse of the British computer hardware industry have also prevented the growth of a strong British software industry outside of a few niches that serve markets for customized software. The chapter includes a critical evaluation of the most recent British government initiative to revitalize the domestic software industry, the Alvey program. Chapter 9 discusses the emergence of a software industry in the economic transition now under way in the Russian Federation. The Russian software industry developed a unique structure during the cold war period, based on independent research institutes' serving the needs of various military services and government agencies in a system that combined impressive theoretical accomplishments with relatively poor computer hardware. The chapter examines recent changes in the policy environment of this emergent industry, focusing in particular on intellectual property reform and on the rapidly expanding web of joint ventures between foreign and domestic enterprises.

Chapter 10 considers one of the most important influences on the development of the computer software industry, intellectual property rights. As the chapter makes clear, computer software poses significant challenges to the existing regime of copyright and patent protection that prevails throughout the industrial world. Moreover, the economic risks associated with excessively restrictive intellectual property protection may be more significant in this industry than in many other high-technology industries, because of the unique nature of the production technology and of software as a product. Chapter 11 provides a brief conclusion that outlines some of the important issues that remain for managers and policymakers concerned with this industry. Here as elsewhere in this volume, the preliminary nature of our conclusions and the tentative nature of any policy implications cannot be emphasized too strongly.

Computer software is a young industry that has experienced rapid change in market structure and rapid growth in output. Although many of the influences on industry structure and competitition discussed in this volume will remain important in the future, their precise effects on industry structure, especially in the face of revolutionary change in computer hardware technology, remain uncertain. Nevertheless, this volume should serve to spark the curiosity and intellectual energy of scholars who for too long have ignored the traded computer software industry.

NOTES

1. I am indebted to Dr. Sara Beckman, former manager of strategic planning in corporate manufacturing for Hewlett-Packard, for this observation.

2. Moreover, much of the software development activity carried out by users is likely to be reported as part of their R&D spending. Identical activities performed by independent software firms may or may not be similarly reported, leading to bias in national R&D statistics.

3. For example, data from the OECD and IDC that are cited elsewhere in this chapter and in this volume do not always agree on the types of services included under the heading "computer services" and therefore may yield different estimates of the size of a broadly defined software industry (that is, one that includes services a well as traded software).

4. Swann and Gill (1993) analyze data from 1987 on the leading producers of PC software in each of twenty-seven product categories and find very little overlap among the leading firms in each, concluding that "the proliferation of software categories can be seen as a deconcentrating force in the development of the software market" (176). This observation, however, applies mainly to applications. The emergence of dominant operating systems, of course, has increased producer concentration in this segment of the software industry.

5. For example, the statement in the December 1993 study of world packaged software markets by the International data Corporation noted that "custom software, produced by consultants and system integrators, constitutes a greater percentage of the software market in all regions of the world except the United States" (IDC 1993, 7). Differences in market structure also may result in some underestimation of Japan's domestic consumption, since a larger share (than in the United States and Western Europe) of Japanese software is supplied in bundled form by computer manufactures (see chapt. 5)

6. "Tools" are "programs used to generate applications to retrieve, organize, manage, and manipulate data" (IDC 1993, 65) and include database programs, programmer tools, and computer-aided software engineering products. "Applications" include "programs designed to solve specific problems inherent across all industries or in a particular industry or business function," e.g., standard office tools, such as word processing and spreadsheet software, as well as applications specific to a given industry, such as banking or finance. The last category,

"System-level software," includes operating systems and software controlling network operations.

7. In von Hippel's terms (1994), much of the necessary knowledge for custom software innovation is "sticky" and may not be easily accessible for a foreign firm.

8. In mid-1984, sales of Microsoft's "Windows NT" operating system, which was intended to support networking and provide a point of entry into large systems, had fallen well short of the firm's projections for first-year sales (Clark 1994). The introduction of the new version of Windows for personal computers in 1995/1996 may extend Microsoft's presence into on-line services.

REFERENCES

Abernathy, W. J., and J. M. Utterback. 1978. "Patterns of Industrial Innovation." *Technology Review* 80: 40–47.

Clark, D. 1994. "Microsoft, AT&T Broaden Push to Make Windows NT a Standard for Big Jobs." *Wall Street Journal,* 19 August.

Cusumano, M., Y. Mylonadis, and R. S. Rosenbloom. 1990. "Strategic Maneuvering and Mass-Market Dynamics: The Triumph of Beta over VHS." Working paper 90-5, Consortium on Competitiveness and Cooperation, Haas School of Business, U.C. Berkeley.

Freeman, C. 1987. *Technology and Economic Performance.* London: Frances Pinter.

International Data Corporation (IDC). 1993. *1993 Worldwide Software Review and Forecast.* Framingham, Mass.: IDC.

———. 1994. *1994 Worldwide Software Review and Forecast.* Framingham, Mass.: IDC.

Lundvall, B.-A. 1992. *National Systems of Innovation—Towards a Theory of Innovation and Interactive Learning.* London: Frances Pinter.

Mowery, D. C. 1995. "The Boundaries of the U.S. Firm in R&D." In N. Lamoureaux and D. Rapp, eds., *The Coordination of Economic Activity within and among Firms.* Chicago: University of Chicago Press for NBER.

Nakahara, T. 1993. "The Industrial Organization and Information Structure of the Software Industry: A U.S.-Japan Comparison." Center for Economic Policy Research, Stanford University. Duplicated.

Nelson, R. R. 1993. *National Innovation Systems: A Comparative Analysis.* New York: Oxford University Press.

Organization for Economic Cooperation and Development (OECD). 1985. *Software: An Emerging Industry.* Paris: OECD.

———. 1989. *The Internationalisation of Software and Computer Services.* Paris: OECD.

Swann, P., and J. Gill 1993. *Corporate Vision and Rapid Technological Change.* London: Routledge.

Teece, D. J. 1986. "Profiting from Technological Innovation: Implications for Integration, Collaboration, Licensing, and Public Policy." *Research Policy* 15: 285–305.

Utterback, J. M. 1994. *Mastering the Dynamics of Innovation.* Boston: Harvard Business School Press.

Von Hippel, E. 1994. " 'Sticky Information' and the Locus of Problem Solving: Implications for Innovation." *Management Science* 40: 429–39.

2

The U.S. Software Industry:
An Analysis and Interpretive History

W. Edward Steinmueller

INTRODUCTION AND ECONOMIC FOUNDATIONS

Over the past fifty years innovations in semiconductors, data storage devices, computer architecture, software, and data communications have revolutionized information collection, storage, processing, and distribution, creating new industries and transforming industries inherited from past industrial eras. Explanations of this revolution in information technology have focused on the extraordinary reductions in the cost of the hardware components,[1] largely to the neglect of the role of computer software in these developments. Nonetheless, every application of information technology has required complementary "software"—computer instructions that transform the *tabula rasa* of computer hardware into machines that perform useful functions.[2]

This chapter offers answers for several basic questions about the historical development of the U.S. software industry. First, what determines the division of labor in software production among hardware producers, computer users, and the companies that produce software as their primary business, the "independent software vendors"? Second, have key events in the history of the U.S. software industry created a distinctly "American" system of software production that need not or cannot serve as a model for the development of the software industries in other nations? Third, what economic effects follow from the high fixed costs of initial software creation and the low marginal costs of reproducing software? In answering these questions this chapter draws upon economic theory as well as descriptive material from industrial and technological commentaries.

Several definitions and distinctions are useful in setting the stage for answering our main questions. In this chapter, software is a general term of reference for instructions that control the operation of information technology hardware. Programmers are people who devise specific collections of instructions called software programs or, simply, programs. The use of the word "systems" is ubiquitous and unavoidable; it is used here to refer to either complementary combinations of hardware and software or to collections of software programs that are "interoperable," that is, programs that operate together and exchange information. The technologies for acquiring, storing, processing, and transmitting information are collectively referred to as "information technology" and include both hardware and software components.

Software is classified as a "business service" in the U.S. income and product accounts despite the fact that "packaged software" products more closely resemble personal computer peripherals or books in their methods of distribution and reproduction. Software that is delivered as part of a business service can and should be distinguished from software that is sold as a product. Software services are performed within the programming services (SIC 7371) and integrated computer systems (SIC 7373) industries, although the latter industry performs hardware engineering design activities in addition to creating software. Sales of software as a distinct product are recorded as output of the packaged software industry (SIC 7372). Although the production of software is a labor-intensive activity, in principle software is *reproducible* at very low costs relative to the costs of its creation, a characteristic that is unusual in the service industries. This means that companies engaged in selling programming services will seek opportunities to reuse part or all of the software created for previous clients in selling service to new clients.[3] A software program that is produced only once should be viewed as a service output, while a program that is reproduced dozens or millions of times has development and marketing characteristics closer to those of manufactured goods. Understandably, such distinctions are not made in assembling statistics in U.S. income and product accounts, and the output of the packaged software (SIC 7372), programming services (SIC 7371), and integrated computer system design (SIC 7373) sectors contain an unmeasured mixture of "one-off," "reused," and reproduced software in each subsector.[4] Of course, creation of software for extensive reproduction is a primary aim in the packaged software (SIC 7372) subsector.

A second important distinction that is relevant in examining the software industry is the division of output between intermediate and final goods. Intermediate goods are used to produce other goods and services, while final goods are sold to consumers. With the recent, and nearly simultaneous, arrival of home computers, information services, and programmable consumer electronics systems (for example, video game systems), independent software producers and system producers' sale of software as a final good have become a major industry. Indeed, the conceptual and technological distinctions between such "consumer" software products as games, and those historically considered to be "entertainment" such as music and video products, are rapidly fading as suggested by the increasing frequency of the term "multimedia" to refer to hybrids of video, sound, and software. Nonetheless, most of our attention in this chapter, as in the other chapters in this volume, is devoted to software that is an intermediate good, employed by businesses in the production of other goods and services or sold for the same purposes to other enterprises. We ignore many of the problems of producing and marketing consumer-oriented software.

A third important distinction is between software and the production of other economic commodities. On the one hand, software, like other commodities, requires inputs that have alternative uses and, once produced, has economic value as an intermediate or final good. But, software is also an unusual economic commodity because its marginal costs of reproduction are very low or negligible. The low costs of software reproduction imply that society must grant businesses some right to control reproduction (and charge higher prices than the cost of reproduction) if investments are to be made in software creation, especially packaged software. Otherwise, third parties would make a business of reproducing software, and competition would drive the costs of software to the low marginal cost of its reproduction.[5] As a result, intellectual property protection is a key policy influence on firm strategy and evolution in this industry, as chapter 10 points out, and the respective political influence of hardware manufacturers, custom software and service providers, and producers of packaged software may influence the structure of software-related intellectual property protection.

Computer producers, users, and independent software vendors each have distinct incentives to produce software. Computer system producers have incentives to produce software because software is an economic complement to the sale of computer systems—that is, the availability of software will increase the sale of computers. Ideally, computer producers can receive revenues from the sale of both computers and software. In practice, hardware producers in the United States, with the notable exception of IBM, have received a diminishing share of their revenues from software production.[6] U.S. hardware producers' involvement in software creation has followed a pattern of vertical "dis-integration," favoring user-produced software and the entry of independent software producers.

Despite the incentives to combine hardware and software production, the ability of computer producers to understand and solve specific user problems is limited. The presence in the United States of an enormous variety of industries that use information technology has been a stimulus to the creation of a correspondingly large volume of user-created software. However, as in other nations, users have little incentive to sell the software they develop to rivals.

The potential profits from widespread sales of particular software products have encouraged the entry of a third group of producers, "independent software vendors" (ISVs).[7] The boundary in software-producing activities among ISVs, computer producers, and users is determined by limits in the abilities of computer producers' ability to increase their "span of control" of joint hardware and software creation and by limits in the capabilities and incentives of users to produce software for sale to other firms. These factors, along with the design and marketing abilities of ISV firms, constitute the "infrastructure" of software creation in any particular nation and differ across nations with different patterns of industrial development. For example, the diversity of user industries in the United States has made it difficult for computer manufacturers to pursue vertical market strategies similar to those pursued by some European computer manufacturers.[8] This was not because such strategies were unavailable but because computer manufacturers' gains from a more exclusive pursuit of hardware improvement (combined with the vertical "dis-integration" of software production) were greater than their gains from controlling integrated software and hardware development in a large number of vertical markets. For example, Digital Equipment Corporation (DEC) abandoned its early position as a leading producer of integrated hardware and software systems for newspaper publishing, ceding the hardware integration and software development of such systems to other companies.

In the U.S. market, most hardware vendors have retreated from software production, and as described below, recent entrants into computer production are minor participants in software production. The most likely explanation for their behavior is that U.S. computer producers have found that ISV entry results in a greater supply of software than would otherwise be available. The U.S. software industry has also benefited from the prior existence of an enormous number of small contract programming companies that originated from the needs of larger companies and governments for custom software production. This infrastructure has played a major role in the growth of the U.S. packaged software industry, through its development of human capital (noted as a problem of the European industry in chapter 7 of this volume) and its pioneering development of particular applications.[9] In the U.S. market, ISV participation appears to have fostered a faster sales growth than computer producers could have realized from joint production of hardware and software. For users, the presence of ISVs offers an alternative to internal production.

Change in the solutions to the "make or buy" problems of computer producers and users, solutions that are *unique to different stages of the of evolution of the U.S. computer market,* along with some key legal and policy decisions, explain the changing division of labor among producers of software in the United States. In other words, our working hypothesis is that there is no "natural" industrial structure for software production; the structure and evolution of a nation's software industry depends upon particular historical and institutional events. This chapter examines this hypothesis by exploring the development of the U.S. software industry, beginning with the period before its birth. During this period, the design and construction of computers as scientific instruments were commingled with writing computer instructions. I bring this discussion to the present day when independent software companies produce and sell packaged software for large installed bases of particular computer "platforms." Although it is tempting to simplify this account by discussing only the independent companies that produce software "products," that approach would obscure the enormous economic significance of software production by other organizations, including producers of hardware and the users of information technology. Because the specifics of history, institutions, and participants are important, a study of the software industry's evolution must begin at the national or regional level, rather than in the "global market."

The outcome of these evolving make-or-buy decisions of computer users and producers in the U.S. market in recent years can be briefly summarized. Virtually all of the people involved in the information technology industry, from electronic component producers to users, write software. Software written for internal use within companies has historically been the largest single source of investment in software creation; this type (which is not separately captured in the U.S. national income accounts) is followed by software produced by design service and software firms and software "embedded" in electronic systems.[10] In 1987 the receipts of U.S. software programming service companies (SIC 7371) were $14.2 billion, the receipts for computer integrated systems design (SIC 7373) were $7.1 billion, and the receipts from prepackaged software (SIC 7372) sales were $5.9 billion. The preponderance of revenues from programming services and a large share of integrated systems design revenues are derived from the production of "specialized" software solutions that are unique to individual companies. By contrast, packaged software is an intermediate good or "tool" that provides applications solutions or entertainment for large numbers of users.

In assaying the size of the software industry, it is important to understand that the sale of software services and packaged software does not include the investment in software creation (programming) *within* organizations. Some indication of the magnitude of these activities is available by analyzing the patterns of employment of software engineers, which are available for broad industry groups. For example, "business services" (SIC 73) includes prepackaged software, software programming services, and computer integrated systems design, as well as other information processing-intensive subindustries such as credit reporting, advertising, and mailing services. In 1990 the "business service" employment of system analysts and programmers was 74,000 and 130,940 respectively. In 1988 and 1989, by comparison, 217,310 system analysts and 264,110 programmers were employed in manufacturing and the other service industries (including state and local government). In other words, establishments outside the business service sector employed many more computer-related professionals (individuals who bear a major responsible for specifying and creating software) than did firms within the software industry. Obviously, programmers and system analysts engaged in business services (within SIC 73), manufacturing, and all service sector activities (excluding SIC 73) are not engaged solely or even primarily in writing software. Nevertheless, the "in-house" employment of these occupational classes is so large that it raises the possibility that in-house software may account for a larger share of total U.S. software production than the output of firms producing for the (custom or packaged) market.

This chapter addresses the development of the software industry chronologically, beginning with the origins of software creation and the early history of the software industry from 1950 to 1965, a period when computer producers dominated software production. During the critical 1965–70 period rapid growth in the utilization of computers, antitrust litigation, and delays in some key technological improvements fostered enormous growth in user-produced software and the birth of an independent software vendor sector. Two themes that shaped developments in the 1970s were the growing dissatisfaction of users with the productivity and effectiveness of their internal software development efforts and the impact of smaller-scale "minicomputers," which altered both the distribution of software-creating activities and the use of computers within organizations. The chapter then discusses the role of the personal computer and the rise of "software publishing" and introduces the final element of the story to date, the role of consulting companies and information system integrators in addressing the problems of internal software development. The final section summarizes these historical developments and identifies some of the forces that are shaping developments during the 1990s. This history addresses two elementary questions noted earlier: (1) What determines the division of labor in software production among hardware producers, computer users, the companies that produce software as their primary business, and the "independent software vendors"? and (2) What key events in the history of the U.S. software industry have created a distinctly "American system" of software production?

The third question this chapter addresses is, Why has software persistently been identified as a "bottleneck" in the growth of information technology markets and as a drag on the realization of productivity gains from utilization of information technology? This question has both a general answer dealt with briefly here in the introduction and specific answers for the United States, which are main themes later in this chapter. The basis for this question is the observation of rapid rates of growth in the level and share of software costs for information technology systems (see, for example, OECD 1985). The growth of the cost share of software has been linked to the "craft production" techniques in the software industry that allegedly cannot match the pace of hardware performance improvement (Baumol, Blackman, and Wolff 1989). The purported result is rapidly rising costs of information technology due to the "bottleneck" of increasing software costs, a consequence may help explain the low measured productivity gains from investments in information technology.[11]

Do recent data on hardware and software expenditures support the "bottleneck" characterization? The sales of packaged computer software and services as a share of computer sales from 1970 to 1993 are depicted in Figure 2–1 using current dollar revenues.[12] Figure 2-1 suggests that during the 1970s expenditures on packaged software and software services grew *at the same rate* as hardware expenditures. Thus, unless it can be established that the *amount* of purchased software utilized during the 1970s *decreased* (which is unlikely), price increases do not provide a plausible explanation for that decade's trends in software expenditure. In other words, for the bottleneck hypothesis to be valid, software use would have had to decrease. The microcomputer revolution of the 1980s accelerated growth in software sales, pushing software's share above 50 percent by 1988 and close to 75 percent by 1993. During the 1980s, the enormous growth of low-priced "packaged software" for personal computers mean that growth again cannot be explained with a cost-push or price-increase model that is consistent with the bottleneck view.[13] Outward shifts in demand and relatively elastic demand appear to better explain increasing expenditures on software than does a tightening bottleneck. This analysis, however, does not address the costs of internally produced software.

Although it is an inaccurate general characterization of U.S. industrial experience, the bottleneck problem has shaped the interactions among hardware producers, computer users, and independent software vendors and has motivated some of the key institutional and policy events in the U.S. industry's development. Institutional reforms have been directed at sources of cost growth, particularly the development costs and maintenance expenses of internally produced software. Thus, specific responses to the software bottleneck in the United States included changes in the organization of the delivery of information processing services (such as the growth of system integration and outsourcing services) as well as the deployment of specific types of hardware (such as minicomputers). In both cases, efforts were directed at widening a bottleneck, although this bottleneck may be more accurately characterized as organizational rather than stemming from software per se.

EARLY DEVELOPMENTS: ORIGINS UNTIL 1965

The development of computers during and immediately after World War II was directed toward scientific and technical rather than business objectives.[14] Like their

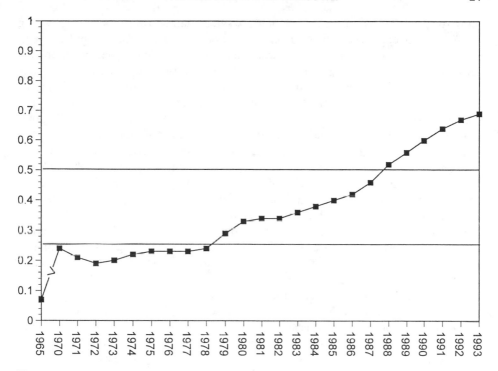

Figure 2-1. Software and service sales revenue as a proportion of computer sales revenue, 1965 and 1970–93. *Source:* Juliessen and Juliessen 1990, 10.3–10.4.

electromechanical business machine precursors, early computers were programmed by rewiring and thus were highly specialized to particular information processing tasks (see Austrian 1982). After the war, Alan Turing and John von Neumann's ideas for a stored program computer created the possibility of a general-purpose problem-solving device that could be "programmed" to emulate and replace more specialized data processing machines.[15] Programmability and the possibility of "reusable" software gave general-purpose computers an advantage over the large installed base of punch-card data processing equipment.[16] Maurice Wilkes, director of Cambridge University's Mathematical Library expressed prescient views on the economic importance of reusable software: "There would be almost as much capital sunk in the library of sub-routines as the machine itself and builders of new machines in the future might wish to make use of the same order code as an existing machine in order that the sub-routines could be taken over without modification" (quoted in Bashe et al. 1986, 322). In short, the problems of software "lock-in" and the incentive for creating machines that could emulate the operation of earlier machines were present at the start of the industry.[17]

An important early demonstration that computers could be used for purposes other than scientific computation was the development of the SAGE air defense system whose software requirements led to the founding of the System Development Corporation in 1956. The early commercial use of computers in the 1950s, however, also gradually stimulated a market for software services. Producers of computer systems such as IBM provided programming services and software tools.[18] Providing these complements accelerated adoption of new general-purpose computers, reinforced links between computer producers and users, and laid a foundation for the reuse of software in future machines. If software instructions could be made less machine-specific, the costs of adopting new machines could be reduced.[19] Computer system manufacturers accordingly focused on producing the tools for creating applications programs rather than developing application programs themselves.[20] Corporations using computers thus needed to develop software for their own information processing applications. As noted above, computer producers have an incentive to stimulate the production of any and all software that will increase the value of computers and enhance their sales of computers. Accordingly, IBM also supported the formation of users groups such as Share, which, as the name implies, was devoted to the exchange of software routines.[21] Computer system producers that offered services and software to stimulate the use of computers, users that developed applications for their own use, and users that cooperated in the exchange of programming routines and methods formed the early economic organization for software development activities. The structure of this organization heavily favored the "make" rather than the "buy" choice in the acquisition of software.

Larger companies scaled up their in-house software development to utilize faster processing capabilities and substantial improvements in peripheral devices such as tape drives, printers, and disk drives. In-house development was facilitated by growing use of higher-level languages. One of the first and most successful of these, Fortran (for "formula translator"), was introduced in 1957, and a 1958 survey of twenty-six Share user installations found that over 50 percent of these sites employed it for the majority of their problems, a rate of use that soon accelerated with further improvements in available compilers (Bashe et al. 1986, 357). The substantial improvements in programmer productivity made possible by Fortran lessened the severity of bottlenecks in in-house development efforts, extended the range of feasible applications, and freed users to consider new machines with compatible language features. Higher-level languages reduced the costs of in-house development, further tilting the make-or-buy decisions toward the "make" outcome because they reduced the requirement for in-house creation of highly specialized (machine-specific) "machine language" programs, freeing programmer resources that would otherwise have slowed developments and forced many companies to employ external programming services.

While Fortran was used for a wide range of applications, the demand for a high-level language for accounting and other business applications was keenly felt by the user community (ibid., 364). These developments, as well as the sponsorship by the Defense Department of a committee to develop a "common business language," led to the specification of a new language, Cobol (common business-oriented language) in 1960, and two years later IBM offered Cobol for several of its 1401 models, including one of the smallest such systems (see Sammet 1985; Flamm 1988; Bashe et al. 1986, 366; and chapter 3 in this volume). Growth in Cobol usage was even more rapid than had been true of Fortran. IBM estimated that while Fortran use peaked in 1965, Cobol continued to grow rapidly growth through 1975, accounting for about 50 percent of software usage and displacing Fortran and assembler languages beginning in 1965 (OECD 1985, 31). The development of higher-level language support for IBM computers was an important factor in delaying the growth of an external market for computer software. Despite rapid growth in applications demand and centralized computer facilities, these higher-level languages supported productivity gains in software development that blunted the demand for external programming services of large organizations with in-house software developers.

In 1960 IBM introduced the IBM 1401, a less expensive general-purpose machine addressing the needs of the medium-sized user. This machine was sold with a new high-level software language, RPG, whose operations resembled those of punched card systems and thus could be employed by individuals without costly retraining in the more abstract Fortran and Cobol languages (Bashe et al. 1986, 480).

By 1965 IBM as well as its competitors, including Burroughs and Control Data, had stimulated a market for programming services, software products, and professional services of $500 million in annual revenues. In 1965 the total value of shipments of U.S. computer manufacturers were estimated to be between $2.4 billion and $2.8 billion.[22] Much of the $500 million in revenues went to "service bureaus," companies that specialized in developing applications software such as payroll systems *and* selling information processing services to other, usually small, companies. By contracting externally for information processing services, client companies avoided investments in both computer hardware and software, albeit at the cost of having to redefine their information processing requirements to fit the solutions offered by service bureaus. One of the leading service bureau companies, Automatic Data Processing (ADP) was established in 1949 and by 1964 had revenues of $4.7 million, which grew to $20 million by 1968 (Fisher, McKie, and Mancke 1983, 321). The McDonnell Automation Center was formed in 1960 and merged with McDonnell Douglas's California computer operations (following the 1970 merger of McDonnell and Douglas aircraft); it recorded $47 million in revenue in 1970 (ibid., 320). These and other computer service bureaus were competitive alternatives to the purchase of computer hardware and the in-house development or purchase of software. While many of these companies had strong sales growth in the latter half of the 1960s, the period was also marked by the rapid diffusion of smaller-scale computers, such as IBM's 1401, that offered medium and smaller-sized organizations their own computer facilities; almost all larger business organizations had installed computers by the end of the decade (Phister 1976).

Early commercial applications of computers were associated with in-house programming using higher-level languages; service bureaus were an alternative supplier of computing services. This structure for the supply of software, in which computer manufacturers created "tools" for applications development, users developed applications software, and a residual of users employed service bureaus for their data processing needs was short-lived. Developments between 1965 and 1970, including IBM's success with the System/360 and IBM's decision to unbundle software from its supply of computers,[23] increased the market for multi-installation software sales. The new entrants that formed the base of the independent software vendor (ISV) industry included software tool and utility program suppliers as well as "vertical market" software companies, which provided applications for particular industries and for common software needs such as accounting systems. For these reasons, 1965–70 were the pivotal years in the emergence of the current structure of the U.S. software industry.

EMERGENCE: 1965–70

The number of independent software vendors grew rapidly during the late 1960s. Lawrence Welke, president of International Computer Programs, Inc. (ICP) testified in *U.S. v. IBM* that, by 1965, forty to fifty major independent suppliers of software and programming services and several hundred smaller organizations had been established. Welke stated that these companies derived most of their revenues from work with the U.S. government and from systems development work on behalf of computer manufacturers (Fisher, McKie, and Mancke 1983, 322). The largest of these companies, Computer Sciences Corporation (CSC), formed in 1959, had revenues of $5.7 million in 1964, $17.8 million in 1965, and $82 million in 1970. Much of CSC's growth in the late 1960s reflected the firm's development of multi-client software packages for accounting, ticketing, income tax preparation, commercial loans, and system operations. Similarly, Informatics, Inc., an early database producer began offering its product, Mark IV, in competition with IBM's unpriced "generalized retrieval system" in 1967 (ibid., 326). By 1969, the revenues of Informatics, Inc., were $19.8 million from sales of computer service and software, and there were over 170 installations with the Mark IV program (ibid.). Welke estimated that the 1965 population of forty to fifty major and several hundred smaller companies had by 1969 grown to more than 2,800 such organizations. This enormous growth was focused on contract programming services, which accounted for $600 million of these companies' revenues in 1969; in contrast, their revenues from software products amounted to only $20–25 million (ibid., 323).

Although many companies were founded before this period, 1965–70 marks the beginning of the U.S. independent software industry. Earlier, software companies were small and relied on government contracts and system development work for hardware companies. In contrast with the service bureaus, software companies had little direct contact with users other than the federal government and therefore had a difficult time marketing their services. Welke estimated that user expenditures on software creation skyrocketed from $200 million in 1960 to $3–4 billion in 1965 and continued upward to $8 billion in 1970 and $12 billion in 1975 (ibid.). Thus with the contract programming and software sales of $625 million in 1969 noted above, users acquired less than 10 percent of their needs externally in the late 1960s.

Three events made it possible for independent software vendors to improve their position in the 1970s. The first was the 1964 introduction of the IBM System/360 "family." The System/360 unified the operating system software of the IBM product line, allowing users to develop software applications that could operate on systems ranging in monthly rental price from $8,800 to $60,000, with corresponding increases in computational power. The unification of software within the System/360 product line encouraged users to define a "migration path" from smaller to larger mainframe computers that would maintain the value of their software development effort as their use of software and computers intensified. These same opportunities supported the growth of computer service companies whose regional processing operations could be expanded through migration to System/360s with greater computational capacity as their business expanded. But the System/360 also provided the first instance of a broad "installed base" of computers with a single operating system. Independent software vendors had, for the first time in the industry's history, the opportunity to market the same product to a variety of users. By the late 1960s, the independent software industry still accounted for a small share of U.S. software creation activities despite rapid growth during the previous decade.

The second important event supporting the growth of the independent software sector was IBM's decision to unbundle the sale of hardware and software during 1969. IBM, which by various estimates accounted for between two-thirds and three-quarters of computer sales and installations, had previously offered software tools for creating user applications as part of the computer systems it leased and sold. Because IBM systems accounted for 66–75 percent of mainframe sales and leases during this period, its software "bundling" policy was highly influential. The practice was terminated on June 23, 1969, for new orders and January 1, 1970, for existing installations. The shock from this change was cushioned by IBM's announcement that it would continue to provide system software and previously produced applications and development tool software to both new and established users.

The motives for IBM's unbundling decision are disputed. One interpretation is that IBM's actions were made in response to anticipated litigation.[24] Fisher, McKie, and Mancke dispute this view, noting that no direct evidence of a relation between the announcement and the DOJ antitrust action was discovered during subsequent litigation (1983, 176–77). These analysts instead argue that IBM's costs of software support were increasing rapidly. The costs of developing the System/360 operating system software had been traumatic for the company and seemed to foreshadow still further cost increases.[25] In addition, the growth of independent software vendors made it possible by the late 1960s for IBM to consider separate pricing for software and to retreat from its commitment to provide all of the software tools that users might need in order to purchase or lease IBM computers.

The third important event of the late 1960s for the software industry was the development of the minicomputer industry. Although IBM dominated sales of the mainframe computers that occupied a central position in the data processing activities of their customers, centralization of computer operations had disadvantages. The inflexibility and inconvenience of mainframes imposed costs on users who wished to develop new applications based on real-time computer control, research and development problem solving, and other specialized problems. For these users, the mainframe computer was a barrier to gaining exclusive and intensive access to computing time, achieving rapid turnaround in the development process, and linking devices such as scientific instruments under computer control. These problems persisted despite the frequent existence of excess computational capacity within mainframe computer installations.

Digital Equipment Corporation (DEC) pioneered the minicomputer market with its introduction of the PDP-8 in 1965. The PDP-8 could be rented for $525 a month, 6 percent of the cost of IBM's smallest System/360, the Model 30. The PDP-8 performed commercial-type computational tasks more slowly, at about 6 percent of the speed of the Model 30, and scientific computation at 22 percent of the speed of the

Model 30.[26] By compromising speed in order to achieve a very low cost, the PDP-8 tapped user needs that were not well served by the competing technological solution, time sharing, which had floundered in the late 1960s.[27] At one-seventh the cost of a mainframe, users could afford to let the PDP-8 stand idle, dedicate it to a single task, or share it among a small team engaged in a development effort.[28] The minicomputer also extended the application of "real time" control—that is, applications in which a computer directly controls scientific instruments or electromechanical systems.[29] Moreover, minicomputers could be used in dedicated data processing applications such as data collection and entry.

The ability to develop entirely new computer system architectures in which tasks were "distributed" provided a basis for networked computing, a means for combining computers of different sizes and computational capabilities and optimizing the system for both computational performance and response time. First developed in the late 1960s, distributed computing had its greatest impact during the 1970s. Minicomputers also made it possible for small organizations to begin to purchase and use their own computers. In a 1968 survey, U.S. manufacturing companies with fewer than five hundred employees or less than $10 million in sales reported no use of larger computers (Phister 1976, pt. 2, 453). In the same year about 30 percent of companies with 200–499 employees or $5–10 million in sales were using smaller computers, including the smaller System/360 mainframes and comparable machines, including minicomputers. Applications and affordability were responsible for rapid growth in the minicomputer sector during the late 1960s, the period when time-sharing operating systems for mainframes were floundering. By 1970, as the CBEMA estimates in Table 2-1 indicate, minicomputer unit shipments exceeded those of mainframes and, consistent with their price, were achieving about one-seventh of mainframe revenues.[30]

To summarize the remarkable developments affecting the software industry of the late 1960s: IBM decided to unbundle hardware and software as its System/360 moved to a dominant position in the market for mainframe general-purpose computers, independent software suppliers began to carve out a market by competing in quality with IBM software products, programming services and service bureaus grew rapidly as they improved their self-developed software and benefited from price-per-unit performance reductions in computer equipment, and the advent of the minicomputer created an enormous range of affordable commercial applications for computer systems. Although disentangling the relative contributions of each of these developments appears to be an impossible task, their collective impact, according to Welke, was to raise investments in user software creation from the $3–4 billion level in 1965 to $8 billion in 1970. In the same five years, CBEMA estimates that software product and services revenue increased more than tenfold, from $200 million in 1965 to $2.5 billion in 1970 (see Table 2-2).

GROWTH AND ITS DISCONTENTS: THE 1970s

By 1970 annual sales of computers and peripheral equipment (SIC 7573) were approaching $5 billion, or nearly 4.75 percent of domestic business investment in equipment and structures.[31] Software product and service revenue were $2.5 billion

Table 2-1. Estimates of U.S. domestic mainframe and minicomputer shipments by number and value, 1960–90

	Mainframes (no.)	Mainframes ($ million)	Minicomputers (no.)	Minicomputers ($ million)
Phister estimates				
1960	1,500	560	300	30
1961	2,300	850	400	30
1962	3,100	1,060	400	30
1963	3,800	1,220	400	80
1964	5,100	1,570	500	100
1965	5,300	1,910	800	150
1966	7,000	3,200	1,000	130
1967	8,500	3,900	2,000	130
1968	7,400	4,650	3,500	185
1969	6,600	4,642	6,700	277
1970	5,040	4,073	9,500	282
1971	8,560	3,975	9,350	300
1972	10,970	5,170	15,100	450
1973	14,000	5,405	24,700	540
1974	8,900	6,220	34,000	810
CBEMA estimates				
1960	1,790	590	na	na
1965	5,350	1,770	600	66
1970	5,700	3,600	6,060	485
1975	6,700	4,960	26,990	1,484
1976	6,750	5,060	39,320	1,887
1977	8,900	6,940	56,780	2,780
1978	7,500	6,230	68,340	3,690
1979	7,200	6,340	81,250	4,712
1980	9,900	8,840	105,870	6,238
1981	10,700	9,640	121,990	7,290
1982	10,600	9,860	128,000	7,770
1983	9,980	9,780	146,800	8,979
1984	11,330	11,900	205,400	12,817
1985	10,910	11,890	190,800	11,696
1986	10,990	12,200	198,200	11,872
1987	11,200	12,660	205,800	12,080
1988	11,540	13,270	218,100	12,656
1989	11,890	13,790	227,700	13,093
1990	12,130	14,190	232,000	12,650

Sources: Phister 1976; CBEMA estimates from Juliussen and Juliussen 1990.
Note: na means not available.

in 1970, 50 percent of hardware revenues in that year. The entry of numerous software companies during the late 1960s had created an industry structure that was so fragmented that estimates of the number of firms vary from 1,500 to 2,800. Of the $2.5 billion in 1970 software product and service revenues, these firms may have divided less than $1 billion in revenue in a market that was still dominated by IBM and other system producers such as Burroughs and Control Data.[32] This implies that average firm revenue would have been $350,000 to $700,000, an amount that could

Table 2-2. Estimates of U.S. domestic software and service revenues, 1965–88 ($ million)

Year	Processing services	Software products	Professional services	Total
1965	na	na	na	200
1970	1,200	500	800	2,500
1975	3,300	1,000	2,200	6,500
1980	10,800	2,850	4,350	18,000
1981	11,550	3,950	5,500	21,000
1982	12,650	4,900	5,950	23,500
1983	14,400	6,900	6,900	28,200
1984	17,150	10,000	8,100	35,250
1985	19,310	12,120	9,270	40,700
1986	20,750	14,150	10,100	45,000
1987	23,600	18,500	11,750	53,850
1988	26,900	27,850	13,300	68,050

Source: CBEMA, as cited in Juliussen and Juliussen 1990.
Note: na means not available.

support no more than about a dozen employees. In the early 1970s independent software development and sales was a "handicraft" industry in which extensive division of labor or specialization was impossible. Moreover, users faced enormous problems in sorting out the offerings and capabilities of these companies. This fragmentation of software and service suppliers helped sustain the growth of larger computer service companies such as Computer Sciences Corporation, McDonnell Douglas, ADP, and EDS.[33]

Early in the 1970s, improvements in hardware technology allowed faster "real time" access, an impetus for software industry growth. IBM introduced the System/370 in 1971 with new hard disk technology (the 3330 disk storage unit, also introduced in 1971) that made it possible for user on-line disk storage to exceed on-line tape storage for the first time in the history of the industry (Pugh, Johnson, and Palmer 1991, 532). This development dramatically improved the response time of time-sharing systems, significantly increasing the performance of a system architecture that had been a great disappointment in the late 1960s and allowing the growth of time-sharing service companies as a new source of software creation activities.[34]

As IBM's System/370 extended the capabilities of centralized data processing, DEC and its competitors in minicomputers developed the market for decentralized data processing. Minicomputer and mainframe shipments had been approximately equal in number (but not in revenues) in 1970. By 1976, almost six minicomputers were sold for each mainframe, and by 1980 more than ten minicomputers were sold for each mainframe (see Table 2–1). Each of these minicomputers required software, often of a very specialized nature requiring extensive user development efforts. For example, the oil refinery business was a major source of minicomputer use, sparking rapid expansion in the demand for complementary specialized software.[35]

Each different use of minicomputers—as primary computers in smaller organizations, as "front ends" for mainframes, in data communications systems, and in process control systems—required very different software. Although total demand for minicomputer software was very large, the diversity of minicomputer applications meant that the size of individual markets for "packaged" minicomputer software was limited. Small market size limited the economies of scale from software packages and led to the development of a minicomputer software industry structure that closely resembled that of the mainframe software industry, in contrast to the "mass market software publishing" that emerged with the personal computer in the 1980s.

The fragmentation of the minicomputer industry is indicated in Table 2-3, which reports on the results of *Datamation*'s 1977 user survey of satisfaction with packaged software. In the 1977 survey, 199 packages were rated by five or more users, the survey report's threshold of use for reporting the name of the software package. Mainframe package software applications dominated these "multi-user" packages, accounting for 72 percent of applications for which the computer system could be identified. By comparison, non-IBM minicomputer package software, most of which was system software, accounted for only ten packages in the survey, the same number of software packages that were listed for IBM's System/3 minicomputer. Collectively minicomputer software packages accounted for only 20 percent of the products mentioned by five or more respondents to the survey.[36] Thus, despite the far larger "installed base" of minicomputers, the relatively small number of packaged software products for minicomputers indicates continued fragmentation in the minicomputer software market as of 1977, despite rapid growth in the number of machines and users during the previous decade.

For the software industry as a whole, the 1970s were a period of broad-based growth accompanied by growing concerns about productivity in software develop-

Table 2-3. Packaged software and computer systems: the *Datamation* 1977 survey of computer software

Computer system type	Number	% of total
Mainframe computers	138	72
IBM System/3 and 32	20	10
Minicomputer systems	19	10
Cross platform or high-level language	10	5
Other (for example, IBM 1130)	5	3
Total	192	100
Cannot determine	7	
Total in listing	199	

Source: Gepner 1977.

Note: Datamation, at that time the leading business publication in the data processing industry, mailed surveys to 30,000 computer installations and received 5,813 usable responses. *Datamation* then reported names and other information about software packages, including user satisfaction for software packages mentioned by five or more respondents. Although 1,200 packages were mentioned by users, only 199 were mentioned by five or more users. This tabulation is based on the information about computer system compatibility from the description offered. In some cases it was not possible to determine for which computer system the sofware package was designed, and in many cases the class of computers is inferred from other information—for example, operating system compatibility.

ment. Growth of software-related activities was led by a ninefold expansion in data processing service revenues; but sales of software products and professional services also expanded by factors of 5.5 and 7 respectively during the decade (see Table 2-2). For mainframe computers, the 1970s were a period of intensive rather than extensive growth. By 1970, growth in the number of firms with mainframe computer systems, computers per dollar of revenue, and computers per employee had all decelerated from the high growth rates of the 1960s (Phister 1976, pt. 1, 129). The organizations that had adopted mainframes by 1970 were developing application programs that would more intensively use their existing mainframe computers rather than increasing the number of mainframes used in their organizations. Growth in the use of minicomputers was both intensive (within firms) and extensive (in new user firms) during this period.

In both mainframe and minicomputer applications the problems of software development and maintenance received growing attention during the 1970s. Users began to experience significant problems in managing their in-house programming efforts. The problems noted in the technical and management literature of the time include efforts by programmers to shelter their positions by creating software with high maintenance costs,[37] the intractability of deriving meaningful measures of software and system performance metrics for increasingly complex systems (Kolence 1971; Boehm 1973, 1981), the hurdles of properly specifying large software systems (Larsen 1973), the frustrations of organizational politics in managing such efforts (Keen and Gerson 1977), and the growing disappointment with software quality.[38]

Problems with software did not prevent the 1970s from being a period of enormous growth in computer applications and perhaps contributed to employment growth in data processing. As early as 1972, computer equipment accounted for almost 23 percent of producer durables sold in the United States (CBEMA 1983, 14). The concerns about software noted above reflect continued growth in this investment, whose share of producer durables increased to more than 33 percent by 1982.[39] Occupations related to data processing grew relative to both noncomputer service and manufacturing sector employment throughout the 1970s (Baumol, Blackman, and Wolff 1989, chap. 7). New methods for organizing the growing investment in data processing equipment lagged behind the investment itself.

As the costs of supporting this new form of physical capital became more apparent, new structures for decision-making and oversight were needed. The efforts to deal with these issues were increased attention to software and system performance, software specification, organization of software creation, and quality assurance. But because software was becoming the repository and mediator of information flows, productivity problems competed for managerial attention with the problems of extending access and utilizing a rapidly expanding flow of information.

THE REVOLUTION: SOFTWARE IN THE 1980s

The 1980s were an extraordinarily complex period of evolution and growth for data processing. Two major developments distinguish the 1980s from the previous decade: the death of time sharing as it was known in the 1970s, and the retreat of computer manufacturers *except IBM* from software and service activities.

The process of creative destruction during this period razed an entire sector of the data processing industry during the decade, the time-shared service company. Tables 2-4 and 2-5 report on the largest data processing companies in 1980 and 1991 that derived the majority of their revenues from software and services. In 1980 there were eight major time-sharing services companies (as well as dozens of smaller regional companies), including Dun and Bradstreet, which is primarily identified with business services and software. By 1991 seven of these companies had fallen out of the *Datamation* 100, while the eighth (Dun and Bradstreet) retained some on-line information services. Information service companies such as Prodigy (a joint venture among Sears, IBM, and other companies), Compuserve, and America Online have filled part of the vacuum left by the time-sharing service companies, and the sale of processing time on remote computers is still an active but highly fragmented market. But remote computation services are now more closely tied to companies that offer system integration or vertical market (specialized by industry) consulting services. Thus software creation activities for particular industry segments that might have been provided by time-sharing service firms are now provided by more specialized service providers. These services may still be organized as a remote computing activity (for example, ADP now receives much of its data from users electronically rather than on paper forms), but the 1970s-style time-sharing company that offered a collection of applications within a single time-sharing system has virtually disappeared.

During the 1980s the software activities of computer manufacturers also underwent dramatic change, as the importance of software and service activities declined significantly for computer manufacturers other than IBM. Table 2-6 shows software and services revenues for the major computer manufacturers for 1981 and 1991, excluding the IBM plug-compatible companies (for example, Amdahl) that have never been prominent in software production. Computer manufacturers' total revenues from software almost doubled over the decade, but almost all of this increase was attributable to IBM; software's contribution to its total revenue grew from 17 to 20 percent. While DEC expanded its software revenues as well, by 1991 software accounted for only one-third of DEC's software and services revenue while IBM derived 84 percent of its 1991 software and services revenue from software.

U.S. computer manufacturers, with the exception of IBM, withdrew from software development during the 1980s through several different paths. For Unisys (formerly Sperry and Burroughs), NCR (now a division of AT&T), and Hewlett-Packard, 1991 software and services revenues fell below their 1981 levels and plummeted as a fraction of the firms' total computer-related revenues. Other firms, especially new entrants into workstations, minicomputers, and personal computers (such as Sun, Tandem, Prime, and Apple) specialized in selling hardware rather than software.[40] These developments reflected the maturation during the 1980s of the independent software industry. Sales of computers no longer required manufacturers to provide software other than a basic operating system. Instead, other companies (including those whose own users developed the software they needed) provided these complementary inputs.

The following sections discuss three major developments of the 1980s that have affected the software industry. The emergence of the personal computer at the beginning of the decade provided a new and revolutionary organizing principle, mass publication of packaged software. The introduction of the workstation in the middle of

Table 2-4. Independent software and services companies, 1980

Among the *Datamation* 100, the 100 largest U.S. data processing companies based on EDP revenue, 25 companies were predominantly engaged in the provision of software or services in 1980.

Primary source of revenue	Number
Software and programming services	4
Time-sharing and on-line services	7
Systems integration	2
Specialized services	12

These 25 companies, by type, were:

Company type	1980 data processing revenue ($ million)	*Datamation* 100 rank	Comment or specialized service (if applicable)
Software and programming services			
SDC	187	43	Large software systems
Informatics	126	56	Large software systems
Dun and Bradstreet	97	67	"Nomad" database product
Management Sciences America	53	96	Finance and human resource products
Timesharing and on-line services			
General Electric	475	17	
McDonnell Douglas	280	25	
Tymshare	211	38	
Boeing	125	57	
United Telecom	115	61	
Comshare	88	68	
Martin Marietta Data Systems	78	74	
Systems integration			
Computer Sciences Corp.	560	15	
EDS	408	18	
Specialized services			
ADP	505	16	Accounting/payroll services
General Instruments	172	45	Wagering systems
Bradford National	143	50	Financial services
Planning Research	127	55	Government services
Reynolds and Reynolds	118	59	Auto dealer services
Shared Medical Services	106	64	Medical and hospital pharmacies
The Sun Company	87	69	Financial and disaster recovery
Interactive Data Corporation (subsidiary of Chase Manhattan)	69	81	Financial and data services
Commerce Clearing House	67	83	Tax preparation
Anacomp	57	89	Financial services
National Data Corporation	53	94	Cash management services
First Data Resources (subsidiary of American Express)	53	95	Credit card authorizations

Source: Datamation 1981.

Table 2-5. Software and services companies, 1991

Among the *Datamation* 100, the 100 largest U.S. data processing companies based on EDP revenue, 41 companies were predominantly engaged in the provision of software or services in 1991.

Primary source of revenue	Number
Software and programming services	17
Time-sharing and on-line services	0
Systems integration	13
Specialized services	11

These 41 companies, by type, were:

Company type	1991 Revenue ($ million)	*Datamation* 100 rank	Category-specific annotation
Software and programming services			*Platform*
Microsoft	2,276	12	Personal computer
Computer Associates	1,438	23	Mostly mainframe
Oracle	1,085	29	Mini and mainframe
Lotus	829	40	Personal computer
Novell	710	44	Network software
Dun & Bradstreet Software	549	56	Mainframe
WordPerfect	533	57	Personal computer
Borland	502	60	Personal computer
Mentor Graphics	400	67	Specialized workstation
ASK Computer Systems	395	68	Minicomputer
Cadence	353	73	Workstation
SAS Institute	295	79	Mini and mainframe
Autodesk	285	82	Personal computer
Adobe	230	92	Personal computer
Sterling Software	229	93	Mainframe
Legent	208	97	Mainframe
Information Builders	202	99	Mini and mainframe

Time-sharing and on-line services
(No companies were listed in the 1991 *Datamation* 100. The new leading companies were Prodigy, Compuserve, and America Online.)

Company type	1991 Revenue ($ million)	*Datamation* 100 rank	Parent company
Systems integration			*Parent company*
EDS	3,666	7	
Andersen Consulting	2,260	13	Accounting firm
Computer Sciences Corp.	1,945	15	
Price Waterhouse	733	43	Accounting firm
Science Applications Intl.	653	46	
Planning Research	623	49	
SHL Systemhouse	601	50	
Coopers & Lybrand	571	52	Accounting firm
Martin Marietta	561	53	
Ernst & Young	551	54	Accounting firm
Systematics Information	377	70	
MAI Systems	329	76	
Computer Task Group Inc.	285	81	

Company type	1991 Revenue ($ million)	*Datamation* 100 rank	Predominant service
Specialized services			*Predominant service*
ADP	1,933	18	General
American Express/First Data	995	33	Transactions processing
Nynex	601	51	Telecom and financial
Bell Atlantic	550	55	Maintenance
Shared Medical	439	66	Hospitals

(*continued*)

Table 2-5. (*continued*)

Company type	1991 Revenue ($ million)	*Datamation* 100 rank	Category-specific annotation
Policy Management Systems	342	75	Insurance
Boeing Information Services	325	77	Aerospace (services to Boeing were 80% of company revenue)
American Management Systems	285	80	Telecom and financial
Fiserve	281	84	Financial
Reynolds and Reynolds	233	90	Auto dealers
National Data	221	95	Financial

Source: Datamation 1992.

the decade fueled the creation of a large new class of software applications that exploited the workstation's sophisticated graphics and numerical computation capabilities. The productivity and organizational problems that first appeared in the 1970s supported the rapid growth during the 1980s of system integration companies and "outsourcing" of corporate data processing activities and management.

The Personal Computer Revolution

A succession of products introduced from 1975 to 1981 was overshadowed by IBM's introduction of its personal computer (PC) in August 1981.[41] IBM succeeded in learning from all of the experiments that had been undertaken in the first six years of the industry and introduced a machine that combined a reasonable level of computational power and an operating system that facilitated application development. Customers quickly endorsed the new product, purchasing more than 13,000 of the machines in its first year (Langlois 1992, 23). Although Apple and Tandy machines continued to outsell IBM for several years, IBM had attained 26 percent of the personal computer market by 1983. The market for personal computers grew very rapidly during the 1980s. Table 2-7 reports IDC's data on U.S.-based computer industry shipments by value and volume for the decade. By 1984 personal computer sales accounted for more revenue than IDC's large, medium-sized, or small computer market segments, with shipments of 9.7 million personal computers for a total revenue of some $17 billion, bringing the installed base in 1984 to 23 million machines.

The rapid growth in the installed base of personal computers provided a homogenous market for operating systems and applications of unprecedented size. In 1984, the installed base of both large and medium-sized computers was less than 200,000 units, and about 1.9 million small-scale systems were in use; there were 23 million personal computers in use in that year. The enormous size of the personal computer market created unprecedented scale and profit opportunities for software producers that were simply unavailable in the markets for larger computers, even though software in the latter markets often had higher price tags.

Three new software companies emerged in the early years of rapid growth in the personal computer market. By 1985, Lotus, with annual revenues of $226 million, had become the sixtieth largest U.S. data processing company (*Datamation* 1986, 62). Microsoft, with revenues of $163 million, ranked seventy-eighth, and

Ashton-Tate, with revenues of $110 million, ranked one hundredth (ibid.). These companies were joined in 1988 by WordPerfect Corporation, whose sales in that year were $179 million. Each company's revenue was dominated in 1986 by a single product that had penetrated a large share of the installed base of personal computers and dominated a class of software—spreadsheets for Lotus, operating systems for Microsoft, databases for Ashton-Tate, and word processing for WordPerfect.

Although the arithmetic of corporate size in the personal computer industry is straightforward, it is less immediately obvious why a single product in any application class should garner a dominant share of personal computer installations. In practice, however, several network externalities can cause a single software product to become the de facto standard for an application.[42] First, there are advantages in establishing a single operating system standard. IBM's endorsement of the PC-DOS operating system provided Microsoft with an enormous advantage that it quickly converted into a position as the dominant supplier of operating systems for IBM and IBM-compatible personal computers.[43] Second, it is desirable for a user firm to

Table 2-6. Software and services revenues of major computer manufacturers, 1981 and 1991

Company	Software and services revenue	Software and services revenue as % of total revenue	Software revenue	Services revenue
	1981			
IBM	1,480	17.0		
DEC	911	25.4		
Control Data	1,154	37.2		
NCR	1,029	33.5		
Burroughs	838	28.6		
Sperry	695	25.0		
Hewlett-Packard	545	29.1		
Honeywell	835	47.1		
Xerox	209	19.0		
Data General	130	17.0		
Total	10,826	22.9		
	1991			
IBM	12,542	20.0	10,524	2,018
DEC	2,366	16.6	796	1,570
Hewlett-Packard	345	3.2	345	0
AT&T (includes NCR)	850	10.4	250	600
Unisys (includes Burroughs and Sperry)	1,200	15.0	600	600
Apple	250	3.8	250	0
Sun	175	5.1	175	0
Xerox	220	7.5	100	120
Tandem	140	7.2	110	30
Prime	247	17.9	247	0
Data General	210	17.3	210	0
Control Data	460	39.2	160	300
Total	19,005	15.5		

Sources: Datamation 1982, Datamation 1992.

Note: Honeywell's computer division was spun off and purchased by Bull of the United Kingdom in 1987.

Table 2-7. U.S-based company computer industry shipments, 1980–90

Year	Large-scale shipments (no.)	Large-scale shipments ($ million)	Medium-scale shipments (no.)	Medium-scale shipments ($ million)	Small-scale shipments (no.)	Small-scale shipments ($ million)	Personal computer shipments (no.)	Personal computer shipments ($ million)
1980	2,380	7,880	16,100	7,300	197,800	7,700	486,000	1,642
1981	1,510	6,150	19,200	9,160	212,500	8,800	905,000	2,707
1982	2,300	11,140	24,100	9,100	248,300	9,100	3,775,000	5,358
1983	3,390	14,460	28,000	9,530	282,390	9,800	7,623,000	11,304
1984	3,750	16,100	38,650	13,400	338,800	11,100	9,670,000	17,168
1985	3,240	16,970	39,650	14,610	325,400	12,320	8,828,000	19,070
1986	3,260	17,560	44,900	15,750	354,700	13,500	9,816,000	20,720
1987	3,380	18,340	49,900	17,500	391,200	14,980	11,130,000	22,650
1988	3,530	19,360	56,000	19,600	447,000	16,810	12,380,000	25,150
1989	3,750	20,520	63,000	21,850	512,300	18,720	13,500,000	27,800
1990	4,000	21,900	68,900	24,000	582,800	20,500	14,560,000	30,100

Source: IDC 1992.

choose a single application product within a particular class so that information created by one user may be shared by another. Lotus Development's spreadsheet application, Lotus 1-2-3, was chosen by many business users of IBM personal computers (for which it had been carefully optimized, as chapter 6 notes) and rapidly displaced the VisiCalc spreadsheet program. Third, the accumulation of skills, training materials, and add-on products that facilitate the use of the product reinforce its dominant position. The development of numerous specific applications written for the dBase II and, later, dBase III and IV products of Ashton-Tate, as well as training materials and the accumulation of consultant skills in these products, are examples of such externalities. Fourth, widespread use of a specific software product creates externalities in the labor market; more individuals are available with skills in widely used application programs. The widespread use of Lotus 1-2-3 in business schools and corporations made it possible to hire individuals who required no training in the use of the product, encouraging companies to expand their use of the product and erecting a substantial entry barrier to other products.

Collectively, these effects have propelled specific applications to dominance in their class. Between 1981 and 1985, the share of the fifteen largest independent software vendors increased from 37 percent to 72 percent of total personal computer software revenues. The three largest companies, Lotus, Microsoft, and Ashton-Tate, accounted for 35 percent of the total in 1985 (*Business Week* 1986, 129). There are, of course, limitations to the impact of network externalities as the disappearance of Ashton-Tate through merger with Borland and the 1994 acquisition of WordPerfect by Novell suggest. In particular, major differences in the functionality of products fragment user choices and create fewer positive externalities.

Personal computer word processing software illustrates the limits of these externalities in permanently establishing market dominance. WordStar, produced by MicroPro International, originally competed against a number of products with more readily understandable user interfaces (such as MultiMate) or with more features (such as XyWrite). But WordStar and its competitors were displaced by WordPerfect, which provided extensive features and an attractive user interface. WordPerfect, in turn, has been unable to dislodge Microsoft Word as the primary word processing application on Apple's Macintosh and now faces major competition from the recent success of Microsoft's new operating system Windows, for which Microsoft Word is a commonly chosen word processing application. The acquisition of WordPerfect in March 1994 by Novell reflects the growing problems of competing against Word and Windows. Ashton-Tate's dBase products were challenged late in the 1980s by a new line of database products such as Paradox, leading to Ashton-Tate's acquisition by Borland, which had previously acquired one of Ashton-Tate's primary competitors. Thus, positive externalities reinforce the establishment of a single product standard for a class of personal computer applications, but they do not guarantee the emergence of a single standard.

The market in personal computer software resembles many aspects of publishing and mass entertainment. The similarity of promotion and distribution methods to those of the book and music recording industries is especially marked.[44] Use of independent distributors that could provide stocks of popular software to immediately satisfy demand for a "hit" product so that users' needs could be immediately satisfied became an important competitive weapon. The growth of personal computer magazines, with extensive advertising for software and hardware, further strengthened the similarities between this new software market and the recording and publishing industries. The retail distribution channels that had been established to sell personal computers also supplied their software, while mail order suppliers and direct distribution provided a convenient source for more specialized products and served as discount outlets for the major products. Major software companies supplemented these promotion and distribution methods with direct sales efforts similar to those used for earlier packaged software.

The economic advantages for a firm of creating and maintaining a leading software product were enormous. Most of the costs in the packaged software market were the fixed costs of product development. When amortized over millions of users, very large development efforts could be financed from current revenues. During the 1980s the largest personal computer software companies invested 10–11 percent of their revenues in R&D (Hodges and Melewski 1991). Their development efforts led to ever more sophisticated products that could utilize the increasing capacity of personal computers.[45] High development costs have introduced elements of monopolistic competition into the personal computer software industry, as the costs of software development have begun reduce the high gross margins of producers.[46]

The huge size of the market for personal computers also created dynamic markets for complementary hardware products, which in turn created new opportunities for applications markets. Markets for hard disks, display monitors, modems, and printers all grew rapidly during the 1980s. The storage capacity of hard disks enabled software producers to deliver larger programs and created a demand for utility software to maintain the larger collections of files stored on personal computer systems. Similarly, display monitors encouraged the creation of more sophisticated graphic display programs, and communication modems increased the demand for personal computer communications programs. Perhaps the most important development came from the improvement of printer technology. Canon's laser printing engine, used by Apple and Hewlett-Packard to produce laser printers, provided a raw capability to place images on a page at the resolution of 300 dots per inch. Many of the software programs of the late 1980s were devised to take advantage of this capability, and an entirely new segment of personal computer use, desktop publishing, emerged as a means to take advantage of the high-resolution printing in the creation of announcements, newsletters, and other "print shop" quality documents, all of which could be produced by a single personal computer.

By the end of the 1980s, personal computer users were able to choose from thousands of programs for specialized applications and dozens of major software products for more general applications. The resulting software network is certainly as complex as the network of software applications that has been developed for all other types of computer systems. Although personal computers have been used as terminals for mainframe and minicomputer systems, limitations in transferability of information across systems have, until recently, limited the use of the personal computer as a node in the larger network of computational resources available in modern businesses. Recent efforts to "reintegrate" the personal computer into a corporate computer network that itself has become more "distributed" between mainframe and smaller computers is discussed in the conclusion of this chapter.

The Workstation: Continuity and Change

The workstation, introduced by Apollo in 1981 and Sun Microsystems in 1982, was a hybrid of the personal computer and minicomputer. Like the personal computer, the workstation took advantage of dramatic reductions in the price per unit of performance of microprocessor integrated circuits. Like the minicomputer, the architecture and peripherals attached to the workstation's central processing unit provided high performance in computation and display. IBM compromised the computational capabilities of its PC to penetrate the mass market for desktop computers; by contrast, workstation producers entering the market at roughly the same time sought to attract engineers and other technically sophisticated users who would otherwise use minicomputers or mainframe computers.[47] A major appeal of the workstation was its graphics capability. Graphics-intensive applications involving computer-aided design (CAD) and computer-aided engineering (CAE) had been developed for minicomputers but suffered from limitations in graphic display capability and the fragmentation in the minicomputer software market.

The most successful of the workstation companies, Sun Microsystems, adopted a corporate strategy based on "open" standards involving the use of Unix, a widely available operating system that had first been developed at Bell Laboratories. Sun's version of Unix had been modified by computer science researchers at the University of California, Berkeley, with support from the Defense Advanced Research Projects Agency (DARPA) (see Flamm 1987 and chapter 3 in this volume). Unix was already widely used on minicomputers, and Sun Microsystems' strategy was to persuade technical users and software developers that applications for its workstations would be "portable" to ever more powerful workstation products, imitating IBM's System/360 marketing strategy. Along with liberal licensing of its microprocessor architecture (see chapter 4), this strategy proved enormously successful in inducing investment in software for Sun workstation products.

From 1985 to 1990 the number of suppliers listed in Sun Microsystems' Catalyst guide to software for Sun workstations grew from 177 to 1,325, despite a major revision in the Sun operating system that interrupted the growth of suppliers in 1989.[48] The majority of companies offered a single software product.[49] Their products were, in turn, often specialized, high-performance solutions to problems such as oil field management, molecular modeling, and electronic circuit design. The growth in applications software spurred further sales of Sun's workstations in the same "virtuous cycle" that supported sales of IBM PC and the Apple Macintosh personal computer products. A larger installed base stimulates software development, and the availability of software stimulates the purchase of additional hardware platforms compatible with that software. Although a similar cycle operated in the market for mainframes and minicomputers, the relevant installed base of both workstations and personal computers was vastly larger, even in specialized markets, because of their lower price per unit of performance. The "virtuous cycle" dynamic thus operated with greater speed and economic impact.

The Rise of System Integration and Outsourcing

The personal computer of the 1980s did not have the performance or capacity to replace mainframe computers, and organizations continued to face the problems of maintaining and expanding mainframe software applications. Solutions to these problems appeared to require a sophisticated corporate business operation within the company whose major output was data processing services. Many companies discovered that these internal capabilities quickly drained their investment resources and, even more important, distracted them from the business activities necessary to the company's success. The continued growth in the intensity of computer operations during the 1970s and 1980s provided a growing challenge for internal development capabilities. In many cases, internal bureaucracies ossified or were simply unable to keep up with the pace of technological change. Accordingly, firms began to reconsider the make-or-buy decision for their entire data processing activity. If another firm could provide the technological knowledge and human resources to implement specialized software solutions, choose among complex competing hardware offerings, and deliver useful information services to internal users, why not buy these services rather than produce them in-house? The growing complexity of data processing technologies and markets pushed companies toward the "buy" solution and a number of companies emerged to satisfy this demand.

During the 1970s, as was noted in Table 2-4, two companies had developed large system integration operations. These companies, Computer Sciences Corporation and EDS, originally established as computer services firms, delivered large-scale system solutions to the federal government and to many state governments. By 1991 thirteen system integration companies had joined the ranks of the *Datamation* 100, the largest U.S. data processing companies (see Table 2-5). Among these companies were four of the "big eight" accounting firms, the 1970s leaders EDS and Computer Sciences Corporation, and seven other companies, most of which had been involved in providing computer programming and consulting services on a smaller scale during the 1970s. Among these companies, EDS is noted for the extensiveness of its intervention in building data processing departments, managing the requirements specification, subcontracting for software creation, and eventually staffing the day-to-day data center operations of client companies.[50] By comparison, most of the other companies have chosen a more limited role with regard to clients, alternately providing consulting, programming services, "change" management, or other specific services in varying proportions over time in partnership with client company data processing personnel.

The size and scope of these new outsourcing and computer service firms appears to signal an important change in the methods of developing large corporate information systems. Unlike the computer service bureaus and time-sharing services, software development and system design are performed in partnership or on behalf of single corporate users. This method of delivering programming services creates software that is not only organization-specific but that also benefits from the supplier's multi-client business. The large computer service organization is able to amortize the fixed costs of large-scale software development and accumulation of specific technical competences in hardware and software over a large number of customers. The computer service organization can also have major impact on the supply of published software by negotiating multi-client site licenses and requesting specific software modifications for their clients' needs. Earlier computer service bureaus and time-sharing services pursued economies of scale by investing in computer hardware and the delivery of "remote" computing; the new service organizations achieve these economies through organizational economies of scale that allow "direct" delivery of their services. Their success, however, is likely to attract competition from computer manufacturers, software suppliers, and perhaps a new generation of time-sharing services using improved data telecommunications.

Summing Up the 1980s

The 1980s were a complex period in the development of the U.S. software industry. The growth in mainframe and minicomputer applications and sales continued through the decade, but additional layers of complexity were introduced by the widespread adoption of workstations and personal computers. The variety and volume of hardware and software mushroomed, and so too did problems of compatibility and complexity in organizing and managing the much larger installed base.

The common theme of 1980s developments was the creation of methods for realizing economies of scale in the development of software. Personal computer software companies achieved economies of scale in software development with a "publishing" approach that tapped the immense installed base. The leading firms' positions were further reinforced by the positive externalities in skills and data compatibility. The large installed base of workstations and the use of Unix as a common operating system supported the development of specialized, computationally intensive software. For mainframes, new service organizations achieved scale advantages by creating organization-specific software. In each of these areas, software developed the characteristics of a mature industry, with established actors, large-scale organizations, effective distribution methods, and a stable population of users. Although user-produced software continued to absorb substantial resources, the viability and stability of the independent software vendor industry seemed assured.

The developments of the 1980s have many implications for the future of software creation, organizational design, and hardware and software markets. They also played an important role in the U.S. software industry's international position.

U.S. SOFTWARE IN THE INTERNATIONAL MARKET AND THE 1990S: SIGNS OF REINTEGRATION?

The rapid pace of change in hardware and software markets has given the U.S. software industry an advantage in international competition. In packaged software, U.S. independent and system software producers hold very strong positions in domestic and foreign markets. According to IDC (1993), one of the leading market research companies in the industry, in 1992 the U.S. domestic market share of U.S. independent software companies in packaged software was 58 percent, and the share of U.S. system companies was 30 percent. In Europe, U.S. independent software companies held a 60 percent share of the market, 34 percent from independent suppliers and 26 percent from system vendors. Software in Europe is often delivered by hardware manufacturers and service companies, and therefore it is possible that U.S. companies hold a smaller position in the European market than the above figures would indicate (see chapter 7 in this volume). It is true, however, that European packaged software consumption is comparable to that of the United States and many of the U.S. service companies, such as Arthur Andersen, have strong positions in the European market. In Japan, U.S. independent software companies hold a 27 percent share of the packaged software market and system companies a 33 percent share. The overall level of packaged software sales in Japan is, however, only one quarter that of Europe and the United States (see chapter 5 in this volume). U.S. service companies have a smaller position in the Japanese market (see Siwek and Furchtgott-Roth 1993).

The most obvious explanation for the international competitive position of U.S. companies is that they have enjoyed a first-mover advantage in all of the software industry's market segments. European and Japanese computer production and rates of utilization have historically lagged behind those of the United States, leaving their domestic software producers with smaller markets and fewer economies of scale advantages than those available to U.S. firms. First-mover advantages were generated not only by commercial activity but also by government R&D policy and the early development of computer science education in U.S. universities. The importance of software for national defense systems led to generous U.S. government support for basic and applied research in software, often through the Defense Advanced Research Projects Agency (DARPA).[51] The Association for Computing Machinery (ACM), a professional association, played an important role in developing curricular standards for college-level study of computer science and aided in the rapid growth of university courses and degree programs in software engineering.

By the end of the 1980s U.S. companies were engaged in another major advance in information technology, the linking of personal computers to create extensive networks. Electronic mail (e-mail), file transfer, and "work group" software applications provided one impetus for networking efforts. Another impetus was the continuing importance of mainframe computers as repositories of organizational databases "of record" that were updated, edited, and analyzed by users of personal computers. In addition to interuser and mainframe communications, networks provided companies with new opportunities for sharing software and computational resources and for servicing and maintaining software within the organization. U.S. software development in the 1990s will be influenced by these growing network capabilities, reinforcing the U.S. software industry's position in international markets. One of the largest U.S. software companies currently is Novell, which provides the leading local area network operating system.[52] Many database programs have introduced features that permit their use on networks (such as record locking, which prevents two users from simultaneously changing database information.) These developments are likely only the first attempts at deriving value from the rapid growth in networking.

Networks provide new entry points for externally produced software in a user organization. Instead of convincing each individual user to adopt a particular software solution, software companies can market applications for many users at a single site or in a single organization and thereby generate higher revenues from a single purchase decision. In many respects, this marketing approach resembles the direct sales approach of earlier periods in the software industry. But it also allows software producers to deal with the problems of coordinating software needs within a firm. As noted earlier, system integration and consultant companies currently are addressing these coordination and compatibility problems. To the extent that users find software applications that help them coordinate computer use in the network, the need for external services may decline. The result may be greater competition between system integrator companies and larger software producers who can add consulting activities to their software development, assisting a company in decisions on the complementary purchases necessary to use their application or operating system software. This competition may influence the structure of the software industry as consulting companies and software producers merge or acquire one another.

Assuming that security problems do not block the further extension of networking in software and computer systems, the reintegration of personal computers with other data processing resources within organizations and the linking of these resources through data communication pathways will become more important in the next decade. In principle, this process should result in new software systems linking manufacturing companies with their suppliers and customers to manage delivery schedules, improve the efficiency of ordering and pricing procedures, and reduce the costs of managing the flow of material and labor inputs. Such gains will require the development of new technical compatibility standards for software such as EDI (electronic data interchange) and the creation of software applications that facilitate interorganizational links. It seems likely that these developments will ensure growth in the market for externally developed software solutions at the expense of internal development efforts.

Alternative techniques for software development are also likely to flourish in the coming years. The personal computer revolution has demonstrated the substantial advantages of using standard application programs. These application programs, however, have not eliminated the need for user organizations to develop custom applications software tailored to their specific needs. How these applications are developed and whether they can benefit from new techniques will be major concerns in coming years. For example, there are two current approaches for improving the custom applications software development process.[53] The first approach uses computer-aided software engineering (CASE) methods to simplify, document, and maintain software. The second approach uses a new class of object-oriented programming (OOP) languages to provide standard modules for the creation of more complex software systems, including application programs.

From an economic viewpoint, the two approaches suggest somewhat different principles. A main objective of CASE is to reduce the costs of creating custom software while maximizing the flexibility and heterogeneity of traditional approaches to this task. Expanded use of CASE will accelerate the growth of customized software applications by lowering development costs. But the flexibility that makes CASE attractive also may limit its application. Flexibility allows programmers to address virtually any problem but also reproduces some of the productivity problems of earlier custom software. For example, although CASE techniques simplify code generation, they do not necessarily encourage the use of well-tested code modules. Thus CASE techniques can lead to errors and inconsistencies similar to those of custom programs where programmers frequently reinvent (often with error) the methods of performing commonly performed functions.

OOP presents an entirely different trade-off. An "object" can be used across units within an organization and across organizations. Application programs are assemblies of objects, some of which are custom coded for a particular organization's needs. A measure of flexibility is embedded within the design of each object. This approach can generate the same sorts of externalities that were created by the mass market for personal computer software, as frequently reused objects are optimized for specific environments and as users improve their skills in the use of such objects. Moreover, as the software network of the corporation integrates objects, the opportunity for external suppliers to enter is enhanced.[54] But realizing advantages and funding the costs of developing sophisticated objects requires widespread adoption of a limited number of object libraries. Independent software vendors will offer many different object libraries in an attempt to become dominant suppliers, and unless a "shake-out" reduces their number, a classic monopolistic competitive equilibrium (in which the costs of differentiation absorb potential profits) is likely to occur. Such an outcome would divert resources from the incremental improvement of object libraries and user skills toward efforts to secure user adoption of one of many competing object libraries. The latter would likely result in object libraries that are more specialized to particular classes of users, and the outcome would be similar to existing product differentiation within application programs. OOP may thus move the long-established tension between standardization and customization in applications software to a new level, without eliminating it.

The contest between CASE and "object" approaches to software development is only one example of the new trade-offs that flow from the enormous installed base of personal computers and the growing use of networks. The contest between efficieny derived from custom solutions and the broad adoption of "standard" approaches that rely on the economies of mass reproduction are of growing importance in explaining the rate and direction of technical change in software. A better economic understanding of the emergence of technical compatibility standards and the conflicts between variety-enhancing competition and cost-reducing coordination are needed to more fully understand these developments.

Future developments in the U.S. software industry are likely to be shaped by the mature character of the supply "infrastructure" for software creation and the large installed bases of particular information technology systems such as personal computers. The U.S. software industry emerged from a complex "infrastructure" involving the interaction of computer producers, users, and independent software vendors. These actors were joined, for a time, by the time-sharing vendors and, more recently, by the computer service consulting companies. The complexity of this infrastructure provides the United States with an enormous variety of possible solutions to new challenges presented by changes in hardware and application needs. Although there is no fundamental reason why other nations cannot, in time, develop similar infrastructures for software creation, the United States has an enormous lead that it is likely to maintain. The sources of U.S. diversity were important events unique to the U.S. market, including the early creation of an independent software vendor sector as a result of IBM's software unbundling decision, the creation of new computer "platforms" that have stimulated complementary software development, and the aggressive adoption of information technology by public and private U.S. institutions. These events were reinforced by early U.S. development of computer science education and widespread investment in on-the-job training in the use of software systems, generous funding of software research and development by the U.S. government, and the enormous U.S. market for hardware and software.

We now know that large and potentially large installed bases of computer systems enhance investment in software development. Software in turn supports the sales of compatible computer hardware. Change in the software industry is likely to be driven by the proliferation of computational "platforms," such as widely accepted personal computer and workstation models, and the associated demand for large investments in software development to support application of these platforms. Many of the platforms that will influence software development in the coming years are not yet available. The recent introduction of personal digital assistants (PDAs), handheld computers that accelerate the trend toward portability, and plans for the development of customer equipment, including PDAs, that will allow access to services offered over a "national information infrastructure" of fiber optic telecommunication networks, suggest that the coming decade will initiate another cycle of investment in software creation that involves all of the actors that have emerged to date and perhaps new ones as well.

NOTES

The author is grateful to the Markle Foundation and the Center for Economic Policy Research for financial support underlying this research, to David Mowery for his substantial intellectual and editorial contributions to this chapter, and to others who have helped me develop the ideas and expression of this chapter, including Timothy Bresnahan, Franco Malerba, Tom Cottrell, Salvatore Torrisi, Yasunori Baba, Peter Grindley, and Robert Merges.

1. For example, Gordon (1990) estimates that the annual rate of decline reduction in computer hardware costs averaged 19 percent for the 1954–84 period.

2. There is no clear boundary between hardware and software. Any information processing operation that can be achieved with "instructions" can also be achieved by a hardware subsystem. For example, systems may be designed that use software instructions for finding the square root of a number; alternatively, an electronic component can be constructed that performs the same function within the system. Similarly, many electronic systems employ "programmable" components, components whose instructions are permanently built in at the time of system manufacture. The software in these systems is "embedded" in the electronic system. The economics and industrial structure implications of embedded software, while of growing importance, are not considered in this chapter.

3. The ability to reuse may, on occasion, be contractually limited.

4. The term "reused" refers to the use of large blocks of instructions in the delivery of multiple outputs. Reuse allows software producers to "customize" software for clients more economically than designing from scratch. While reuse is assumed to be quite frequent, there is little evidence about its actual extent.

5. This has happened in nations with no effective intellectual property right protection for software. At the same time, the rents available from protection are limited by the competition of "noninfringing" substitutes.

6. Moreover, although all software is complementary in demand with hardware, some software may raise the level of hardware demand more than others (for example, software that demands intensive use of the computational or mass storage hardware), and we expect to find hardware producers more active in these areas than in other areas (for example, in areas that permit users to conserve on their use of hardware).

7. Information goods that can be protected from copying can command prices in excess of the marginal costs of reproduction. If a given product's price provides more than sufficient revenues to recover the costs of developing, marketing, and maintaining the product, the pro-

ducer will earn economic profits. Entry of independent producers is therefore likely if such entrants can overcome advantages of computer producers in the simultaneous design of hardware and if software and computer users are disinclined to offer or relatively inefficient at offering their internally produced software to others. As we will see, all of these conditions eventually were fulfilled.

8. See chapter 7 in this volume.

9. For example, one of the pioneering relational database products, dBase II, III, and IV, originated in a program developed at the Jet Propulsion Laboratory.

10. Unfortunately, embedded software cannot be covered here. Of the features discussed, the only one of particular relevance to embedded software is the role of feedback in accelerating the advance of user interfaces, discussed in the section on the personal computer revolution below. Chapter 5 in this volume attempts to estimate the size of the "user-produced" software sector in Japan.

11. See Roach 1987 and Strassmann 1990 for reviews of this issue.

12. In addition to the information provided in Figure 2-1, other sources provide some evidence about earlier periods and suggest some qualifications to the empirical conclusions suggested by Figure 2-1.

For information on the pre-1970 relative expenditures on hardware and software, see Phister (1976). Phister reports results of a series of *Datamation* facility surveys that indicate that purchased software costs only became significant in 1967 when they were 0.1 percent and gradually increased to 1.4 percent by 1974, the ending date of his report. More significant, costs of system analysts and programmers accounted for 20.9 percent of system operating costs in 1955 and gradually rose to 32.3 percent by 1970 and remained near that level for the remaining four years of data he reports.

Two snapshots are available in OECD 1985, 82. Between 1979 and 1985 total software expenditures more than doubled (from $51.9 billion to $113.3 billion, and the share of software expenditures increased from 15 percent to 19 percent.

There has, however, been some controversy over the extent of software cost increase. Gurbaxani and Mendelson (1987) note that the software costs reported to IDC (a leading consulting company) by data processing managers are a stable fraction of total EDP (electronic data processing) budgets. There are, however, three problems with this analysis. The first is that the growing deployment of computer hardware should engage economies of scale in software use for the shared systems under DP manager control, easing cost increases in this portion of the company's computer budget. Second, EDP budgets are often only a portion of the software investments because many companies have active departmental computing programs and the share of software in departmental budgets may differ from department data processing expenditures. Third, it is unclear how EDP department personnel costs should be assigned because many of these personnel are involved in programming activities. Because personnel costs are the most rapidly increasing portion of costs, accounting for internal software production would raise the share of software in corporate EDP costs for the years reported.

13. Even with very high costs of developing such programs as Lotus 1-2-3 and Word-Perfect, the number of purchasers for these programs was unprecedented, and the increase in returns must surely be attributable to these products. Moreover, in the software industry the costs of failure cannot be passed on to consumers by increasing the price of some other product; instead they are borne by investors.

14. Histories of the origins of the computer industry include Flamm 1988 on the government role in the creation of the computer, Bashe et al. 1986 on IBM's early computers, and Williams 1985 on the technological history of computing devices (including precursors to the electronic computer).

15. The Univac I, Remington Rand's commercialization of a computer designed by Eck-

ert and Mauchly, and the IBM 701 launched the first generation of general-purpose commercial computers.

16. In 1928 the five largest manufacturers of data processing equipment based on punched cards recorded profits of $32 million on sales of $180 million, and the same companies recorded lower profits ($19 million) on an equal sales volume in 1937. The annual prewar revenues in this market were larger than the value of the installed base of general purpose computers in 1956, the era of the first generation (vacuum tube) computer (Beniger 1986).

17. For an exploration of the role of lock-in as an influence on user choice see Greenstein 1991. An explanation of how lock-in was partially overcome through the growth of "niche" markets is developed in Bresnahan and Greenstein 1992.

18. For example, IBM supplied interpreters, programs that ease the problem of machine language programming by translating "assembly code" instructions into machine-readable computer codes.

19. Of course, this process also increases the substitutability among all types of computers. Programs such as operating systems (many of which are machine-specific) therefore may play a special role in the strategies of computer system manufacturers.

20. IBM and its competitors provided significant assistance in software through the sales function. In IBM's approach, an application with significant value was identified and IBM and company engineers worked cooperatively to implement the software, often in cooperation with external contractors.

21. Bashe et al. 1986, 347–49. Although Share fell short of early expectations, it became important with the introduction of IBM's 704 in 1955 and accumulated a library of three hundred programs.

22. Estimates of the value of domestic software and services market from CBEMA 1983 as excerpted in Juliussen and Juliussen 1990.

23. IBM would also spin off its service bureau operations to Control Data (DeLamarter 1986, 87, 94).

24. On December 6, 1968, IBM announced that significant changes in IBM marketing practices would be made in the following year. On December 11, 1968, Control Data Corporation (CDC) sued IBM for antitrust violations following two years of gathering data on IBM's practices, data that CDC shared with the Department of Justice. *U.S. vs. IBM* was filed a month later with claims similar to those offered by CDC (Brock 1975, 170). The protracted resolution of *U.S. vs. IBM* certainly prevented IBM from reconsidering its unbundling decision during the 1970s.

25. Pugh, Johnson, and Palmer (1991, 331–45) employ the term "trauma" to describe this experience. For a summary of System/360 system software development see Brooks 1975, especially pp. 47–48.

26. Both comparisons are drawn from Phister 1976, pt. 2, 343–44 and 350–51. The speed comparison is based on the machines' relative Knight index, a measure based on the speed of executing instructions in different types of applications where the frequency of particular instructions is used as a weight on their execution speed.

27. Experiments with time sharing had begun when John McCarthy and his colleagues at MIT sought a means to address their own software development needs during 1960 and 1961 (Pugh, Johnson, and Palmer 1991, 355–56). IBM launched several experimental time-sharing system software development efforts including the System/360 Time Sharing System (TSS) in 1967. Despite these efforts, the performance goals demanded of time sharing were not met. A history of IBM concludes, "Having been victimized by over-optimism, time sharing temporarily floundered during the last half of the 1960s" (Pugh, Johnson, and Palmer 1991, 364). While part of IBM's problems with developing time-sharing systems stemmed from failure to embrace computer architectures optimized to this application and the shortcomings of its early time-sharing operating systems, companies such as General Electric that had overcome both

hurdles fared little better. General Electric's 265 system was adopted by MIT and Bell Laboratories and was responsible for GE's leading position in the time-sharing services market of the late 1960s. Nonetheless, this system (as well as IBM's) experienced accelerating decline in performance as users were added and, by several measures, was more expensive than batch computing on mainframe computers (see Sharpe 1969, 509–17).

28. Two contemporary viewpoints on decentralization were those of Tomaszewksi (1972), who advocated mobile "gypsy" development teams for centralized computers, and Wagner (1976), who argued that dedicated use of cheaper computers makes sense even with enormous unused capacity. Wagner's hardware-based solution prevailed, largely because of the reductions in hardware costs made possible by the minicomputer.

29. Such real-time systems had previously been developed for cost-insensitive applications such as the control of military and space missions. The minicomputer allowed similar techniques to be employed in commercial applications.

30. Growth in U.S. shipments in minicomputers depends upon classification. Table 2-1 includes estimates of both Phister and the Computer and Business Equipment Manufacturers Association (CBEMA). Phister's inclusion of smaller and more specialized machines raises his estimate and pushes the date of first shipments of minicomputers back in time to 1957.

31. To be precise it was 4.738 percent. The 1970 output of the computer and peripheral industry (SIC 7573) was $4,984 million while gross private domestic nonresidential investment $105.2 billion.

32. *Datamation* estimated IBM's 1975 software revenues at 10 percent of its $11.1 billion revenues (*Datamation* 1976).

33. During the 1970s, EDS began to provide on-site data processing services for large clients.

34. The enhanced computational capabilities of the System/370 were complemented by its use of integrated circuit memory, which proved to be faster and ultimately cheaper for storage of data and software instructions than ferrite core memory. (See Pugh 1984 for a detailed history of ferrite core memory, the critical technology for computer memory until the 1970s.)

35. The petrochemicals sector led the demand for minicomputers; installations grew from 300 in 1964 to 2,000 in 1974 (see Phister 1976, pt. 1, 134.

36. Unfortunately, Gepner (1977) did not report user characteristics. He does report that 30,000 surveys were sent out and 5,813 returned, a response percentage of almost 20 percent. Unless the mailing list was biased, this is a large enough sample to capture a significant share of the minicomputer users of the period.

37. For example, one software entrepreneur noted: "It is not at all uncommon for a programmer to threaten resignation, while simultaneously generating the type of undocumented programs that increases management's dependence on him. Thus he is in a position of strength from which he can (and, in the aggregate, often does) use mild blackmail to achieve greater status, money or dominance over management" (Brandon 1970). See Kraft 1977 for the alternative view, that programmers' work was becoming "deskilled" and routinized.

38. The quality shortcomings of software were a frequent subject in the trade press and in conferences of the 1970s. For example, at the 1974 National Computer Conference the president of the American Federation of Information Processing Societies "accused the data processing industry of ignoring the growing inability of the programming profession to produce enough good software." (See Dolotta et al. 1976 for the quoted paraphrase of G. Glaser's remarks and the cite to Glaser 1974, the published version of the speech.) One example from *Datamation,* of many in the trade press, quotes Tom Steel of Equitable Life Assurance: "Quality is, of course, a complex attribute, but by whatever measure one chooses, current software scores low. It is usually inadequate functionally, inconsistent between actuality and documentation, error-ridden and inexcusably inefficient. Beyond all that, it costs far too much. I can

think of no other products (aside, perhaps, from pornography and telephone service in New York) that have all these failings to anything like the degree found in software" (Kirkley 1974, 65).

39. Its share continued to grow until well into the 1980s, eventually leveling off at about one-half.

40. Note that Apple Computer's operating system software for its Macintosh computers was bundled with the sale of the hardware and thus is not recorded as software revenue.

41. Langlois (1992) provides a concise history of the early development of personal computers before and including IBM's introduction of the PC.

42. See chapter 6 for additional discussion. Network externalities increase the value of participation in a particular network. The telephone network is the archetypal example of network externalities; the value of a telephone connection increases as the number of others connected to the telephone network increases. A de facto standard is established by market outcomes, in contrast to a de jure standard, which is established by some deliberative process.

43. IBM initially retained a proprietary advantage in the embedded software of the IBM PC that disappeared when small software companies succeeded in duplicating its functionality, a development that launched the PC-compatible or "clone" market.

44. The Software Publishers Association, established in the early 1980s, immediately began to publish information about the unit shipments of particular products and award "gold" and "platinum" status to best-selling products. See Software Publishers Association 1988, 1989, and 1990 for examples.

45. A major transition in the personal computer industry occurred when Compaq and IBM introduced new MS-DOS-based computers based on the Intel iAPX 386 microprocessor. The iAPX386, also called the 80386, employed a memory addressing method that made it possible to develop software programs far larger than those that could be created for previous models of IBM and IBM-compatible computers. In combination with the greater availability of high-capacity hard disk drives, the iAPX386 and its successors made it possible to devise much larger and more complex software products for the personal computer, including Microsoft's Windows.

46. Nonetheless, the gross margins of Lotus Development and Microsoft were 81 percent and 74 percent respectively in 1989. These are impressive margins, even with the higher product development (R&D) costs of 14–15 percent experienced in the late 1980s (see *Business Week* 1990).

47. Langlois (1992, 22) reports that IBM eschewed using the 8086 microprocessor for the IBM PC to avoid creating a machine that would compete more directly with other IBM products.

48. From research notes by Carolyn Judy, Center for Economic Policy Research, Stanford University.

49. For each year from 1985 through 1990, the percentage of vendors offering a single product were 68, 67, 69, 66, 61, and 60 (calculated from research notes provided by Carolyn Judy; see previous note). The lower percentage in 1989 and 1990 may reflect the change in Unix used for Sun's operating system, a change that was supposed to encourage software development.

50. EDS is also active in the market for more limited services.

51. See chapter 3 for more discussion of U.S. government programs.

52. Another example of software developed specifically for networks include Lotus Development's Notes, which provides a means to distribute and comment on documents over networked computers.

53. See Cusumano 1991 and Nakahara 1993 for different views of the Japanese approach to the same problem.

54. The intellectual property debates over "look and feel" and the alleged infringement

by Microsoft Windows on Apple's operating system were only the beginning of these kinds of disputes; as users seek to construct a web of interactions among their programs they will undoubtedly become more frequent.

REFERENCES

Austrian, Geoffrey D. 1982. *Herman Hollerith: Forgotten Giant of Information Processing.* New York: Columbia University Press.

Bashe, Charles J., Lyle R. Johnson, John H. Palmer, and Emerson W. Pugh. 1986. *IBM's Early Computers.* Cambridge, Mass.: MIT Press.

Baumol, William J., Sue Anne Batey Blackman, and Edward N. Wolff. 1989. *Productivity and American Leadership: The Long View.* Cambridge, Mass.: MIT Press.

Beniger, James R. 1986. *The Control Revolution: Technological and Economic Origins of the Information Society.* Cambridge, Mass.: Harvard University Press.

Barry W. Boehm. 1973. "Software and Its Impact: A Quantitative Assessment." *Datamation.* May: 48–59.

Boehm, Barry W. 1981. *Software Engineering Economics.* Englewood Cliffs, N.J.: Prentice Hall.

Brandon, Dick H. 1970. "The Economics of Computer Programming." In George F. Weinwurm, *On the Management of Computer Programming.* New York: Petrocelli Books.

Bresnahan, Timothy F., and Shane Greenstein. 1992. "Technological Competition and the Structure of the Computer Industry." Center for Economic Policy Research, Stanford University, CEPR Publication #315, Palo Alto, Calif.

Brock, Gerald W. 1975. *The U.S. Computer Industry: A Study of Market Power.* Cambridge, Mass.: Ballinger.

Brooks, Frederick P., Jr. 1975. *The Mythical Man-Month: Essays on Software Engineering,* Reading, Mass.: Addison-Wesley.

Business Week. 1986. "Software: The Growing Gets Rough." 24 March, 128–34.

———. 1990. "Software: It's a New Game." 4 June, 102–6.

Computer and Business Equipment Manufacturers Association (CBEMA). 1983. *The Computer and Business Equipment Industry Marketing Data Book.* Washington, D.C.: CBEMA.

Cooper, John D. 1978. "Corporate Level Software Management." *IEEE Transactions on Software Engineering* SE-4, no. 4 (July): 319–26.

Cusumano, Michael A. 1991. *Japan's Software Factories: A Challenge to U.S. Management.* New York: Oxford University Press.

Datamation. 1976. "The Top 50 Companies in the Data Processing Industry. June, 49.

———. 1981. "The Datamation 100." June, 91.

———. 1982. "The Datamation 100." June, 115.

———. 1986. "The Datamation 100." 15 June, 43ff.

———. 1989. "The Datamation 100." 15 June, 7.

———. 1992. "The Datamation 100." 15 June, 12.

DeLamarter, Richard Thomas. 1986. *Big Blue: IBM's Use and Abuse of Power.* New York: Dodd, Mead.

Dolotta, T. A., M. I. Bernstein, R. S. Dickson, Jr., N. A. France, B. A. Rosenblatt, D. M. Smith, and T. B. Steel, Jr. 1976. *Data Processing in 1980–1985: A Study of Potential Limitations to Progress.* New York: John Wiley.

Fisher, Franklin M., James W. McKie, and Richard B. Mancke. 1983. *IBM and the U.S. Data Processing Industry: An Economic History.* New York: Praeger.

Flamm, Kenneth. 1988. *Creating the Computer: Government, Industry, and High Technology.* Washington, D.C.: Brookings Institution.

Gepner, Herbert L. 1977. "User Ratings of Software Packages." *Datamation* (December): 118.

Glaser, G. 1974. "Keynote Address, 1974 National Computer Conference." Montvale, N.J.: American Federation of Information Processing Societies.

Gordon, Robert J. 1989. "The Postwar Evolution of Computer Prices." In Dale W. Jorgenson and Ralph Landau, eds., *Technology and Capital Formation.* Cambridge, Mass.: MIT Press.

————. 1990. *The Measurement of Durable Goods Prices.* Chicago: University of Chicago Press.

Greenstein, Shane. 1991. "Lock-in and the Costs of Switching Mainframe Computer Vendors: What Do Buyers See?" Faculty Working Paper 90–1718, Political Economy Series #48. Champaign: University of Illinois.

Gurbaxani, Vijay, and Haim Mendelson. 1987. "Software and Hardware in Data Processing Budgets." *IEEE Transactions on Software Engineering* SE-13, no. 9 (September): 1010–17.

Hodges, Judith, and Deborah Melewski. 1991. "Top 50: Profiles of the Leading Independent Software Companies." *Software Magazine,* June, 23.

International Data Corporation (IDC). 1992. *Computer Industry Reports: The Gray Report.* Framingham, Mass.: IDC.

————. 1993. *Application Development Tools: 1993 Worldwide Software Review and Forecast.* Framingham, Mass.: IDC.

Juliussen, Karen, and Egil Juliussen. 1990. *The Computer Industry Almanac: 1991.* New York: Simon and Schuster.

Keen, Peter G. W., and Elihu M. Gerson. 1977. "The Politics of Software Systems Design." *Datamation* (November): 80–84.

Kirkley, John L. 1974. "The Critical Issues: A 1974 Perspective." *Datamation* (January): 64–67.

Kolence, Kolence. 1971. "Software View of Measurement Tools." *Datamation* (January): 32–38.

Kraft, Philip. 1977. *Programmers and Managers.* New York: Springer-Verlag.

Langlois, Richard N. 1992. "External Economies and Economic Progress: The Case of the Microcomputer Industry." *Business History Review* 66 (Spring): 1–50.

Larsen, Gerald H. 1973. "Software: A Qualitative Assessment." *Datamation* (November): 60–66.

Nakahara, Tetsushi. 1983. "The Industrial Organization and Information Structure of the Software Industry: A U.S.-Japan Comparison." Center for Economic Policy Research, Stanford University, CEPR Publication #346, Palo Alto, Calif.

Organization for Economic Cooperation and Development (OECD). 1985. *Software: An Emerging Industry.* Paris: OECD.

Phister, Montgomery, Jr. 1976. *Data Processing Technology and Economics.* Santa Monica, Calif.: Santa Monica Publishing Co.

Pugh, Emerson W. 1984. *Memories That Shaped an Industry: Decisions Leading to IBM System/360.* Cambridge, Mass.: MIT Press.

Pugh, Emerson W., Lyle R. Johnson, and John H. Palmer. 1991. *IBM's 360 and Early 370 Systems.* Cambridge, Mass.: MIT Press.

Roach, Stephen S. 1988. "America's Technology Dilemma: A Profile of the Information Economy." Special Economic Study. New York: Morgan Stanley. April 22.

Sammet, J. E. 1985. "Brief Summary of the Early History of COBOL." *Annals of the History of Computing* 7: 288–303.

Sharpe, William F. 1969. *The Economics of Computers*. A Rand Corporation Research Study. New York: Columbia University Press.

Siwek, Stephen W., and Harold W. Furchtgott-Roth. 1993. *International Trade in Computer Software*. Westport, Conn.: Quorum Books.

Software Publishers Association. 1988. *Publishers' Software Sales Report: 1988 Annual Report*. Washington, D.C.: SPA.

———. 1989. *Publishers' Software Sales Report: 1989 Annual Report*. Washington, D.C.: SPA.

———. 1990. *Publishers' Software Sales Report: 1990 Annual Report*. Washington, D.C.: SPA.

Strassmann, Paul A. 1990. *The Business Value of Computers*. New Canaan, Conn.: Information Economics Press.

Tomaszewski, L. A. 1972. "Decentralized Development." *Datamation* (November): 61–64.

Wagner, Frank V. 1976. "Is Decentralization Inevitable?" *Datamation* (November): 86–97.

Williams, Michael R., *A History of Computing Technology*. Englewood Cliffs, N.J.: Prentice-Hall.

3

The Federal Government Role in the Development of the U.S. Software Industry

Richard N. Langlois and David C. Mowery

The development of the U.S. computer software industry has been powerfully influenced by federal government policy during the postwar period. Its importance for the demands of cold war defense, especially strategic air defense during the 1950s, meant that the software industry received considerable federal R&D and procurement funding throughout the postwar period. But the very novelty of computer technology and software meant that a substantial portion of the defense-related spending in software was allocated to the creation of an infrastructure that would support a new area of R&D, training, and technology development. Federal support for the creation of this infrastructure provided important benefits to the commercial U.S. software industry. From the earliest years of the postwar era, private industry has been responsible for a great deal of innovation in software; but by the 1960s, these industrial innovations drew on research and manpower that had been generously supported by federal government funds.

Because of the complex and changing relationship between software and hardware technology during the postwar period, much of the influence of federal government policies on the software industry was channeled through programs affecting the computer industry as a whole. For example, for much of the postwar period federal agencies' development and procurement expenditures for hardware included spending on software.

Federal policy toward the U.S. software industry in many ways resembled the history of federal support for other postwar high-technology industries. As it did for airframes (Mowery and Rosenberg 1982), semiconductors (Levin 1982), and computer hardware (Katz and Phillips 1982; Flamm 1987), defense-related support for both R&D and procurement accelerated the early development of the industry. And as it did in those other industries, the influence of defense-related procurement on the commercial software industry declined as defense needs diverged from those of a burgeoning commercial market. Indeed, throughout the 1980s, Pentagon policymakers sought ways to tap commercial software applications and operating systems for military use. There are also some important differences between the software and other high-technology industries, however, most notably in the nature and evolution of military-civilian spillovers and in the role of federally funded university research.

Rosenberg (1992) has argued that the computer is one of the most significant examples of a large class of scientific instruments that have been developed in universities and widely applied in industrial economies. Rosenberg's observations concerning the "instrumental" nature of the computer are borne out by the history of federal policy in software innovation in at least two ways: (1) the key role of the university within the software industry; and (2) the importance of federal support for universities' adoption of the mainframe computer, the critical instrument for software research and innovation.

In contrast to their stereotypical role as performers of basic research, university researchers pioneered in the development of computer technology well in advance of industry in both the United States and Great Britain. British and U.S. universities, and research institutes affiliated with them, were responsible for important advances during the late 1940s and early 1950s in computer architecture and hardware, including the stored-program concepts that were the origins of software. Much of the federal government's early postwar efforts to develop computer technology relied on university researchers.

In both nations, but especially in the United States, technological advances and researchers from universities entered the domestic electronics industry, and industry came to dominate the development of subsequent generations of hardware. Universities remained important, however, in many software advances from the mid-1950s onward. The contributions of U.S. universities to these developments relied on the growth of a new academic discipline, computer science. The creation of this academic field was aided by federal support during the 1950s and 1960s for the purchase of the scientific instrument that was indispensable to computer science research, the mainframe computer.

The software industry, like other postwar high-technology U.S. industries, drew on defense-related support for applications development and basic research. Direct "spillovers"—that is, widely adopted civilian versions of software developed initially for military applications—did appear, but these were supplemented by advances from the private sector (Flamm 1988, 26). Other advances (including several important programming languages and operating systems) were developed in universities with federal funding.

Growing concern in the Department of Defense about the soaring costs, project delays, and unreliability of complex, software-intensive weapons systems were heightened by the Strategic Defense Initiative of the 1980s. Efforts to reduce the cost of defense-related software spawned two Department of Defense (DoD) initiatives during the late 1970s and 1980s—a program in "software engineering," and (some years earlier than similar efforts in other dual-use technologies) efforts to utilize commercial software for military applications. The second of these initiatives has had only limited success.

Throughout the postwar period, the federal government has accounted for a large share of total U.S. demand for software. Flamm estimated that the federal government was the largest single U.S. customer for traded software in 1982 (1987, 122–23). More recent data on market trends are not available, but it is likely that the federal government's share of the U.S. market for traded software has declined since then. A great deal of defense-related software procurement has involved the purchase of "embedded" software. There are relatively few examples of major "standard" operating systems, programming languages, or applications being developed initially for federal agencies. But the development of custom software and services for federal purchasers was for much of the 1960s and 1970s a rapidly growing industry in Washington, D.C., and environs.

This discussion of the federal role in the U.S. software industry focuses primarily on policies that directly affected the industry (not including intellectual property protection, which is covered in another chapter of this volume). We begin with a description of the earliest years of federal involvement in the U.S. computer industry, a period during which software scarcely existed as a distinguishable technology or as a focus of development effort. We then examine the federal role in supporting the emergence of computer science as an academic discipline, a discussion that spans 1955–90. The role of the DoD during this period is the subject of the next section. We briefly discuss the activities of another important U.S. agency in software development and procurement, the National Aeronautics and Space Administration (NASA). The concluding section summarizes our argument and points out how the U.S. experience has differed from those of other industrial economies.

THE EARLY YEARS

Software technology did not develop in a political or institutional vacuum; nor was government policy unaffected by changes in the nature of software technology. Despite a number of prewar precursors, the history of computer hardware and (eventually) software development begins with World War II. During the war years, the American military sponsored a number of projects to develop computers to solve special military problems. The ENIAC (electronic numerical integrator and computer)—generally considered the first fully electronic digital computer—was funded by Army Ordnance, which was concerned with the computation of firing tables for guns. MIT's Whirlwind computer, which was introduced in 1951, grew (after a difficult adolescence) out of a project begun in 1943 to create an analog-computer flight simulator for pilot training.

In the earliest days of postwar computer technology, software was literally indistinguishable from hardware. Software was effectively born with the advent of the von Neumann architecture for computers. In the summer of 1944, the mathematician John von Neumann learned by accident of the Army's ENIAC project. Developed by J. Presper Eckert and John W. Mauchly at the Moore School of the University of Pennsylvania, the ENIAC did not rely on software, but was hard-wired to solve a particular set of problems. Von Neumann began advising the Eckert-Mauchly team, which was working on the development of a new machine, the EDVAC (electronic discrete variable computer).

Out of this collaboration came the concept of the stored-program computer: instead of being hard-wired, the EDVAC's instructions were to be stored in memory, facilitating their modification. As we would now say, the computer could be programmed by software rather than hardware. Von Neumann's abstract discussion of the concept circulated widely and served as the logical basis for virtually all subsequent computers (von Neumann 1945). But even after the von Neumann scheme became dominant, which occurred rapidly in the 1950s, software remained closely bound to hardware. During the early 1950s, the organization designing the hardware generally designed the software as well. As computer technology developed and the market for its applications expanded after 1970, however, users, independent developers, and computer service firms began to play prominent roles in software development (see chapter 2).

Although military support for the ENIAC and Whirlwind projects began with narrowly defined goals, these programs produced general principles and technologies that found much broader application. Indeed, in the case of Whirlwind, the Navy never obtained its hoped-for flight simulator (Redmond and Smith 1980). Jay Forrester, who took charge of the project in 1943, became embroiled in a prolonged struggle with the Office of Naval Research (the primary postwar Navy research funding agency) over his desire to shift the project to the development of a general-purpose digital computer rather than a flight simulator. The Whirlwind project, which was by far the most expensive of the early postwar federal computer programs, was spared only when the U.S. Air Force adopted it as the basis for the SAGE (semi-automatic ground environment) air-defense system that began in the early 1950s.[1] In addition to driving the development of a reliable large computing system and the communications technologies necessary to link these computers with radar networks, SAGE was among the earliest programs in large-scale software development (Tropp 1983).

The development of a U.S. software industry really began only when the first stored-program computers begin appearing in significant numbers. The first fully operational stored-program computer in the United States was the SEAC (Standards Electronic Automatic Computer), a machine built on a shoestring by the National Bureau of Standards in 1950 (Flamm 1988, 74). A number of important machines followed. Among these, in addition to Whirlwind and ENIAC, were:

- the IAS computer, in 1951, built by von Neumann at the Institute for Advanced Study and "cloned" at the Rand Corporation and four national labs. Funding came from the Army, the Navy, and RCA, among others.
- Univac (universal automatic computer), 1953, built by Remington Rand, which had bought the rights to the Eckert-Mauchly technology. Early customers included the Census Bureau and other government agencies as well as private firms.
- the IBM 701, in 1953, developed by IBM and influenced by the IAS design. It was originally developed as a scientific computer for the Defense Department, which bought most of the first units.

The most commercially successful machine of the decade, with sales of 1,800 units, was the low-priced IBM 650 (Fisher, McKie, and Mancke 1983, 17). The

650, often called the Model T of computing, thrust IBM into industry leadership (Katz and Phillips 1982, 178; Flamm 1988, 83). Even in the case of the 650, how-ever, government procurement was crucial: the projected sale of fifty machines to the federal government (a substantial portion of the total forecast sales of 250 machines) influenced IBM's decision to initiate the project. The large commercial market for computers that was created by the 650 provided strong incentives for industry to develop software for this architecture.

Programming all of these early machines was a tedious process that resembled programming a mechanical calculator: the programmer had to explicitly specify in hardware terms (the memory addresses) the sequence of steps the computer would undertake. This characteristic tied program development closely to a particular ma-chine, because programmers had to understand its hardware architecture. Since few models of any single machine were available, programming techniques developed for one machine had very limited applicability. This was one reason the commercial success of the IBM 650 was crucial to advances in software and in programming techniques. The 650 created a generic "platform" for the development of programs that could run on a large installed base.[2]

Perhaps the main bottleneck of this "machine-language programming," how-ever, was the difficulty of changing a program. Inserting new data or instructions into the sequence required changing most, if not all, memory references. In response to this problem, programming tools—rudimentary languages—appeared. For exam-ple, researchers at IBM and in the Whirlwind group at MIT developed symbolic assembly languages in which coded statements referred to "symbolic" addresses that the computer converted to specific hardware locations (Sammet 1969, 3; Bashe et al. 1986, 323–38).

In general, the direction of technological advance was toward higher-level lan-guages—that is, languages employing a relatively user-friendly notation that software could later translate into machine language. These advances included assemblers, interpreters, and compilers. The last is a program that translates a higher-level "source" code into a machine-language "object" code that a specific computer can understand. In this way a higher-level language can become machine-independent; different compilers can translate the same source code into different machine lan-guages. The first commercial compiler was the A-0, developed for the Remington Rand Univac by Grace Murray Hopper, who described it as a means to support "automatic programming," using the computer to automate some of the tasks of machine-language coding (Hopper 1954, cited in Bashe et al. 1986, 431; see also Sammet 1969, 13, and Hopper 1981, passim).

Much of the early work on automatic programming was conducted not at univer-sities but at the laboratories of computer makers and users. Hopper, a veteran of the wartime military Mark I project at Harvard, was supported by Remington Rand in developing the A-0 compiler. The assembler most widely used on IBM machines was developed by a user (United Aircraft) and disseminated through an IBM users' group called Share (Bashe et al. 1986, 358). Fortran (for formula translator), the first genuine higher-level language, also was developed by IBM researchers (Backus 1981). And the earliest IBM operating system—the program that stage-manages the execution of programs and the use of peripherals—was written at the General Motors Research Laboratories (Bashe et al. 1986, 359). An important exception to this general pattern was MIT, where in the early 1950s the Whirlwind group developed not only a symbolic assembler but also an operating system and an algebraic compiler that anticipated some of the capabilities of Fortran (Flamm 1988, Table A4; Backus 1981). But the unique architecture of Whirlwind and its operation solely as a research instrument meant that the automatic-programming techniques developed for Whirlwind had significantly less influence than their private sector counterparts.

The federal government influenced the development of early automatic programming techniques by supporting the dissemination of information. The U.S. armed forces, from the earliest days of their support for the development of computer technology, were surprisingly eager for technical information about this innovation to reach the widest possible audience, in some contrast to the military in Great Britain or the Soviet Union.[3] The Office of Naval Research organized seminars on automatic programming in 1951, 1954, and 1956 (Rees 1982, 120). Along with similar conferences sponsored by computer firms, universities, and the meetings of the fledgling Association for Computing Machinery (ACM), the ONR conferences circulated ideas within a developing community of practitioners who did not yet have journals or other formal channels of communication (Hopper 1981). The ONR also established the Institute for Numerical Analysis at UCLA which made important contributions to the overall field of computer science (Rees 1982, 110–11).

The private sector took some of the first steps to build the discipline of computer science within U.S. universities. Computer manufacturers recognized that their support of higher education would reap public-relations benefits and increase demand for their products at universities (Fisher, McKie, and Mancke 1983, 169). Academic computing would attack the software bottleneck by training more programmers and would "lock in" future users and buyers of computer equipment.[4]

For example, in addition to offering price discounts on its machines, Control Data Corporation (CDC) offered research grants, free computer time, and cash contributions to U.S. universities (Fisher, McKie, and Mancke 1983, 170). In addition to donating computer time to establish regional computing centers at MIT and UCLA in the mid-1950s, IBM rented some fifty of its model 650 computers to universities at reduced rates (Galler 1986; Fisher, McKie, and Mancke 1983, 170–72).[5] For example, the IBM 650 at the Carnegie Institute of Technology's new Graduate School of Industrial Administration, which was used by Herbert Simon, Allen Newell, and Alan Perlis in their early work on artificial intelligence, was acquired with funds from private foundations, although Simon and others also received support as consultants to the Rand Corporation (Bach 1986).

The institution-building efforts of the National Science Foundation and the DoD came to overshadow private sector contributions by the late 1950s. In 1963 about half of the $97 million spent by universities on computer equipment came from the federal government, while the universities themselves paid for 34 percent and computer makers picked up the remaining 16 percent (Fisher, McKie, and Mancke 1983, 169).

The federal government's expanding role in supporting R&D during the 1950s, much of which was located in U.S. universities, was supplemented by procurement spending on military systems. The government's different needs from those of the commercial sector had important implications for the "production technologies" employed in defense and commercial software. Initially, defense-related demand for software (outside of logistics applications) was aimed not at general-purpose automatic programming tools but at special-purpose, large-scale software for specific defense applications, such as air defense.

The most conspicuous early example of defense-related software development and procurement was the SAGE air-defense system, the computerized early-warning system developed and deployed in the 1950s. It involved by far the largest programming effort of the day. In 1950 the Air Force established the MIT Lincoln Laboratories to develop air-defense technology. This effort absorbed MIT's Whirlwind project and evolved into SAGE. Although the Whirlwind had long since severed its connection to the flight simulator project, it had been designed for real-time command-and-control applications rather than for batch processing and was one of the first examples of a "mission-critical" defense computer. Successful tests of the SAGE system on Cape Cod led to a full-scale development effort in 1953, coordinated by Lincoln Labs. Lincoln Labs chose IBM to produce operational computers that were based on the Whirlwind model; AT&T developed the communications system that linked the radar units; and Burroughs built peripheral equipment. A division of the Rand Corporation that soon spun off to become System Development Corporation (SDC) took up the massive programming task.[6]

The Rand group that became SDC started out as a psychological testing unit engaged in simulating interactions between humans and machines in radar-defense installations. In addition, Rand in 1955 already employed what one official estimated to be 10 percent of all the qualified programmers in the country—about twenty-five people (Baum 1981, 23). By 1959 SDC had more than 800 programmers working on SAGE (ibid., 35). By 1963 SDC had 4,300 employees (not all of whom were programmers) and, more significantly, some 6,000 former employees spread throughout the computer industry (ibid., 47). One of the greatest contributions of SAGE was its training of a large cadre of educated systems programmers. Indeed, because SDC was restricted by Air Force pay scales and because it sought to play this training role, the company encouraged turnover, which ran to 20 percent per year (ibid., 51). As one SAGE veteran noted in the early 1980s, "the chances are reasonably high that on a large data processing job in the 1970s you would find at least one person who had worked with the SAGE system" (Benington 1983, 351).

SAGE also contributed to the embryonic discipline of software engineering. Although many claim that this discipline was born at a 1968 NATO conference (Naur, Randell, and Buxton 1976), SDC developed many of the programming and organizational techniques later associated with software engineering. These included modular design techniques that facilitated task decomposition and organized the division of labor in large projects.

SAGE was the first of many large-scale government programming projects. After SAGE, SDC undertook the development of a command-and-control system for the Strategic Air Command that required a then-astounding one million lines of code. SDC also developed JOVIAL (Jules's own version of the international algebraic language), a higher-level programming language for command-and-control applications that was widely used in industry. (JOVIAL was named for Jules Schwartz, whose idea it was and who led the development team at SDC). By 1960, however, SDC began to face competition from the vertically integrated software divisions of large firms such as Boeing and TRW and from the more than 2,000 firms that had begun to enter the contract-software business (Cusumano 1991, 121). SDC abandoned its nonprofit status in 1969 and eventually merged with Burroughs in 1981.

The federal government remained a major purchaser of contract software well into the 1980s. By one estimate, the Defense Department spent some $4–8 billion on contract software in 1982 (Flamm 1987, 123).

COMPUTER SCIENCE AND THE SOFTWARE INDUSTRY: CREATING AN ACADEMIC DISCIPLINE

The other chapters in this volume emphasize the role of universities in the growth of the software industries of Western Europe, Japan, and Russia. Universities have been important sites for both applied and basic research in software and have contributed to the development of new hardware. In addition, the university training of engineers and scientists active in the software industry has been extremely important. Universities, with their relatively "open" research and operating environment that emphasizes publication, their relatively high levels of turnover among research staff, and their production of graduates who seek employment elsewhere, can serve as sites for the dissemination and diffusion of innovations throughout the global software industry.

U.S. universities provided important channels for cross-fertilization and information exchange between industry and academia, and also between defense and civilian research efforts in software and in computer science generally. In Britain a lack of interchange between military and civilian researchers and engineers weakened the early postwar British computer industry;[7] the very different situation in the United States enhanced the competitiveness of this nation's hardware and software industry complex. In Japan and the Soviet Union the more modest role of universities in computer science and software-related research activities also reduced the exchange of knowledge and hampered the pace of technological progress in those nations' software industries (see chapters 5, 6, and 9).

Federal policy contributed to the central role of U.S. research universities in the advancement of hardware and software technologies. As pointed out earlier, universities were among the first developers of computers, supported by wartime and early postwar R&D contracts from the federal government. But even after the rise of a substantial private sector computer hardware industry, federal R&D support aided the creation of the new academic discipline of computer science. But the creation and legitimation of a new academic discipline, particularly in the applied and engineering sciences, is itself not novel. Partly because of their decentralized structure and financing, U.S. universities frequently have responded to the demands of industry (and, in some cases, the state governments that supported so many U.S. universities) by developing new academic departments and disciplines in areas such as chemical engineering, electrical engineering, and aeronautical engineering (Rosenberg and Nelson 1994; Mowery and Rosenberg 1993). Private firms also supported the early development of academic computer science, but their contributions and support soon were outweighed by those of the federal government. Much of the government financial support was motivated by defense concerns.

Although comprehensive data on federal R&D support for academic research in computer science are difficult to obtain, the data in Figure 3-1 display trends in total

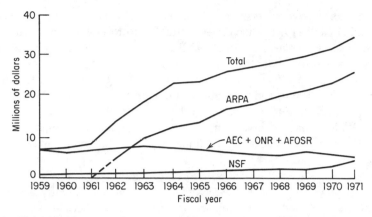

Figure 3-1. Federal R&D support for computer science, fiscal years 1959–71. AEC, Atomic Energy Commission; ONR, Office of Naval Research; AFOSR, Air Force Office of Scientific Research. *Source:* National Science Foundation 1970.

federal support for computer science R&D between 1959 and 1971 and show how important DoD-related sources of funding were throughout this period. Figure 3-1 points out the rapid rise of the Advanced Research Projects Agency (ARPA) support for computer science R&D. (ARPA was established in 1958 to conduct long-range R&D of interest to all of the armed services. It was renamed DARPA in 1972 and re-renamed ARPA in 1992.) Since its data include federally supported R&D performed outside of universities, the figure understates the importance of the National Science Foundation (NSF) as a funder of academic computer science research. Nevertheless, according to Yudken and Simons (1988), defense-related agencies accounted for more than 50 percent of academic computer science R&D from fiscal year 1977 through the mid-1980s, and defense-related support for applied computer science research grew rapidly after fiscal year 1983.

The foundations for the contributions of U.S. universities to the growth of the software industry were laid during the 1950s by two federal agencies: NSF and ARPA. The approaches taken by these agencies to building a new academic discipline complemented each other: NSF's support was distributed broadly and ARPA's was concentrated in a few leading research universities.

During the early 1950s, NSF support for computer science was modest and was channeled through its mathematics research program (Aspray and Williams 1993a). This picture changed after the 1956 endorsement by the Advisory Panel on University Computing Facilities (chaired by John von Neumann) of a specialized NSF program for the support of computer science, the 1957 launch of Sputnik, and the 1958 passage of the National Defense Education Act. NSF support for computer science research grew rapidly after 1958, and was especially important in meeting the critical need of academic researchers for computer equipment. Between 1957 and 1972, the National Science Foundation gave $85 million to more than 200 universities for the purchase of computer hardware.

In an emergent discipline that depended on access to state-of-the-art equipment to conduct much of its research, these facilities grants for equipment literally laid the foundations (and in other cases, provided the equipment that was placed on those foundations) for many universities' computer science departments. According to Norberg and O'Neill (1992), "there were virtually no formal programs" in computer science in U.S. universities as of 1959. By 1965 the Association for Computing Machinery reported that more than fifteen universities offered doctorates in computer science and seventeen offered bachelor's degrees (ACM Curriculum Committee on Computer Science, 1965), and the number of degree holders rapidly expanded. Facilities grants peaked in 1967 and began to decline thereafter as a paradoxical consequence of White House intervention to create an Office of Computing Activities within NSF, which assigned a higher funding priority to computer education than to facilities.

The National Science Foundation also supported academic research in software. Figure 3-2 displays the growth of NSF funding for research in software and related areas between 1956 and 1980, which cumulatively amounted to more than $250 million (1987 dollars).[8] Among the contributions supported in part or entirely by NSF grants were the development of Pascal (a popular computer language), pathbreaking work in principles of software engineering, and early object-oriented programming languages, such as CLU.

The support of NSF for computer science research was organized along classic "basic research" principles of peer review and individual support. Because or in spite of this structure, NSF support was widely dispersed among U.S. universities.[9] The distribution and consequences of NSF's R&D programs contrast with those of ARPA computer science funding.[10]

Rather than being spread among many universities, ARPA support was concentrated among leading U.S. research universities, primarily Carnegie-Mellon, MIT, Stanford, and the University of California at Berkeley.[11] ARPA funding was intended to support the long-term development of institutional and team strengths and therefore was not allocated exclusively on the basis of individual performance or promise. Although expert panels played an important role in overseeing and reviewing its research programs, ARPA's support for computer science research was less tightly controlled by peer review than that of NSF. This flexible management approach was highly responsive to the needs of academic researchers.[12]

For much of ARPA's existence, its support for academic computer science research was channeled through IPTO, whose budget for the fiscal years 1965–85 is shown in Figure 3-3 (IPTO was disbanded in 1986). ARPA funding of academic computer science research contributed a number of important innovations in software and computer architecture, including computer time sharing (based on a project begun at MIT in the early 1960s when campus demand for computer time began to outpace the available supply), artificial intelligence architectures and software (including the LISP program), computer networking and communications (the ARPANET, forerunner of the NSFNET that underpins national and international electronic mail, was undertaken by ARPA as a means of linking researchers at its scattered "centers of excellence"),[13] and important modifications to the Unix operating system to improve its performance in computer networking applications. As we discuss in more detail below, during the late 1970s and early 1980s, ARPA also undertook a major initiative to improve software development and maintenance practices.

ARPA's concentrated research funding also made important educational contributions. ARPA research support for computer science in these universities, major

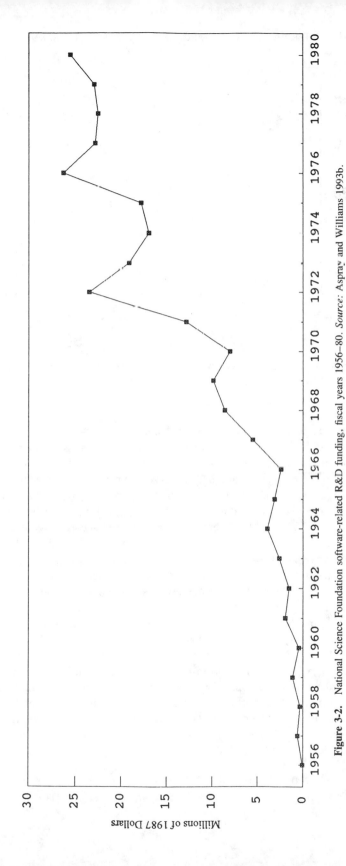

Figure 3-2. National Science Foundation software-related R&D funding, fiscal years 1956–80. *Source:* Aspray and Williams 1993b.

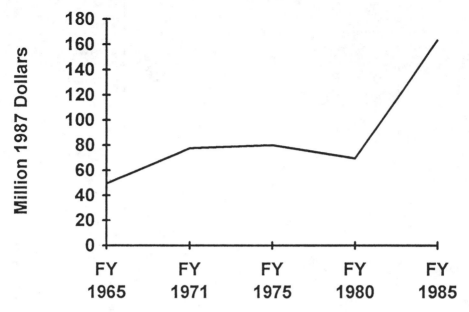

Figure 3-3. ARPA Information Processing Techniques Office R&D funding, fiscal years 1965–85. *Source:* Norberg and O'Neill 1992.

producers of academic researchers, had a substantial impact on computer science research and education in other U.S. universities. According to Norberg and O'Neill (1992, 140–41), in 1990, 26 percent of the faculty in the forty leading U.S. university departments of computer science had received their computer science Ph.D. degrees from one of the three major universities supported by ARPA—Stanford, Carnegie-Mellon, or MIT. The influence of these three institutions was even greater among the top ten U.S. computer science departments, where 42 percent of the tenured faculty and 53 percent of the nontenured faculty had received their Ph.D.s from one of these three universities.[14] Other Ph.D. graduates of these universities also found employment in senior positions in firms such as Silicon Graphics, Microsoft, and Sun Microsystems. Many faculty at these institutions also entered into formal and informal consulting relationships with private firms, and others were directly involved in the foundation of such important hardware and software firms as the Carnegie Group, Ingress, and Thinking Machines.

　　The original aim of ARPA support for academic research in computer science was the creation of a basic research infrastructure in this new discipline, which was already being exploited by defense agencies for applications. This infrastructure-building goal incorporated support for training of personnel and for research. ARPA's educational goals also influenced its academic research programs. Support for computer time sharing, for example, was motivated by a desire to allow universities to train undergraduate and graduate students in computer science as much as by direct defense needs.

　　After the late 1960s, the mix of IPTO projects and funding shifted in favor of applications. This shift was a response to the growing budget of IPTO, the diminishing tolerance of congressional and executive branch policymakers for fundamental research programs within the defense budget, and demands from the uniformed services for near-term solutions to such challenges as software development and maintenance. The increase of $10.5 million (more than 35 percent) in the IPTO budget during fiscal years 1971 through 1975, for example, masked an absolute decrease in the most fundamental research areas and increases in support for more applied projects. According to Norberg and O'Neill:

> The IPTO budget in FY 1971 represented 60% for basic research and 40% for exploratory development. By FY 1975, the numbers were approximately reversed: 43% for basic research and 57% for exploratory development. The split remained essentially the same for the FY 1980 budget, 42% and 58%, respectively. (1992, 8–9)

Defense-related support for academic computer science research continued to shift toward applied research through the mid-1980s. The effects of this shift were enhanced by the growth of defense-related R&D within overall federal computer science R&D funding. This source of academic R&D funding, which was more development-oriented than federal R&D funding from other sources, tilted academic computer science research toward applications. Yudken and Simons argued that:

> An increasing percentage of the nation's applied computer science research is being performed in universities and colleges. In 1987, academia received about 40% of all computer science federal obligations, an increase of approximately 25% since 1982. Academia's share of federal funding for applied computer science research has increased to 33% in 1987, up from 11.8% in 1982. However, its share of federal support for basic computer science research dropped from 78% to 66%. (1988, 62–63)

During the 1980s, ARPA began to develop a new "bridging" institution, the Software Engineering Institute (SEI), to facilitate and accelerate the movement of academic computer science research results, especially those relevant to software, into industry. The development of the SEI implied some shift in the relationship between academic research and defense-related software development. Support for university research alone no longer provided the infrastructure necessary to solve serious problems in defense-related software management. A new organization was needed to conduct applied research and to support the dissemination and application within industry of the results of this and other research.

ARPA wanted to locate SEI in or near a research university, but it would provide a "halfway house" between academic research and application, supporting and accelerating the transfer of advances in software engineering and design from computer science research to application in commercial and defense-related firms.[15] The establishment of SEI appears to have reflected some concern that the returns to the large DoD investment in research were not being realized to a sufficient extent or with sufficient speed in defense-related applications. The 1984 announcement of the formation of SEI, located at Carnegie-Mellon University, projected a five-year DoD contribution to the SEI budget of $103 million. DoD funding for the institute expanded from $5 million in 1985 to almost $20 million annually during the late 1980s; since 1992, the annual DoD contribution has been roughly $15 million.

In contrast to the SAGE air defense system, a tightly targeted development project whose management was shifted by MIT to the semiautonomous Lincoln Labs,

SEI focused on development and dissemination of generic tools and techniques for software engineering with defense applications. Its establishment seems to reflect some divergence between the mainstream of academic research in computer science and defense-related requirements for software innovations. Although U.S. universities developed a number of key innovations in computer hardware and software during the 1950s and 1960s, the establishment of SEI suggests that the future relationship between universities and defense-related software development may be less close.

DEFENSE-RELATED PROGRAMS AND THE U.S. SOFTWARE INDUSTRY

Defense-related procurement and R&D programs supported the growth of a number of postwar U.S. high-technology industries, including commercial aircraft, semiconductors, and computer hardware for much of the postwar period. Although the computer software industry benefited from large DoD programs for R&D and procurement, the effects of these programs differed somewhat from other postwar high-technology industries. In the semiconductor industry, for example, DoD R&D programs produced few of the major technical advances embodied in commercial (or military) products (Tilton 1971; Levin 1982; Mowery and Steinmueller 1994). Private firms accounted for numerous advances in software, but defense-related R&D programs, notably those of ARPA, supported important advances in fundamental knowledge of computer architecture, software languages, and design that found applications in both the civilian and defense sectors of the emergent industry.

Spillovers from defense to civilian use nevertheless were important in software. Of forty-five advances in computer software during 1950–80 listed by Flamm as having originated in the United States, the development of eighteen was funded by the federal government, and all but one drew on funding from the Pentagon and related military services (Flamm 1988, Table A-4). Of the eighteen innovations funded by the federal government, nine were developed in universities (including MIT's Lincoln Labs, the developer of the SAGE air-defense computer system). Among the postwar U.S. industries characterized by high military R&D and procurement spending, the central place of universities in defense-civilian spillovers is unique to software.

The spillovers identified in Flamm's tabulation were of two types: (1) innovations that were first sold to federal agencies; and (2) innovations that were first sold to private firms. Most of the defense-civilian technological spillovers in other industries and technologies fall into the first of these two categories. Fourteen of the eighteen innovations that were developed with federal funds were first sold to federal agencies; four of them were first applied outside of the federal government. Examples of the second category of defense-civilian spillovers in other postwar U.S. industries are rare, perhaps because defense-related R&D in these other industries emphasizes specific mission applications.

But a mere count of these spillovers says little or nothing about their economic significance. The innovations listed in Table 3-1, however, do include a number of major advances. The compiler that was developed for the MIT Whirlwind, for example, contributed to the development of higher-order languages such as Fortran.[16] Co-

Table 3-1. Defense-to-civilian "spillovers" in the U.S. software industry, 1950–75

Year	Innovation	Federally funded	First sale to federal agency	Developer
Unknown	Project Rye	Yes	Yes	Sperry Rand for the National Security Agency
Early 1950s	APT language	Yes	Yes	MIT Whirlwind
1954	Whirlwind batch operating system	Yes	Yes	MIT Whirlwind
1957	SAGE time-sharing system	Yes	Yes	MIT Lincoln Labs/System Development Corp.
1959	Cobol language	Yes	Yes	Developed primarily by IBM, Sylvania, and Remington-Rand to DoD specifications
1959	JOVIAL	Yes	Yes	System Development Corp. for DoD
1962	MIT time-sharing system	Yes	Yes	MIT with DARPA funding
1963	Q-32 time-sharing system	Yes	Yes	System Corp. for DoD
1963	Multiprocessor system	Yes	Yes	Burroughs for D-825 military computer
1963	JOSS dedicated time-sharing system	Yes	Yes	Rand for DoD
1964	Culler-Fried time-sharing system	Yes	Yes	TRW for DoD
1966	Project Genie general time-sharing system	Yes	Yes	U.C. Berkeley for Scientific Data Systems with DoD funding
1968	MULTICS advanced time-sharing system	Yes	Yes	MIT with DARPA funding
1972	TENEX time-sharing system	Yes	Yes	Bolt, Beranek, and Newman, an engineering consulting firm, with DARPA funding
1953	Algebraic compiler	Yes	No	Whirlwind at MIT
1956	Share assembly program	Yes	No	United Aircraft and distributed through IBM's SHARE program
1963	Carnegie Institute of Technology remote job entry system	Yes	No	Carnegie Institute of Technology with DARPA funding
1964	Basic	Yes	No	General Electric and Dartmouth with NSF funding

Source: Flamm 1988, Table A-4.

bol, which was described in 1972 as one of the two languages (the other being Fortran) that "into the foreseeable future" would dominate "most of the world's serious production programs" (Rosen 1972, 591), is a high-order programming language developed to specifications formulated by a committee of industrial and military experts that was sponsored for much of its life by the Defense Department. DoD support for the committee reflected military policymakers' growing concern about the costs and usefulness of the rapidly expanding military investment in software for data-processing applications, as opposed to the "mission-critical" applications in weapons systems that inspired the development of the defense programming language of the 1980s, Ada.[17] Another important spillover from defense to civilian software technology, noted above, was the Defense Department training during the 1950s of the programmers who created the software for the SAGE air-defense computer system.

The interaction between defense and civilian applications and technological developments in the emergent U.S. software industry differed from that in other U.S. high-technology industries in the postwar period for at least two reasons. First, defense-related demand for software remained high for a longer period of time than than it did for the products of other industries, such as semiconductors. According to Fisher (1978), annual DoD software expenditures amounted to $3–3.5 billion in 1973. In 1977 total software industry revenues were no more than $4.2 billion (Siwek and Furchtgott-Roth 1993, 15), so defense demand accounted for a substantial fraction of software industry revenues in the early and mid-1970s. As late as the early 1980s, some thirty years after the beginnings of software production, military demand may have accounted for 50 percent of total software industry revenues.[18] By contrast, only ten years after the commercialization of the integrated circuit in 1958, defense-related demand, which had accounted for 100 percent of industry shipments in 1962, accounted for only 37 percent of the market (Mowery and Steinmueller 1994, 211–13).

Second, defense demand throughout the postwar period has been primarily for highly specialized custom and embedded software. This characteristic of military demand may well have reduced product-embodied "spillovers" (as opposed to spillovers based on defense R&D). In the 1950s and 1960s, however, when a large share of DoD funding in computer science focused on fundamental R&D rather than development, many of the military-civilian spillovers in software were generic rather than product-specific, and were developed in universities. Thus, because this divergence has existed since the industry's earliest days, the different characteristics of products demanded by the military and those demanded in the commercial market that has affected such U.S. industries as semiconductors and aircraft may prove to be less significant in software.

There is no reliable time series of DoD expenditures on software procurement that employs a consistent definition of software—for example, that separates embedded software from custom applications or operating systems and packaged software. The data on software expenditures in Figure 3-4 are also inconsistent in their treatment of DoD expenditures on software maintenance and those for procurement. Nevertheless, the trends in these data are dramatic: in constant-dollar terms, DoD expenditures on software increased more than thirtyfold in just over twenty-five years, from 1964 to 1990. Throughout this period, DoD demand was primarily for custom software, and DoD and federal government demand for custom software accounted for a substantial share of the total revenues in this segment of the U.S. software industry. Much of the rapid growth in custom software firms during the 1969–80 period that is discussed in chapter 2 reflected expansion in federal demand, which in turn was dominated by DoD demand.[19]

This rapid growth in DoD software expenditures, coupled with other developments in DoD programs and in the structure of the U.S. software industry, gave rise to concern within the Pentagon about "productivity bottlenecks" in software production. Software support and maintenance—that is, changing programs to adapt to new

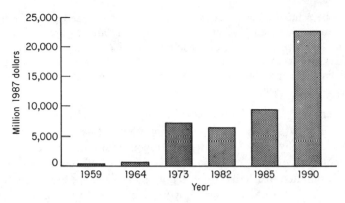

Figure 3-4. Department of Defense software procurement, 1959–90. *Source:* 1959 and 1964 estimates from Phillips 1985; 1973 from Fisher 1978; 1982 from U.S. Department of Defense 1982; 1985 from U.S. Department of Defense 1987; 1990 from U.S. Department of Defense 1992.

mission requirements, eliminate errors, or improve performance—grew rapidly as a share of total software and hardware costs. By 1985 software support alone was estimated to account for at least 50 percent of the cost of complex defense computer systems, a significant increase from its original share of less than 10 percent in the early 1960s (Defense Systems Management College 1990, 2–3). Policymakers also worried about the availability of skilled software engineers and the ability of any technical staff to maintain the rapidly growing, aging, and extremely heterogeneous installed base of software in DoD weapons systems. The Strategic Defense Initiative, with its requirements for large amounts of highly reliable, error-free software, made all of these problems more acute and visible.[20] These concerns led to several initiatives in the 1980s, including the development of the Ada high-order language for defense applications, expanded programs in software engineering that included the STARS (Software Technology for Adaptable, Reliable Systems) program, and SEI.

The complexities of DoD software procurement and maintenance were exacerbated by the importance of "embedded" software, software contained in instruments or in components of larger weapons systems. This type of software accounted for more than 55 percent of total DoD software expenditures in 1973.[21] Embedded software brought with it considerable costs and benefits. Software enabled much greater flexibility, and often much greater speed, in modifying deployed weapons systems for new missions. The 1982 Joint Services Task Force on Software Problems estimated that modifying the capabilities of the Air Force F-111 aircraft through software rather than hardware enabled a fiftyfold savings in cost and a threefold acceleration in the deployment of the modified aircraft (U.S. Department of Defense 1982, 5).[22] But this "mission-critical" embedded software also had to meet requirements for reliability and quality control that were far more demanding than those associated with conventional data processing operations.

Perhaps the greatest cost associated with its widespread use was due to the fact that most of the embedded software employed in weapons systems developed before 1982 was specific to a given weapons system or contractor; such a lack of standards implied a lack of compatibility.[23] Moreover, the dominance of custom applications within military software minimized incentives to create generic tools or languages:

There has been little incentive for individual projects to expend the effort and resources necessary to provide facilities that would be generally useful, especially when there are few, if any, other projects using the same programming language. This may also account for the lack of off-the-shelf software. . . . At least 450 general-purpose programming languages and (incompatible) dialects are used in DoD embedded computer applications— and none is widely used. (Fisher 1978, 26)

Maintenance and support of defense software were especially difficult: idiosyncratic programs for specific systems and applications could remain in service for years or even decades, and they were frequently developed with limited documentation.

When confronted with a similar problem in 1959, DoD had supported an industry-led committee that laid out the requirements and specifications for a higher-order language, Cobol, to be developed by private firms. In response to similar difficulties with "mission-critical" software, the Defense Department launched a major effort to develop an "official" standard for its software procurement in 1974. It appointed the committee charged with defining the requirements and evaluating the suitability of existing languages to meet them. After determining that no satisfactory language existed, it held a competition for a new language. The winner, developed largely by Honeywell-Bull on a DoD contract, was the Ada language, announced in 1981 and required in all major DoD procurement programs.

The Ada initiative was an effort by DoD to create a standardized software environment that would create a "virtuous cycle" similar to that associated with the growth of a "dominant design" in the civilian microcomputer market, in which the diffusion of the IBM PC supported growth in the production of low-cost packaged software for a huge variety of applications (See chapters 2 and 5 in this volume). In contrast to Cobol, Ada has not been extensively employed thus far in nondefense systems, partly because it was developed to meet requirements that had few civilian counterparts.[24]

In the early 1980s a broader effort to enhance the efficiency of defense-related software development and procurement led to increased DoD funding for generic software engineering research and related activities. Beginning with the report of the Joint Services Task Force on software development and procurement, a succession of studies reviewed DoD software policies and agreed on three goals:[25] (1) control the costs of software procurement and maintenance; one way to achieve this goal was to (2) exploit the resources and products of the civilian software industry (so-called COTS—commercial off-the-shelf software) for defense-related software needs;[26] and (3) fund expanded research on and dissemination of software engineering techniques. In contrast to the Ada initiative, which defined a defense-specific set of requirements that produced a "dedicated" DoD high-order computer language, these efforts of the 1980s attempted to bridge the gap between defense and civilian technological developments and "unify" the civilian and defense industrial base in software. Another motive for efforts to link the civilian and defense-related software industries more closely was growing concern by IPTO and ARPA managers with the international competitiveness of the U.S. computer and electronics industry complex. This concern led to large programs in "strategic computing," which included expanded research in software development.

As originally planned, the STARS program and SEI had a hardware complement in the very high speed integrated circuit (VHSIC) program, which also sought to exploit civilian technological capabilities in the semiconductor industry for defense-related applications (Martin 1983). The STARS program was intended to develop better methods for defining software requirements and specifications in a flexible manner that would also enhance reuse of software code. Among STARS' goals were computer-aided software engineering tools for developing Ada and other software. In December 1989 ARPA increased the involvement of commercial software vendors so as to draw more heavily on civilian software products and be able to sell the new products in civilian as well as military markets. This change was associated with new requirements that STARS contracts involve commercial software vendors.[27]

The combination of sharp cuts in the Strategic Defense Initiative budget and across-the-board reductions in defense spending after 1989 reduced defense-related R&D spending in software, at the same time that civilian agencies such as the National Science Foundation increased their computer science research budgets. The defense share of federal computer science R&D funding declined from almost 60 percent in fiscal year 1986 to less than 30 percent in fiscal year 1990 (Clement 1987, 1989; Clement and Edgar 1988), and by the early 1990s, defense demand accounted for a declining share of industry markets.

Although the historical pattern of military-civilian interaction in the software industry is different from that in other U.S. high-technology industries, the present relationship between civilian and military software technology appears to resemble that of other industries. Defense-related demand is declining, and technologies developed for civilian applications promise higher performance at lower cost. In response, the Defense Department has attempted to strengthen its links with the commercial sector of the software industry, just as it now seeks to do with the development of flat-panel displays (small, high-resolution screens for computers, instruments, and video monitors) (Davis and Zachary 1994).

One of the most important impediments to the development of such links, defense contracting policies on the ownership of code, has scarcely been addressed, however (Zraket 1992, 310–11). The Ada initiative defined a set of requirements and an entire language that has thus far produced few spillovers or "spin-on" benefits for the civilian software industry, and few new entrants have been attracted to the military software market. The creation of the Software Engineering Institute to develop and disseminate software engineering techniques for defense-related applications alone risks contributing to further divergence between defense and nondefense software development techniques and products.

There is also divergence between defense and commercial technologies in software engineering. Until recently DoD has addressed the "software bottleneck" problem by focusing on the development of large-scale software systems that require very low error rates in code in organizations resembling "software factories" (SAGE was one prototype). As originally developed by SAGE contractor System Development Corporation (SDC), the goal of the software factory was to increase productivity and reduce errors by systematically reusing parts of code on similar but not identical large-scale projects.[28]

The software factory and related techniques of software engineering remain relevant to the creation of complex, customized defense software, especially embedded, "mission-critical" software that cannot tolerate errors in code. But in the commercial software industry, standardization of platforms and languages, rather than code reuse, has been the key to great increases in efficiency and profitability. Many of the techniques of the software factory are unnecessary for mass-market, packaged software, early releases of which often are riddled with errors. In the commercial sector, where the problems of sharing code across (proprietary) organizations are serious, object-oriented programming may provide a way to share and reuse code in new ways and more effectively (Lavoie et al. 1992). But DoD has not pursued object-oriented techniques for software development. Ada is not an object-oriented language, and because it is used only in DoD applications private developers have not been interested in diverting their investment and effort away from the far more widely used commercial operating systems and languages.[29]

Unless DoD radically changes its underlying weapons design and procurement philosophy, from one that emphasizes performance above all else to one that stresses the use of standard hardware components and platforms, military efforts to exploit commercial software are likely to remain ineffective. Even if it did so, the experience with software suggests that the development of closer links between the defense-related and civilian sectors of high-technology U.S. industries would be difficult and take considerable time.

This discussion of federal policy extends only through 1990, but developments since that date nonetheless merit a brief comment. Since 1992 ARPA has explicitly followed a policy in which DoD and other federal agencies will support projects that have both commercial and defense applications (Alic et al. 1992; Bingaman and Inman 1992). (As we noted, this policy has been articulated within the agency since at least 1980 but rarely stated publicly.) Although ARPA's fundamental R&D support in software produced important advances in both civilian and defense application, there are ample gounds for skepticism about the possibilities for such "spin-on" benefits from development funding. The differences between defense and commercial requirements and markets in software remain so great that genuinely dual-use benefits from technology development spending are likely to be rare.

NASA SOFTWARE PROGRAMS

Another federal agency with significant software-related activities is the National Aeronautics and Space Administration (NASA), which required complex flight-operations software (both on the spacecraft and on the ground) for its manned space exploration missions and embedded software for its unmanned planetary satellites. As Figure 3-5 shows, NASA's software requirements for the Space Shuttle and other manned spaceflight missions were more complex (measured in terms of the number of instructions) than any single U.S. weapons system, including the B-1 bomber or the AWACS airborne air-defense radar system. These demanding, mission-specific requirements forced NASA and its civilian contractors to develop advanced techniques of software engineering.

In the manned spaceflight program, NASA's first software contractor was MIT's Instrumentation Laboratory (later known as Draper Labs), which was chosen by NASA on the strength of its performance in developing guidance systems for the Polaris nuclear missile (Tomayko 1988). Although the Apollo software program was eventually successful, the enormous difficulties associated with the effort led NASA

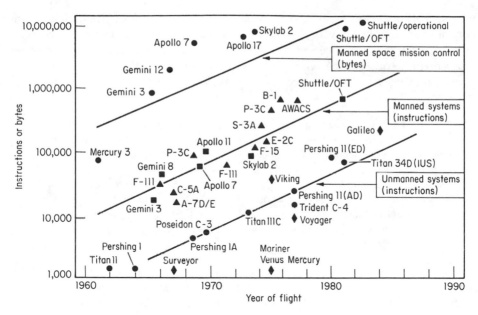

Figure 3-5. Trends in spaceflight software complexity, 1960–84. *Source:* Defense Systems Management College 1990.

to seek an on-site contractor in later programs for the development of flight opera
tions and ground-based control software.[30]

Because the space and weight requirements of NASA's manned and unmanned
spaceflight missions were so demanding, most of the on-board computer hardware
and software was unique to these missions. As a result, the software developed for
on-board applications yielded relatively few spillovers to commercial applications.
The ground-based computer systems that managed the extremely complex tasks of
launch and communications, however, were exploited far more extensively as "off-
the-shelf" hardware. Moreover, many of the techniques of software development for
these applications were employed in broader commercial markets by the primary
vendor, IBM's Federal Systems Division (now known as the Federal Systems Company).[31] IBM, which located a large software development facility near the Johnson
Space Center in Houston, was the major supplier of software for ground control
systems throughout NASA's manned spaceflight program and later became the prime
contractor for the Space Shuttle's software. Beginning with the Mercury program,
IBM's development of computer systems and software for ground control applications yielded important commercial spillovers:

> For IBM and NASA, the development of the Mercury control center and the network was
> highly profitable. . . . Large central computers with widely scattered terminals, such as
> airline reservation systems, have their basis in the distant communications between Wash-
> ington and a launch site in Florida. (Tomayko 1988, 248)

Other important architectural advances spurred by IBM's experience as the prime
contractor for ground-control hardware and software include the design principles
that underpinned the innovation of virtual memory and major improvements in IBM's

internal software engineering practices and guidelines.[32] All of these yielded important commercial spillovers for IBM and for the broader U.S. software industry.

Although they were valuable for the development of complex, custom software programs, the software engineering advances supported by IBM's NASA experience were less relevant to the packaged software market that became so important during the 1980s:

> The [IBM NASA software development] process is an excellent fit for the environment: a dedicated customer, a limited problem domain, and a situation where cost is important but less of a consideration than zero defects. For the wide range of commercial software developers that do not operate in this type of environment, the . . . complete FSC Houston approach is not feasible, although variations of the process are clearly possible and used at other IBM sites and other companies. . . . Drawing upon this success in process improvement and quality delivery, the IBM Federal Systems Company has also created a team that now goes out and consults on the software development process. (Smith and Cusumano 1993, 19)

In spaceflight no less than in defense-related procurement, large government software contracts now appear to yield fewer benefits for vendors in the commercial market, underlining the two sectors' different requirements and strategies. IBM's 1993 divestiture of its Federal Systems Company seems to confirm the limited relevance of the large-scale software factory for developing commercial software (which accounted for $11 billion in 1993 corporate revenues, according to the firm's *Annual Report*).

CONCLUSION

The federal government's role in the development of the U.S. software industry is broadly similar to its role in the development of such other postwar high-technology industries as semiconductors, computer hardware, and commercial aircraft. In all of these cases, federal expenditures on R&D and procurement were motivated primarily by defense concerns in the context of the cold war. And in all of these areas defense-related expenditures produced important spillovers for commercial applications. Especially in semiconductors, computer hardware, and software, federal procurement also supported significant entry by many startup firms.

But the apparent similarities between software and other postwar dual-use industries mask some important differences in federal policy toward the software industry. For example, throughout the brief history of the software industry, defense-related demand for (largely custom) software has accounted for a much larger share of the total market than was true of semiconductors. Federal funding of university research and development activities appear to have been more important to the evolution of the software industry than of semiconductors or aerospace. Unlike these industries, which drew on established academic disciplines even as they transformed them, the software industry relied on the creation of a new academic discipline, computer science. Federal policymakers in agencies such as ARPA focused their R&D support on universities because of the need for a new academic infrastructure of training and research in a technology with numerous defense-related applications. Moreover, because computer science findings "targeted" specific institutions and focused on the defense missions of federal agencies, the policies and criteria used to select the recipients of research support were unlike the peer review system more commonly associated with federal support for fundamental academic research. The contrasting postwar histories of the British and U.S. computer industries appear to stem in part from the very different policies adopted by each nation's military establishment for the support of university research and education in computer science.

The National Science Foundation also helped build the infrastructure through its funding of computer purchases by U.S. universities, and thereby complemented the focused policies of ARPA. The important role of universities within the software industry of federal financial support for the research facilities of these universities suggests some interesting similarities between the U.S. software and biotechnology industries. In biotechnology the National Institutes of Health have played an indispensable role in supporting fundamental research and equipment acquisition that have yielded major commercial applications.

Although ARPA's R&D support focused on specific areas in computer science, federal R&D support in software-related fields did not focus on specific civilian applications, or even on civilian technology development, in contrast to the ambitious programs mounted in Europe and Japan.

The history of federal policy in the software industry supports a strong role for public funds in the creation of a research infrastructure, including support for the production of trained personnel rather than the development of specific technologies for civilian applications. It also suggests the value of support for institutions, facilities, and individual investigators in spurring the growth of new academic disciplines. In all of these respects, the lessons of postwar federal policy in the software industry closely resemble those of federal technology policy in other sectors (see Nelson 1985; Mowery and Rosenberg 1989). Paradoxically, the national security rationale for much of the DoD and ARPA funding, especially the ARPA funding of university "centers of excellence," may have insulated these programs, which did not operate solely via peer review, from the distributional politics that otherwise might have forced the use of very different criteria for allocation.[33] The lack of a "civilian competitiveness" rationale for them may have increased the contribution of these federal R&D programs to the U.S. software industry's competitiveness.

Although military-civilian spillovers were important in the software industry, they differed somewhat from those associated with other postwar dual-use industries. In other postwar industries, government R&D support and defense-related procurement often yielded commercial applications during the earliest stages of a technology's development. With the maturation of the technology and the emergence of a commercial industry, however, government procurement needs diverge from those of the commercial market, especially if this market becomes larger than the government market (See Mowery and Rosenberg 1989; Cowan and Foray 1994). When this happens the spin-offs from defense-related government spending on R&D and procurement are often reduced, and military applications come to rely more heavily on "spin-ons" from the commercial sector.

This transition occurred quite early in the development of the U.S. software industry. The early experimental machines at universities, such as Whirlwind and the IAS computer, yielded a number of generic software concepts and tools. But very soon the private sector, notably IBM, began producing standard platforms in large volume. At the same time, the commercial sector, responding to the resulting growth in the market for standard commercial applications, began to provide generic programming tools and languages. Private firms also extended some financial support for computer science and developed end-user capabilities through user groups. In the mid-1950s, as in the current software industry, standardized hardware platforms supported the growth of commercial production of software, although independent software vendors now play a much more prominent role in the commercial sector (see chapter 2).

Also in the 1950s, rapid growth in defense-related demands for software, and for science and technology in general, expanded government spending on software and computer science. Government funding stimulated the creation of a university-based infrastructure for the development of "generic" technology and abstract principles, many of which were applicable to both military and commercial software. Software-related spillovers frequently flowed from defense-related support for fundamental research, and universities were important sources of such spillovers. Had private firms retained the primary responsibility for the "legitimation" of computer science, this process would probably have taken considerably longer and might have restricted the diffusion of university-based research.

The differences in military and commercial software needs have not been significantly reduced by the development of Ada and are not likely to increase military use of commercial software products. Indeed, the shift in defense-related R&D support toward applied research may reduce the future spillovers to commercial applications formerly generated by this research funding. The creation of the Software Engineering Institute, which initially was intended to supplement the role of U.S. universities in defense-related software R&D, has weakened the relationship between DoD R&D programs and academic research that has generated a number of civilian technologies. Whereas the SAGE program of the early 1950s, whose management was controlled by MIT through its Lincoln Laboratories, sought to use academic computer science to develop a specific, large-scale system, ARPA established the Software Engineering Institute to develop defense-relevant applications from advances in computer science. The very need for such a "bridging" institution suggests that the links between basic research and defense applications have been considerably attenuated since 1970.

The political and economic circumstances within which these federal agencies influenced the early development U.S. software industry were in many respects unique. Although federal support for its university infrastructure will remain vital, the software industry has achieved sufficient scale and economic vitality that federal R&D policy will exercise less direct influence over its future technological development.

Federal policy toward the software industry appears to have been highly successful without "targeting" support for civilian applications. Instead, federal support contributed to the creation of a large industry and university research infrastructure, which has exploited the rapid diffusion of computer hardware in the U.S. economy to spawn a vigorous software industry. This "infrastructure-oriented" technology policy contrasts with the prescriptions of some policymakers, who seek to harness federal R&D support of the development of specific civilian or "dual-use" applications (see, e.g., Tyson 1992). The history of the software industry suggests that long-term, stable support for infrastructure and human capital formation may be an extremely powerful impetus to the growth of a new industry.

NOTES

We are grateful to Jay Adams, William Aspray, Bruce Bruemmer, Bonnie Chen, Larry Druffel, Andrew Goldstein, Randy Katz, George Mazuzan, and Scott Wallace for invaluable assistance in the preparation of this chapter. Support for the second author's research was provided by the U.S.-Japan Industrial Technology Management Program, sponsored by the Air Force Office of Scientific Research; by the Center for Research in Management of the Haas School of Business; and by the Alfred P. Sloan Foundation.

1. The Whirwind's cost of $3 million substantially exceeded the average cost of $650,000 for the other systems described below (Redmond and Smith 1980).

2. "Prior to this system [the 650], universities built their own machines, either as copies of someone else's or as novel devices. After the 650, this was no longer true. By December 1955, Weik reports, 120 were in operation, and 750 were on order. For the first time, a large group of machine users had more or less identical systems. This had a most profound effect on programming and programmers. The existence of a very large community now made it possible, and indeed, desirable, to have common programs, programming techniques, etc." (Goldstine 1972, 331).

3. Goldstine, one of the leaders of the wartime project sponsored by the Army's Ballistics Research Laboratory at the University of Pennsylvania that resulted in the Eckert-Mauchly computer, notes that "a meeting was held in the fall of 1945 at the Ballistic Research Laboratory to consider the computing needs of that laboratory 'in the light of its post-war research program.' The minutes indicate a very great desire at this time on the part of the leaders there to make their work widely available. 'It was accordingly proposed that as soon as the ENIAC was successfully working, its logical and operational characteristics be completely declassified and sufficient publicity be given to the machine . . . that those who are interested . . . will be allowed to know all details' " (1972, 217). Goldstine is quoting the "Minutes, Meeting on Computing Methods and Devices at Ballistic Research Laboratory, 15 October 1945 (note 14). Flamm makes a similar point with respect to military attitudes toward classification of computer technology (1988, 224–26).

4. "The grants were in IBM's interest, because the corporation felt a strong concern with supporting and maintaining a close relationship with universities, and because an entire generation of students and faculty would associate computers and computing with 'IBM' " (Galler 1986, 37.) Fisher, McKie, and Mancke suggest, however, that this hoped-for lock-in effect might in fact have been illusory (1983, 169).

5. In 1957 IBM made a model 704 computer available free of charge to MIT seven hours a day and to twenty-four other New England universities another seven hours a day. IBM itself used the remaining ten (nighttime) hours (Wildes and Lindgren 1985, 336–37.)

The IBM educational allowance program began in October 1955, with 60 percent reductions in lease rates to universities. In May 1960 IBM changed the allowance to 20 percent for administrative use and 60 percent for academic use. In 1963 the company abandoned the administrative/academic distinction and reduced all allowances to 20 percent on new orders. In 1965 IBM set up a sliding scale of allowances on the new 360 series, ranging from 20 percent on the base model to 45 percent on a high-end system. By 1969 the allowance had been reduced to 10 percent (Fisher, McKie, and Mancke 1983, 172).

6. According to some accounts, the Rand group got the programming job only after MIT, IBM, and AT&T had all declined it (Baum 1981). IBM, for example, was concerned about how it would employ some 2,000 programmers once the project ended.

7. "Indeed, despite what was in many respects a first-rate network of contacts, the NRDC [National Research and Development Corporation] was not even aware of some of the military computer developments taking place in the 1950s and early 1960s. Nor were the people carrying out these developments in many cases aware of work on the commercial front. In America, in contrast, communications between different firms and laboratories appear to have been very good, even where classified work was involved." (Hendry 1990, 162)

8. The data in Figure 3-2 are taken from Aspray and Williams (1993b) and include all NSF research funding in numerical analysis, computer theory, architecture, theoretical computer engineering, graphics, software, artificial intelligence, databases, and communications. We are indebted to Professor William Aspray and Dr. Andrew Goldstein of the IEEE Center for the History of Electrical Engineering for these data.

9. "NSF wanted to develop a broad academic base for science education and scientific research. Thus it supplied facilities not only to the top research universities, but also to other universities, liberal arts colleges, junior colleges, and even some high schools. While NSF was building a broad national infrastructure for science, DARPA was constructing a high-powered experimental computer science research program." (Aspray and Williams 1994, 28).

10. This account draws on the excellent history of DARPA's Information Processing Techniques Office (IPTO) by Norberg and O'Neill (1992).

11. A 1985 study by an ACM committee found that average DoD funding per faculty member in the computer science departments of these four universities was $279,000; average funding was $42,000 per faculty member in departments ranked 5–12. In contrast, NSF funding per faculty member in the top four departments was $31,000, $46,000 per faculty member in departments ranked 5–12, and $41,000 per faculty member in departments ranked 13–24 (Gries, Miller, Ritchie, and Young 1986, 878).

12. "IPTO strove to develop a few centers of excellence in order to stimulate the computer science field in substantial ways, rather than by making a large number of small contracts. Contracts written for this purpose were brief. They specified in general ways the nature of the research to be pursued, the equipment to be purchased if needed, and the length of time of the contract. . . . Manager rather than peer review made possible this rapid evaluation of proposals and issuance of an intent to contract with an institution." (Norberg and O'Neill 1992, 122–23).

13. The ARPANET packet-switching architecture and supporting software were developed by Bolt, Beranek, and Newman, an engineering firm that had spun off from MIT, rather than solely by academic researchers. Nonetheless, academic computer science researchers were very active participants in ARPA's early development of requirements for what became the ARPANET, as well as in the testing of the system. In 1989 ARPA turned over the network technology to NSF, which became the lead agency of an executive branch consortium guiding the future of the Internet.

14. These data omit data for Ph.D. production from the University of California at Berkeley, which for much of this period did not grant Ph.D.s in computer science (a division of the university's department of electrical engineering), although it was a major recipient of ARPA funding for computer science research. By virtue of this omission, these data understate somewhat the "true" influence of the top four ARPA-funded research universities in computer science.

15. "An institute like the SEI could play several influential roles. It could collect and integrate existing tools into common, unified, software life-cycle support frameworks. Such an institute could act as an integrative agent by energetically soliciting community opinion and helping the community to achieve a consensus on critical new suspects of shared infrastructure for the 1990's. Additionally, it could furnish effective institutional support for the technology insertion process. This process needs to be carefully planned and managed, and if it is not vigorously supported, an essential part of the overall job cannot be accomplished.

"A key feature of technology transfer is to have people from the DoD, industry, and academia rotating through the institute. Such rotation would have the additional benefit of keeping the institute fresh and vital over time. It would thus be a magnet for top talent without being a talent sink." (Boehm and Standish 1983, 34)

16. Moreover, the Office of Naval Research supported information exchange, workshops, and informal cross-fertilization that enabled the compiler, first developed by J. Halcombe Laning and Neal Zierler at MIT, to be quickly exploited by John Backus of IBM in creating Fortran: "During the first part of 1954, John Backus began to assemble a group of people within IBM to work on improved systems of automatic programming. . . . Shortly after learning of the Laning and Zierler system at the ONR meeting in May, Backus wrote to Laning that 'our formulation of the problem is very similar to yours: However, we have done no programming or even detailed planning.' Within two weeks, Backus and his co-workers Harlan Herick and Irving Ziller visited MIT in order to see the Laning-Zierler system in operation. The big problem facing them was to implement such a language with suitable efficiency. . . .

"By November 1954, Backus's group had specified 'The IBM Mathematical FORmula TRANslating system, FORTRAN.'" (Knuth and Pardo 1980, 241)

17. According to Phillips (1985), "In early 1959 there were 225 computer systems in the [DoD] business area alone, with annual costs of over $70 million . . . the total number of computers in DOD was estimated at 1046 with costs of about $443 million. On a rough approximation, DoD estimated that about half of these costs could be attributed to (1) systems design, (2) flowcharting, (3) programming and coding, and (4) 'debugging.' With direct 'software' costs of about $35 million, which grew to over $200 million in the next five years, DoD obviously had an interest, as well as a position of stature, in the subject. Certainly, if such a project offered a hope of reducing 'software' costs, it would provide a strong motivation as well.

"Two other items were of concern to DoD at that time: compatibility and the interchange of computer programs; we might really consider them as two parts of the same basic problem. This problem was clearly evident in the supply and logistics area, which represented about 85 percent of DoD business-type applications in 1959." (Phillips 1985, 305)

18. According to the U.S. Department of Commerce (1984), total U.S. software industry revenues amounted to $10.3 billion in 1982; in that year, the DoD Joint Service Task Force on Software Problems estimated that total Pentagon spending on software amounted to $5–6 billion (Department of Defense 1982, 6). A portion of the revenues included in these estimates are excluded from the Commerce Department measure of industry revenues (and these revenue estimates may be low, judging from the OECD data cited in chapter 1), and the orders of magnitude suggest that defense-related demand figured much more prominently within the software industry than in computer hardware. Fisher notes that "at one time DoD was a major innovator and consumer of the most sophisticated computer hardware, but now it represents only a small fraction of the total market. In software, that unique position still remains: a significant fraction of the total software industry is devoted to DoD-related programs—and this is true in even larger proportion for the more advanced and demanding systems" (Fisher 1978, 24).

19. "In 1966 the FB-111 required an on-board computer memory of roughly 60,000 words but by 1988 the B-1B Bomber was approaching on-board computer memory requirements of about 2.5 million words. Current and future systems will greatly exceed these memory requirements, with large-scale software systems being the norm." (Defense Systems Management College 1990, 2-2)

20. The congressional Office of Technology Assessment estimated that as of June 1987 the software development activities of the Strategic Defense Initiative Organization (SDIO) accounted for more than $275 million in expenditures. The estimate does not cover a single fiscal year's expenditures; instead, "it shows money that at that time had been spent since the

inception of the program, that was then under contract, or that was expected soon to be under contract" (U.S. Congress, Office of Technology Assessment 1988, 248).

21. Fisher (1978) estimated that embedded software accounted for 56 percent, data processing software 19 percent, scientific software 5 percent, and "other and indirect software costs" 20 percent, of total DoD software expenditures in 1973 (25).

22. Other examples cited by the task force included modifications in the targeting accuracy of the Minuteman III nuclear missile and an emergency modification in the guidance systems of the British Sea Wolf antiaircraft missiles made to adapt them to the needs of the Falkland Islands conflict in 1982 (U.S. Department of Defense 1982).

23. In 1978, "at least 200 models of computers are used in embedded computer systems at DoD. In many applications, the computers must be installed in configurations that are incompatible with general-purpose installations" (Fischer 1978, 25).

24. One other indication of this "divergence by design" is the fact that Ada does not incorporate object-oriented programming design concepts or tools, which now are widely employed in the civilian software industry.

25. Following is a partial list of the major reports of the 1980s and early 1990s: the Joint Services Task Force Report on Software Problems (U.S. Department of Defense 1982); the report of the Software Engineering Institute Study Panel (Institute for Defense Analyses 1983); the Defense Science Board Task Force report on Military Software (U.S. Department of Defense 1987); the Department of Defense Software Master Plan (U.S. Department of Defense 1990); and the Department of Defense Software Technology Strategy (U.S. Department of Defense 1992). This list excludes the numerous studies of software issues in the Strategic Defense Initiative program. Pentagon studies of its software needs, of course, substantially predate the 1980s—the Joint Services Task Force report lists twenty-six previous studies in an appendix.

26. "Migration to commercial support spreads the maintenance costs for software technology across a much larger base than DoD. It is thus a major leverage factor for DoD software technology products. Even greater cost-effectiveness leverage can be obtained by stimulating existing commercial technology products to address DoD needs." (Department of Defense Software Technology Strategy 1991, ES-23)

27. "The goal of the STARS program is to improve productivity while achieving greater system reliability and adaptability. Meeting this goal requires a very broad attack to improve the environment in which software is first developed and then supported. The DoD's 'Ada' program provides an initial focus for the development of a common, sharable software base. The STARS program broadens the scope of attention to the entire environment in which software is conceived and evolved." (Druffel, Redwine, and Riddle 1983, 10) The 1992 "Software Technology Strategy" report of the Defense Department noted that "the STARS prime contractors (IBM, Unisys, and Boeing) are developing these [software environment frameworks] in concert with their commercial counterparts (in-house for IBM and Unisys; DEC for Boeing) and a number of tool vendor subcontractors for computer-aided software engineering (CASE). The primary program objectives are that STARS products are commercially, supported, responsive to particular DoD needs (support of very large, embedded, real-time, and Ada software applications), and built using common open interfaces to facilitate CASE tool portability and interoperability." (U.S. Department of Defense 1991, 3–4)

28. The DoD's January 1992 Software Technology Strategy called for increased reuse of code in addition to improvements in software engineering and the use of more commercial software (Burgess 1992). Despite the substantial DoD investment in software engineering, the commercial sector (especially in microcomputers) appears to be ahead of the defense sector in many of these techniques. For example, Microsoft is far ahead of traditional large-scale software houses (including IBM's now independent Federal Systems Division) in the use of such techniques as rapid prototyping (Smith and Cusumano 1993).

29. In 1991 DARPA funded a $22 million project on object-oriented databases. The participants include Texas Instruments, the National Institute of Standards and Technology (NIST), and several universities (Stix 1992). The April 1994 request for proposals for the ARPA-led Technology Reinvestment Program listed "object-oriented technology for rapid software development and delivery" as one if its areas of interest.

30. "The realization that software is more difficult to develop than hardware is one of the most important lessons of the Apollo program. So the choice of memory should be software driven, and designers should develop software needed for manned spaceflight near the Manned Spacecraft Center. The arrangement with MIT reduced overall quality and efficiency due to lack of communication. Also, more modularization of the software was needed." (Tomayko 1988, 62)

31. "The story of computers in manned mission control is largely the story of a close and mutually beneficial partnership between NASA and IBM. There are many instances of IBM support of the space program, but in no other case have the results been as directly applicable to its commercial product line. When Project Vanguard and later NASA approached IBM with the requirements for computers to do telemetry monitoring, trajectory calculations, and commanding, IBM found a market for its largest computers and a vehicle for developing ways of creating software to control multiple programs executing at once, capable of accepting and handling asynchronous data, and of running reliably in real time. . . .

"The company maintained its lock on mission control contracts through Gemini, Apollo, and the Shuttle. At each point, some experienced personnel were transferred to other parts of the company to share lessons learned. Several individuals contributed to OS/360, the first multiprogramming system made commercial available by IBM. One became head of the personal computer division." (Tomayko 1988, 243–44)

32. "IBM reacted to the increased complexity [of the Gemini program's data and mission control requirements] in several ways. Besides adding more manpower, the company enforced a strict set of software development standards. These standards were so successful that IBM adopted them companywide at a time when the key commercial software systems that would carry the mainframe line of computers into the 1970s were under construction." (Tomayko 1988, 252)

33. Sapolsky's comment on the changing role of the U.S. Office of Naval Research is relevant and prescient in this regard:

> National security rationales are no longer very important in the support of basic research. . . . But without the protection of national security rationales, science is vulnerable to political pressures in ways that undermine its integrity and productivity. When vital defense interests are not at stake, politicians wonder why their districts are not benefiting from the federal research largess much more than when they are. Less favored institutions and disciplines find the urge to employ pork barrel tactics impossible to resist. The network of elites that binds together the scientific community and provides its priorities cannot contain the desire for equity and opportunity that is so much a part of the political process. The Navy and the other armed services may not regret their reduced role in basic research, but science no doubt will." (Sapolsky 1990, 121)

REFERENCES

ACM (Association for Computing Machinery). 1965. ACM Curriculum Committee on Computer Science. "An Undergraduate Program in Computer Science—Preliminary Recommendations," *Communications of the ACM* 8: 543–52.

Alic, J. A., L. W. Branscomb, H. A. Brooks, and A. Carter. 1992. *Beyond Spinoff*. Boston: Harvard Business School Press.

Arrow, Kenneth J. 1962. "Economic Welfare and the Allocation of Resources to Invention." In Richard R. Nelson, ed., *The Rate and Direction of Inventive Activity: Economic and Social Factors*. Princeton, N.J.: Princeton University Press.

Aspray, William. 1990. *John von Neumann and the Origins of Modern Computing*. Cambridge, Mass.: MIT Press.

Aspray, William, and Bernard O. Williams. 1993a. "Computing in Science and Engineering Education: The Programs of the National Science Foundation." Paper presented at the IEEE Electro/93 conference, Edison, N.J., April 27–29.

———. 1993b. "The National Science Foundation's Computer Science Research Program." Duplicated.

———. 1994. "Arming American Scientists: The Role of the National Science Foundation in the Provision of Scientific Computing Facilities for Colleges and Universities." *Annals of the History of Computing 14*.

Bach, G. L. 1986. "A Computer for Carnegie." *Annals of the History of Computing* 8: 39–41.

Backus, J. 1981. "The History of Fortran I, II, and III." In Richard L. Wexelblat, ed., *History of Programming Languages*. New York: Academic Press.

Bashe, Charles J., Lyle R. Johnson, John H. Palmer, and Emerson W. Pugh. 1986. *IBM's Early Computers*. Cambridge, Mass.: MIT Press.

Baum, Claude. 1981. *The System Builders: The Story of SDC*. Santa Monica, Calif.: System Development Corp.

Benington, H. D. 1983. "Production of Large Computer Programs." *Annals of the History of Computing* 5: 350–61.

Bingaman, Jeff, and Bobby R. Inman. 1992. "Broadening Horizons for Defense R&D." *Issues in Science and Technology* 9 (Fall): 80–85.

Boehm, B., and T. A. Standish. 1983. "Software Technology in the 1990s: Using an Evolutionary Paradigm." *IEEE Computer* (November): 20–37.

Brosgol, B. M. 1992. "Ada." *Communications of the ACM* 35 (November): 41–42.

Burgess, Angela. 1992. "DOD Budget Embodies New Acquisition Plan." *IEEE Software* 9 (May): 99.

Clement, J. R. B. 1987. "Computer Science and Engineering Support in the FY 1988 Budget." In Intersociety Working Group, ed., *AAAS Report XII: Research & Development, FY 1988*. Washington, D.C.: American Association for the Advancement of Science.

———. 1989. "Computer Science and Engineering Support in the FY 1990 Budget." In Intersociety Working Group, ed., *AAAS Report XIV: Research & Development, FY 1990*. Washington, D.C.: American Association for the Advancement of Science.

Clement, J. R. B., and D. Edgar. 1988. "Computer Science and Engineering Support in the FY 1989 Budget." In Intersociety Working Group, ed., *AAAS Report XIII: Research & Development, FY 1989*. Washington, D.C.: American Association for the Advancement of Science.

Cowan, R., and D. Foray. 1994. "Quandaries in the Economics of Dual Technologies and Spillovers from Military to Civilian Research and Development." Duplicated.

Cusumano, Michael. 1991. *Japan's Software Factories: A Challenge to U.S. Management*. New York: Oxford University Press.

Davis, B., and G. P. Zachary. 1994. "Electronics Firms Get Push from Clinton to Join Industrial Policy Initiative in Flat-Panel Displays." *Wall Street Journal*, 28 April, A16.

Defense Systems Management College, U.S. Department of Defense. 1990. *Mission Critical Computer Resources Management Guide*. Washington, D.C.: U.S. Defense Department.

Druffel, L. E., S. T. Redwine, and W. E. Riddle. 1983. "The STARS Program: Overview and Rationale." *IEEE Computer* (November): 21–29.

Feldman, M. B. 1992. "Ada Experience in the Undergraduate Curriculum." *Communications of the ACM* 35 (November): 53–67.

Fisher, D. A. 1978. "DoD's Common Language Programming Effort." *IEEE Computer* 11 (March): 24–33.

Fisher, Franklin M., James W. McKie, and Richard B. Mancke. 1983. *IBM and The U.S. Data Processing Industry*. New York: Praeger.

Flamm, Kenneth. 1987. *Targeting the Computer*. Washington, D.C.: Brookings Institution.

———. 1988. *Creating the Computer*. Washington, D.C.: Brookings Institution.

Flamm, Kenneth S., and Gary L. Denman. 1994. "Testimony before the Subcommittee on Defense." Committee on Appropriations, U.S. House of Representatives, 13 April.

Galler, Bernard A. 1986. "The IBM 650 and the Universities." *Annals of the History of Computing* 8, no. 1: 36–38.

Goldstine, H. H. 1993. *The Computer from Pascal to von Neumann*, 2d ed. Princeton, N.J.: Princeton University Press.

Gries, D., R. Miller, R. Ritchie, and P. Young. 1986. "Imbalance between Growth and Funding in Academic Computer Science: Two Trends Colliding." *Communications of the ACM* 29: 870–78.

Hendry, J. 1990. *Innovating for Failure*. Cambridge, Mass.: MIT Press.

Hopper, G. M. 1981. "Keynote Address." In Richard L. Wexelblat, ed., *History of Programming Languages*. New York: Academic Press.

IBM Corporation. 1993. *Annual Report*. Armonk, N.Y.: IBM.

Institute for Defense Analyses. 1983. *Report of Findings and Recommendations—Software Engineering Institute Study Panel*. Alexandria, Va.: Institute for Defense Analyses.

Katz, Barbara, and Almarin Phillips. 1982. "The Computer Industry." In Richard R. Nelson, ed., *Government and Technical Progress: A Cross-Industry Analysis*. New York: Pergamon Press.

Knuth, D. E., and L. T. Pardo. 1980. "The Early Development of Programming Languages." In N. Metropolis, J. Howlett, and G.-C. Rota, eds., *A History of Computing in the 20th Century: A Collection of Essays*. New York: Academic Press.

Lavoie, Don, Howard Baetjer, William Tulloh, and Richard Langlois. 1992. *Component Software: A Market Perspective on the Coming Revolution in Software Development*. Special Research Report, Patricia Seybold Group, Boston.

Leslie, S. 1993. *The Cold War and American Science*. New York: Columbia University Press.

Levin, Richard C. 1982. "The Semiconductor Industry." In Richard R. Nelson, ed., *Government and Technical Progress: A Cross-Industry Analysis*. New York: Pergamon Press.

Levine, Bernard. 1994. "Largest Funds Emerge So Far for TRP Wins." *Electronic News*. 28 February, 1.

Martin, E. W. 1983. The Context of STARS." *IEEE Computer* (November): 14–17.

Mowery, David C., and Nathan Rosenberg. 1982. "Government Policy and Innovation in the Commercial Aircraft Industry, 1925–1975." In Richard R. Nelson, ed., *Government and Technical Progress: A Cross-Industry Analysis*. New York: Pergamon Press.

———. 1989. *Technology and the Pursuit of Economic Growth*. New York: Cambridge University Press.

———. 1993. "The U.S. National System of Innovation." In R. R. Nelson, ed., *National Innovation Systems: A Comparative Analysis*. New York: Oxford University Press.

Mowery, David C., and W. E. Steinmueller. 1994. "Prospects for Entry by Developing Countries into the Global Integrated Circuit Industry: Lessons from the United States, Japan, and the NIEs, 1955–1990." In D. C. Mowery, *Science and Technology Policy in Interdependent Economies*. Boston, Mass.: Kluwer Academic Publishers.

National Science Foundation, Office of Computing Activities. 1970. "Director's Program Review: December 15, 1970." Program Review Office, National Science Foundation, Washington, D.C. Duplicated.

Naur, P., B. Randell, and J. B. Buxton, eds. 1976. *Software Engineering Concepts and Techniques: Proceedings of the NATO Conference*. New York: Petrocelli/Charter.

Nelson, R. R. 1985. *High-Technology Policies: A Five-Nation Comparison*. Washington, D.C.: American Enterprise Institute.

Norberg, A. L., and J. E. O'Neill, with contributions by K. J. Freedman. 1992. *A History of the Information Processing Techniques Office of the Defense Advanced Research Projects Agency*. Minneapolis, Minn.: Charles Babbage Institute.

Phillips, C. A. 1985. "Reminiscences (Plus a Few Facts)." *Annals of the History of Computing* 7: 304–13.

Redmond, Kent C., and Thomas M. Smith. 1980. *Project Whirlwind: History of a Pioneer Computer*. Bedford, Mass.: Digital Press.

Rees, M. 1982. "The Computing Program of the Office of Naval Research, 1946–53." *Annals of the History of Computing* 4: 102–20.

Rosen, S. 1972. "Programming Systems and Languages, 1965–78." *Communications of the ACM* 15: 591–600.

Rosenberg, Nathan. 1976. *Perspectives on Technology*. New York: Cambridge University Press.

———. 1992. "Scientific Instrumentation and University Research." *Research Policy* 21: 381–90.

Rosenberg, N., and R. R. Nelson. 1994. "American Universities and Technical Advance in Industry." *Research Policy* 23: 323–48.

Sammet, J. E. 1969. *Programming Languages: History and Fundamentals*. Englewood Cliffs, N.J.: Prentice-Hall.

———. 1985. "Brief Summary of the Early History of COBOL." *Annals of the History of Computing* 7: 288–303.

Sapolsky, H. 1990. *Science and the Navy*. Princeton, N.J.: Princeton University Press.

Siwek, S. E., and H. W. Furchtgott-Roth. 1993. *International Trade in Computer Software*. Westport, Conn.: Quorum Books.

Smith, S. A., and M. A. Cusumano. 1993. "Beyond the Software Factory: A Comparison of 'Classic' and PC Software Developers." Sloan School of Management working paper #96-93, Massachusetts Institute of Technology, Cambridge, Mass.

Stix, Gary. 1992. "Objective Data: DARPA Nudges Development of Object-Oriented Data Bases." *Scientific American* 266 (March): 108.

Tilton, J. E. 1971. *The International Diffusion of Technology: The Case of Semiconductors*. Washington, D.C.: Brookings Institution.

Tomayko, J. E. 1988. *Computers in Spaceflight*. Washington, D.C.: National Aeronautics and Space Administration.

Tropp, H. S., ed. 1983. "A Perspective on SAGE: A Discussion." *Annals of the History of Computing* 5: 375–98.

U.S. Congress, Office of Technology Assessment. 1988. *SDI: Technology, Survivability, and Software*. Washington, D.C.: U.S. Government Printing Office.

U.S. Department of Commerce. 1984. *A Competitive Assessment of the United States Software Industry*. Washington, D.C.: U.S. Government Printing Office.

U.S. Department of Defense. 1982. Joint Services Task Force on Software Problems. *Report of the DOD Joint Services Task Force on Software Problems*. Washington, D.C.: U.S. Department of Defense.

———. 1987. Under Secretary of Defense for Acquisition. *Report of the Defense Science*

Board Task Force on Military Software. Washington, D.C.: U.S. Department of Defense.

———. 1990. Defense Acquisition Board. *Department of Defense Software Master Plan*. Washington, D.C.: U.S. Department of Defense.

———. 1992. Director of Defense Research and Engineering. *Department of Defense Software Technology Strategy*. Washington, D.C.: U.S. Department of Defense.

U.S. House of Representatives, Committee on Science, Space, and Technology. 1989. *Bugs in the Program: Problems in Federal Government Computer Software Development and Regulation*. (Washington, D.C.: U.S. Government Printing Office.

von Neumann, John. 1945. "First Draft of a Report on the EDVAC." Reprinted in William Aspray and Arthur Burks, eds., *Papers of John von Neumann on Computing and Computer Theory*. Cambridge, Mass.: MIT Press, 1987.

Wildes, Karl L., and Nilo A. Lindgren. 1985. *A Century of Electrical Engineering and Computer Science at MIT, 1882–1982*. Cambridge, Mass.: MIT Press.

Yudken, J. S., and B. Simons. 1988. "Computer Science Research Funding: Issues and Trends." *Abacus*: 60–66.

Zraket, Charles A. 1992. "Software: Productivity Puzzles, Policy Challenges." In John A. Alic, L. W. Branscomb, H. A. Brooks, and A. Carter, *Beyond Spinoff*. Cambridge, Mass.: Harvard Business School Press.

4

Tails that Wag Dogs: The Influence of Software-based "Network Externalities" on the Creation of Dominant Designs in RISC Technologies

Jonathan Khazam and David C. Mowery

Innovation in the computer workstation hardware and software industry has been rapid since the development of workstations in the early 1980s. Workstations based on reduced-instruction-set computing (RISC) microprocessors recently have challenged (and in some cases have overtaken) those designed around complex-instruction-set computing (CISC) processors. This chapter explores the history and development of RISC and the commercialization strategies of Sun Microsystems, the former MIPS Computer Systems, and other producers of microprocessors and workstations.

As other chapters point out, the complementarity between software and hardware in many segments of the information technology industry gives rise to "network externalities," in which an individual's decision to adopt a given design is influenced positively by the number of other adopters (Katz and Shapiro 1986). In RISC technology, however, as in other hardware innovations in the microcomputer industry, network externalities have less to do with physical interconnection than with the ability of an emergent dominant design to create a "bandwagon effect" among the independent software developers who create many of the standardized applications programs for competing hardware architectures (Arthur 1988). These network externalities and bandwagon effects have been especially important in RISC and other microcomputer products because few of the developers of the hardware architectures are vertically integrated into the creation of applications software that is compatible with their products. As a result, hardware innovators must attract the necessary "swarms" of software developers to their particular architecture in order to become or remain viable.

The hardware-software complementarities and resulting externalities that are discussed in this chapter now are important across a broad spectrum of information technology products. Not only desktop computers and software, but also videocassette recorders, interactive home media, and compact disc players, to name only a few, have been powerfully influenced by the availability of software for their operation. In discussing commercialization strategies in RISC, we hope to shed some light on a broader class of issues in technology management that is likely to grow in importance.

THE CREATION OF RISC

Reduced-instruction-set computing was born in IBM's Thomas J. Watson Research Center in the mid-1970s. Engineers at IBM theorized that optimizing a microprocessor to execute a reduced number (set) of commonly used instructions very fast could enhance the overall processing speed of the system. Their prototype RISC machines supported this theory, running some programs twice as fast as comparable IBM machines on the market.

IBM chose not to introduce RISC-based machines for almost ten years after its pioneering research, presumably to avoid cannibalizing its existing product lines.[1] Another disadvantage of the new computer architecture was its need for new software, which rendered obsolescent IBM's extensive software library (or at least required a very significant level of investment to revise it). Although the results of IBM's work were not published until 1982, rumors of the IBM project spread through parts of the academic community shortly after the original experiments.

These rumors, as well as the complexity of current chip designs and computer architectures, the paucity of empirical academic research on computer architectures, and their wish to reduce the design effort necessary to construct high-performance computers, all led professors David Patterson and Carlos Sequin of the University of California at Berkeley to pursue research on RISC.[2] In a 1980 paper Patterson and graduate student David Ditzel introduced RISC to the computer architecture community, and sparked a controversy (Patterson and Ditzel 1980). The steady fall in the costs of computer hardware relative to those of software had created strong incentives for computer designers to utilize hardware-intensive, complex instruction technologies more intensively;[3] Patterson and his collaborators suggested the opposite. Stanford University engineering professor John Hennessy also conducted research on RISC architectures with DARPA support during the early 1980s. Hennessy's work on optimizing compiler technology and CPU architecture produced MIPS, the "Microprocessor without Interlocked Pipelined Stages" (Patterson 1985; Hennessy 1984; Hennessy et al. 1981).

Although its most significant impact may have been on the commercialization strategies of RISC microprocessor producers, the software environment within which RISC and CISC microprocessors were developed also influenced their design. The established CISC architectures (for example, the Intel x86 microprocessor family) were developed during the late 1970s, when software developers used assembly language in programming and often included special instructions (which are rarely if ever used by compilers) to assist these programmers. RISC microprocessors, however, were designed for programmers using high-level languages and compilers, and their instruction sets are tailored to work efficiently with compilers.[4]

COMMERCIALIZATION STRATEGIES IN RISC

Commercialization strategies in RISC microprocessors have followed a different path from those associated with the dominant CISC microprocessors (the Intel x86 and the Motorola 68000 families). The most popular current RISC designs were developed by major Intel and Motorola customers, such as Sun Microsystems and Hewlett-Packard (HP). This user-based innovation was facilitated by the diffusion of the basic principles of microprocessor design and fabrication associated with less complex architectures like RISC, and by the increased sophistication of commercial design and development tools.[5]

Retention of their dominant positions in CISC microprocessor technology hinges on the ability of Intel and Motorola to quickly improve their complex chip designs. These producers also benefit from their large "installed base" of microprocessors in workstations and microcomputers and the vast operating system and applications software libraries that have been developed to serve this installed base. This advantage is much more compelling for Intel, because of its dominant position in PCs, than for Motorola, which faces erosion of its CISC components' share of the workstation market (Ristelhueber 1990). The importance of applications software libraries differs between the PC and workstation markets. The workstation market consists of technically sophisticated users, who place a greater premium on performance than most PC users. Workstation users are often able to modify software to facilitate the conversion from one hardware platform to another. PC users, however, depend on off-the-shelf, standardized software and lack the tools to create or modify software to run on multiple hardware platforms. As a result, users of workstations can switch more easily between hardware platforms, and the advantages for hardware producers of a large applications software library are less significant.

Key Industry Players and Strategies

Sun Microsystems

Sun Microsystems embarked on its RISC development program out of concern that new, more powerful generations of CISC microprocessors would not appear quickly enough to keep pace with the company's future product development plans (*Electronics* 1987). Exploiting the greater simplicity of RISC designs, Sun developed SPARC, Scalable Processor ARChitecture, a microprocessor that was competitive with those of Motorola and Intel. University research and researchers played an important role in the technology development work that led to SPARC in 1985.

Rather than integrating backward into the production (as opposed to the design and development) of components, Sun licensed other firms to produce SPARC. The Japanese electronics firm Fujitsu was the first of several licensees of SPARC chips.[6] Other licensees include Cypress Semiconductor, LSI Logic, Texas Instruments, and

N. V. Philips. Liberal licensing of the chip architecture ensured competition in the manufacture of SPARC microprocessors and prevented Sun from depending exclusively on any single supplier.[7] Sun's substantial market share in workstations and its encouragement of entry by other SPARC system producers attracted independent software developers to this architecture, helping to establish SPARC as a dominant design in the workstation industry.

Although Sun's encouragement for "cloning" its workstation architecture risked some loss of market share, the firm retained important competitive advantages. Sun and its licensees offered the SPARC chip design to other systems vendors in an effort to attract clones, but Sun continued to compete vigorously and has dominated the SPARC-compatible systems market since its introduction of this architecture.[8]

MIPS Computer Systems

MIPS Computer Systems was founded in 1984 by professor John Hennessy of Stanford, Edward Stritter of Motorola, and John Moussouris of IBM to exploit the MIPS RISC design developed by Hennessy. The firm intended to enter the systems business with a proprietary CPU design, but shifted to licensing its microprocessor design while producing workstations for the OEM market. MIPS's disappointing performance in the OEM market contributed to losses during the second and third quarters of 1991, resulting in its 1992 acquisition by Silicon Graphics, a workstation manufacturer (see *Business Week* 1991b, 52).

MIPS's licensing strategy, like Sun's, allowed the firm to focus on microprocessor design and avoid the expense of manufacturing its own chips. Licensing also encouraged other semiconductor and systems manufacturers to adopt the MIPS architecture, which challenged SPARC as the dominant RISC design during 1989–92. Because MIPS manufactured its workstations exclusively for the OEM market, adopters of its RISC chip faced a smaller threat of direct competition from the designer of a critical component for their systems. Unlike Sun, however, MIPS retained control over the chip design, delivering only masks to its semiconductor licensees. This approach more closely resembled a classic "second-sourcing" strategy than that of Sun. Although MIPS's approach ensured pin-compatibility among MIPS-architecture chips and made it easier for MIPS licensees to "ramp up" their production, it limited its licensees' ability to implement designs tailored to specific market segments.

By 1991 MIPS's semiconductor licensees included LSI Logic, NEC, and Siemens; Toshiba soon followed. Its systems licensees included Silicon Graphics and Digital Equipment Corporation. Working with its licensees, MIPS attempted to use an alliance strategy, in contrast to the market-based approach of Sun, to establish its architecture as a dominant design. In 1990 the firm joined DEC, Compaq (then an investor in Silicon Graphics), the Santa Cruz Operation (a supplier of Unix operating system software), Silicon Graphics, and Microsoft to form an alliance, the Advanced Computing Environment (ACE), dedicated to the development of a hardware and software standard that would encompass PC and workstation systems based on either Intel CISC or MIPS RISC architectures. ACE, however, proved incapable of developing a credible, "consensus" architecture, as Compaq dropped out of the RISC market to focus on its PC product lines (which faced intense price competition from PC clones) and DEC withdrew to pursue an independent commercialization strategy with its Alpha RISC architecture. MIPS's licensing business, while profitable, rapidly declined in 1991 because of delays in developing its R4000 component (*Business Week* 1991b, 52).

The strategies of these two RISC insurgents, Sun and MIPS, differed significantly. Sun adopted a liberal licensing policy, effectively conceding control over its intellectual property, in order to reap the returns to RISC through sales of its workstation. MIPS, on the other hand, adopted a licensing strategy that followed the prescription of Teece (1986), seeking to gain access to "complementary" assets by licensing its technology under tighter controls to firms manufacturing workstations. MIPS subsequently sought to develop a new software "platform" for its workstation through the unsuccessful Advanced Computing Environment (ACE) consortium. The implications of these contrasting strategies are discussed later.

Other major computer firms have entered the RISC market with internally developed microprocessors. Two of these, IBM and Hewlett-Packard, were among the first to apply RISC architectures in their systems and used proprietary RISC designs, rather than the commercially available architectures associated with Sun or MIPS. This "proprietary strategy" enabled its developer to retain control of a technology. It limited the number of systems utilizing the architecture, however, and fewer independent software developers have developed products for these systems. Both IBM and HP have licensed their architectures more widely in order to attract independent software developers. Digital Equipment, the latest entrant, has pursued a similar approach.

IBM

Overcoming its initial reluctance to pursue commercial applications of RISC, IBM introduced the RISC-based RT PC to the technical and engineering market in 1986. Despite its compatibility with key components of other IBM PC products (the AT bus), the RT PC was not marketed to the business PC market because of concerns over compatibility with other IBM products in that market and because of the small amount of applications software for it. The RT PC was not successful, partly because it did not offer significant improvements in performance or cost-effectiveness over competing systems (Sexton 1990). With its introduction of the RS/6000 workstation in 1990, IBM became an important player in the technical and engineering workstation market.

In 1991 IBM and Apple teamed with Motorola to pursue development of a new RISC-based microprocessor. (Motorola had failed to develop its own successful RISC microprocessor for microcomputer applications, largely because of internal conflicts.) The "PowerPC" was based on the RISC architecture used in IBM's RS/6000 but is aimed at both the workstation and PC markets. Penetration of the PC market requires extensive software libraries and some ability to operate applications programs originally written for IBM PC–compatible and Apple personal computers. In order to meet these software requirements, IBM and Apple formed a joint venture (Taligent) in 1992 to create a new operating system and software development tools for this new platform. These tools are intended to attract independent software developers to create applications for PowerPC systems.

PowerPC-based systems are expected to combine the performance and cost advantages of RISC with some ability to exploit the applications software libraries written for CISC-based Apple and IBM hardware PC platforms. But the PowerPC's compatibility with Apple-, DOS-, and Windows-based applications software is incomplete. The PowerPC runs Apple and DOS/Windows applications software less efficiently than the CISC-based Motorola and Intel microprocessors that operate the Apple and DOS/Windows-compatible microcomputer platforms. This architecture thus faces obstacles like those confronted by the MIPS RISC chip and other microprocessor architectures (CISC and RISC) seeking to compete with the Intel-dominated DOS standard.

There is one other significant difference between the situation faced by MIPS and that of the PowerPC: this new architecture has the formal support of the world's two largest PC manufacturers. Apple and IBM jointly account for over 20 percent of global sales of PCs. Apple introduced a new line of products based on the PowerPC architecture in 1994, and Motorola teamed with Microsoft to develop a version of its Windows/NT operating system for the PowerPC. IBM has continued to develop new Intel-based PCs, however, and does not yet offer PowerPC-based systems to the Intel-dominated PC market.[9] The marketing capabilities of its sponsors enhance the prospects that the PowerPC could attract the independent software developers that are critical to its success. These prospects would be far brighter, however, with stronger IBM support for the PowerPC architecture. IBM's June 1995 introduction of a PowerPC-based line of personal computers was delayed by more than one year because of internal divisions over the risks of cannibalizing the market for its CISC-based systems (Ziegler 1995).

Hewlett-Packard Company

Hewlett-Packard (HP) began developing its Precision Architecture (PA) RISC systems in the early 1980s as the centerpiece of a far-reaching overhaul of the firm's computer product lines and introduced the first HP RISC system in 1986. Nevertheless, no PA-RISC workstation product appeared until 1991, partly because it was so difficult to create a "migration path" that could support conversion of the software developed for earlier HP workstations to this new architecture.[10] Like the RS/6000, the HP products initially retained a proprietary CPU architecture, which hampered the development of new applications software. HP now is licensing its PA-RISC architecture in an effort to gain broader acceptance of the architecture, but its licensing strategy has been very cautious. As of mid-1993, HP and its licensees, which include semiconductor manufacturers Hitachi and Samsung, had yet to offer PA-RISC microprocessors in the merchant market. Hitachi introduced its first PA-RISC chip only in late 1993, three years after licensing HP's architecture. HP also has wavered in its commitment to obtain a version of Microsoft's Windows/NT operating system for its RISC architecture. As a result, PA-RISC is used in very few other firms' workstations and therefore has attracted relatively few independent software developers; it remains essentially captive to HP.

DEC

The Digital Equipment Corporation (DEC) launched several RISC development projects during the 1980s, but abandoned them to pursue an alliance with MIPS that underpinned the ACE consortium. DEC's Alpha development project began in 1989, in order to serve as a complement to DEC's MIPS-based systems. In 1992, however, DEC decided to use its newly developed Alpha chip in its workstations and related products, severely undercutting ACE. DEC, like other entrants into the RISC competition, has sought out licensees for the production of its Alpha chip, although the firm also produces the component in-house. DEC's late entry into the RISC competition has hampered its efforts to attract licensees. Many of the strongest semiconductor manufacturers already had licensed other RISC chips and were reluctant to commit to the production of another line of RISC chips because of the low profits on their other licensed RISC products. Only in March 1993 did DEC reach a licensing agreement with Mitsubishi Electric Corporation.

All of the major developers of CISC or RISC microprocessors seek the creation of a large software applications library in order to establish (or retain) a position for their products as a dominant design in the large PC market. New entrants must convince software developers that licensing and other policies will make their hardware architecture ubiquitous. MIPS, DEC, and IBM supported the development of PC operating systems that are compatible with their RISC architectures in order to penetrate this market. The PowerPC alliance set out to use the marketing strength of IBM and Apple to directly challenge the dominance of Intel-based PCs. Sun uses its software library to maintain dominance in the workstation market and prices its systems aggressively in continuing efforts to penetrate the PC market. Intel, under pressure from numerous entrants, is working to improve its x86 architecture through successive generations that can operate all of the enormous library of Intel-compatible applications software.

The other major incumbent in desktop computing, Microsoft, remains remarkably well positioned to benefit from either Intel's continued dominance or its unseating by any of a number of RISC entrants. Microsoft's enviable position seems to reflect its role as the "gatekeeper" to the most valuable complementary asset in the architecture competition, the applications software library.

Market Performance in RISC

The market for RISC microprocessors has grown rapidly since the late 1980s. In 1989, according to International Data Corporation (1993), CISC-based workstations accounted for 70 percent of workstation shipments (Table 4-1). Shipments of RISC-based workstations grew more than fivefold during 1989–94, however, and by 1993 RISC-based workstations accounted for 84 percent of shipments. Although IDC projected that shipments of these workstations would grow more rapidly than shipments of CISC-based systems, CISC-based systems in fact gained considerable market share during 1994 (see Table 4-1). These gains were largely due to the rapid penetra-

Table 4-1. Worldwide workstation/workstation server unit share by processor type, 1989–94 (percent)

Processor	1989	1990	1991	1992	1993	1994
RISC	30	60	70	81	84	73
Motorola 680x0	46	31	22	12	7	3
Intel x86	4	<1	<1	<1	5	22
Proprietary (non-RISC)	20	11	8	7	4	2

Source: International Data Corporation 1991, 1992, 1993, 1994, 1995.

tion of Intel Pentium-based systems into market segments formerly dominated by RISC workstations.

Some sense of the success of the strategies of the competing firms in the RISC market is conveyed by Table 4-2, which gives the shares of the 1989–94 global RISC workstation market (excluding RISC-based minicomputers, supercomputers, and embedded applications) captured by each of the competing architectures. Sun's SPARC architecture dominates the RISC workstation market, while MIPS lost market share to both Hewlett-Packard PA-RISC and IBM's RS/6000 architecture and the Power chip. HP's market share in RISC systems exceeds its position in workstations, since the Precision Architecture has been applied in both HP minicomputers and workstations. If additional systems beyond workstations were included in Table 4-2, HP's market share would be significantly larger.

Workstation market shares (Table 4-3) present a slightly different picture. In 1994 Sun controlled the largest single share of the workstation market (32 percent), although this represented a decline from its 1991 peak of 39 percent.[11] Silicon Graphics, which uses MIPS chips, accounted for 6 percent of the market, and HP (including Apollo) had a share of 17 percent (HP shipments of workstations included some CISC-based products). IBM, which performed the seminal research that contributed to the RISC concept, accounted for only 6 percent of the workstation market.

But the global workstation market (639,000 units and revenues of $11.1 billion in 1993) is dwarfed by the market for PCs, which was more than $73 million (39 million units) in 1993. Even in the recessionary PC market of the early 1990s, annual *growth* in PC unit shipments was nearly ten times as large as the total *market* for workstations. As we noted earlier, much of the competitive jockeying in the workstation industry has been motivated by the desire to penetrate the much larger PC market. By 1994, however, it appeared that more powerful PC systems were encroaching on the workstation market, based largely on the success of Intel's newest microprocessor.

RISC, ENTRY BARRIERS, AND HARDWARE-SOFTWARE COMPLEMENTARITY

RISC architecture enabled several systems producers to design their own chips, reducing the competitive value of the dominant microprocessor firms' in-house design

Table 4-2 Worldwide workstation/workstation server unit share by type of RISC processor, 1989–94 (percent)

Processor	1989	1990	1991	1992	1993	1994
SPARC	55	64	63	53	48	47
MIPS	22	18	16	18	15	12
HP PA-RISC	1	<1	6	15	21	23
IBM RS/6000	5	8	8	9	9	8
Motorola 88x00	1	3	1	1	na	na
Other RISC	16	7	5	5	3	<1

Source: International Data Corporation 1991, 1992, 1993, 1994, 1995.
na = not available.

Table 4-3. Workstation unit shipment share by
vendor, 1990–92 (percent)

Vendor	1990	1991	1992
Sun	38	39	38
Hewlett-Packard	20	17	17
DEC	17	14	12
IBM	4	6	7
Silicon Graphics	3	3	5
Other	18	21	21

Source: International Data Corporation 1991, 1992, 1993.

capabilities for complex chips.[12] By lowering the barriers to entry into the microprocessor market, RISC has reduced the power of the dominant microprocessor suppliers, encouraged the emergence of several competing hardware architectures, and
threatened Motorola in particular. The severity of this threat contributed to Motorola's decision to participate in the Apple-IBM alliance.

RISC threatens Intel less than it does Motorola, because Intel's strength derives
from its position in the personal computer market, not the workstation market. Nevertheless, Intel is heavily dependent on microprocessors, having lost much of its dominant position in peripheral chips (graphics, chipsets, etc.) to smaller, nimbler competitors and having exited from production of DRAM memory chips in the mid-1980s.
If PC manufacturers were to switch in large numbers to RISC microprocessors, Intel's position would be threatened. As we note below, the licensing strategies of
MIPS and IBM were aimed at penetrating the PC market.

The network externalities that influence the success of competing microprocessor architectures operate in a circular fashion. The success of an operating system
(OS), like that of a microprocessor, depends on the variety of applications software
libraries that it can run, as well as the size of the installed base of the hardware
platforms it supports. In order to attract applications developers, OS vendors strive
to support hardware platforms with large current or expected installed bases. Independent software developers focus their efforts on operating systems and hardware platforms that are most extensively used.

The interdependence of the installed hardware base and operating systems with
the activities of independent software developers explains the efforts of Microsoft,
which dominates PC operating systems, to modify its Windows/NT operating system
for microprocessor architectures other than the Intel x86. These factors also influenced the decision of SunSoft (Sun's software subsidiary) to modify its Solaris Unix
operating system to run on Intel's x86 architecture and IBM's PowerPC, in addition
to SPARC.[13] If operating systems, such as Windows or Windows/NT, are modified
successfully (that is, without severe performance penalties) to run on a wide variety
of hardware platforms, the high switching costs that formerly supported the dominant
microprocessor architectures will fall, and producers such as Intel will be weakened.
The enduring dominant design in desktop computing thus eventually may be soft-
ware- rather than hardware-embodied. Until genuinely platform-independent software
emerges, however, the success of OS and applications software vendors will be

linked to the size of the hardware platform base they choose to support, which remains heavily weighted in favor of Sun SPARC in workstations and Intel x86 in PCs.[14]

These interdependencies create serious challenges for firms like Sun, whose hardware products rely on operating systems produced by wholly owned software subsidiaries. Sun's efforts to modify its operating system to run on other hardware platforms undermines its SPARC architecture. Sun's hardware division is to an increasing extent competing against its software division, because successful modification of Sun's operating system means that SPARC hardware no longer will be necessary to exploit this operating system and its applications library. Thus far, fragmentation in operating systems in the workstation market, combined with Sun's large market share, has muted this conflict, but the problem may grow more acute with the passage of time.

EVALUATING COMMERCIALIZATION STRATEGIES

The decisions by Sun, MIPS, and other RISC vendors to license their RISC chips had at least three advantages. First, these firms avoided or shared the tremendous investment in complementary assets required to manufacture and reap the returns to their innovations.[15] Second, the lower technological barriers to entry into RISC design meant that a more restrictive approach to dissemination of their technologies might have invited additional entry and competition. Indeed, the tendency for RISC to erode design- and production-based entry barriers reinforces the logic of Sun's decision to reap the returns to its SPARC chip through sales of its workstation, rather than through manufacture and sale of the chip.[16] Third, licensing their components established multiple production sources for these new microprocessors, reducing costs and risks for their users, ensuring strong competition among suppliers, and contributing to declines in price-performance ratios that accelerated market penetration.[17] By accelerating adoption of their architecture, licensing attracted independent software developers to write the applications packages necessary to support the diffusion of RISC-based workstations and PCs.

This commercialization strategy was based on the premise that software, rather than design and manufacturing expertise, was the critical complementary asset for profiting from RISC, especially in the enormous PC market. In contrast to the engineering and scientific workstation market, most PC users prefer desktop computers with an extensive library of applications software to higher-performance machines that lack extensive applications software; they rely on the large software libraries developed for the Intel and Motorola CISC microprocessor designs. Sun's liberal licensing policy and strong market share supported the creation of a large number of applications programs for the SPARC architecture in workstations. One industry analyst suggested in 1990 that Sun's workstation had perhaps 40–60 percent more applications programs than the competing HP workstation.[18] Sun's large applications software library has helped the firm maintain its dominant market share since 1990, despite the appearance of competing architectures with significant performance advantages. In the case of the PowerPC, the prospect of access to PC platforms marketed by Apple and IBM has attracted the interest of independent software developers in this architecture.

The SPARC component is an interesting example of a user-developed innovation whose returns are realized through the sale of a product incorporating it—von Hippel's "output-embodied" source of returns (1989). Von Hippel predicted that innovative users seeking "output-embodied" returns to their innovations would retain tight control over them, which Sun has not done. The reason for these differences between predicted and observed strategies, of course, is the importance of the applications software library in establishing SPARC as a dominant design.

In contrast to Sun's focus on establishing dominance in workstations, MIPS sought to establish its RISC architecture as a dominant component design, and controlled its licensees more closely. MIPS fell between two stools. The firm was not well positioned to reap output-embodied returns to its innovative component through OEM production of workstations. Nor did MIPS seek to produce its chips and reap the returns to its innovation through component sales. The problems faced by MIPS suggest that a "pure licensing" strategy remains a problematic entry route in this technology. Unfortunately for MIPS, its alternative "alliance" strategy—the ACE consortium—also was unsuccessful.[19]

The wide licensing of these architectures has important implications for domestic and international competition in the microprocessor industry. Liberal licensing has enabled European and Japanese semiconductor manufacturers to enter the 32-bit microprocessor market (both Fujitsu and Siemens are RISC licensees). These foreign manufacturers, as well as several domestic semiconductor manufacturers, view RISC as an opportunity to break the Intel-Motorola stranglehold on the microprocessor market. Nevertheless, their production of RISC microprocessors thus far has not been highly profitable, possibly because no single architecture has yet established a position of dominance comparable to that of the Intel x86 or early Motorola 680x0.

EMBEDDED SYSTEMS

As was noted earlier, the success of Sun's commercialization strategy in RISC has been driven mainly by the interaction of hardware producers and independent developers of applications software. Where this interaction is less important, as in the "embedded systems" market for microprocessors, commercialization strategies assume very different forms. "Microcontrollers," microprocessors modified for applications in embedded systems in automobiles, home appliances, and telephone switching systems, yielded revenues of $8.2 billion in 1994 (2.6 billion units), nearly as large as the $11.7 billion in revenues (177 million units) for microprocessors in other applications (In-Stat 1995). This represented a sharp shift in the relative size of the microcontroller and microprocessor markets from 1991, when they respectively accounted for $4.9 billion (1.8 billion units) and $3.3 billion (134 billion units). As these data suggest, the unit revenues of microprocessors also grew significantly during 1991–94.

The application of RISC-based microcontrollers within embedded systems requires design tools for hardware and software, as well as supporting logic devices. Independent software developers, however, are less pivotal to the success of new components in this market, because software for these applications generally is highly customer-specific. Penetration of the embedded systems market by RISC therefore does not depend on the availability of a large standardized applications software library. Moreover, the lack of a mass market for packaged software means that independent software vendors are less important in embedded systems, diminishing the role of network externalities and "bandwagon effects."

Because Sun does not reap large returns from its licensees and does not manufacture the SPARC component, it is not well positioned to reap the returns to RISC in the embedded systems market.[20] The more restrictive licensing strategy of MIPS, on the other hand, made it difficult for its licensees to adapt MIPS's RISC components to embedded systems applications for which MIPS did not provide design solutions.

Reflecting the fact that this market will reward a more conventional commercialization strategy that exploits control of "downstream" assets, Intel, Motorola, and other established semiconductor manufacturers (for example, Advanced Micro Devices) have moved aggressively to serve embedded systems designers, drawing on their many years of experience and close ties with customers in this market. For Motorola in particular, this market has been an important source of revenues for its 68000 and other components. Moreover, because Intel retains exclusive production rights to its RISC components for embedded applications, it may well earn more from RISC microprocessor sales than any other single producer of these components (see *RISC Management Newsletter* 1991).

CONCLUSION

The literature on strategic management of technology commercialization (classic treatments include Teece 1986 and Abernathy and Utterback 1979) has devoted little attention to strategies that influence the emergence of a dominant design. The availability and performance of complementary technologies clearly are important influences, however, and in the desktop computer industry, software is among the most important complementary technologies. Moreover, the success of firm strategies for RISC commercialization has been determined in large part by their ability to attract the independent developers of complementary software for their hardware products. In this sense, the workstation and microcomputer industries' software "tail" wags the "dog" that is technology commercialization in hardware.

This phenomenon is hardly new in the microcomputer industry, of course, nor is it unique to this industry. The emergence of the IBM PC as a dominant design, for example, had as much to do with its relatively open architecture (relying on standard components, using the standard DOS operating system, and extensive, public technical documentation) as the firm's established marketing assets and product image. The essential factor in the emergence of the IBM PC architecture as a dominant design proved to be the availability of complementary applications software.

IBM's marketing strength and credibility proved far less effective in establishing the PS/2 as a dominant design. Interestingly, the firm spared few efforts to protect the design and architecture of the PS/2, which restricted entry by imitators and made the system less attractive to independent developers of peripheral equipment and software.[21] In consumer electronics, the victory of Matsushita over Sony in the VCR "standards wars" hinged on Matsushita's greater willingness to license its technology

(Cusumano et al. 1990). Matsushita created a broader supplier base for its VHS-compatible videocassette machines, and this proved more attractive to the packagers of the entertainment "software" that was a critical complementary technology.

The importance of a "bandwagon-creation" strategy like Sun's also was influenced by the lack of vertical integration between producers of the innovation (the SPARC and other RISC chips) and the producers of the complementary technologies (applications software). In particular, the mass market for standard, packaged software is key, because it supports entry by the independent software vendors, whose perceptions and behavior create software-based "bandwagon effects." Where there are no such markets for software, as in embedded systems, Sun's strategy has been less effective. Higher levels of vertical integration between producers of applications software and systems might favor a different approach to commercialization. Since 1985, the acquisitions of recorded music and film producers by Sony Corporation, Philips, and Matsushita, whose success in consumer electronics technologies hinges on the availability of entertainment software, are attempts to pursue a vertical integration strategy.

Vertical integration into the development of applications software for microcomputers and similar products, however, is likely to remain very difficult. The progressive "dis-integration" of hardware and software development has been driven in large part by rapid declines in the cost and power of computing hardware, which have accelerated diffusion of desktop computing hardware into a much broader array of uses. As the array of potential applications has expanded, it has become more difficult for hardware producers to develop software for all of the proliferating and increasingly specialized market niches. Although many of these packaged software niches are small markets, they are large enough to allow independent software developers to recover their development costs and return a profit, and therefore will attract entry.

This discussion of technology commercialization in products that derive much of their functionality from software also illustrates the ineffectiveness of formal non-market mechanisms for establishing technical standards (see Grindley 1990, for a more detailed discussion). The failure of the Advanced Computing Environment consortium highlights this point: It is very difficult to establish consensus among competitors on technical standards in an industry characterized by very rapid technological change. The complexity of the technology and the conflicting commercial incentives of the partners may create similar problems in developing standards for software and hardware in the Apple-IBM-Motorola PowerPC alliance.

The complementarity between software and hardware that has underpinned the workstation commercialization strategies of Sun, MIPS, and other firms now may be weakened somewhat. Both software and hardware vendors are striving to develop "platform-independent" products, which would reduce their reliance on a particular microprocessor or operating system. If producers of microprocessors, operating systems, and software applications achieve true independence, the competitive position of smaller firms like Sun, historical producers of differentiated systems products, could be weakened.

A new arena of competition between RISC and CISC architectures now is opening up in "personal digital assistants" (PDAs), handheld wireless communication and computing devices, and in video games. The PDA, models of which are produced by AT&T, Apple, and other firms, currently does not rely on the extensive software libraries developed for PCs. Instead, independent software vendors are developing distinct versions of their software tailored for these devices. The PDA's "software-independence" removes an important barrier to entry into this market. The PDA market also holds out the prospect of high sales volumes, although rapid growth is likely to require the development of a more extensive applications software library and a market shakeout that results in fewer competing, incompatible designs. Among the chips being produced or designed for PDAs are products from ARM (Advanced RISC Machines), Hitachi, Motorola/IBM PowerPC, and Intel. The dynamics of competition in this market are likely to resemble those observed in desktop computing—the prospect of mass-market applications means that the architecture that attracts the greatest library of applications software is likely to prevail.

The video game industry also may present opportunities for new RISC entrants, because 32-bit RISC microprocessors and CD-ROM technology will significantly improve graphics and displays. The installed base of 16-bit video games and their software cannot compete effectively with this next generation, which therefore offers another potentially large market to semiconductor manufacturers of RISC chips.

The rapid growth of independent applications software firms in the United States and in other industrial economies thus has transformed the strategies of firms seeking to commercialize a broad and growing array of electronics technologies. As more and more of the features and functions of these electronics products derive from the availability of applications and operating system software produced by third parties, "bandwagon" strategies will play a larger role in commercialization strategies. In this context, the tradeoff between stringent protection and more liberal dissemination of intellectual property emerges as a central issue in technology strategy. In other applications, however, where the relevant software remains "embedded," liberal licensing and dissemination strategies may prove less effective.

As markets for such electronics products become global in scope, so too will the market for their complementary packaged software. This will likely create more niches of sufficient size to support entry by independent software vendors, perhaps through alliances with large vendors of "dominant designs" of operating systems or major applications (such as spreadsheets). Independent software vendors and their bandwagons thus are likely to remain a central element in the electronics industry, and in the commercialization strategies of manufacturers of electronics systems, for the foreseeable future.

NOTES

This chapter draws on Khazam and Mowery 1993. Research for this paper was completed while the first author was a graduate student at the Haas School of Business. Support for the second author's research on this paper was provided by the Alfred P. Sloan Foundation. We are grateful to Richard Nelson, Keith Pavitt, Richard Rosenbloom, W. Edward Steinmueller, David Teece, and the other participants in the International Computer Software Project for valuable comments and suggestions.

1. George Radin, head of the IBM research team, observed in an interview that IBM executives were "somewhat concerned" by the incompatibility of RISC with the large installed

base of IBM systems: " 'IBM executives had a difficult problem,' he said. 'IBM's customers have a vast backlog invested in our current architecture. It is very difficult to make the decision to embark on another incompatible product line' " (Burke 1990, S/13).

2. "In 1980 we started the RISC project at Berkeley. We were inspired by an aversion to the complexity of the VAX and Intel 432, the lack of experimental evidence in architecture research, rumors of the 801 [IBM RISC] project, and the desire to build a VLSI machine that minimized design effort while maximizing the cost/performance factor" (Patterson 1985, 20). Patterson and Sequin's research was supported by the Defense Advanced Research Projects Agency (DARPA), continuing its pattern of support for academic computer science research with significant commercial "spinoffs" (see chapter 3 in this volume).

3. "At a time when software costs were rising as fast as hardware costs were dropping, it seemed appropriate to move as much function to the hardware as possible" (Patterson 1985, 8–9).

4. Assembly language programs are low-level programs that use mnemonics that represent microprocessor instructions. These mnemonics are translated into machine language, the binary language of the microprocessor. High-level language programs, such as those written in C, Fortran, Cobol, or Pascal, use a compiler to translate the high-level language into machine code. RISC instruction sets are also optimized to take advantage of advances in computer design techniques, including pipelining, superpipelining, and superscalar approaches. These techniques can be implemented on CISC microprocessors, but the task is much more difficult when done as an "afterthought" to instruction set design.

5. This "user-active" pattern of innovation contrasts with the analysis of Abernathy and Utterback (1978), who said that users play a prominent role in developing new applications at an early stage in the evolution of a technology. The development by users of RISC in microprocessors, a technology that is two decades old, is an exception to this generalization.

6. Fujitsu was unable to enter the U.S. market for 32-bit microprocessors because of policies against second-sourcing adopted by Intel and Motorola in the mid-1980s. Fujitsu was a member of the TRON project, a cooperative Japanese research effort established to develop a CISC-based 32-bit microprocessor, but this project appeared unlikely as of 1985 to yield tangible results, a prospect borne out by subsequent developments.

7. Each Sun licensee was free to implement its own design for SPARC, a freedom that has led to pin-compatibility problems on some SPARC chips (that is, one chip cannot be simply substituted for another within a system, meaning that a given system producer may become dependent on a sole source for SPARC chips).

8. Sun's extensive direct sales force was one important competitive asset, and its aggressive pricing strategy made entry by producers of Sun clones less profitable than imitators of IBM's PC. In addition, Sun continued to develop new products, and restricted the licensing of its peripheral chips (complements to the SPARC microprocessor), which meant that many SPARC clones were unable to match the performance of Sun's SPARC systems (Poole 1991). Some systems producers resisted adopting the SPARC architecture because they did not wish to become dependent on a competing systems producer for critical component designs. This concern, as well as Sun's marketing, pricing, and technology development policies, almost certainly slowed the growth of the SPARC-based "clone" market.

9. IBM is also selling and enhancing a line of microprocessors that is compatible with Intel's 486 architecture and has been rumored to be planning the development of hardware that is compatible with both the PowerPC and Intel's x86 architecture. In other words, IBM appears to be hedging its bets on the evolution of microprocessor architecture, recognizing the powerful influence of Intel's installed based of microprocessors and applications software libraries.

10. One of the most serious challenges in creating conversion protocols was the need to

avoid serious degradation in the performance of applications software originally written for the Motorola 68000, the basis of earlier HP workstations.

11. Consistent with our earlier discussion, the market share of producers of clones of the SPARC workstations has grown relatively slowly. In 1991 SPARC clones accounted for roughly 12 percent of the SPARC workstation market (Wrona 1992). Projections compiled by the WorkGroup Technologies forecasting firm, however, forecast that sales of SPARC clones would grow more rapidly (47 percent average annual growth) than sales of Sun workstations (15 percent average annual growth) during 1990–95.

12. The chip design and development capabilities of firms like Sun and MIPS do not allow these firms to compete with Intel and Motorola on the scale or in the complexity of their components. Indeed, the control by Intel and Motorola of both design and production provides another source of competitive advantage within CISC components. Instead, RISC provides an avenue to improve systems performance that requires somewhat fewer engineering and financial resources for design and development.

13. The development of a genuinely standard, platform-independent version of Unix would unify this operating system's installed base, making it potentially as attractive for independent software developers as Apple's System 7. The present fragmentation among Unix operating systems severely reduces the attractiveness of this operating system as a target for the efforts of independent software developers.

14. According to Hudson and Bannon (1992), the purchases of equity positions in Machines Bull by IBM and in Olivetti by DEC are responses to the increasing portability of software across different RISC architectures. IBM and DEC invested in these important European customers for their RISC components as a means of retaining them as major promoters of their respective architectures in the face of declining switching costs.

15. The costs of new manufacturing capacity in the microprocessor industry continue to rise; Intel Corporation announced in April 1993 that it would invest $1 billion in manufacturing capacity expansion. Cost escalation has driven every manufacturer of high-performance microprocessors, except Intel, to seek manufacturing partners.

16. The fact that all of the major producers of workstations have unique RISC chip architectures illustrates this point; each workstation vendor has elected to design its own architecture rather than use architectures furnished by a competing workstation producer or by a merchant semiconductor firm.

17. Market projections for RISC and CISC microprocessors compiled by Dataquest forecast an average annual rate of decline in average selling prices of 15.7 percent for CISC microprocessors for the 1988–94 period, well below the projected average annual rate of price decrease of 23.2 percent for RISC microprocessors (Dataquest 1990).

18. " 'The most critical component of Sun's success is the availability and variety of third-party software support,' said Kathleen Hurley, an analyst at Dataquest.

" 'Even though Hewlett-Packard and Apollo have merged, Sun still maintains the leading market share,' she said. 'If I purchased a Sun workstation, there would be 1,400 or 1,600 applications available.'

" 'Sun's major competitors—Digital Equipment and Hewlett-Packard Co.—each have approximately 1,000 applications available,' said Hurley" (Spiegelman 1990, S/4). Sun's very liberal approach to licensing the SPARC architecture, however (recall the point made earlier concerning pin-compatibility problems), has led some industry observers to raise questions about whether all "SPARC applications" software can run on all SPARC workstations (see Slater 1991).

19. The apparent failure of the ACE consortium suggests the dangers of using a broad alliance to develop a new product, in contrast to the success of using alliances to conduct precommercial technological or basic research. The development-oriented alliances that (thus

far) have been viable in RISC commercialization strategies (for example, the IBM-Apple-Motorola undertaking) involve a narrower focus and a smaller number of stronger participants.

20. If rapid growth in applications of the SPARC chip in the embedded systems market results in lower prices for SPARC components, Sun will benefit indirectly, but the magnitude of this benefit remains uncertain.

21. More recent efforts by IBM to liberalize the financial terms of licenses for the PS/2's architecture reflect a shift in strategy to one that more closely resembles that of Sun. The changing attitude of IBM toward "cloners" of its original PC and its subsequent PS/2 product illustrates the tensions between tight protection of technology and the establishment of one's product as a dominant design. Cusumano et al. (1990) present a similar assessment of the contrasting strategies of Sony and Matsushita in the competition to establish a VCR standard. Swann's discussion of second-sourcing of microprocessors (1987) mentions this issue as well. Finally, the efforts of Apple Computer in 1994 and 1995 to license its operating system and architecture reflect a renewed effort to attract more software developers to this design.

REFERENCES

Abernathy, W. J., and J. M. Utterback, 1978. "Patterns of Industrial Innovation." *Technology Review* 80: 40–47.

Arthur, W. B. 1988. "Competing Technologies: An Overview." In G. Dosi, C. Freeman, R. Nelson, G. Silverberg, and L. Soete, eds., *Technical Change and Economic Theory*. London: Frances Pinter.

Bambrick, R. 1985. "Barrage of 32-Bit Alternatives Challenges Motorola, Intel MPU Supremacy." *Electronic News,* 18 February, 1.

Burke, S. 1990. "The Soul of a Newer Machine: Recalling RISC's Roots." *PC Week,* 2 April, S/13.

Business Week. 1991a. "Congratulations, It's a Clone." 15 April, 69–70.

———. 1991b. "MIPS Computer Has a Great Future behind It." 5 October, 52.

Card, D. 1987. "How Intel and Motorola Missed the Sun Rise." *Electronic Business,* 1 November, 32–34.

Cusumano, M., Y. Mylonadis, and R. S. Rosenbloom. 1990. "Strategic Maneuvering and Mass-Market Dynamics: The Triumph of Beta over VHS." Working paper 90–5, Consortium on Competitiveness and Cooperation, University of California, Berkeley.

Dataquest. 1990. "The 32-Bit Microprocessor Forecast: RISC to Account for 48 Percent of Market by 1994." Research Report, San Jose, Calif.

David, P. A. 1985. "Clio and the Economics of QWERTY." *American Economic Review Papers and Proceedings* 75: 332–37.

David, P. A., and S. Greenstein. 1989. "Compatibility Standards and Information Technology—Business Strategies, Market Development, and Public Policies. Center for Economic Policy Research, Stanford University, CEPR Publication #159, Palo Alto, Calif.

Electronics. 1987. "Why Sun Designed Its Own RISC Chip." 3 September, 72–73.

Electronics Buyers News. 1991. "SPARC Boosts Risc Standard." 21 January, 30.

Gannes, S. 1985. "Back-to-Basics Computers with Sports-Car Speed." *Fortune,* 30 September, 98.

Grindley, P. 1990. "Winning Standards Contests: Using Product Standards in Business Strategy." *Business Strategy Review* (Spring): 71–84.

Hennessy, J. L. 1984. "VLSI Processor Architecture." *IEEE Transactions on Computers* C-33, no. 12 (December): 1221–46.

Hennessy, J. L., N. Jouppi, F. Baskett, and J. Gill. 1981. "MIPS: A VLSI Processor Architecture." Proceedings of a Carnegie-Mellon University Conference on VLSI Systems and Computations. Rockville, Md.: Computer Science Press, October.

Hudson, R. L., and L. Bannon. 1992. "Digital Hopes to Rule Europe's RISC Market with Olivetti Gambit." Wall Street Journal Europe, 29 June, 1.

In-Stat. 1991. "Overview of the Microcontroller (MCU) Market." Scottsdale, Ariz. November.

———. 1995. "1994 Micro Logic Summary." Scottsdale, Ariz. January.

International Data Corporation. 1991. "1990 Workstation/Workstation Server Market: The Year in Review." January.

———. 1992. "1991 Workstation/Workstation Server Market: The Year in Review." January.

———. 1993. "1992 Workstation/Workstation Server Market: The Year in Review." January.

———. 1994. "1993 Workstation/Workstation Server Market: The Year in Review." January.

———. 1995. "1994 Workstation/Workstation Server Market: The Year in Review. January.

Judy, C. 1991. "Competitive Developments in the Computer Workstation Industry." Presented at the Technology, Organizations, and Productivity Workshop, Stanford University, 5 March.

Katz, M., and C. Shapiro. 1986. "Technology Adoption in the Presence of Network Externalities." Journal of Political Economy 94: 822–41.

Khazam, J., and D. C. Mowery. 1993. "The Commercialization of RISC: Strategies for the Creation of Dominant Designs." Research Policy 22: 89–102.

Patterson, D. A. 1985. "Reduced Instruction Set Computers." Communications of the ACM, January, 8–21.

Patterson, D. A., and D. R. Ditzel. 1980. "The Case for the Reduced Instruction Set Computer." Computer Architecture News, 15 October, 25–33.

Patterson, D. A., and C. H. Sequin. 1982. "A VLSI RISC." IEEE Computer, September, 8–21.

Poole, G. A. 1988. "Sun in Their Eyes." Unix World, October.

RISC Management Newsletter. 1991. 28 January.

Ristelhueber, R. 1990. "Motorola, Intel Push Defensive Measures." Electronic News, 5 February, 1.

Sexton, T. 1990. "IBM Raises the Ante in High-Stakes RISC Game." PC Week, 2 April, S/8.

Slater, M. 1991. "The Value of Standards, Part 3." Microprocessor Report, 12 June, 3.

Spiegelman, L. L. 1990. "Sun Focuses on SPARC to Fend Off Growing Competition." PC Week, 2 April, S/4.

Swann, G. M. P. 1987. "Industry Standard Microprocessors and the Strategy of Second-Source Production." In H. G. Gabel, ed., Product Standardization and Competitive Strategy. Amsterdam: Elsevier.

Teece, D. J. 1986. "Profiting from Technological Innovation: Implications for Integration, Collaboration, Licensing and Public Policy." Research Policy 15: 286–305.

———. 1990. "Innovation and the Structure of Industry." University of California, Berkeley. Duplicated.

von Hippel, E. 1977. "The Dominant Role of the User in Semiconductor and Electronic Subassembly Process Innovation." IEEE Transactions on Engineering Management (May): 60–71.

———. 1989. The Sources of Innovation. New York: Oxford University Press.

Wrona, T. 1992. "Vendors Vie for VARs." Computer Reseller News, 6.

Ziegler, B. 1995. "New IBM PCs Are Superfast, But Might Be Too Late," Wall Street Journal, 16 June, B4.

5

The User-Driven Evolution of the Japanese Software Industry: The Case of Customized Software for Mainframes

Yasunori Baba, Shinji Takai, and Yuji Mizuta

The Japanese software industry has many facets, which differ sharply in structure and performance. Although some observers have argued that the software houses of the major computer vendors are more productive than their American counterparts (Cusumano 1991), most Japanese software houses are growing relatively slowly and appear to be somewhat less innovative than those in the United States. Faced with an increasing number of bankruptcies, in 1993 Japan's Ministry of International Trade and Industry (MITI) declared that the software industry had been seriously affected by Japan's recession, thus entitling it to special subsidies and other preferential treatment. The Japanese software industry is a paradox, at once highly productive and yet unsuccessful. What does this paradox suggest? Is there an unified Japanese software industry, or are there several software industries?

In this chapter we define the software industry broadly as including all firms and parts thereof that have software capabilities.[1] We present an analytical framework called the "hub structure," which has two advantages over previous analytical tools. It includes all actors involved in software development in Japan: the users, the computer vendors, and the software houses; and it graphically illustrates the interactions through which software is developed. The internal capabilities of software users are at the hub of this structure, as the coordinating component, and they are surrounded by the capabilities of the computer vendors and the software houses. The framework, though general, is especially relevant to Japan, where customized software developed through the cooperation of firms dominates the market. The primary focus of this chapter is mainframe software (for a discussion of Japan's microcomputer software industry, see chapter 6 in this volume).

We attempt to provide a clear picture of the structure of the industry, using published data to identify the hub structure, and describe how leading users contributed to the formation of the structure. We analyze the features of the hub structure, especially the division of labor, that are created by exclusive business relations. Most of the activities of software firms in this segment of the market are devoted to the development of customized software for the users; the packaged software business is less fully developed because it presupposes a more competitive market. Customized software development has created organizational mechanisms for highly interactive user-supplier relations to produce "finely tailored" software; we refer to this as the "user-driven paradigm." We consider the factors that gave rise to these structural and functional features of the Japanese software industry, and more specifically, we examine how the Japanese government, universities, and other institutional influences, such as intellectual property laws, shaped the evolution of the industry and promoted business activities and competition.

In our conclusion we argue that the evolution of the Japanese software industry has been heavily influenced by its unique institutional environment. Many features of this environment, especially government policy, have contributed to the development of a strong Japanese manufacturing sector and may also have supported Japanese software development practices that have enhanced productivity through tight quality control. Other elements of this environment have proven less beneficial for the software industry, and without far-reaching revisions in policy and changes in industry structure, the Japanese software industry will encounter intense international competition and weak innovative performance in the fastest-growing segments of the domestic market.

DEFINITION AND DESCRIPTION OF THE "HUB STRUCTURE"

Market Structure

The first Japanese software houses were established during the second half of the 1960s. Before that time, most computer programs had been internally developed by the users or supplied free of charge by computer vendors. Widespread adoption of computers increased users' demand for software, triggering the establishment of software houses as separate companies. In the early stages, most of the founders of these firms were systems engineers who had been in charge of software development within a vendor or a user company. Following the example of their American counterparts, Japanese computer vendors formally "unbundled" software and hardware in 1977. The resulting software houses were established by computer vendors and created from the data processing sections of user companies. The early growth of the software market in Japan was driven by the rapidly increasing demand for new user programs, and the primary participants were the users and the computer vendors.

Previous studies of the Japanese software industry have focused almost exclusively on the contracts and interactions between users and software houses. The surveys of domestic service industries published by MITI, for example, provide data for only the most narrow definition of a software market. Although the "external" software market (that is, the market outside the firm) has grown rapidly since the 1960s, an "internal market," based on the development of software by users and computer vendors, remains very important in Japan. Users' operations usually include confidential matters and complicated procedures specific to each company, and basic programs like the operating system are closely connected, both technologically and strategically, with their hardware. Therefore, many user companies still develop their core programs internally, and the computer vendors supply more or less differentiated basic programs.

This chapter examines the characteristics and size of external and internal software development activities and shows how these activities are interrelated in the overall software market, .through the "hub structure" (see Figure 5-1). In the hub structure framework, users' internal activities are at the center, surrounded by the computer vendors' internal activities and the activities of the software houses. The software houses can be classified into three groups according to the type of company that spawned them. These three groups are maker spin-offs, user spin-offs, and independent software houses. The maker spin-off receives more than 50 percent of its capital from a computer vendor or is under a vendor's explicit control. The user spin-off has a similar relationship with a user company, such as a bank. The independent software houses are independent of users or computer vendors. Each group's contribution to total software sales is discussed in the following sections, using estimated values from 1990.

The external software market in Japan

The total size of the software market in 1990 was estimated at 3,457,947 million yen, based on sales data published in the MITI report on the information service industry in Japan (Ministry of International Trade and Industry 1990). This MITI report was based on a survey of 7,042 firms and contains the most comprehensive database on the Japanese software industry.

We estimated the software sales revenues of each company group from other sources, because the MITI report provides no firm-level software sales data. We grouped Japan's top 100 information service firms into the maker spin-off, user spin-off, and independent categories (*Computopia* 1989, 1990, 1991). The reported sales of these firms include revenues from computer services and consulting as well as software. In order to estimate the net sales of software alone, the data were multiplied by 0.589, which is the average ratio of the software sales to the total sales revenues

Figure 5-1. The hub structure of Japanese software development.

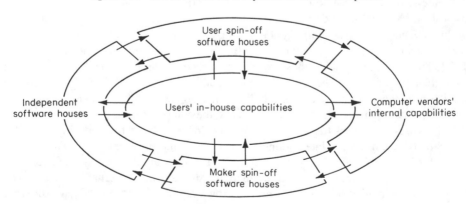

of the information service industry, as reported in the MITI survey. Net software sales were estimated at 511,934 million yen for seventeen maker spin-off firms, 765,999 million yen for fifty-three user spin-off firms, and 410,202 million yen for thirty independent software houses. This sum amounted to 1,688,135 million yen, or almost 50 percent of Japan's total domestic software sales in 1990.

We estimated sales data for the remainder of the Japanese software industry by using data from a survey of another 243 firms conducted by the Japan Information Service Association (JISA). These results showed sales of 235,385 million yen (13.3 percent of the total) for the maker spin-off firms, 553,951 million yen (31.3 percent) for the user spin-off firms, and 980,476 million yen (55.4 percent) for the independent software houses.[2] Combining the estimated sales from these three sources gives the following figures: the independent software houses have the highest sales, 1,390,678 million yen, followed by the user spin-off firms, with 1,319,950 million yen, and the maker spin-off firms, with software revenues of 747,319 million yen. The first group's sales revenues are about twice as large as those of the third group.

Estimate of Computer Vendors' Internal Activities

Our estimates of the magnitude of the software-related activities of the six major computer vendors, namely Fujitsu, Toshiba, Hitachi, NEC, Mitsubishi Electric, and IBM Japan, assumed that these activities were focused mainly on the development of customized software for mainframe computers. At the moment, none of the major vendors reports software sales. In order to estimate revenues from software sales, we relied on the published ratio of sales of software and related services to total computer sales. IBM Japan reported that the share of software and related services in total computer sales exceeded 30 percent in the 1980s. Hitachi and Fujitsu reported 32 percent (1991) and 34 percent (1992), respectively (*Nikkei* 1993). Total computer sales were multiplied by 0.3 (the average ratio of software sales to total computer sales) and by 0.589 (the average share of software sales in total computer services revenues, which include services and consulting), to obtain an estimate of the computer vendors' software revenues. We estimated total software sales by computer vendors to be 1,548,093 million yen in 1990.

Estimate of the Value of Users' Internal Activities

Finally, we estimated the value of software developed internally by users. We based this estimate on the average ratio of users' internal software development expenses to payments by users for software produced by a computer vendor or a software house, based on data from another MITI survey series (Ministry of International Trade and Industry 1979, 1984, 1989). This MITI report series tabulated expenses for in-house computer-related personnel and payments for external computer-related personnel, the development and purchasing costs of the software, and the operating charges paid to external vendors. These data yielded an internal-external ratio of 0.486, and the value of user-developed software was estimated to be 4,744,863 million yen in 1990, nearly as large as the estimated revenues from external software sales (Figure 5-2)[3].

These results allow us to describe the hub structure of the Japanese software

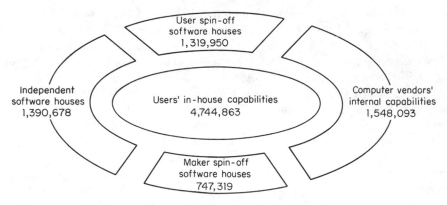

Figure 5-2. The market structure of the Japanese software industry, 1990 (million yen). *Source:* MITI 1979, 1984, 1989.

industry qualitatively and quantitatively. Adding the estimated figures yields an estimated total for the value of marketed and internally developed software of 9,750,903 million yen. This amount is smaller than the output of the textile industry (13,300 billion yen) in the same period but exceeds that of the shipbuilding industry (6,200 billion yen) and approaches the value of output of the paper manufacturing industry (9,700 billion yen) and the nonferrous metals industry (10,600 billion yen). The estimated value of the software industry's output amounted to about 2.2 percent of nominal gross national product (GNP) (434,200 billion yen) for fiscal year 1990.

Development of the Hub Structure

The origins of the user spin-off software houses

Japanese high-technology firms frequently spin off operations when they exploit new technological or market opportunities that differ substantially from their main lines of business (Gerlach, forthcoming 1995), and similar tendencies are clear in the software activities of computer vendors and users. To build up the hub structure, leading computer vendors have created independent software houses to develop or maintain close relationships with specific customers. These major user industries also have been an important source of software firms and development expertise. Japan's steel industry made a significant contribution during the early stage, and in recent years banks and other financial companies have done the same.

During the period of industrial recovery after the war, the government designated shipbuilding as a key industry. This decision triggered expansion and the development of production processes in the steel industry, and its computerization in the early 1960s substantially contributed to the advancement of the Japanese computer industry. In the mid-1960s, the old batch production systems were placed under the control of computers. The major steel producers also computerized other activities, such as production and marketing management. In addition, as a result of computerization, continuous casting technology replaced the previous production processes. These advanced process technologies required huge programs in order to operate smoothly. For instance, while the software needed for a third-generation on-line banking network requires 5 to 10 million lines of code per bank, a steel manufacturer requires more than 90 million lines of code to control its plants (*Toyo Kezai* 1991).

But the immature state of development of the Japanese software industry meant that steel producers had to train their own engineers to develop the software to control their complex production technology. In-house software development became the rule in the steel industry, and each firm accumulated extensive knowledge and know-how. Baba and Seike's discussion (1991) of computerization in Japanese industry focused on the installation of mainframes between 1973 and 1988 and revealed substantial interindustry differences in the extent of in-house software development. Between 1973 and 1980 the steel industry recorded the largest increase among all Japanese industries in its investment in in-house software and computer services expertise, as measured by the ratio of expenses for in-house computer personnel to total software-related expenses. The increase in its in-house software-related expenses occurred during a period of rapid growth in total computer-related investments (related to the post-1973 increase in energy costs) by Japanese firms; the average reported computer-related costs per firm almost doubled during these seven years. This "in-house development ratio" continued to grow in many manufacturing industries during the 1980–88 period, but in the steel industry it decreased. Nevertheless, by 1988 the ratio was still the highest among the manufacturing industries for which data were available (0.37). The electric machinery industry (with a ratio of 0.31) ranked second, followed by chemical products (0.30). The transportation machinery industry had the lowest ratio (0.24). This early commitment to internal software development explains why Japan's steel manufacturers established so many software houses.

Around 1980 service industries such as banks and other financial companies overtook the steel industry in software development. Japanese banks began to computerize their operations in the mid-1960s. In the 1970s, the banks invested approximately 30 billion yen per firm in the automation of networkwide clearing operations and the establishment of a countrywide interbank network. They made another large investment during the 1980s for a third-generation computer network. It is estimated that each major bank spent about 150 billion yen, and large local banks spent about 30 billion yen apiece. In total, the banking sector invested 3,000 billion yen on computerization through the 1980s (Ministry of International Trade and Industry 1992).

In 1988 the banking sector's computer-related investments equaled those of the information service industry and were more than twice as large as those of the third largest investor, the electric machinery sector. The banking sector continued to increase investments in computing technology at a very high rate until 1990. In 1991 these investments fell 10 percent because the third-generation network was complete and because the Japanese economy entered a recession. The great expansion in software development in the banking sector during the 1980s, like that of the steel industry in the 1970s, spawned many software houses.

The Japanese packaged software market

The small size of Japan's market for packaged software has hindered the development of this segment of the Japanese software industry (see Nakahara 1993). Two factors have contributed to the slow growth of Japan's packaged software market. The first is that operating system software is still not unified around a single "dominant design" or standard in the Japanese market (see chapter 6 in this volume). Each Japanese computer vendor has developed a unique architecture (in part as a means of meeting the demand for Japanese-language text processing capabilities), and each vendor has developed a different version of the MS-DOS operating system software based on bilateral contracts with Microsoft. As a result, the products of different vendors are largely incompatible, and the packaged software market remains divided. For the software houses, segmentation makes it difficult to spread the high fixed costs of entry and product development across a large number of buyers of any single software program.

A second problem is that very little venture capital flows into the Japanese software industry, especially by comparison with the United States. According to a survey in 1989, 11 percent of American venture capital went to the American software industry; in Japan this industry's share of a smaller stream of venture capital was only 0.04 percent (*Nikkei* 1992c). The lack of venture capital almost certainly is linked to the underdeveloped domestic market for packaged software, which has provided the most attractive possibilities for U.S. start-up firms. In addition, the limited technological assessment capabilities of Japanese venture capital managers may make it difficult to evaluate investments in a complex industry such as software. Japan has spawned few innovative firms in the packaged software segment of the industry. As a result, packaged software sales amounted to only 16 percent of total Japanese software sales in 1990 (Ministry of International Trade and Industry 1990), and as chapter 1 points out, still accounted for less than 25 percent of domestic sales in 1992. Moreover, much of this domestic demand for packaged software is met through imports.

Employment and Level of Skills

In this section we discuss the number, qualifications, and working conditions of the software engineers employed in the hub structure. According to the 1990 MITI survey of the Japanese information service industry, the total number of workers was 458,462 in 1990 (excluding managers and other nontechnical personnel). Within this total, 357,752 were classified as "software engineers," using a broad definition of this occupational category that includes researchers, systems engineers, programmers, operators, and keypunch operators (Ministry of International Trade and Industry 1990). A narrower definition (counting systems engineers and programmers only) yields an estimate of 279,533 software engineers. These figures cover only the external market discussed in the previous section; no satisfactory data are available on the number of engineers working in the systems sections of computer vendors or user companies.

According to another survey conducted by the Industrial Structure Council of MITI in 1987, the total number of software engineers in Japan was 428,000, an estimate that included 165,000 systems engineers and 263,000 programmers (MITI 1987). About 35 percent of these engineers were employed by software houses, 58 percent by user companies, and 7 percent by computer vendors. Assuming that the share of total employment of systems engineers accounted for by users, computer vendors, and independent software houses remained constant, these data can be combined with those from the 1990 MITI survey to infer that roughly 463,000 engineers were employed by user companies and 56,000 by computer vendors in 1990. These figures suggest that total employment of software engineers in Japanese industry, based on a narrow definition of this occupation, amounted to 800,000 in 1990.

The importance and functions of systems engineers

Although it discusses only the external market for software, the 1990 MITI report suggests how the characteristics of software engineers have changed since 1980. The proportion of qualified engineers has increased rapidly. The share of systems engineers and programmers (the narrow definition of the "software engineer" occupation) within the broad definition of software engineers increased from 48.2 percent in 1980 to 78.2 percent in 1990. The number of systems engineers increased more than tenfold during this period, and their share of the broad software engineering workforce increased from 19.6 percent to 41.4 percent. Another MITI survey of the computerization process in Japan shows growth in the number of software engineers working at user companies (Ministry of International Trade and Industry 1979, 1984, 1989). The average number of software engineers employed within companies grew from 20.3 in 1979 to 29.3 in 1989, an increase of about 40 percent, and the rate of growth was especially high during 1984–89. According to the 1989 MITI report, 34.5 percent of these in-house software engineers had duties that resembled those of a systems engineer, indicating some growth in the complexity and demands of the in-house engineering tasks.

Despite this growth in employment of software engineers with more advanced qualifications, other data suggest that the quality of Japanese software engineers needs improvement. The productivity of the workforce of Japanese software houses, for example, has grown more slowly than total sales. Total sales in the external market grew 400 percent during 1985–90, but sales per employee increased by only 30 percent during the same period. The rapid growth of Japan's information business, especially software development activities, has been achieved mainly through employment growth rather than productivity growth (Figure 5-3). In order to elaborate on these observations, we now turn to a discussion of the tasks and corresponding skill requirements of employment in each component of the hub structure. We begin by discussing the educational backgrounds and training of the engineers in each group.

Systems engineers' qualifications and training

Most software houses recruit new graduates from universities and professional schools, but many recruits are underqualified. The JISA survey of the information service industry says that of the graduates who started work in software houses in April 1991, only 0.4 percent had a master's degree, and 35 percent had a bachelor's degree (Figure 5-4). The rest graduated from technical colleges, professional schools, and high schools (JISA 1992). The modest educational qualifications of entry-level employees do little to improve the quality of in-house systems engineers, who need a broad knowledge of scientific disciplines in order to deal with business procedures and user needs appropriately. Even the largest Japanese software houses find it difficult to recruit qualified computer science graduates. According to Recruit Research, among the students with a bachelor's degree or above who started work in the infor-

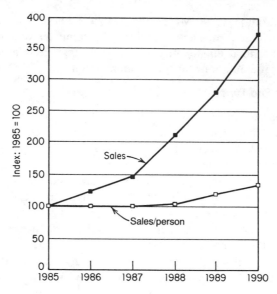

Figure 5-3. Growth of the information service industry in Japan, 1985–90. *Source:* MITI 1990.

mation service industry in April 1990, 58.6 percent had majored in economics, law, and other subjects in the social sciences and humanities, and only 3.6 percent were from a computer science department (Recruit Research 1990).

Japan has three primary problems associated with the training of software engineers. First, few software houses have systematic, formal training programs, perhaps because of a lack of consensus on what skills are required, and there are very few competent instructors. Second, and as a consequence of the first problem, most software engineers develop their specialized skills through improvised on-the-job training. In fact, most customized computer programs are jointly developed by the internal personnel of a user company and engineers dispatched from a software house. If necessary, newly hired employees are trained by the user personnel. Third, because

Figure 5-4. Academic background of employees in the Japanese software industry, 1989–91. *Source:* Japanese Information Service Industry Association 1989, 1990, 1991.

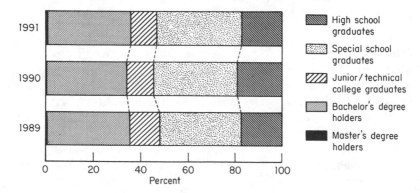

of the rapid growth in software demand, many inexperienced engineers are assigned to tasks that are too difficult given their limited formal training and experience. Most individuals classified as software engineers once had at least ten years' experience as programmers, but this training period now lasts no more than three years on average (Baba and Takai 1990). This shorter period of on-the-job experience and training makes it difficult for software engineers to overcome the consequences of their lack of formal training.

Most of the small number of computer science graduates are employed by computer vendors and manufacturers of electronics equipment. They are engaged mainly in the development of operating systems and other special software rather than in application programs for business. By contrast, many large user companies assign software-related tasks to junior employees with varied backgrounds. For example, large electronics firms are known to assign 40–60 percent of all newly hired university degree holders, regardless of their field of study, to programming jobs. The tasks of these new employees consist largely of software maintenance, although they include some software development and improvement.

The Roles of the Different Groups within the Hub Structure

Dominant developers by market segment

This section discusses the types of software that are developed by the different company groups within the hub structure. As illustrated in Figure 5-5, software is classified as either operating system (OS) or application software (customized or packaged), and the hardware platforms for software are grouped into mainframe, minicomputer (including workstations), and microcomputer categories.

Because OS programs are developed for a specific hardware platform in order

Figure 5-5. Dominant developer by market segment.

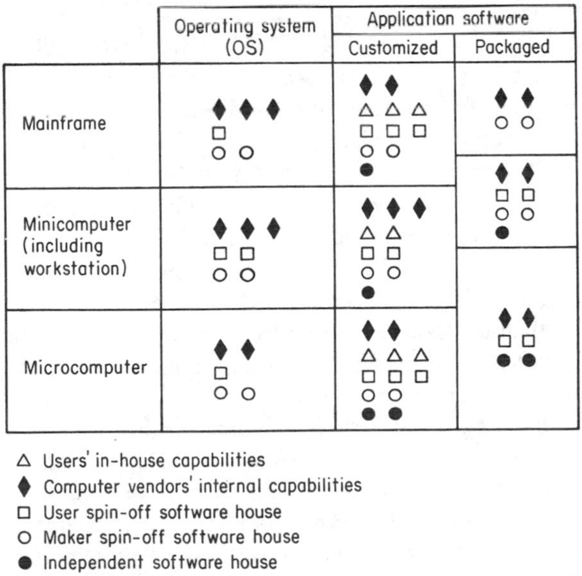

△ Users' in-house capabilities
◆ Computer vendors' internal capabilities
□ User spin-off software house
O Maker spin-off software house
● Independent software house

to attain maximum performance, development is usually done by the computer vendors with assistance from the maker spin-off software houses. On the other hand, most packaged programs are for microcomputers and are often developed by independent software houses. Packaged software for mainframes and minicomputers, however, is often produced by computer vendors and maker spin-off software houses. In fact, the major vendors, such as Fujitsu and NEC, have assigned a high priority to the packaged software business. As we discuss later, customized programs for mainframes are jointly developed by computer vendors, the user companies, and software houses.

International comparisons

In order to compare the quality of Japanese software products with their American counterparts, one must distinguish among product areas such as finance, games and amusement, operating systems, office automation, science and technology, telecommunications, and defense. The main users of finance-related software in Japan are the major banks, which are large global firms that have long promoted internal computerization through large-scale software investments. Apart from their ever-increasing demands for on-line networking, Japanese banks demand extremely high technical standards and require advanced and unique systems. One reason for their demanding requirements is the limited use of bank checks in Japan, which means that the use of automated-teller machines (ATM) is extremely heavy. The quality of Japanese software in this sector is widely judged to be comparable to that in the United States.

In amusement, especially in game software for family computers, Japan is strong. Each of the major producers, Nintendo and Sega, produces hardware with unique specifications. Because their hardware shares depend on software sales, these companies invest heavily in software development. Both of these firms support large teams of in-house systems engineers working under optimum conditions and closely monitor external software development. All software houses that wish to develop game software must complete a special license contract with the hardware company, ensuring high-quality products.[4] Since 1983, when the first family computers were released, both hardware and software sales have increased rapidly and a large amount of software is exported to Europe and the United States.

In the other five software product areas, the United States seems to be in a superior position. All commercial OS programs in Japan are modified products of their American forerunners. Although Japan is working on some original programs (for example, the real-time operating nucleus, or TRON), they are still at the experimental stage (see chapter 6 in this volume). New office automation concepts for microcomputers and local area networks (LANs) have thus far originated in the United States rather than in Japan, because of differences in the applications environment in the two countries and in the marketing strength of each nation's software firms. Furthermore, the American software industry has benefited from long-standing, close ties between industry and academia. U.S. government agencies with high technological standards, such as NASA and the Department of Defense, have supported expansion in university research and training in computer science, which have made American software for scientific and engineering applications far more advanced than Japan's. The situation is the same in telecommunications; although

NTT and other companies have sought to develop core technologies to enhance their infrastructure, there are still insufficient capabilities for commercialization. In the area of military applications the U.S. software industry is far ahead of the Japanese, although little of the defense-related software has thus far yielded direct civilian applications (see Flamm 1988 and chapter 3 of this volume).

OPERATION OF THE HUB STRUCTURE

The Division of Labor among Software Developers in Mainframe Software

The company groups that make up the hub structure have established a complex subcontracting system to develop customized programs for mainframes (see Figure 5-6). User companies, especially large firms, assist the computer vendors and software houses in the development of custom software by clarifying specifications and requirements for complex products, and often, by designing the basic structure. At the same time, computer vendors manage software development planning and often rely on their spin-off software houses for design and production. The maker spin-off software houses obtained 71 percent of their revenues from such orders in the second half of 1980s (Totsuka, Nakamura, and Umezawa 1990). "Lower-end" activities such as system production, testing, and maintenance are entrusted to user spin-off software houses, which obtained 74 percent of their revenues from their parent companies during the late 1980s. Although independent software houses originally were close partners of the computer vendors, a growing share of their contracts is derived from users. During the late 1980s, 33.2 percent of the independent software houses' orders came from the computer vendors, 34.7 percent from the users, and 21.4 percent from other software houses (ibid.).[5]

The current division of labor may require structural reform in order to deal

Figure 5-6.   Division of labor among Japanese software developers.

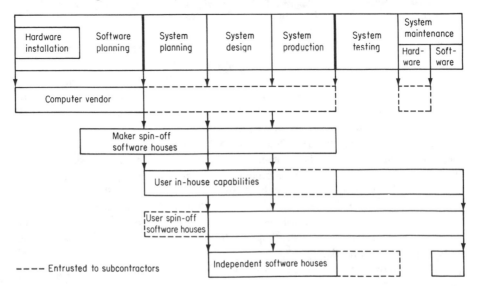

---- Entrusted to subcontractors

with emerging technologies. In fact, a number of new companies, so-called system integrators, have already appeared to provide software and computer services that include activities ranging from the basic specification and design of integrated systems to system maintenance, all drawing on their accumulated know-how in hardware and software technologies.[6]

The Structure of Transactions: Semideveloped Markets and the User-Driven Paradigm

The discussion in the previous section explains that the various company groups in the hub structure are involved in different tasks. Suppliers' development of customized software for specific users in particular fosters long-lasting relations among the participants, and these user-supplier relationships support the creation of "finely tailored" software in Japan. But this interaction has also hindered the full development of the software market. This section explores this interaction in greater detail.

In the 1970s a decisive factor in the creation of stable relations between producers and users was the active participation by Japanese computer vendors in software development for users. The Japanese computer vendors dispatched systems engineers to clients for extended periods of time. The computer vendors expected this assistance to generate future sales, and some clients relied on the vendors' support because they lacked their own internal development capabilities. As a consequence, computer vendors employed a large number of systems engineers and, in response to growing demand, assigned these employees and their activities to separate firms. These eventually became independent software houses, many of which maintained their affiliations with the computer vendors that gave them their start.

Another reason for the limited development of the packaged software market in Japan was the general attitude of vendors toward the software business. The commercial value of computer systems was attributed almost exclusively to the hardware, and software programs were considered to be a supplement. Losses incurred by computer vendors on services and software engineering were offset by their profits from hardware sales. Pricing and product marketing strategies for software products thus were of secondary importance.

How do firms customize software, its modification, and its maintenance for a user's mainframe? The whole process is a joint effort involving the user's personnel and external software engineers, but the user takes the initiative (Baba and Takai 1990). Before creating a system design, the user must specify how existing procedures are to be computerized. In Japan, the identification of specifications is usually made through the collection of shop-floor data and experience, and the problem-solving is done by trial and error in a typically "bottom-up" decision-making process. The design stage and subsequent stages, including development and maintenance (a euphemism for postdelivery development), are "spiral-overlapped" (Imai, Nonaka, and Takeuchi 1985). That is, if it becomes clear that the development costs will exceed the original estimate, the design is modified; if the user finds deficiencies after introduction, the system will be improved or a new system will be designed. These adjustment processes make it possible for the user to have a system that is finely tailored to its needs.

The development and modification of customized software thus depend on the knowledge and initiative of the user; we call this a "user-driven paradigm," which accumulates and utilizes knowledge through a number of channels. First, personnel from a wide range of development processes acquire the knowledge and skills necessary for development and improvement through on-the-job training. Second, since the operation and maintenance of the new system are usually done by the user or user spin-off software house, the accumulated shop-floor knowledge facilitates the internal upgrading of the system and its software.

Conversely, the small size of Japan's "arm's-length" software market impedes the development of the hub structure and the application by users of their accumulated know-how and experiences. The form of cooperation and the exploitation of accumulated knowledge are very path-dependent, and the resulting structure has slowed the growth of an efficient software market in which standard products are supplied through price competition among producers.

Toward a New Paradigm

Recent structural changes in the computer hardware business reflect the widespread downsizing from mainframes to smaller computers and the introduction of operating systems software that is more "platform-independent." From 1987 to 1992 the share of mainframes in total Japanese computer consumption decreased to 50 percent. Downsizing has also increased the popularity in Japan of the Unix operating system. An increasing number of users demand packaged programs and comprehensive systems for the qualitative improvement of their business. All of these trends mean that packaged software and other innovative software technologies for workstations, networks, and personal computers will play a more important role in the upcoming decade.

Although Japanese software sales have grown more than 15 percent annually for more than a decade, the growth rate has dropped considerably since 1990. The future of the Japanese software business will be determined in large part by the ability of the company groups in the hub structure to adapt to change, to meet continually evolving user needs, and to enter promising new markets. This section discusses the present trends and future prospects for software houses and computer vendors.

According to the journal *Computopia,* the top 100 firms in the Japanese information service industry account for about 50 percent of total Japanese software sales (see Figures 5-7 and 5-8).[7] The 1988 and 1990 data reveal remarkable changes in the composition of this group. The number of user spin-off software houses increased from forty-eight in 1988 to fifty-three in 1990, while the number of independent software houses decreased from thirty-five to thirty. The share of total sales attributable to user spin-off firms was 45.4 percent in 1990, an increase from 42 percent in 1988. There were only seventeen maker spin-off software houses in this group throughout the 1988–90 period; their share of sales grew from roughly 28 percent in 1988 to 30.3 percent in 1990, with each firm recording relatively large sales. The maker spin-off software houses appear to have maintained a strong position, and the user spin-off firms have expanded their margin over the independent firms.

The top 100 companies had average sales per employee of 23 million yen in 1990, more than twice the 1990 average of about 10 million yen in the information service industry as a whole (*Computopia* 1990) (Table 5-1). But these data reveal

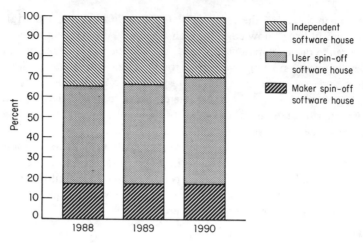

Figure 5-7. Composition of the top 100 Japanese software houses, 1988–90. *Source: Computopia* 1989, 1990, 1991.

substantial differences among the company groups. In 1990 the user spin-off software houses average about 29.4 million yen per employee, the maker spin-offs 26.6 million yen per employee, and the independents 15.7 million yen per employee. In other words, this measure of the overall productivity of the user spin-off software houses is almost twice as large as that of the independent software houses. Furthermore, during the period 1988–90 the maker spin-off software houses showed the largest increase in labor productivity, 22 percent, followed by the user spin-off software houses with 16 percent, and the independents with 10 percent.

Japanese software houses share similar management systems, and these productivity differences reflect differences in the allocation of tasks and the associated distribution of development skills. The productivity of the independent software houses is low because most of these companies are small or medium sized and have not developed

Figure 5-8. Market share of the top 100 Japanese software houses, 1988–90. *Source: Computopia* 1989, 1990, 1991.

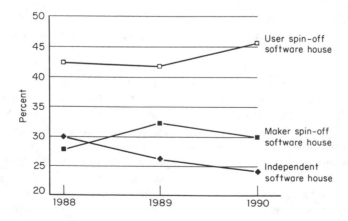

Table 5-1. Labor productivity & software houses in Japan, 1988–90
(thousand yen)

Firm type	1988	1989	1990
Maker spin-off software house	21,843(100)	26,372(121)	26,581(122)
User spin-off software house	25,384(100)	26,455(104)	29,386(116)
Independent software house	14,307(100)	14,671(103)	15,723(110)
Average	19,872(100)	21,867(110)	23,639(119)

Sources: Computopia 1989, 1990, 1991.
Note: 1988 = 100.

satisfactory human resource management policies. According to a 1991 survey of university students by Recruit Research, 67.9 percent of the students preferred employment with a company that would enrich its human resources, and 62.3 percent hoped to participate in extensive training programs (Recruit Research 1991). Major computer manufacturers and user spin-off software houses can meet these desires, but independent software houses often have no choice but to pay higher wages than the others to retain workers. Large salaries compensate for insufficient R&D and training courses but also weaken the financial position of the independent firms, many of which find it impossible to participate in large projects. Bankruptcies of software firms almost tripled from 1989 to 1991: thirty-two software houses went bankrupt in 1989, forty-five in 1990, and eighty-seven in 1991 (Tokyoshoko Research 1988, 1990, 1991). The total debt of these firms amounted to 19,300 million yen in 1991, 4.5 times more than the previous year. Most of the bankrupt companies were independent software houses with capital of less than 10 million yen and a few hundred employees each.

An increasing number of user spin-off and maker spin off software houses are trying hard to enhance the skills of their personnel. For example, IIII Systems Technology, a user spin-off firm (spun off by Ishikawajima Heavy Industries), paid higher wages and bonuses than the parent company, IHI, as a way of attracting highly qualified engineers. User spin-off and maker spin-off software houses also have the opportunity to improve their skills in management of large projects by developing systems for their parent companies. Because the software houses are usually allowed to develop the core programs and may be able to modify their components for use elsewhere, these products can be quite profitable. In order to fully utilize their strengths, the user spin-off firms are accumulating knowledge of business procedures, and the maker spin-off firms are developing advanced systems and package programs.

Although the total number of maker spin-off firms within the top 100 companies did not change during the 1988–90 period, their composition did (Figure 5-9). The number of maker spin-off software houses founded by (or under the influence of) a computer vendor increased from ten in 1988 to twelve in 1989 and to fourteen in 1990. During 1988–90, these firms increased their share of the top 100 firms' sales from 15.4 percent to 21.9 percent. About 50 percent of the user spin-off firms were founded by (or were under the influence of) a financial company. In 1988 there were twenty-one firms belonging to that group, twenty-two in 1989, and twenty-three in 1990. In 1990 these firms accounted for 34.1 percent of the top 100 firms' sales, the computer spin-off firms for 21.9 percent, the telecommunications spin-off firms for

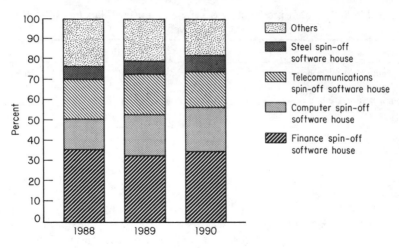

Figure 5-9. Market share of Japanese software spin-off firms, 1988–90. *Source: Computopia* 1989, 1990, 1991.

17.5 percent, and the steel spin-off firms for 7.9 percent (an increase from their 1988 share of 6.4 percent).[8] Although they account for a relatively small share of the sales of this group of firms, the steel spin-off firms have maintained their position because of their accumulated software knowledge dating from the 1970s.

In recent years, most computer vendors have expanded their activities in software, because the profitability of their hardware business has declined and become more unstable. Many computer vendors have expanded into the packaged software business. Fujitsu, for instance, thus far has developed more than 600 products for its own hardware; its popular products can be installed in other computer platforms. Others have established collaborative ventures or merged with other firms. For example, Hitachi has collaborated with Nomura Research Institute on software development, and NEC joined the network in 1992 to develop a CASE (computer-aided software engineering) toolset. Recent joint projects have imposed very demanding criteria for partner selection. NEC, for example, nominates ten candidates for a partnership, according to their previous achievements and personnel capabilities, and selects only one firm from this list.

THE INSTITUTIONAL FRAMEWORK

The Role of Japanese Universities in Computer Science Education

Most U.S. universities have computer science departments that train computer engineers and conduct research that often is applied in the U.S. software industry. In Japan, however, there are only a few such departments in the national universities, and they have been established only since the 1980s. Their own organizational rigidity prevents the universities from building new academic courses or disciplines. Instead, many universities teach computer-related subjects within an unchanged organizational framework. The classes demonstrate conventional theories and programming techniques, and the curriculum is much less sophisticated than the computer science courses in American and European universities. Although many private universities have begun to establish departments specializing in computer-related areas, little else has changed. The computer science courses at professional schools teach high school graduates ordinary programming languages such as Cobol and bear little resemblance to university-level computer science courses in other countries.

Faced with this critical state of affairs, in 1992 the Ministry of Education formed a committee of the leading Japanese computer scientists to find a solution. They proposed transplanting the American core computer science curriculum to the Japanese universities. But because very few major national universities have succeeded in recruiting or training qualified computer science faculty, Japanese companies must hire "programmers" who have been taught little more than the most basic programming techniques. One approach to routinizing the development of software, and thereby reducing the skill requirements for programmers, is the "software factory" approach, wherein Japanese software developers import and adapt software engineering technology from the United States (see Cusumano 1991). The "factory techniques" appear to be most successful for some forms of large-scale, customized software but have been far less valuable in developing standard packaged software, the fastest-growing segment of the Japanese market.

Most firms continue to believe that personnel should learn company-specific procedures, and however formal their organization of code creation, they employ essentially trial-and-error methods of requirements definition and software engineering. This craft approach often means that qualified engineers are not assigned to appropriate jobs because supervisors or managers do not understand the requirements of the jobs or the technical analysis of the engineers.

The subordinate position of computer science in Japan has also given rise to the common practice of pricing software according to the number of engineering man-months it took to create or the program size (for example, the number of steps). In Japan the prices of software are usually established on the basis of product costs and little else.

The Limits of Industrial Policy

Since the first half of the 1970s, the Japanese government has pursued a large-scale promotion program for the domestic computer industry. The industrial policy initially consisted of supporting joint development projects and establishing favorable taxation and finance policies (Anchordoguy 1989). Since 1982 the Institute for New Generation Computer Technology (ICOT) and other organizations have supported the Fifth-Generation Computer Project, which seeks to establish an innovative data processing system that emulates human reasoning, known as "parallel inference" (PI). This project has received about 54 billion yen (roughly $360 million at 150 yen per dollar) and has developed a special computer language and an operating system. ICOT has also developed various PI-type programs for experiments. The software and results obtained from the PI system, however, are not up to commercial standards, and MITI and ICOT recently decided to disclose and provide free of charge the PI-type software (now about seventy programs) in the hope that research institutes and companies will bring the system to the commercial level (*Nikkei* 1992a).

Despite its current problems, ICOT believes it will enjoy a worldwide reputation by the turn of the century, given the increasing interest in the PI-type computers. The project has made some research advances in such basic areas as artificial intelligence, but so far it has not attained its technological or industrial goals.

The software industry has received other forms of assistance from MITI. Five joint projects during the 1980s received 83,700 million yen (approximately $560 million). Between 1985 and 1990 a total of 21,800 million yen (approximately $145 million) was invested in the SIGMA (Software Industrial Generalization and Maintenance Aids) Project, a national network to support technology and tools transfer and the promotion of standard tool interfaces to enable software interoperability. Many domestic computer vendors and software houses were invited to develop technologies based on the Unix standard. The project thus far has few technological or commercial results, having completed sixty programs whose yearly sales currently are only 30 million yen. The SIGMA System, a company established to commercialize results from the SIGMA Project, recorded a loss of 260 million yen (*Nikkei* 1992b).

Thus far, these collaborative projects, which resemble earlier Japanese programs in semiconductors and other industries, have not been effective. The basic design—joint development by private firms with guidance from public agencies—will face serious difficulties in dynamic and uncertain markets. In the software industry, the winning technology is decided by market forces only after fierce technological competition among firms. And as lead times become shorter, program design and administration become even more complicated. The near failure of the SIGMA Project reflected inflexible planning in a project that required unusual flexibility to deal with a very fluid technology. The basic software selected for SIGMA's software development program was obsolete after being on the market for only five years.

In software, the user decides which technology is the winner, and this decision may not coincide with the specifications or targets of government programs. Consumer choices have influenced the success and failure of other Japanese technology programs, but software appears to be subject to much more fundamental uncertainty than such technologies as DRAM (dynamic random access memory). In the case of the Fifth-Generation Computer Project, demand shifted to smaller computers and fewer people were interested in mainframes, despite the new possibilities developed by the project. The rapid rate of change of computer technologies means that public software programs should be managed flexibly, so that technological developments can be monitored and necessary adjustments made.

Japanese government policy thus far has been remarkably unsuccessful in stimulating the growth of a competitive domestic software industry. Fundamental change is needed in current policies, and this will require that MITI and other government organizations revise their basic premise, that hardware production is more important than software production. Most Japanese government policies in the computer industry have assigned priority to expansion in hardware production and sales, and little effort has been made to establish the software business as an independent sector. Close links between mainframes and customized software benefit both technologies, and most Japanese software houses have supported themselves until quite recently by participating in software development programs organized by the computer vendors. But in desktop computers and packaged software, these relationships are less strong.

Despite (or because of) their strong competitiveness in hardware production, many Japanese manufacturers appear ill-prepared for a postindustrial economy. For example, high-value-added services such as visual media, telecommunications, and especially software as a whole are far behind the United States. This critical state has pushed MITI toward direct promotion of the software industry.

The Slow Progress of Intellectual Property Rights

Japanese intellectual property policies in software have also hampered the growth of a vigorous market in packaged software. Discussion about whether and how to protect computer programs started in the 1970s. MITI proposed that software should be protected under a new law, but the Agency for Cultural Affairs of the Ministry of Education believed that software should be covered by existing copyright laws. The two organizations eventually agreed to amend the copyright law, but the amendment was not enforced until 1986. The slow progress suggests that protection of software intellectual property rights was of secondary importance in Japan, and debate continues over whether computer programs, commercial products in many cases, should be covered by the current copyright law (see chapter 10 and Toyota 1992 for further discussion).

Other sensitive questions also remain unresolved. First, how should Japan treat the expression and identification of independently developed programs? Some effort has been made to resolve this problem by relying on the judgment of American legal authorities. For example, an American court decided in 1985 that reverse engineering of software violates copyright protection. This decision has been criticized in Japan, however, because it makes the contents of a program dependent on its expression and hinders the creation of new ideas. Second, how should one treat copyrights held by a company or some other legal entity? According to the present copyright law, a legal entity is entitled to possess the copyright of any program developed as a part of its business. Thus, for example, the copyright of an externally developed program belongs primarily to the subcontractor. When engineers in a software firm establish a separate company, their use of their own previous knowledge and experience is severely restricted.

In the 1980s in addition to copyright protection, patent protection was extended to Japanese software.[9] A typical software patent registers the programming processes. Most of the patent applications in this category are for software development processes and chemical production processes.

SUMMARY

In the United States the software industry has evolved in parallel with innovations in computer hardware (see also chapters 2, 3, and 4 in this volume). In Japan, by contrast, advances in hardware provided far less technological impetus for the software industry. National policies for the development of capabilities in computer hardware focused on mainframe development, and the very success of these policies contributed to the fragmentation of Japan's domestic software market and to the dominance of custom software. The supply of innovative software also has been hampered by a lack of computer science in Japanese research universities. The effect of these factors was to assign disproportionate importance to the "user side" of computer technologies; the goal of policy and firm strategy was to enable users to procure information technologies and introduce them into their operations. Maintaining shop-floor usability, rather than stressing new technological innovation, is Japan's most salient characteristic, and this has slowed the growth of a strong traded software industry.

Japanese users emphasize shop-floor knowledge when computerizing their operations and do not hesitate to alter the programs to fit existing procedures. Because even Japanese companies that belong to the same industrial sector usually have different management policies and organization, it makes more sense for the processes and their supporting software to be customized than to be purchased as prepackaged programs. Japan's emphasis on customized software has discouraged systematic training for software engineers. Software personnel often have no formal computer science education and acquire their professional skills through on-the-job training. After a brief exposure to programming classes, newly hired employees are assigned tasks as junior systems engineers and acquire practical skills through day-to-day experience. In the United States, by contrast, computer science is a widely and systematically taught university discipline. As it is in other industries, knowledge in the software industry is locally accumulated in Japan and is primarily exploited within the boundaries of a firm.

The evolution of the Japanese software industry gave rise to the hub structure, which has certain advantages. First, it provides software that is finely tailored to user needs, albeit at a high price. Second, it has helped create a synergy between mainframes and customized software, which is lacking in Japanese software development for desktop computers. The software departments of computer vendors, using their hardware capabilities, import advanced software engineering technology from the United States and, after some modification, have introduced useful techniques to their own shop floors. These "software factories" have become highly productive by applying rigorous technical standards and process management and quality control regimes to software production (Cusumano 1991). Unfortunately these factory techniques are less applicable in the rapidly expanding packaged software market.

Third, the hub structure provides some insulation from competitive pressures. Internationally, the focus on customized rather than packaged software makes penetration of the Japanese market by foreign firms difficult, because customized software is essentially nontradable. Domestically, the status quo in software is reinforced by the conservative attitudes of user firms. As long as software is custom-developed for specific mainframes, software houses with experienced engineers have little incentive to renovate their business practices.

Although historically the Japanese software industry has benefited from its unusual path of development, the industry now faces a transformation in the technological and industrial regime that is forcing it to revise its competitive strategies. The present downsizing trend, that of building networks of small computers based on internationally standardized operating systems, will increase Japanese domestic demand for packaged software programs. The most popular products in this segment of the industry almost always are developed and produced by non-Japanese firms, which have started to invest in the Japanese market.

But the institutional inertia of the hub structure may limit the Japanese industry's ability to adapt to the new industrial environment. First, the hub structure hinders the development of an open market, which could expand demand for Japanese packaged software. Only an open market makes it possible for software houses to develop profitable, standardized programs and allows users to select the most suitable software product at a lower cost than customized programs.

Second, the classic sources of Japanese competitiveness in the manufacturing sector—decreasing development cycles, high productivity, and low error rates—are well supported by the hub structure but are less useful in the packaged software business. Strategies that emphasize productivity and quality in writing huge numbers of lines of software code neglect the innovative and marketing perspectives that are crucial to the packaged software business. Finally, the reliance of Japan's software industry on learning-by-doing and its neglect of formal computer science training will limit Japan's presence in the packaged software industry.

The Japanese software industry may have little choice other than to co-evolve with its American and European counterparts during this period of computer downsizing. To this end, however, it will need to adopt an institutional framework that differs from the hub structure. For example, government policy could provide greater support for software houses to shift their operations from high-quality custom programming to the development of innovative programs for large-market software products. The university system also must be restructured to support research and training in computer science as a systematic discipline, providing a knowledge and manpower base for innovative Japanese software.

NOTES

The authors are indebted to David Mowery, Franco Malerba, Edward Steinmueller, Bénédicte Callan, Richard Nelson, Keith Pavitt, and Satoshi Nakada for comments.

1. This chapter does not attempt to discuss "embedded" software—software that is incorporated into manufactured products, such as consumer electronics, machine tools, and motor vehicles.

2. In addition to its small sample size, which is less than 5% of the MITI survey, other problems arise in interpreting the results of this survey. Most independent software houses are medium-sized or smaller, measured in terms of capital, sales, and employees; but the companies covered by this survey appear to be somewhat larger than average. If this survey has systematically omitted the smaller software houses, it may in fact understate the total value of the software produced by this segment of the industry.

3. These results contain no information about microcomputer software development expenditures by users. Nevertheless, users of microcomputer software typically rely far more heavily on external sources of supply than mainframe and minicomputer users, so this omission should not significantly affect our estimates.

4. For example, the number of games to be developed and sold by a software house is limited to five per year, and the products cannot be converted for use on other hardware platforms for a specific period. The hardware producer handles the marketing of the externally developed software, enabling the software houses to concentrate on development.

5. Third-level subcontractors that formerly supplied labor to second-level subcontractor software houses are now disappearing.

6. MITI acknowledged the importance of establishing more systems integration firms and in 1989 extended tax breaks to seventy-three companies.

7. Reported sales revenues include those from software products, processing, and professional services. In order to estimate the sales revenues associated solely with software development, these data were multiplied by 0.589, the average ratio of sales of software to total services and software-related revenues in the information service industry.

8. Ninety-nine percent of Japanese telecommunications software sales are accounted for by a single company, NTT Data Communications. It is therefore impossible to assess the competitiveness of software houses spun off from other telecommunications companies.

9. Patent protection guidelines were formulated in 1976 and were implemented in 1982 and 1988. The first guidelines restricted the programs to those that used exclusively the established laws of the natural sciences. This condition was relaxed at the next stage, provided that the whole system, including the hardware, could be regarded as an independent unit. In 1988 software for amusement and word processing was recognized as an invention without reference to hardware.

REFERENCES

Akagi, T. 1992. *SEGA vs. Nintendo*. Tokyo: Japan Management Association Management Center Inc.

Anchordoguy, M. 1989. *Computers Inc.: Japan's Challenge to IBM*. Cambridge, Mass.: Harvard University Press.

Aoki, M. 1986. "Horizontal vs. Vertical Information Structure of the Firm." *American Economic Review* 76, no. 5: 971–83.

Association of Information Processing Development in Japan, 1992. *Jyoho-nka Hakusho* (Whitebook on informatization). Tokyo: Computer Age Ltd.

Baba, Y., and A. Seike. 1991. "Jyohoshori System Donyuniokeru Sangyo Tokusei: Nihonniokeru Mainframe no Jirei" (Industrial characteristics of information processing system introduction: the case of mainframes in Japan). National Institute of Science and Technology Policy. Tokyo. Duplicated.

Baba, Y., and S. Takai. 1990. "Information Technology Introduction in the Big Banks: The Case of Japan." In C. Freeman and L. Soete, eds., *New Explorations in the Economics of Technological Change*. London: Pinter Publishers.

Computopia. 1989. "Jyoho Service Ranking 100 Company" (The top 100 companies in the information service industry). September, 12–13.

———. 1990. "Jyoho Service Ranking 100 Company" (The top 100 companies in the information service industry). September, 20–56.

———. 1991. "Jyoho Service Ranking 150 Company" (The top 150 companies in the information service industry). September, 25–44.

Cusumano, M. A. 1991. *Japan's Software Factories*. New York: Oxford University Press.

Financial Information System Center, ed. 1992. *Whitebook on Financial Information Systems*. Tokyo: Zaikei Shouhou Sha.

Gerlach, M. Forthcoming 1995. "Economic Organization and Innovation in Japan." *Journal of Economic Behavior and Organization*.

Imai, K., ed. 1990. *Software Shinka-ron* (Evolution of the software industry). Tokyo: NTT Press.

Imai, K., I. Nonaka, and H. Takeuchi. 1985. "Managing the New Product Development Process: How Japanese Companies Learn and Unlearn." In K. Clark, R. Hayes, and C. Lorenz, eds., *The Uneasy Alliance: Managing the Productivity-Technology Dilemma*. Cambridge, Mass.: Harvard University Press.

Imano, K., and H. Sato. 1990. *Software Sangyo to Management* (Software industry and management). Tokyo: Toyo Keizai Press.

Japanese Information Service Industry Association, 1989, 1990, and 1991. *Jyoho Service Sangyo Doko Chousa* (Survey on the information service industry). Tokyo: JISA.
————, ed. 1992. *Whitepaper on the Information Service Industry.* Tokyo: Ministry of International Trade and Industry.
Ministry of International Trade and Industry. 1979, 1984, and 1989. *Wagakuni Jyohoshori no Genjo* (The information processing industry in Japan). Tokyo: MITI.
————. 1980, 1985, and 1990. *Tokutei Service Sangyo Jittaichousa: Jyoho-service* (Survey on the service industry: information service). Tokyo: MITI.
————, ed. 1992. *Pasocon Hakusho* (Whitebook on personal computers). Tokyo: Computer Age Ltd.
————, Industrial Structures Council, ed. 1987. *2000-nen-no Software Jinzai* (Expected employment related to software development in 2000). Tokyo: Computer Age Ltd.
Nakahara, T. 1993. "The Industrial Organization and Information Structure of the Software Industry: A U.S.-Japan Comparison." Center for Economic Policy Research, Stanford University, CEPR Publication #346, Palo Alto, Calif.
Nikkei Keizai Shinbun. 1992a. "Dai 5 sedai Densanki Jitsuyoka no Suishin" (Promoting the commercialization of the fifth-generation computer), 23 May.
————. 1992b. "Kokka Durojekuto Genso" (Illusion of national project), 10 June.
————. 1992c. "Tenki ni tatsu Jyoho Sangyo: Sofuto Shijo no Mondaiten, Jo" (Information industry at a turning point: problems in software market, first half), 24 November.
————. 1993. "Sofuto Uirage Hiritsu Raimendo ni 4-wari e" (The share of software sales will be 60 percent next year), 7 August.
Recruit Research. 1990. "Research on Employment of Japanese Undergraduates: March 1990." Tokyo: Recruit Research.
————. 1991. "Research on Employment of Japanese Undergraduates: March 1991." Tokyo: Recruit Research.
Shimoda, H. 1990. *Software ga Nihon o Kaeru* (Software transforming Japan) Tokyo: PHP Kenkyujyo.
Tokyoshoko Research. 1989, 1990, 1991. *Edemiru Tosan* (Bankruptcy in a graphic view). Tokyo: Tokyoshoka Research.
Totsuka, H., K. Nakamura, and T. Umezawa. 1990. *Nihon no Software Sangyo: Keiei to Gijyutsushu* (Japan's software industry: management and engineers). Tokyo: Tokyo University Press.
Toyota, M. 1992. *Software to Tokkyoken* (Patent rights for software). Tokyo: Diamond Press.
Toyo Keizai. 1991. "Business Aspect 500-Shin-Nippon Seitetsu." Toyo Keizai Shinpo-sha, 3 August, 3–8.

Appendix 5-1. The Top 100 Japanese Software Houses, 1990

Company	Affiliation			Sales (million yen)	Employees	Sales per employee (10,000 yen)
	Independent	Maker spin-off	User spin-off			
CSK	O			80,205	7,803	1,027.9
QUICK	O			68,356	528	12,946.2
INTEC	O			58,308	2,479	2,352.1
AINES	O			40,838	1,882	2,169.9
TKC	O			29,036	900	3,226.2
Japan System	O			26,984	916	2,945.9
Japan Time Share	O			26,138	1,780	1,468.4
NJK	O			24,308	1,485	1,636.9
Tranca Cosmos	O			22,856	3,801	601.3
SRA	O			22,202	1,209	1,836.4
CEC	O			21,819	1,375	1,586.8
Japan System Development	O			20,455	1,901	1,076.0
Japan Computer System	O			19,942	943	2,114.7
CATENA	O			19,616	912	2,150.9
Nihon Electronic Development	O			18,151	1,337	1,357.6
Japan Systemware	O			18,008	1,644	1,095.4
Mitsubishi Research Institute	O			17,779	827	2,149.8
SCC	O			16,667	1,505	1,107.4
Japan Information Industry	O			15,500	1,700	911.8
TST	O			14,837	1,709	868.2
MIC	O			14,135	881	1,604.4
MKC	O			13,294	646	2,057.9
ALGO-Technos 21	O			11,899	829	1,435.3
TDI	O			11,502	1,426	806.6
Japan System	O			11,410	530	2,152.8
Computer Applications	O			10,922	670	1,630.1
Hokkaido Business Automation	O			10,847	623	1,741.1
Fuji Software	O			10,470	1,267	826.4
JACOS	O			10,368	102	10,164.7
Software Development	O			9,586	683	1,403.5
Hitachi Information Systems		O Computer		103,757	3,755	2,763.2
Hitachi Software Engineering		O Computer		72,263	3,981	1,815.2
Nihon Electric Software		O Computer		53,964	988	5,461.9

Company	Industry			
Fujitsu F-I-B	○ Computer	49,195	2,398	2,051.5
Toshiba Information System	○ Computer	48,137	3,028	1,589.7
Nihon Electric Software	○ Computer	36,580	2,700	1,354.8
Fujitsu B-S-C	○ Computer	18,119	1,414	1,281.4
Kansai Nihon Electric Software	○ Computer	15,700	1,140	1,377.2
Hitachi System Engineering	○ Computer	15,365	1,709	899.1
NEC Techno-Information System Development	○ Computer	14,722	407	3,617.2
NEC Management-Information System Development	○ Computer	13,100	447	2,930.6
Kobayasi Electronic Industry	○ Computer	13,084	750	1,744.5
Fujitsu Social Science	○ Computer	12,593	1,050	1,199.3
Fujitsu Kansai System Engineering	○ Computer	10,062	528	1,905.7
NTT Data Communications	○ Telecommunications	344,914	7,220	4,777.2
Nihon Information Communications	○ Telecommunications	35,200	560	6,285.7
OMRON Software	○ Electronics	12,403	623	1,990.9
ENICOM	○ Steel	58,824	2,700	2,178.7
NK—EXA	○ Steel	30,146	1,450	2,079.0
Kwatetsu System Development	○ Steel	25,697	1,153	2,228.7
Kobelko System	○ Steel	14,851	510	2,912.0
Central Computer Service	○ Steel	10,785	385	2,801.3
Sumitomo Metal System Development	○ Steel	10,767	623	1,728.3
Nitetu Hitachi System Engineering	○ Steel	10,388	313	3,318.3
Nikkei Information System	○ Steel	10,016	432	2,318.5
Komatsu Software Development	○ Machinery (shipbuilding)	16,940	821	2,063.3
Mitsui Shipbuilding System	○ Machinery (shipbuilding)	14,600	686	2,128.3
HZS	○ Machinery (shipbuilding)	14,109	607	2,324.4
RKK	○ Machinery (shipbuilding)	12,791	1,350	947.5
Bridgestone Software	○ Chemicals	11,605	282	4,115.2
Ryouka System	○ Chemicals	11,127	462	2,408.4
Nomura Research Institute	○ Finance	139,620	2,678	5,213.6
Nihon Research Institute	○ Finance	71,040	2,571	2,763.1
Toyo Information System	○ Finance	60,551	2,217	2,731.2
Yamaichi Computer Center	○ Finance	50,621	650	7,787.8
Daiwa Research Institute	○ Finance	45,154	1,125	4,013.7
Fuji Research Institute	○ Finance	41,128	2,050	2,006.2
JIP	○ Finance	36,071	1,560	2,312.2
Nikkou System Center	○ Finance	33,982	516	6,585.7
Sumisyo Computer Service	○ Finance	32,542	1,121	2,902.9
Central Systems	○ Finance	23,789	1,345	1,768.7

(continued)

129

Appendix 5-1. The Top 100 Japanese Software Houses, 1990 (*continued*)

Company	Affiliation			Sales (million yen)	Employees	Sales per employee (10,000 yen)
	Independent	Maker spin-off	User spin-off			
AST			O Finance	23,434	604	3,879.8
Diamond Computer Service			O Finance	21,821	837	2,607.0
Mitsui Information Development			O Finance	20,009	620	3,227.3
CRC			O Finance	19,228	845	2,275.5
Tousyo Computer System			O Finance	17,512	270	6,485.9
Mitsuigin Software Service			O Finance	17,506	750	2,334.1
Nomura System Service			O Finance	15,586	246	6,335.8
KCS			O Finance	14,625	960	1,523.4
Daiichikangin Computer Service			O Finance	12,506	689	1,815.1
Nissei Computer			O Finance	11,419	951	1,200.7
Sumisyo Computer Service			O Finance	11,038	822	1,342.8
Daiichikangin System Development			O Finance	10,919	863	1,265.2
L S			O Finance	10,148	641	1,583.2
Railway Information System			O Transportation	17,472	350	4,992.0
Yamato System Development			O Transportation	17,257	1,100	1,568.8
Ryobi Systems			O Transportation	10,415	868	1,199.9
Seino Information Service			O Transportation	9,638	280	3,442.1
OG Information System			O Electric power	24,080	425	5,665.9
Tokyo Count Service			O Electric power	23,877	952	2,508.1
Kansai Sogo-denshi-keisan			O Electric power	19,454	730	2,664.9
TG Information Network			O Electric power	16,280		
Touden Software			O Electric power	12,850	460	2,793.5
I S I D			O Mass communication	23,563	366	6,438.0
Daie Information System			O Mass communication	19,369	407	4,759.0
Seibu Information Center			O Mass communication	13,339	494	2,700.2
M&C System			O Mass communication	11,078	283	3,914.5
JT Soft Service			O Other	51,916	332	15,637.3
Toppan			O Other	19,660	504	3,900.8
Misawa Van			O Other	17,365		

Source: Computopia 1991.

6

Standards and the Arrested Development of Japan's Microcomputer Software Industry

Thomas Cottrell

This chapter examines the development of the Japanese microcomputer software industry and compares it with the evolution of the U.S. industry. The central contrasting factor is the relationship between the hardware and software industries in each nation. The fragmented hardware standards environment in the Japanese microcomputer industry, I argue, has slowed the development of a vigorous microcomputer software industry in Japan. The more unified architectural environment of the U.S. microcomputer marketplace has (along with other factors) contributed to dramatic growth in this nation's microcomputer software industry. Surprisingly, in view of the great powers ascribed to its role in other postwar industries, Japanese government policy has been relatively unsuccessful in altering the domestic standards environment to support the growth of the microcomputer software industry.

Historical antecedents (both cultural and technological) also have played an important role in the development of the Japanese software industry; they include the challenges of language processing, the structure of distribution channels, and the oligopolistic mainframe market structure.

A COMPARATIVE OVERVIEW OF THE U.S. AND JAPANESE INDUSTRIES

Market Size and Standardization

Computer software is purchased in a variety of ways. Packaged software, the off-the-shelf, shrink-wrapped package that we associate with retail sales of software, accounts for a large share, 60–70 percent, of U.S. software industry revenues. Customized software accounts for a much larger share of software industry revenues in Japan than in the United States or Europe (see Figure 6-1).

By 1985, packaged software sales as a percentage of the total had increased for all countries, although Japan's packaged sales continued to lag (see Figure 6-2). More recent data show that the packaged software market has continued to grow, but the estimated proportion of packaged to total software sales remained at 20 percent in 1991 (Cortese and Morrissey 1993).

Microcomputer software accounted for about 26.7 billion yen (51.6 percent) of Japan's software market in 1988 (Siegmann 1988), which is consistent with a 1993 estimate that it accounted for 50 percent of the software market (JISA 1993). The Japan Personal Computer Software Technology Research Institute estimated that the 1989 revenues of Japan's 1,500–2,000 manufacturers of personal computer software were 167.8 billion yen (ibid.) (Figure 6-3 shows market segment size), and recent estimated sales of PC packaged software are 263.8 billion yen. By comparison, 1989 U.S. software industry revenues were $21.8 billion (3.1 trillion yen), of which $4.8 billion (672 billion yen) were derived from microcomputer software, and 1993 micro-computer software revenues exceeded $10.9 billion (Data Analysis Group 1990, 391). While these amounts ignore "embedded" software, an area in which the Japanese do quite well, they do indicate an important difference in the Japanese and U.S. markets for computer software.

The Japanese microcomputer hardware market also differs significantly from the U.S. market in size, structure, and kinds of applications. Most obviously, the size of the installed base of microcomputers is smaller: there are 3 million personal computers in Japanese businesses and 23 million in U.S. businesses.[1] The revenues generated by a small percentage of the U.S. market are seven to eight times greater than the revenues from the same percentage of the Japanese market. And that payoff comes at a smaller unit cost, because the U.S. microcomputer hardware market is relatively homogeneous, dominated as it is by IBM-compatible microcomputers (see below). In the business sector, the market for 16-bit computers is evenly distributed across platforms, while a cursory analysis of the entire PC market indicates that *three* groups are dominant.[2]

An important issue in this chapter is standardization of computer software at the binary compatibility level (binary compatibility occurs at the most fundamental level of computer operations). Although many of the PC platforms in Japan can run MS-DOS, selection of a single operating system is not sufficient to guarantee standardization;[3] compatibility is a matter of degree rather than of kind. Following the introduction of the IBM microcomputer, competing microcomputer hardware firms advertised the manufacturer of their Basic Input Output System (BIOS) to assure customers that the product was "100 percent IBM-compatible." Because the IBM BIOS was protected by copyright, hardware manufacturers had to demonstrate that they had separately developed their own BIOS; copying the "IBM-compatible" BIOS violated copyright law. By selling chip sets that contained an "independent" BIOS, these firms could assure hardware vendors that their BIOS conformed to the IBM standard. In the United States, sales of IBM-compatible microcomputers created a large installed base for this architecture, whether the computers were made by IBM or other "clone" manufacturers. Although NEC's microcomputers account for more than 53 percent of the Japanese market,[4] the key issue is the size and mix of the installed base

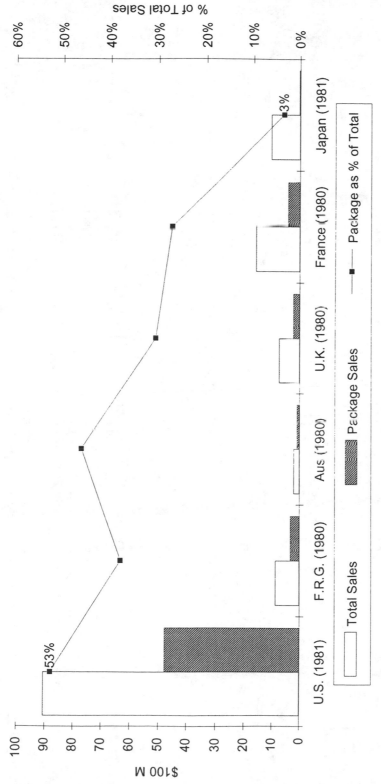

Figure 6-1. Software sales in the United States, Europe, Australia, and Japan, 1980. *Source:* OECD 1985.

133

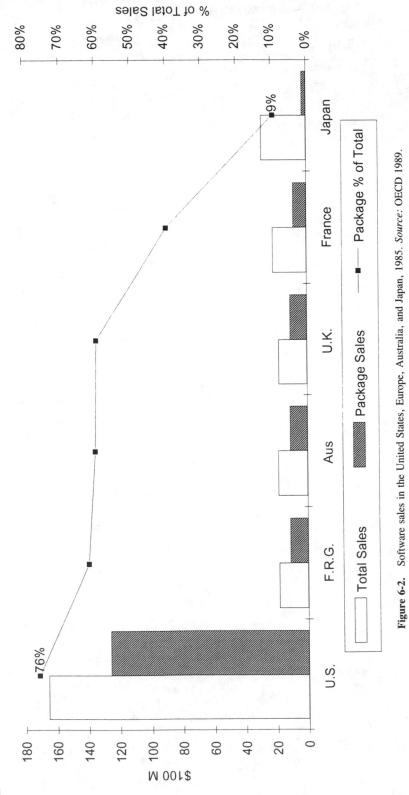

Figure 6-2. Software sales in the United States, Europe, Australia, and Japan, 1985. *Source:* OECD 1989.

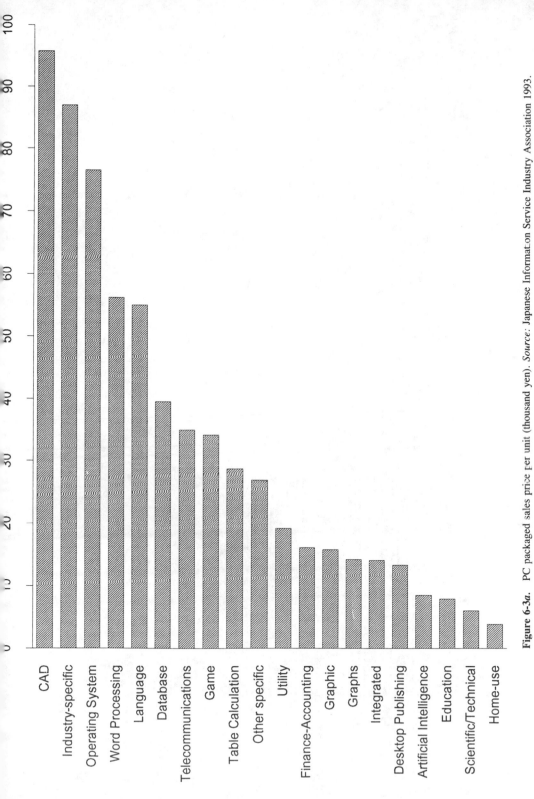

Figure 6-3a. PC packaged sales price per unit (thousand yen). *Source:* Japanese Information Service Industry Association 1993.

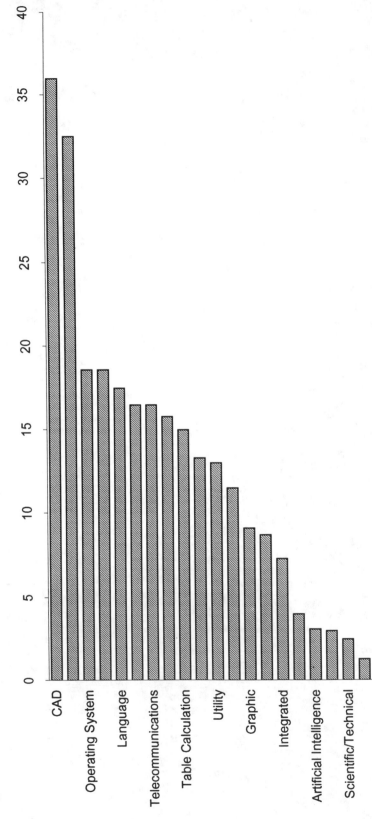

Figure 6-3b. PC packaged software revenues (billion yen). *Source*: Japanese Information Service Industry Association 1993.

of microcomputers, rather than the shares held by IBM and NEC. In this respect, the U.S. market is both larger and more homogeneous; IBM-compatible microcomputers accounted for more than 80 percent of the installed base in 1993.

If software developers use only high-level DOS functions, then virtually any MS-DOS machine will run their program. Unfortunately, using only these functions virtually guarantees that the software will be slow or lack the "sparkle" that one's competitors offer by optimizing for a particular platform. In this discussion, then, standardization refers to more than simply the operating system or the microprocessor. A systemwide standard is critical.

FORCES THAT DRIVE FRAGMENTATION OF STANDARDS

Standards and Network Externalities

The market for practically all computer technology is strongly affected by "network externalities." In the case of telephone networks, for example, the value to an individual of having a phone is greatly enhanced by expansion in the size of the network.[5]

Connections to the network require a "standardized interface"; standards make it possible for consumers to "mix and match" components and systems (Matutes and Regibeau 1987), and they have been crucial to the evolution of the microcomputer industry. For example, the IBM PC first offered a monochrome monitor that displayed only text. A separate company, Hercules, developed a monitor and card that facilitated display of graphics on a monochrome system. Both Hercules and IBM benefited from this development, which was facilitated by standardized interfaces, an advantage of the PC's "open architecture." Software that directs the hardware in performance of tasks also works on a wide variety of platforms that conform to a standardized environment.

A second sort of network effect is apparent in "positive consumption" externalities; prospective purchasers of a good are concerned about the number of other purchasers of the same good. One widely understood example is that of VCR (videocassette recorder) technology. In the early 1980s, consumers choosing between Beta and VHS formats for their VCRs were concerned that there be a large "installed base"— that is, lots of *other* people with VCRs that used the same format. The motive for this concern is founded on the expectation of competition in secondary markets. For example, the larger the number of VHS VCRs, the greater the market for movies in VHS format. Although there are technological developments that can obviate the need for strict compatibility (for example, converters and "gateways," or translators), the inefficiencies of such technologies often make them undesirable. In the face of positive consumption externalities, one entity's (firm's or person's) investment decision may significantly influence an otherwise unrelated entity to choose the same standard.

In the case of family game computers, there are essentially two incompatible standards: Sega and Nintendo. In the absence of a gateway technology, consumers are restricted to the use of software that is "compatible" with their hardware: that is, their initial choice of a standard has a long-term impact. We might refer to this as an instance of "lock-in," reflecting the fact that the hardware is entering an implicit long-term contract in the use of software.[6] If there is only one supplier of the nondurable goods, the purchaser will attempt to avoid making a long-term investment for fear of ex post opportunism by the seller. Standardization of the product, however, reduces the purchaser's risks of commitment to a particular manufacturer because there are alternative manufacturers of complementary goods.

In both mainframes and microcomputers, the choice of a main processor affects a wide variety of complementary asset investments. Compatibility is important for both peripheral hardware (such as IBM "plug-compatible" products for mainframes) and applications and operating systems software. One of the most significant complementary asset investments is in personnel. Once a mainframe purchaser begins the hiring and development of personnel for its management information systems (MIS) department, it becomes more and more expensive to change to an alternative system. This is why the issue of IBM-compatibility historically has been important in the development of computer systems, both in the United States and throughout the world. Clearly, a firm will not make so significant an investment without assurance that the manufacturer will be around for a long time, and this leads customers to place a much greater emphasis on the producer firm's reputation. The firm's reputation is influenced by a number of its practices, including post-sales service, product longevity, fitness for use, and competitive pricing. However, a large installed base may outweigh these concerns.

Human resource development issues are among the most subtle, yet pervasive aspects of computer technology investment. Investments in technologies that require a significant human resource commitment create an investment inertia that can significantly affect the long-term trajectory of the firm (Nelson and Winter 1982, chap. 5; Hannan and Freeman 1989, 66). As investments in complementary assets increase, so do switching costs. This is true for investments in hardware as well as in training to acquire specific organizational skills. In addition, managers may stress the importance of familiarity with a particular technology. As a result a firm may decide not to adopt a superior technology if it makes the skill set of a significant portion of those inside the firm obsolete.

Not all of these issues are unique to networked industries. What is unique are the implications of "positive consumption externalities." The dissemination of information regarding the decisions of early adopters may encourage the emergence of a particular standard and its achievement of a dominant position. Significant inertia is likely to perpetuate a particular standard, even in the face of technological improvements in other architectures (Farrell and Saloner 1987). Arguably, this is the situation in the U.S. microcomputer industry with respect to aspects of both hardware and software.

Standards, Compatibility, and Competition

The concept of network externalities sheds considerable light on the issues facing entrants and incumbents in the microcomputer software industry. A firm whose product has become the de facto standard in an industry with network externalities may expect competition to decline. But the standards and compatibility (S&C) issue is a Faustian bargain for the incumbent. Although S&C makes market entry difficult, thereby protecting incumbents, it also hampers the profitability of software development.[7] The S&C issue is an important factor in the modest position of Japanese firms in the global packaged software industry.[8] The risk and resource commitment involved in new product development for the Japanese microcomputer software market do not have the same potential payoff that they have in the larger U.S. market.

A discussion of the lag in the development of software design engineers (SDEs), the critical input factor for the packaged software industry, illustrates the importance of standards. If all SDEs within a firm could focus on development for a single platform, overall profitability would be enhanced. Instead of devoting energies toward understanding and optimizing code for a variety of platforms, the firm's (limited) total SDE resources could be directed toward other aspects of the development process. Requiring an SDE to know multiple platforms is analogous to requiring a businessperson to be fluent in several spoken languages. Although it is helpful to have such fluency, it comes at a price in training and productivity and consumes significant resources. The fewer or more uniform the platforms, the greater the amount of SDE resources that can be committed to product development.

Thorough knowledge of a single platform contributes to static efficiencies in the software development environment. But if the standards environment changes, the ability to deal with multiple standards could become valuable. Despite the short-term costs, fluency in porting to a variety of platforms and knowledge of different ways of accomplishing the same task are useful when hardware platforms and standards change.

HARDWARE PLATFORMS: MAINFRAMES TO MICROS

A great deal of the work that can be done on an applications software project is circumscribed technologically by the hardware platform: the central processing unit (CPU) and operating system. A discussion of the hardware environment complicates the story because programming skills and techniques are different in different environments (for example, in the mainframe, minicomputer, workstation, and microcomputer).

Production Characteristics

In both the United States and Japan, software development has been a difficult process to manage. Watts Humphrey at the Software Engineering Institute has characterized the progression of software process management as going through five levels to reach maturity (see Baumert 1991). A recent study of twenty-seven sites found that nearly 81 percent of the U.S. firms in the study were at only the first level (Baumert 1991). The development of mainframe software is increasingly done in larger, more structured organizations. In the early development of the mainframe industry, small, entrepreneurial groups supplied most software products. However, as the size and complexity of programs increased, support and maintenance required larger organizations with more formal interactions. Over time, no matter how "entrepreneurial" software development firms may have been, they ultimately became larger, more structured organizations. Mainframe programming requires a highly systematic approach because it is usually beyond the capacity of even a small group to fully comprehend the operating environment. Thus, production teams include specialists in some aspect of the software/hardware challenges (such as user interface, writing the specifications, video output, printer output, and providing end-user support and documentation). Microcomputer software development, on the other hand, is characteristically performed by individuals or very small groups (MS-Basic, MS-DOS, CP/M, Lotus 1-2-3, Pac-Man, DBase, and others were produced by such small groups). While this is changing as the microcomputer industry matures (for example, the development of OS/2 and Lotus 1-2-3, version 3.0, involved relatively large numbers of developers and coordination between two large firms), the "flat," nonbureaucratic entrepreneurial structure is an important legacy. The view that American software designers are "creative" may in part be due to the "entrepreneurial environments" in which microcomputer applications were initially developed.

Cusumano's work on the development of "software factories" indicates that there is a significant difference in the approach to software development in Japan. The factory approach used in many large Japanese software development centers relies on a more carefully managed environment than its typical U.S. counterpart. For example, software functions that are common to many development projects are centralized and codified. A sorting routine might be made available to all developers from its central storehouse. A new SDE would be required to learn the contents of this repository of routines and be tested periodically to demonstrate an understanding of the appropriate use of the routines in day-to-day applications. Although there is some question about the pervasiveness of Japanese factory techniques, the efficiency of such an approach is clear. If these methods can be successfully applied to a microcomputer software development environment, and if Japanese microcomputer software firms employ factory techniques as successfully as their mainframe counterparts, we should see the development of a strong microcomputer software industry in Japan, with or without an "entrepreneurial" phase of the industry. More important, the rise of new software tools for product development, including computer-assisted software engineering (CASE) and object-oriented programming, is making code development much less platform-specific. As this occurs, software developers are likely to manufacture products that are easily portable across a wide variety of platforms (mainframes to micros).

Symbiosis of Hardware and Software: New Platforms

New hardware requires software that will run on it. This has several implications for the design and development of software. (Of course, hardware can be designed around an existing piece of software, but historically that has not been the trend.)[9] The decision to develop new hardware has often signaled the opportunity to make an impact on the economics of network externalities. For example, IBM's PC used Intel 8086 and 8088 microprocessors. Visicalc, one of the first spreadsheet programs, was developed for the CP/M market using Intel 8080 and Motorola 6502 chips. With the rise to dominance of the 8088/MS-DOS combination, Lotus 1-2-3 seized an opportunity to dominate the market. Lotus has maintained this dominant position despite its problems with subsequent versions. Lotus's continued strength illustrates the importance of network externalities and lock-in.

Software development practices differ according to the type of software; operating systems, for example, are evaluated by "performance" metrics that differ from those used for applications software. Moreover, because network externalities are so important, the number of applications that run under a particular operating system is likely to be greater for operating systems that have been in the market longer. Inertia associated with a "platform" can pull the software market along with it. The key influence on this inertia is not where the installed base lies, but the expectations of software developers about its future evolution. Such expectations about the industry are likely to become self-fulfilling, given the long-term nature of the "technological trajectories" mentioned earlier. To the extent that Japanese firms acquire expertise in hardware development, less software for the latest hardware will likely be developed in the United States.

HOW MULTIPLE STANDARDS EMERGED

The emergence of multiple standards in Japanese computer hardware and software markets is critical to understanding the development of Japan's microcomputer software industry. Several factors led to a fragmented standards environment in Japan. I summarize the factors briefly here and expand on them in the section that follows. First, low rates of entry into the Japanese microcomputer markets left mainframe producers as the dominant source of microcomputer technology. These firms' product development incentives differed from those of new entrants, and this affected the evolution of the market: Because mainframe producers have a large investment in centralized computing, their use of the PC was often as an adjunct; new entrants, however, were not constrained to support a centralized computing environment, and thus their product development efforts would not be hampered by the need to provide compatibility or ease of connectivity to a particular computer architecture. Second, once Japan began producing microcomputers, slow sales acceleration permitted the emergence of multiple standards. In the United States, in contrast, hardware sales acceleration and standardization occurred quickly.[10] Third, the complexity of the graphic representation of the Japanese language hampered widespread market acceptance of a PC standard. Finally, Japan's weak intellectual property regime slowed assimilation of a global PC operating system standard.

Mainframe Producer Dominance

The tight, oligopolistic structure of the Japanese computer hardware industry has affected expectations regarding PC development and firms' incentives to develop PC technology. While U.S. minicomputer and mainframe producers were not among the earliest entrants to the U.S. microcomputer market, Japanese computer manufacturers dominated their nation's nascent personal computer industry. The structure of the Japanese mainframe market was an important factor in the development of PCs.

During the emergence of the U.S. microcomputer industry, the U.S. mainframe computer marketplace was dominated by IBM, followed by DEC and the so-called BUNCH (Burroughs, Sperry-Univac, National Cash Register, Control Data Corp., and Honeywell). In Japan, however, no single firm has dominated the mainframe industry (the producer group resembles the BUNCH in the United States). Although

IBM is an important force in Japan, a small group of other computer hardware manufacturers is fiercely competitive.[11]

A brief history of the early development of the microcomputer hardware market illustrates the dominant role played by larger computer manufacturers. In 1976 NEC introduced a microcomputer kit (the TK-80), which played a catalytic role in Japanese markets similar to that which the MITS Altair played when it was introduced in the United States in 1975: it gave birth to the hobbyist microcomputer market. Toshiba, Panfacom, Hitachi, Sharp, and Fujitsu soon followed with kits of their own. In 1977 Sord announced the M200 microcomputer kit (Sord was acquired by Toshiba in 1985). Then, in 1978, Hitachi announced the first Japanese PC, the Basic Master L1. Shortly thereafter, in 1979, NEC introduced the PC-8001 as a computer for business use. The 8001 was the first Japanese PC with a color display and to offer features important for business use: built-in floppy disk drives (much more convenient than cassette tape players) and a high-resolution display (640×400 pixels) showing eighty characters by twenty-five lines. Several products introduced later by NEC were designed for use as "smart" terminals that could be connected to a mainframe. This strategy differed from that of firms in the U.S. market, where PCs were valued for their stand-alone computing capabilities. By the end of 1981 the following firms had entered the Japanese personal computer market: Oki Electric (1980), Toshiba (1980), Fujitsu (1981), Sharp (1981), Matsushita (1981), and Mitsubishi (1981). Of these, all but Sord and Sharp had previously been involved in mainframe and minicomputer manufacture. Later entrants include IBM Japan (1983), Sony (1982), Seiko-Epson (1982), and Ricoh (1983).

The structure of the Japanese mainframe computer industry and the prominent role of mainframe producers in the microcomputer market has affected the development of the PC market in important ways. Each mainframe manufacturer has viewed the role of the PC quite differently and has contributed to diversity in microcomputer architectures.[12] One market research firm reported in 1988 that "Some computer manufacturers see the AX [a proposed PC standard] as a terminal for their own hosts; others peg it as an IBM terminal emulator; and still others are going for the value-added reseller market" (*Electronics* 1988). Industry analysts argue that Fujitsu's minor presence in the Japanese microcomputer market can be explained by the fact that microcomputer sales are linked to sales of Fujitsu's mainframe computer. As I noted earlier, the architecture of Japanese microcomputer market is highly heterogeneous, reflecting its dominance by the mainframe producers, which have also contributed to heterogeneity in mainframe architecture.

Historically, major Japanese hardware companies have considered software to be "a necessary evil" and have devoted much of their effort to developing customized software for specific accounts.[13] Software customization requires devoting substantial resources to software design engineers, although it may offer savings in software maintenance.[14] In contrast, standardized products made for a large market fit many customer requirements imperfectly; in a packaged product environment, the software may be customized by users themselves, or industry consultants, rather than the software producer. In such an arrangement users purchase more of a company's standardized products, but arguably at less cost than a customized product.

In the U.S. market, most computer software developers are independent of hardware manufacturers, and this arm's length relationship between hardware and software producers has proved important to the growth of the U.S. microcomputer software market.[15] Figure 6-4 illustrates the close links between Japanese hardware vendors and software development firms, and Figure 6-5 shows the extent to which software development in Japan is performed on a commissioned basis (indicating "upstream" dominance of the industry).

The Development of an Installed Base

Growth in the Japanese market for packaged software also has been heavily influenced by the lingering dominance of the mainframe in Japanese businesses.[16] The reasons for the slow Japanese transition from mainframe to microcomputer are not clear, but as late as 1988 sales of mainframes still accounted for more than half of computer systems sales in Japan (*Electronics* 1988, 59). As mainframe computers continue to supply what might otherwise be provided by smaller computers, the installed base of PCs grows slowly and the development of uniform standards for personal computers is deferred.

The rapid diffusion of microcomputer technology in the United States aided the process of architectural standardization and provided a strong foundation for growth in the packaged software market. Figure 6-6 shows hardware sales by machine type. Total Japanese sales of "super-small" computers, which are roughly the same as personal computers, were 50,117 in fiscal year 1986. In sharp contrast, one U.S. mail-order entrepreneur alone (Michael Dell of PCs Limited) shipped an estimated 70,000 units that year, a total that accounted for only 2.2 percent of the U.S. PC-compatibles market (*PC Week* 1987, 127).

The Effects of the Japanese Distribution System

In the late 1970s and early 1980s the use of microcomputers spread rapidly into American business via hobbyists and enthusiasts (Benson 1983, 45). As decision-

Figure 6-4.   Japanese software house affiliations. *Source:* Japanese Information Service Industry Association 1989.

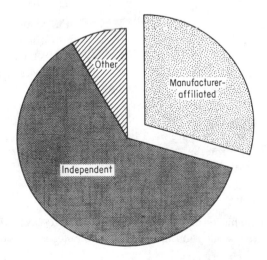

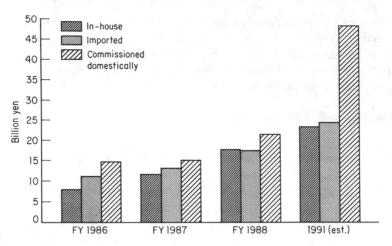

Figure 6-5.   Japanese software sales by development source, 1986–91. *Source:* Japanese Information Service Industry Association 1989.

makers began to recognize their usefulness the role of the microcomputer expanded. A diffusion process of this sort does not require sophisticated distribution channels or extensive on-site product support (although these have taken on greater significance as the market has matured); early adopters of microcomputer technology assumed the risks associated with using it. During the period in which microcomputers were primarily "self-service," the expense of educating potential users about a wide variety of platforms was prohibitive. Thus, the development of mass-market retail channels for microcomputers in the United States favored the rapid distribution and standardization of one or two architectures.

In contrast, Japanese firms were unwilling to assume the risks associated with early adoption of microcomputer technology and required vendors to offer training and support through highly developed original equipment manufacturer (OEM) distribution channels. Support includes installation (for example, connecting the peripherals—monitor, printer, and pointing devices), maintenance, training, and the like. Reliance on OEM channels for training and support in Japan facilitated the growth of a heterogeneous installed base. When microcomputers were designed for office use, connectivity with the mainframe was an important consideration, and thus businesses chose PCs that were compatible with their mainframes. And Japanese OEM's, most of whom were mainframe producers, offered smaller minicomputers called "Offcon" to address the same demand that in the United States was addressed with microcomputers. The use of Offcon computers spread rapidly in the early 1980s and leveled off in 1985–86 as the PC market began to expand. Figure 6-7 illustrates the relative proportions of software revenues by size of platform; the "takeoff" in microcomputer sales lagged well behind the rapid development of the U.S. market by 1988.

The Role of Language in Delaying Standardization

The Japanese ideographic written language, kanji, has delayed development of the PC market and restricted adoption of the U.S. computer architecture standards. One

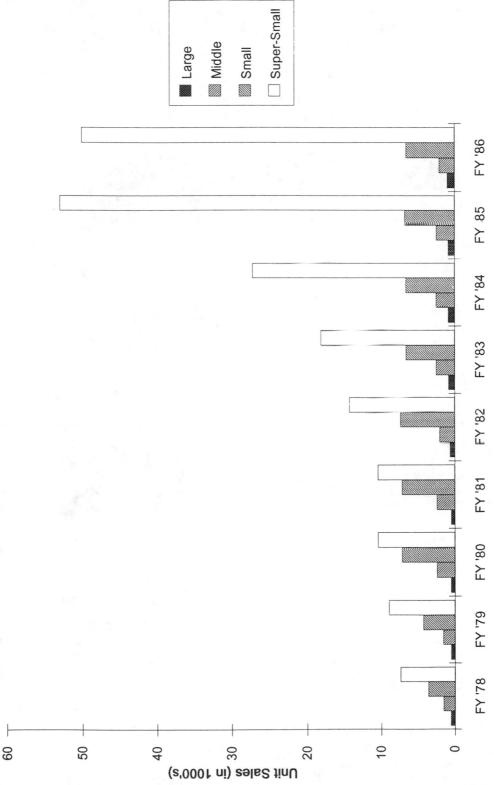

Figure 6-6. Japanese software unit sales by computer type, 1978–86. *Source:* Japanese Information Service Industry Association 1989.

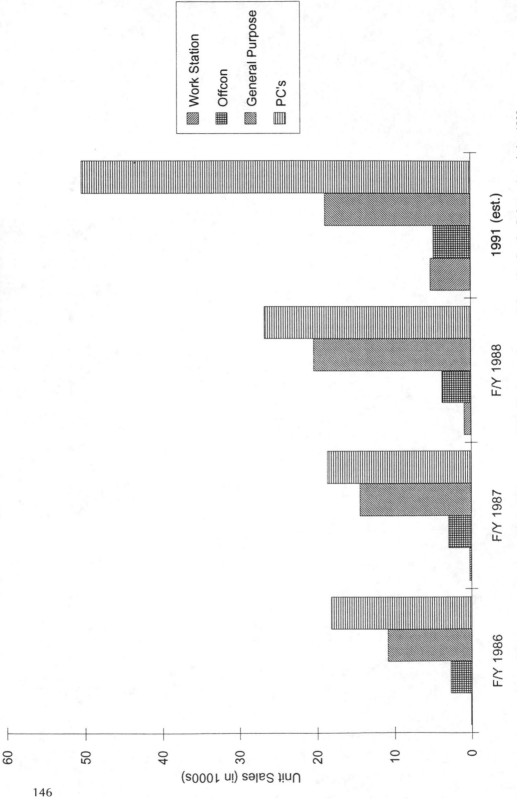

Figure 6-7. Japanese software sales by hardware type, 1986–91. *Source*: Japanese Information Service Industry Association 1990.

important early application of PCs in the United States was in word processing, and sales of microcomputers for this application helped the development of an IBM PC standard. But computer processing of Japanese text is a more challenging technical problem, which manufacturers developed dedicated word processing hardware to handle. These specialized machines siphoned off much of the market demand that in the United States contributed to a larger PC installed base: in 1988 projected gross sales of kanji word processors were nearly $1.9 billion, $3.5 billion for PCs (Dempa Publications 1988). The smaller installed base reduced incentives for manufacturers to produce compatible machines, which dramatically diminished incentives for software producers to develop standard products.[17]

Why didn't Japanese manufacturers simply adopt the IBM PC standard? One view of the Japanese PC market is that computer manufacturers, most notably IBM (whose IBM Japan PC 5550 is not compatible with its U.S. microcomputers), were unable to maintain IBM PC compatibility in a product that would also deal with kanji ideographs.[18] Early Japanese personal computers used the CP/M operating system, and initially both the personal and the business markets were dominated by CP/M-80 and CP/M-86 operating systems.[19] (Although the operating system was standardized, what we are calling "the platform" was not. A standardized operating system helps a great deal but is not sufficient for binary compatibility.) CP/M was the dominant operating system in Japan; but as U.S. standards and products diverged from CP/M, the U.S. and Japanese installed base also diverged. The two markets could have converged during the transition to a new generation of microprocessor (for example, from 8- to 16- to 32-bit microprocessors), but because of the slow adoption of faster computers there was no bandwagon effect in the Japanese market. MS-DOS is expected to become the standard operating system for Japanese 16-bit business machines, but 16-bit machines began to outsell 8-bit machines in Japan only in 1987 (Kurita 1988b, 57)[20]. Thus the market was fragmented by the acceptance of the CP/M standard and the correspondingly slower transition to MS-DOS.

Japanese PC-clones introduced in the U.S. market by 1985 had U.S.-developed software, because most Japanese software was kanji-based. Kanji poses challenges for keyboard design, pattern recognition, graphics display, and memory requirements.[21] The intricate characters and the memory necessary for text manipulation of kanji characters required significantly more sophisticated display and data storage technology than was available from microprocessors in the early 1980s.[22] Japanese research and development has sought economical solutions to these problems, and Japanese advantages in display technology and in high-volume production of DRAMs resulted in part from efforts to deal with the technological challenges presented by the language.

As the DRAM and display examples suggest, efforts by Japan's firms to address technological challenges, especially where they diverge from those facing U.S. firms, may "push" these firms to pursue different trajectories of technological development and technical capability. For example, facsimile technology arose in Japan faster than in the United States because of the need to transmit kanji characters. Japanese developments in character recognition and some aspects of artificial intelligence also reflect efforts to address the problems posed by the language. These efforts by Japanese firms delayed early adoption of standards, but they may create long-term advantages in other areas, such as computing power, graphics, and storage capacity. It is possible that the challenges that face the Japanese microcomputer industry will eventually support capabilities that are more important than the uniform standard in the U.S. PC market.

The Role of Licensing and Intellectual Property Protection

A final reason for the emergence of multiple architectural standards in Japan is that foreign (for example, U.S.) standards were not adopted. An important barrier to earlier adoption of MS-DOS in Japan was the weaker protection of intellectual property rights. Only in 1983, two years after the introduction of the IBM PC, were sixteen Japanese personal computer manufacturers finally able to license Microsoft's MS-DOS operating system. Weak intellectual property protection was one reason for the delay in licensing.[23]

Even if intellectual property protection had been strengthened earlier, it seems unlikely that the IBM PC standard would have become dominant. Japanese purchasers would have expected indigenous firms to succeed in developing Japanese microcomputers and thus have delayed acquisition of foreign products. Japanese government programs had supported indigenous firms in the development of technology (for example, the mainframe industry in the 1960s and 1970s), and the success of a foreign firm or standard in the Japanese market thus was uncertain. Moreover, Japanese firms with long-term ties to a particular computer manufacturer also might have deferred purchasing equipment from a foreign firm because of concerns about its compatibility with that of domestic manufacturers.

IMPACT OF A MULTIPLE STANDARDS ENVIRONMENT

Productivity of Software Design Engineers and "Tailormade Applications"

Extensive reliance on customized software in a multiple standards environment is a drain on the resources for "national" software design engineers (SDEs). SDEs were, and still are, a scarce resource in both Japan and the United States. Indeed, as chapter 4 points out, they are, if anything, scarcer in Japan than in the United States. Some Japanese firms have attempted to improve the production of customized software with small numbers of SDEs by trying to squeeze more code out of their SDEs through careful management and training in reusability (this is discussed extensively in Cusumano 1991). If one measures productivity using a standard (albeit controversial) metric, such as lines of written computer code per hour, Japanese programmers seem highly productive.[24] Nevertheless, the software factories described by Cusumano have not thus far proven capable of supporting more rapid growth in the packaged software industry in Japan.

Sale of Packaged Software

Although Japanese software developers appear to do well in terms of physical productivity, the market structure limits their profitability. No matter how efficient an SDE is at developing code, one-time sale of a custom product limits profitability. If, on the other hand, that code is resold thousands of times, profitability will be higher.

An individual line of code used over and over in packaged products can be sold thousands or millions of times.

According to IDC Japan's Yugi Ogino, Japanese users now are willing to abandon their historic preference for customized software because a shortage of software engineers has made custom software more expensive and less available. Toshiba and the AX group (most notably Mitsubishi Electric, Sanyo Electric, and Sharp) are developing technology that will allow English and kanji software to run on the same hardware (*PC Week* 1988, 81). Success by these firms would remove a barrier to sales of U.S. packaged software in Japan. Finally, developments in operating systems are making software more device-independent. For example, graphic user interfaces such as MS-Windows allow for greater device independence in developing software: improvements in operating systems facilitate the development of software for a variety of platforms. The increased market acceptance of MS-Windows has led to greater market entry by U.S. software manufacturers.

PUBLIC POLICY EFFORTS TO ADDRESS MULTIPLE STANDARDS

The fragmented environment of hardware and software architectures has clearly hampered the development of Japan's packaged software industry, and public policy has largely failed to address this problem. Despite the previous success in "administrative guidance" by Japanese government agencies in other postwar industries, government financial incentives and other programs aimed at establishing a successful software industry have not dealt with this central industry problem.

Government Financial Support for Software Firms

Government programs have been an important part of the development of the information services industry in Japan since at least 1957 (Davidson 1984). The Information Technology Promotion Law, passed in 1970, created the Information Technology Promotion Agency (IPA). From 1970 to 1982, MITI gave IPA nearly $70 million to offset operating expenses and helped software firms obtain more than $450 million in loans for software development and company operations. Software R&D grants through 1975 totaled $12 million (Jeffries 1987, 157). Tax law changes enacted by the IPA in 1979 provided tax breaks to software houses, placing 50 percent of licensing revenues into a five-year tax-deferred "reserve." This reserve could be used before the five-year deadline for software development, with only 25 percent subject to tax (Davidson 1984).

Although there were individual agreements between U.S. software developers and Japanese counterparts before 1986, Japan extended copyright protection to cover software only in that year (*New Scientist* 1987, 30). Initially, copyright protection was extended for only fifteen years, substantially less than the fifty-year protection provided in the United States (Barney 1984, 48). This weak intellectual property regime clearly discouraged U.S. (and Japanese) developers from marketing software in Japan.

As chapter 10 in this volume points out, intellectual property protection is a much more critical issue for software developers than for hardware manufacturers because software is so easy to pirate. The fact that Japanese hardware manufacturers

sold integrated computing solutions that relied on custom software–related intellectual property may have lowered their interest in protection of their software. Hardware manufacturers may even be less concerned with protecting packaged software,
because its wide availability reduces the effective cost of delivering solutions to users
without also reducing hardware sales (see chapters 4 and 10).

SIGMA: R&D collaboration between industry and government

The SIGMA (Software Industrial Generalization and Maintenance Aids) Project
(1985–90), sponsored by MITI, attempted "to overcome problems in the areas of
software productivity, development, and incompatibility" by "applying proven manufacturing automation techniques to the software design process" (Dambrot 1989, 80).
The project expended $194 million of government resources over five years to "auto-
mate software development and create standardized Unix-based data structures, communications interfaces, and applications platforms." The program focuses on tools
and environments for software development, with two important goals: (1) improving
programmer productivity; and (2) developing greater uniformity for greater compatibility through the Unix operating system. The follow-on five-year program, SuperSIGMA, seeks to develop interfaces for incompatible computers.[25]

SIGMA was a major government effort to address the heterogeneous standards
environment within which Japanese software developers must operate: "The ostensi-
ble goal of Sigma is the improvement of software development productivity through
the creation of a standard Unix software development engine that would eventually
network all of Japan's software engineers. . . . Once the Japanese have standardized
the base hardware [that is, the SIGMA workstation], they can develop the software
and specialized peripherals, such as keyboards, displays, mass storage and others,
tailored to specific vertical markets" (Alster 1987, 26).

There is little question that SIGMA was MITI's attempt to move Japanese hardware manufacturers toward a Unix operating system standard in order to reap the
benefits of compatibility (Cohen 1987, 72). Expectations were that promotion of
the Unix operating system standard would also aid Japanese firms' efforts to enter
world markets.[26]

But despite its substantial budget, and perhaps because of its ambitious goals,
the SIGMA program has had little impact on Japan's software industry. Firms continue to use proprietary development tools, and despite progress in promoting Unix,
Japanese hardware firms have been reluctant to market SIGMA systems because they
are not proprietary.

Other Japanese government programs

Other government programs in software have attempted to address the impediments
described earlier. The Japan Software Company was organized by MITI in 1966 as
a joint venture of Hitachi, Fujitsu, NEC, and the Industrial Bank of Japan. The
company sought to create a common software development language to aid the fledgling software industry; but the effort failed completely. The IPA Package Project in
1970 offered financial support for software firms developing packaged software, but
the project did not yield commercially successful packaged software. The Software
Module Project, a four-year project that began in 1973, sought to develop standard-

ized modules for applications programming. A follow-up project, the Software Production Technology Project (1976–81), attempted to develop standardized tools and processes for software development and aid in the development of software factory techniques. This project also was unsuccessful for a variety of reasons, including interfirm rivalry.

This sketch of MITI-sponsored projects indicates that MITI has long been aware of the difficulties of standardization in this market but has had little success at remedying them. The more recent SIGMA project shows greater promise, but its success is by no means assured. Japan's government has also been slow to act in the area of intellectual property protection, which is crucial to the business prospects of independent developers of packaged software. The slow pace with which copyright protection has been extended to cover software has hampered the growth of Japan's packaged software industry, but the lack of such protection also reflects the large political influence of the large producers of mainframe computers: those who specialized in custom software development and stood to benefit far less than commercial producers from stronger protection of software-related intellectual property rights.

University research

Although most software-related R&D is performed in the private sector in Japan, government projects and infrastructure play an important role in the direction and character of research. The Japanese government funds universities and cooperative research laboratories. In 1984 an assessment of the Japanese facilities concluded that:

> Japanese universities have central computer facilities that are remarkable for their equipment and productivity. Not only are the individual sites well endowed, but the national university centers are netted together to provide a national academic computer resource unparalleled in this country. . . . The research environments at the various universities were notably different from those in the United States, testifying to the strong commitment to top quality computer facilities in Japan. These [academic] installations rival Japan's most powerful commercial installations and greatly exceed the capacity of comparable academic computing centers in the United States. Not only are the centers remarkable in themselves, but they are netted together for data and program sharing. (Stone 1984, 26)

This assessment contrasts with the generally accepted view of Japanese universities as poorly funded and inadequately equipped. Nevertheless, there are several barriers to university-industry cooperation in research, most notably central control over all funding of higher education by the Ministry of Education, Science, and Culture.[27] Public financial support has helped focus university research. Most significantly, the computer hardware made available to researchers influences the kinds of problems chosen by university investigators. For example, one 1984 study said that Japanese public funding facilitated research on new computer systems and architectures.[28] The study concluded that Japanese compiler and utilities technology had improved considerably, particularly with respect to parallel processing paradigms: "There is data that suggests the Japanese are writing superior compilers and utilities. . . . U.S. vendors currently dominate the supercomputer market, but superior Japanese software for supercomputers, such as a vectorizing FORTRAN compiler, is increasing the competition (Zelkowitz et al. 1984, 65)."[29]

University-Industry Collaboration: TRON

The Real-time Operating Nucleus (TRON) was conceived in 1981 by professor Ken Sakamura at the University of Tokyo who wanted to design a 32-bit operating system with 2-byte coding to deal with the kanji characters integrally rather than as an add-on. Funding for the project was unique in that "five companies . . . backed it to the tune of perhaps 50 million pounds a year. This makes the project by far the largest example of cooperative research between a university and industry that has ever been undertaken in Japan" (Johnstone 1987, 33). TRON may provide a standardized operating system for future product development; indeed TRON now appears to be focused on the development of standards rather than products per se (see Poe 1987b).[30] The collaboration between university and industry offers an ideal forum for the development of open standards. Japanese computer manufacturers, with the notable exception of NEC and its V-series of microprocessors, are developing TRON hardware.[31]

A COMPETITIVE ANALYSIS OF THE MICROCOMPUTER SOFTWARE INDUSTRIES IN THE UNITED STATES AND JAPAN

Strengths of the U.S. Industry

The American microcomputer software industry is clearly a dominant force in global markets (see OECD 1985 and OTA 1986). The pioneering role of U.S. computer hardware firms and the inertial characteristics of network externalities have left American software firms in a strong position. The U.S. microcomputer hardware market is more homogeneous than the Japanese market, and this accounts for the relatively high profitability and productivity of U.S. software design engineers. Standards and compatibility thus are an important aspect of the U.S. success in computer software, as is market size. Comparable levels of penetration of the U.S. and Japanese microcomputer software markets have very different implications for profitability: having a 10 percent share of the U.S. PC-compatible market may mean a fortune to a U.S. company, whereas 10 percent of the NEC 9800 market in Japan may not allow a company even to reach the breakeven point.

The threat of entry, and companies' ability to make rapid entry, in microcomputer hardware and software has greatly speeded the development of the U.S. microcomputer market. In Japan, where mainframe manufacturers dominate the field, the development of the PC is tied to the overall strategy of the mainframe producers, and in this case slowness and delay have had significant implications (Kurita 1988b, 57). If a mainframe company views the PC as a threat, delayed development of the product can reduce the threat. If PC sales cannibalize sales of higher-margin mainframes and minicomputers, manufacturers of larger computers can be less aggressive in developing their lower-end products. Japanese microcomputer producers—manufacturers of proprietary mainframe computers—emphasized proprietary microcomputer systems that were incompatible with those of rivals. The absence of truly open systems and the focus on products congruent with the parent company's mainframe product line contributed to the slow evolution of standardized products.

In the United States, market entry is less difficult, and independent entrants in

PC software threatened low-end mainframe and minicomputer applications (simple word processing and database, spreadsheet, and financial modeling applications). Some argue that existing computer companies were aware of the opportunities in personal computing but did not seek a role in its development (see Freiberger and Swaine 1984). For one reason or another, Hewlett-Packard, DEC, and Control Data Corp. all considered the opportunity and might have offered a PC product by 1975, but each decided either to wait or to leave the market to other companies. Thus entrepreneurial firms such as MITS, IMSAI, and Apple spurred the growth of the industry in the late 1970s. By the early 1980s, the challenge for incumbent computer manufacturers was to offer any low-end product rather than to develop the product according to an overall company strategy. Low entry barriers offered similar opportunities in the microcomputer software industry. Thus, widespread entry in both hardware and software helped accelerate the overall development of the U.S. microcomputer market. More than just the capabilities of firms that entered, entry and threat of entry forced a response by incumbent computer manufacturers to offer products for the low end of the market without the constraints of a mainframe world.[32]

In addition to ease of entry, U.S. firms were able to form alliances (for example, the one between IBM and Microsoft to develop MS-DOS for the release of the IBM PC) to promote development of standards and products. These alliances were less confining than the long-term relationships observed in the Japanese industrial structure, where Japan's *keiretsu,* or business alliances, operate more like cartels (for example, IBM did not prohibit Microsoft from licensing MS-DOS to run on non-IBM computers). This open U.S. system spurred hardware and software market development. The environment for new firm development in the United States was also facilitated by the strong demand for new products. Investment capital was not limited in the early years of this industry, because in the late 1970s, microcomputer hardware and software were often sold prepaid—sometimes even several months in advance. Thus customers contributed to the financing of new products. This environment, while accompanied by periodic shake-out, has not yet left the industry vulnerable to its more established Japanese counterparts.

Weaknesses of the U.S. Industry

Nonetheless, standardization in the United States is accompanied by certain risks. As the industry matures, inertia may lead businesses to be less flexible in accepting and incorporating new technologies. The difficulties that Lotus faced with version 3.0 of its spreadsheet software illustrate this problem.

Lotus expanded version 1.0 of its spreadsheet product to run on Intel 8088/PC-DOS/IBM-compatible machines, and the result was software that was much faster at recalculation than its competitors. But these changes made it more difficult for Lotus to adapt its product to multiple platforms and environments. Firms that used more general programming tools were able to adapt their product to multiple platforms more rapidly. This may explain why Microsoft's Multiplan has been so much more successful in Europe than in the United States. Multiplan was written in a higher-level language than Lotus and is therefore more adaptable to different platforms and languages.[33]

The success of a successor to DOS, OS/2, has been *significantly* constrained by the size of the DOS installed base. IBM's decision to write a sophisticated operating system for the Intel 80286 chip led to an enormous investment of time and energy in developing a piece of software that has yet to be commercially successful. Some of the difficulties in the OS/2 project were created by Microsoft's effort to retain backward compatibility with DOS applications. In order to retain compatibility, OS/2 must execute a process that Gordon Letwin (Microsoft's OS/2 chief architect) describes as "turning off the engine to shift gears" (Letwin 1988). In the face of emerging multiple standards, this heavy commitment to a single chip and its compatibility challenges might have been unnecessary.

Will dominance of the U.S. microcomputer software industry by a single architecture diminish the industry's adaptability? As new platforms are developed over time, the ability to deal with a new operating environment becomes important. Will the deployment of significantly improved computer technologies be hampered by the huge U.S. installed base of standardized platforms? I overstate the extent to which the U.S. market is monolithic, and the rapid development of products for the new PowerPC architecture suggests that it has considerable adaptability; nonetheless, the initial reluctance of the independent software vendor (ISV) market to develop products for new operating environments (for example, Microsoft's Windows 3.0, or IBM OS/2 EE) can be attributed in larger part to the enormous installed base of 80 x 86 machines.

Weaknesses of the Japanese Industry

The Japanese microcomputer software market is developing rapidly. In order to operate in the fragmented Japanese microcomputer markets, firms must be efficient, and its individual software design engineers are highly productive. The key impediment to the Japanese software industry, as I have noted, remains the fragmented standards environment. But other problems, such as the small supply of professional SDEs, limited sources of capital for entrant firms, and remaining weaknesses in intellectual property protection, also inhibit industry growth.

Strength's of the Japanese Industry

If government policy and market efforts to standardize are effective, then Japanese productivity in computer software engineering could become a potent force in world markets. Even if the standardization effort is not successful, the legacy of the "software factory" may offer long-term advantages. Standardization presents the development process with a series of trade-offs. Where the hardware platform is standardized, SDEs can carefully optimize software for the architecture. Standardization thus facilitates product development by fixing component boundaries and allowing subsystem developers to optimize within those boundaries. Perhaps the simplest example of this comes from the development of microcomputer hardware, but there are important parallels in software development. When the IBM PC was first introduced, it offered only a monochrome display screen that lacked graphics capabilities. Hercules, a Berkeley, California, company, was able to design an interface card and monitor for the PC that could be used to display graphics. This innovation was possible because, while IBM was occupied with the development of hardware, it provided the necessary information (it published the BIOS) to software and hardware engineers for the development of complementary hardware. Thus, standardizing the BIOS and communicating it publicly allowed subsystem (display) optimization.

Over time, however, the graphics capabilities of PCs grew slowly through the evolution of display technology from CGA to VGA and beyond. Consider the impact of the Apple MacIntosh on display technology. Because there was no open architecture to support, Apple was free to provide a highly integrated solution to the development of a graphical user interface. At a time when the IBM PC was incapable of providing a Windows interface, the Apple MacIntosh provided reasonable speed for both display of graphical objects as well as mouse input processing.

Thus, component boundaries present constraints that may become more serious with advances in technological capabilities. And, while development of software for a customized application on a proprietary hardware platform will be somewhat constrained by the need to provide compatibility with an installed base, the software development effort will generally be much less restricted than in standardized environments.[34]

Japanese success in supercomputers illustrates the potential strengths of Japan's computer sector. Although the success has been primarily in hardware (NEC with the SX-3, and Fujitsu with the VPP500), important advances also have been achieved in compiler technology and software tools development. Software and the installed base are less important in supercomputer development because the installed base is smaller, and more specialized applications should lead to smaller network externality effects. The close relationship between new platforms and software suggests that future software development efforts will be more successful as complements to "new" Japanese hardware. But these advantages do not relate to desktop computer systems and packaged software for such systems.

It is possible that the great diversity in the Japanese microcomputer market will reduce the threat created by the obsolescence of any particular platform. Its tight oligopolistic structure may produce more approaches to solutions of a given computing problem than an atomistic industry structure in a homogeneous platform environment, and it may be easier to pursue parallel development of alternatives to some problems within the Japanese market structure. Although Japan's microcomputer industry currently is weak, the very diversity of platforms that has impeded its growth could prove beneficial in the long run.

Recent Developments

A number of approaches to the problem of multiple standards in Japan merit brief discussion. DOS V, a disk operating system that allows both U.S. and Japanese software to run on the same microcomputer, was introduced in 1992. The operating system facilitates the use of double-byte kanji character representation. One difficulty in developing software for multiple Japanese platforms is the varying screen resolution. By conforming to the de facto U.S. VGA (videographics adapter) standard, DOS V addresses the problem posed by the lack of a single standard for monitor resolution in Japanese computer screens, thus facilitating the development of software by both U.S. and Japanese vendors.

Microsoft's Windows 3.1 operating system was introduced in Japan in 1992 and is likely to have a significant impact on industry structure. Windows facilitates device-independent applications development, and version 3.1 contains improvements over prior versions. Device independence is particularly important in Japan because display density and the complexities of kanji representation mean that adapting software to new machines is difficult. The graphical user interface provided in MS-Windows also makes computers easier to learn, which should increase the appeal of the microcomputer in Japan. Sales of Windows 3.1 have increased rapidly, particularly among NEC customers (Hamilton 1993).

Sales of personal computers in Japan have grown to around 2 million units per year; the opportunity for ISVs improves even if this growing installed base remains fragmented among architectures. The entry by U.S. firms in the low-cost end of the Japanese market has accelerated the growth of installed IBM-compatible microcomputers; according to AST Research Japan, one NEC machine costs roughly twice that of an 80486 IBM-compatible microcomputer (Pope and Hamilton 1993). Apple, Compaq, and Dell all have established operations in Japan.

These developments are likely to convey competitive advantage to U.S. software vendors over their Japanese counterparts. The diffusion of U.S. operating systems and computer architectures eases entry by U.S. software firms into the Japanese markets. U.S. vendors already control approximately 50 percent of Japan's $1 billion market in packaged software for business. Japanese software firms will need time to adapt their products to the Windows 3.1 operating system, offering opportunities to the U.S. firms who have developed MS-Windows applications (Tanzer 1992). Because MS-Windows provides greater screen resolution than the NEC 9800 series currently offers, its rapid diffusion in Japan is likely to erode the importance of the 9800's large installed base (in 1993 NEC enjoyed a tenfold advantage in applications software) (Pope and Hamilton 1993). The newer, U.S.-developed next generation operating systems such as OS/2 and Windows NT may be too much for the NEC 9800 architecture (Perratore 1993).

SUMMARY AND CONCLUSIONS

The Japanese microcomputer software industry is paradoxical, since it more closely resembles a "typical" U.S. market structure (a large number of relatively small firms) than a "typical" Japanese market structure (a small number of powerful oligopolies dividing up the market). This is only one of several areas in which the U.S. and Japanese software markets invert the stereotypes often used to describe each nation's high-technology industries. Most puzzling, perhaps, are battles over standards in the Japanese market. A priori, one would expect that the small number of Japanese mainframe producers would cooperate and communicate more effectively than their U.S. counterparts and therefore should have little difficulty in developing standards. Yet in these networked industries, where significant profits can be earned from proprietary systems, the advantages to interfirm cooperation apparently are offset by the expected benefits of market share in the dominant proprietary product standard. Another paradox follows from the normally complementary nature of hardware and software assets: Japanese strength in hardware has not been matched by a strong position in software, despite close links between hardware and software developers.

Unsuccessful efforts at standardization are not unique to Japan. Several U.S. hardware vendors have recently begun to offer "open system" architectures, but interfirm efforts to develop standard architectures (for example, the Archer Consortium, a group of computer hardware and software firms working on a Unix standard) in the United States have been largely unsuccessful. Japanese microcomputer software firms clearly would benefit from a more standardized domestic environment, but the installed base and the Japanese distribution system ensure that multiple computer hardware vendors, and the associated incompatibility, are likely to endure. Customer expectations of "tailormade applications" also will not disappear overnight, and these expectations make it difficult for firms to use their limited software development resources effectively. The success of the industry will likely be determined by its ability to make the transition to a more standardized environment. Indeed, the introduction of DOS and MS-Windows for a variety of platforms will be able to provide this environment without changing the hardware.

Product evolution in the U.S. microcomputer software industry is influenced by the need to provide "backward compatibility" for the large installed base of both desktop computers and applications. The challenge here is to adapt current technology to next-generation technology. In launching its Micro 2000 project in 1988, Intel announced that, whatever else the chip does, it will be compatible with the current 80 x 86 instruction set. Intel now faces an unprecedented challenge from the PowerPC microprocessor, whose success will itself be critically influenced by its ability to attract developers of new applications software and by its backward compatibility with the large libraries of operating system and applications software developed for the IBM PC and Apple MacIntosh architectures. The long-run success of both Micro 2000 and the PowerPC thus will be constrained by the architectural legacy of prior generations.

The computer industry is extremely "path dependent." At present, this path-dependent pattern of development imposes severe handicaps on Japan's microcomputer software industry. Japanese software producers would be better positioned to respond to a competitive environment among desktop architectures if it were less fragmented and more standardized.

NOTES

An earlier version of this chapter was published as Cottrell 1994. The author acknowledges financial support for this research from the Pacific Rim Research Program of the University of California, the Bradley Foundation, and the Sasakawa Peace Foundation. The author also gratefully acknowledges the help of professor David Mowery and the advice of peers. Any remaining errors are my own.

1. "Japanese corporations are making a slower transition from large computer systems to microcomputers than their U.S. counterparts. There are only 3 million personal computers installed in Japanese businesses, according to the Japan Management Association; there are 23 million installed in the United States, according to market researchers Dataquest Inc., in San Jose, Calif." (Siegmann 1988, 124)

2. "In fact, three dominant PC groups have arisen in Japan:—NEC and its clone maker Epson;—the AX project group which aims at providing a unified Japanized version of the IBM PC/AT. The group is jointly promoted by ASCII, Japan Softbank and Microsoft K.K. . . ;— the alliance between Fujitsu and Matsushita Electric Industrial Company Ltd." (Kurita 1988, 57)

3. The term "platform" refers to the microprocessor and operating system for a particular piece of hardware. IBM-compatible means use of the MS-DOS operating system and an Intel 80 x 86 microprocessor in the context of a compatible BIOS (Basic Input Output System). However, use of MS-DOS and Intel 80 x 86 alone does not imply BIOS compatibility.

4. Associated Press, "Apple Gains Market Share as Japanese PC Sales Slip," 31 March, 1993.

5. See Katz and Shapiro 1986 and Farrell and Saloner 1988. Much of following discussion draws on these works.

6. Farrell and Saloner (1987) and Arthur (1985) discuss the impact of "lock-in." See Teece 1986 for a discussion of complementary assets in a slightly different context. Williamson (1985) also provides a discussion of the long-term impact of asset-specific investments, which often lead to concern about lock-in, on contracting behavior and the organization of transactions. But see Farrell and Gallini 1988 for a discussion of the situation in which a monopoly has incentives to make a credible commitment to compete in the secondary market.

7. "Perhaps the greatest barrier to entry for U.S. software developers in Japan is the lack of standards in that market. . . . The most popular hardware standard in Japan is that of NEC Corp.'s 9800 microcomputers. However, there are no clones of that technology. And although the NEC machines run MS-DOS, they are not IBM PC compatible. And in Japan there are competing standards. . . . 'It's a real obstacle,' said Mr. Hosogi [of Microsoft]. 'You have to adapt to NEC, Fujitsu, and IBM Japan.' " (Siegmann 1988, 129)

8. "Still, other than customized computer systems, the Japanese are not producing innovative, general-use systems for the software market. This phenomenon is based more on economics than technology. Where many computer makers are competing heavily, applications are segmented by types of hardware and operating systems. Since normally there are only a dozen or so prospective clients for a single software product, a few hundred for the most general case, it is hardly worthwhile to risk significant losses for general applications products." (Tajima and Matsubata 1984, 43)

9. Japan's "the real-time operating nucleus" (TRON) may be an example of software being developed before hardware (*Electronics* 1985).

10. I am not arguing that one caused the other; they nevertheless appear to be related.

11. "In other countries, IBM, and companies that make machines compatible with IBM's operating systems, dominate the market. This dominance provides a sufficient incentive for independent companies to develop software, called packaged programs, that will run on any compatible machine. In Japan, by contrast, there is fierce competition between half-a-dozen makers of mainframe computers, plus IBM. The result is that there are several different types of computer, but there are not many of each model. Software written for one type of computer will not run on another; it is not economical to develop packaged programs for a single make of machine." (Johnstone 1986, 60)

12. "Executives at Fujitsu, Japan's No. 1 mainframe vendor, clearly see the PC as an integral part of their overall business. 'Low-level machines including personal computers and workstations have very quickly become strong recently, and the future of mainframe computers depends on this trend,' asserts Akira Kuwahara, general manager of the marketing promotion division." (Kurita 1988b, 57)

13. "The industry's main weakness is that it is dominated by big computer manufacturers, such as Fujitsu, Hitachi and NEC, which are interested only in selling hardware. They regard the production of software as a necessary evil." (Johnstone 1986, 60)

14. "The Japanese practice of tailoring applications to each specification is a fundamental difference between the Japanese and the U.S. market (the U.S. abandoned this some time ago). This practice consumes quantities of programmer time and consequently limits the resources available for more innovative work. On the other hand, it is recognized that software maintenance can consume up to 50% or more per year of the original software investment.

Under these conditions, the Japanese may gain more in software maintenance than they lose in tailoring their codes." (Albus et al. 1986, 28)

"Custom-made software should, in theory, be better than packaged software, because it is tailored exactly to the user's requirements. In reality, tight schedules lead to short cuts: programmers reduce the time allowed for design and testing, they press unsuitable modules into service, and then provide only skimpy or (frequently) no documentation at all. The result is a poor product, riddled with bugs, which is difficult to maintain." (Johnstone 1986, 61)

15. "Software companies are usually subsidiaries set up by computer manufacturers to provide programs for their machines. Of Japan's 10 largest software houses, seven are tied to a specific maker. None of the top 10 houses in the U.S. is tied to a computer manufacturer." (Johnstone 1986, 61)

16. "The Japanese market for personal computers, one-tenth the size of the U.S. market, differs from the American computer scene in a number of ways, the [Dataquest] report ["The History of the Japanese Personal Computer Industry"] says . . . [T]he majority of large companies still process most data in a centralized mainframe environment, and departments typically have scant understanding of personal computers. The forces that ordinarily bring PC's into a company, then, are grass roots interests: individual department members who want to use the machines, the report said. . . . As of 1987, however, IBM Japan had captured roughly 12 percent of Japan's 16-bit personal computer market, the report said. Ninety-five percent of IBM's sales have been in large corporations." (Stoll 1988, 96)

17. Kanji requires 2-byte characters, whereas Western languages require only 1-byte characters. This size difference greatly complicates the computer architecture. The machines for processing kanji called for a faster processor than was necessary in the United States. Recently, however, kanji word processing on PCs has become viable as the platform has become more powerful.

18. "Despite the fact that a number of Japanese computer manufacturers have developed IBM PC AT-compatible computers for the U.S. market, the number of IBM PC-compatible machines sold in Japan is minuscule compared to the sales of the NEC PC-9801 series, for example. IBM Japan Ltd. offers its Model 5550 and 5540 workstations, which are popular office computers in many banks and large corporations here. . . . But these computers aren't directed toward the personal computer market, they aren't PC-compatible, and they carry substantially higher price tags than most personal computers. . . . The reason for so few IBM PC and PC AT machines and work-alikes being sold here is no mystery . . . you can't expect to sell a large number of computers in Japan if those computers can't handle the Japanese language. Hardware produced by the leading personal computer manufacturers (NEC, Fujitsu, Oki, Sanyo, Sharp, Hitachi, and others) is very powerful and has undergone a long and arduous winnowing process in the fiercely competitive Japanese market. Demands include extensive and sophisticated Japanese-language processing features that are built into the hardware, as well as more familiar hardware features like fast microprocessors, massive on-board RAM, large floppy disk and hard disk capacities, and extensive interfacing capability." (Raike 1986b, 351)

19. "Here in Japan, the most common and well-known operating systems are CP/M-86 (for 16-bit computers) and CP/M-80 (for 8-bit computers). Despite the many advantages of MS-DOS over CP/M-86, the main Japanese computer manufacturers were slow in introducing Japanese-language versions of MS-DOS for their computers, and most applications software products, including word processors, spreadsheets, and the like, were developed first for the CP/M-86 operating system. The reason for all of this is that the IBM PC never had much impact in Japan, and there has been no stimulus to produce IBM PC-compatible machines here for the domestic market. Consequently, no major forces pushed first-time computer users and buyers into becoming familiar with MS-DOS (or PC-DOS)." (Raike 1986a, 329)

20. "Ever since it was adopted by [IBM] for use in the personal computer, the operating

system MS-DOS has overwhelmed the CP/M. Not only in world markets where the IBM is dominant, but also in Japan the view is that MS-DOS would eventually become the standard operating system of the 16-bit business personal computer." (Dempa Publications Inc. 1988, 104)

21. "Japanese text recognition is clearly more difficult than the recognition of handprinted English. And the challenge is all the more important because a greater percentage of documents in Japan are generated by hand than in the United States. Kanji characters (ideographs) are far less suited to typewriter technology than roman letters." (Stone 1984, 30)

22. "The translation process for kanji software is extremely memory-intensive, both for the dictionary conversion of hiragana to kanji and for the high-resolution display of the corresponding graphics. Conversion requirements have given a strong impetus to the development of extremely dense, inexpensive nonvolatile memory. Japan, in fact, has long been a producer of 128K and 256K ROM chips, which were used early in the display of kanji graphics. . . . Furthermore, kanji requires far greater resolution on the display or printer [than roman text]. Roman text may be displayed adequately with a dot resolution of 8 x 6; and for a relatively good resolution, by a 10 x 8 matrix. Kanji has curves of many different shapes, and characters of great complexity with 10 to 15 strokes are common. . . . Consequently, the Japanese computer manufacturers moved quickly to displays that offer resolution on the order of 20 x 20 or better." (Stone 1984, 30)

23. There may have been other reasons as well. For example, the demand for a disk-based operating system (MS-DOS) lagged in Japan. Cassette tape data storage technology dominated the Japanese market much longer than it did in the United States; diskettes did not take the market by storm as they did in the United States.

24. "This study finds no support for the belief that Japanese skills in software development still appear to be inferior overall to those in the U.S." (Cusumano and Kemmerer 1990, 28)

25. "SuperSIGMA, a five-year extension of SIGMA for which MITI will reportedly request $775,000 (100 million yen) in first-year capitalization, will continue to develop interfaces for incompatible computers. Specifications for a standard operating system will also be devised, and the application of AI and expert system technology to automatic programming will be investigated." (Dambrot 1989, 80)

26. "Actually, there's more than market momentum attracting the Japanese to Unix. Lacking a substantial installed base tied to their own proprietary operating systems and historically unproductive in developing applications for other systems environments, software standardization has long been Japan's chief hope for penetrating world computer markets. Operating systems that have already emerged as standards are supported by well-stocked applications libraries and offer large potential hardware markets. Such are ideal conditions in which the Japanese can best exploit their vertical integration and manufacturing capabilities to concentrate on the production of low-cost hardware. . . . This, to date, has been their strategy in mainframes (with the exception of NEC) and personal computers." (Alster 1987, 24)

27. "Industry pays for roughly 10 per cent of the research done at Japanese universities . . . which is less than 0.5 per cent of total research by the private sector. . . . Why so low? Many industrialists blame the heavy hand of the ministry of Education, Science and Culture, or Monbusho as it is known in Japan. The national universities are Monbusho's creatures, and the ministry likes to keep them on a tight rein. In particular, Monbusho insists that all funding for the universities must go through its hands. Strict regulations and reams of red tape delay applications and discourage industry." (Johnstone 1987, 36)

28. "One result of the difference in the types of facilities is that research in Japan has concentrated on areas different from those in the U.S. Parallel computation and systems construction are two of the areas. Several factors account for this different concentration, and the computer community in Japan finds research in these areas relatively easy to conduct, while

in the U.S. it is relatively difficult. . . . Since 1980, public funding and private subsidies in Japan encourage university exploration in new computer systems and architectures. By contrast, U.S. institutions find it easier to purchase existing hardware and operating systems than to conduct research in these areas. Hence, research in novel architectures for hardware and software is less common in the U.S., where research is directed to problem areas served by existing computer systems." (Stone 1984, 28)

Through the 1980's, we have certainly seen this kind of "novel" research facilitated. However, Stone's qualitative conclusion that Japanese researchers find it relatively easy should not be construed to mean that their U.S. counterparts are blocked from new research. Clearly, the RISC architecture as well as significant work on parallel processing are the products of U.S. institutions.

29. This last point is particularly interesting in light of the concern expressed about maintaining compiler technology in a study of thirty software development houses in the United States and Japan in June 1984: "Many companies seem to contract out compiler development to smaller software houses because the nature of building most compilers is pedestrian. While compiler technology is relatively straightforward and perhaps cheaper to contract to a software house, the implications are far reaching. Software research is heading toward an integrated environment that covers the entire life cycle of software development. Research papers are being written about requirements and specification languages, design languages, program complexity measurement, knowledge-based Japanese fifth-generation languages, etc. All of these depend on mundane compiler technology as their base." (Zelkowitz et al. 1984, 65).

30. "The TRON goals depend fundamentally on open participation. TRON subprojects are aimed at developing 'standards', not products. Many commercial interests are participating, and each standard is intended to enable products of many vendors, although reasonably differentiated, to work together. . . .

"The TRON standards are not developed in a vacuum. They do not conflict with existing international standards, and they interface to these standards where appropriate (e.g. the OSI model, the Ada Language). TRON representatives participate in international standards activities, and the various TRON specifications are likely to be proposed for ISO/IEC JTC-1 standardization when completed. . . . TRON is funded purely by an industrial consortium; it receives no government support. . . . The TRON project was conceived from the start to include five principal subprojects. . . . Four of these subprojects have been well developed to date: ITRON, BTRON, CTRON, and the TRON CPU (or CHIP). Each of these has already led to both detailed specifications and products. ITRON, BTRON, and CTRON are each families of operating system interface specifications. The TRON CPU is a family of microprocessor architecture specifications. The fifth subproject, MTRON (for Macro TRON), is aimed at developing an intelligent distributed control for a complete network. It is in a much earlier stage of development." (Mooney 1991, 20)

31. "Among the exhibitors, all Japanese computer manufacturers were present with the notable exception of NEC. NEC has been reluctant to join the TRON project, because it is successfully marketing MS-DOS/WINDOWS/UNIX machines and because it has developed its own series of Intel compatible microprocessors, the V-series. The MPUs at the lower end are already replacing the Intel processors due to their superior performance. On the software side, NEC is however using ITRON specifications as realtime kernel in its realtime UNIX OS, called RX-UX832." (Wattenberg 1991, 17)

32. Existing computer manufacturers did consider, and some attempted, entering the personal computer market. For example, in 1975 IBM introduced the 5100 as a "portable computer." The 5100 was priced significantly out of the market, around $5,000 for a base system and closer to $9,000 for a more useful system. IBM had made the effort to pioneer the industry, but because its product cost too much or because of its culture was so fundamentally different from that of the computer hobbyists, it was unsuccessful.

33. Lotus 1-2-3 was written in 8086 assembly language, whereas Multiplan was written

162   THE INTERNATIONAL COMPUTER SOFTWARE INDUSTRY

in a higher-level language developed by Microsoft known as P-code (see Ichbiah and Knepper 1991 and Lammers 1986).

34. There are two interesting points here. First, DEC's VAX family was preceded by the PDP line. The VAX CPU development was constrained to retain compatibility with the PDP-"backward compatibility." Compatibility was retained by significantly increasing the size of the CPU instruction set. In the late 1980s, researchers at Thomas Watson Labs discovered that a reduced instruction set can make for much faster computing. The computer jargon for these differences is reduced-instruction-set computing (RISC) versus complex-instruction-set computing (CISC). Thus, all VAX users pay some overhead in reduced efficiency in order to retain PDP compatibility. A second point is that IBM was successful at designing the IBM 360 to retain compatibility.

REFERENCES

Albus, J., et al. 1986. *Japanese Technology Assessment: Computer Science, Opto-and Microelectronics, Mechatronics, Biotechnology.* Parkridge, N.J.: Noyes Data Corporation.
Alster, Norm. 1987. "Unix: Japan Jumps into the U.S. Computer Marketplace." *Electronic Business,* 1 March, 24–28.
Arthur, Brian. 1985. "Competing Technologies and Lock-In by Historical Small Events: The Dynamics of Allocation under Increasing Returns." Center for Economic Policy Research, Stanford University, Discussion Paper #43, Palo Alto, Calif.
Barney, Clifford. 1984. "AEA and EIA of Japan Agree to Joint Action on Software Protection, Investment and Taxes." *Electronics,* 5 April, 48–49.
Baumert, John. 1991. "New SEI Maturity Model Targets Key Practices." *IEEE Software* 8, no. 6 (November): 78–79.
Benson, David H. 1983. "A Field Study of End User Computing: Findings and Issues." *MIS Quarterly* 7, no. 4 (December): 35–45.
Cohen, Charles L. 1987. "Unix in Japan: Late Start, but Picking Up." *Electronics,* 15 October, 72.
Cortese, Amy, and Jane Morrissey. 1993. "Standard DOS Opens Up Japanese Market; U.S. Vendors Ramp Up to Meet Opportunity." *PC Week,* 22 February.
Cottrell, Thomas J. 1994. "Fragmented Standards and the Development of Japan's Microcomputer Software Industry." *Research Policy* 23, no. 2 (March): 143–74.
Cusumano, Michael A. 1991. *Japan's Software Factories: A Challenge to U.S. Management.* New York: Oxford University Press.
Cusumano, Michael A., and Chris F. Kemerer. 1990. "A Quantitive Analysis of U.S. and Japanese Practice and Performance in Software Development." *Management Science* 36, no. 11 (November): 1384–1406.
Dambrot, Stuart M. 1989. "Japan Prepares for Software Crisis." *Datamation,* 1 May, 80–83.
Data Analysis Group. 1988. *Computer Industry Forecasts.* Fourth Quarter (La Mesa, Calif.: DAG).
Davidson, William H. 1984. *The Amazing Race: Winning the Technorivalry with Japan.* New York: John Wiley and Sons.
Dempa Publications. 1988. *Japan Electronics Almanac 1988.* Tokyo: Dempa Publications Inc.
Electronics. 1985. "Will TRON Help Japan Catch Up in Software? (The Real-Time Operating Nucleus)," 22 July, 46–48.
———. 1986. "Systems and Software Emerge from the Laboratories," 4 September, 117–18.
———. 1988. "Overseas Market Report: Japan." 21 January, 59–63.
Farrell, Joseph, and Nancy Gallini. 1988. "Second-Sourcing as a Commitment: Monopoly

Incentives to Attract Competition." *Quarterly Journal of Economics* 103, no. 4 (November): 673–94.

Farrell, Joseph, and Garth Saloner. 1987. "Competition, Compatibility and Standards: The Economics of Horses, Penguins and Lemmings." In H. Landis Gabel, ed., *Product Standardization and Competitive Strategy*. Series eds., A. Bensoussan and P. A. Naert. Vol. 11. New York: North Holland.

————. 1988. "Coordination through Committees and Markets." *Rand Journal of Economics* 19, no. 2 (Summer): 235–52.

Freiberger, Paul, and Michael Swaine. 1984. *Fire in the Valley: The Making of the Personal Computer*. Berkeley, Calif.: Osborne/McGraw-Hill.

Hamilton, David P. 1993. "Technology: Compaq to Intensify PC Battle in Japan by Cutting Prices, Offering Service Plan." *Wall Street Journal*, 3 February.

Hannan, Michael T., and John Freeman. 1989. *Organizational Ecology*. Cambridge, Mass.: Harvard University Press.

Ichbiah, Daniel, and Susan L. Knepper. 1991. *The Making of Microsoft: How Bill Gates and His Team Created the World's Most Successful Software Company*. Rocklin, Calif.: Prima Publishing.

Japanese Information Service Industry Association. 1989, 1990, 1993. *White Paper on the Information Service Industry*. Tokyo: Ministry of International Trade and Industry.

Japan Personal Computer Software Association. 1993. *Japan's Market for Personal Computer Software*. Tokyo: JETRO.

Jeffries, Francis M. 1987. *Understanding the Japanese Industrial Challenge: From Automobiles to Software*. Poolesville, Md.: Jeffries & Associates, Inc.

Johnstone, Bob. 1986. "Japan Tackles Its Software Crisis." *New Scientist*, 30 January, 60–62.

————. 1987. "The Seedy Side of Research in Japan." *New Scientist*, 2 April, 33–36.

Katz, Michael, and Carl Shapiro. 1986. "Technology Adoption in the Presence of Network Externalities." *Journal of Political Economy* 94 (1986): 822–41.

Kurita, Shohei. 1988a. "AI in Japan Closing the Gap with the U.S." *Electronic Business*, 1 January, 110–11.

————. 1988b. "The PC Market in Japan: Where's IBM?" *Electronic Business*, 15 May, 56–57.

Lammers, Susan. 1986. *Programmers at Work: 1st Series*. Redmond, Wash.: Microsoft Press.

Letwin, Gordon. 1988. *Inside OS/2*. Redmond, Wash.: Microsoft Press.

Matutes, Carmen, and Pierre Regibeau. 1987. "Standardization in Multi-Component Industries." In H. Landis Gabel, ed., *Product Standardization and Competitive Strategy*. New York: North Holland.

Mooney, James. 1991. *Office of Naval Research Scientific Information Bulletin*. Arlington, Va.: Dept. of the Navy.

Nelson, Richard R., and Sidney G. Winter. 1982. *An Evolutionary Theory of Economic Change*. Cambridge, Mass.: Belknap Press.

New Scientist. 1987. "Japan Joins Action against the Software Pirates." 23 July, 30.

OECD, Committee for Information, Computer and Communication Policy. 1985. *Software: An Emerging Industry*. Information, Computer, and Communications Policy Series, no. 9. Washington, D.C.: OECD Publications and Information Center.

————. 1989. *The Internationalisation of Software and Computer Services*. Information, Computer, and Communications Policy Series, no. 17. Washington, D.C.: OECD Publications and Information Center.

Office of Technology Assessment. 1986. "SuperComputers: Government Plans and Policies." A Background Paper. Washington, D.C.: U.S. Government Printing Office, March.

PC Week. 1987. 21 July, 127.

Perratore, Ed. 1993. "News: Microbytes: IBM, Others Vie for Japanese PC Market." *Byte,*
    1 January.

Poe, Robert. 1987a. "The Era of Packaged Software Dawns in Japan." *Datamation,* 15 De-
    cember, 30.

———. 1987b. "Japan's TRON Tactics." *Datamation,* 1 October, 76.

Pope, Kyle, and David P. Hamilton. 1993. "New Battleground: U.S. Computer Firms, Ex-
    tending PC Wars, Charge into Japan." *Wall Street Journal,* 31 March.

Raike, William M. 1986a. "Byte Japan: An Innovative Program." *Byte* (May): 329–33.

———. 1986b. "Byte Japan: Perspectives on Hardware and Software." *Byte* (September):
    351–56.

Siegmann, Ken. 1988. "A Wealth of Opportunity Exists in the Japanese Market for U.S.
    Software." *PC Week,* 17 May, 124.

Stoll, Marilyn. 1988. "U.S. Computer Companies Must Meet Japanese on Their Terms, Study
    Says." *PC Week,* 22 August, 96.

Stone, Harold S. 1984. "Computer Research in Japan." *Computer* (March): 26–32.

Tajima, Denji, and Tomoo Matsubara. 1984. "Inside the Japanese Software Industry." *Com-
    puter* (March): 34–43.

Tanzer, Andrew. 1992. "Software on Black Ships: U.S. Dominates the Japanese Packaged
    Software Market." *Forbes,* 21 December.

Teece, David. 1986. "Profiting from Technological Innovation." *Research Policy* 15, no. 6:
    285–305.

Wattenberg, Ulrich. 1991. "Review of TRON-SHOW November '91." *Office of Naval Re-
    search Scientific Information Bulletin.* Arlington, Va.: Dept. of the Navy.

Williamson, Oliver E. 1985. *The Economic Institutions of Capitalism.* New York: Free Press.

Zelkowitz, Marvin V., et al. 1984. "Software Engineering Practices in the U.S. and Japan."
    Computer (June): 57–66.

7

The Dynamics of Market Structure and Innovation in the Western European Software Industry

Franco Malerba and Salvatore Torrisi

THE COMPETITIVE PERFORMANCE OF THE EUROPEAN SOFTWARE INDUSTRY

In 1992 the Western European market for information technologies was $157.2 billion (approximately 36 percent of the world market); in the United States it was $152.5 billion; and in Japan it was $75 billion. Software and services accounted for 41.5 percent of the total European information technologies market, against 59 percent in the United States and 40 percent in Japan (see Table 7-1).

In the European market, American firms such as Computer Associates, Microsoft, Lotus, and Ashton-Tate have a large market share in packaged software. In 1991 U.S. demand for software was 40 percent of the world market, and American firms had an 87 percent share of the world packaged software market. European firms accounted for 16 percent of world production of packaged software and consumed 41 percent. Japanese firms produced 4 percent of software packages worldwide and consumed 11 percent (EEC 1993). Few European independent software houses specialize in software packages; those that do include Software AG (Germany) and SAP (Germany). Most European firms specialize in professional services and custom software rather than software packages; they include Cap Gemini Sogeti (France), Finsiel (Italy), Sema Group (France, U.K.), and SD-Scicon (U.K.).

There are about 13,000 European software and services firms (EEC 1991). American and European hardware manufacturers control about 50 percent of the European market for packaged software (IDC 1990 estimates). In the late 1980s European hardware manufacturers began to devote a large portion of their R&D efforts to

Table 7-1.   World market for information technologies, 1992[a]

| | *Largest OECD markets* | | | | |
	United States	Japan	Western Europe	Rest of world	Total
Value (billion $)	152.5	75.0	157.2	47.5	432.2
Percentage of world market	35.3	17.4	36.5	11.0	100.0

Western European market by type of product

	Total	Hardware	Software and services	Packaged software	Professional services	Processing services	Network services
Value (billion $)	157.2	92.0	65.2	23.0	29.5	11.1	1.2
Percentage of world market	100.0	58.6	41.5	14.8	18.8	7.1	0.8

Packaged software by type of hardware in Western Europe[b]

	Large scale	Medium scale	Small scale	Single user	Total
Value (billion $)	4.9	7.4	7.4	3.7	23.4
Percent of world market	19.0	34.0	31.0	16.0	100.0

Source: EEC 1993, using IDC data.

[a] Information Technologies include office equipment, electronic data processing equipment, software and services. Estimates of information technology markets do not include office equipment. Values are expressed in billions of dollars at 1991 constant exchange rates. Because of rounding not all shares add to 100.

[b] According to IDC classification, mainframes correspond to large-scale computers (129 or more terminals (e.g., the IBM 308x and 3090 series and supercomputers), medium-scale computers include systems that support between 33 and 128 terminals in commercial environment (e.g., IBM system/38s and Dec VAX 11/750), small-scale computers include mini-computers that support an average of 2 to 32 terminals (e.g., IBM system 36 and AS/400 and Dec PDP-11/3X). Single-user computers include workstations such as Sun's, Digital's, and Hewlett-Packard's workstations, and personal computers.

software technology. In custom software and computer services, on the other hand, independent software suppliers control about 80 percent of the market (IDC 1990). Because of the high number of firms in this industry, producer concentration in the main European markets is relatively low. In 1989 the largest European specialized software house—Cap Gemini Sogeti (CGS), with $889.2 million in sales—had a European market share of only 2 percent, whereas the ten largest firms controlled about 10 percent of the European market. Among the four largest European markets, Italy has the highest market concentration (the ten largest firms controlled 33.6 percent of the market), while Germany has the lowest (the ten largest firms controlled 11.1 percent of the market) (see Table 7-2).

Most European firms sell primarily in their domestic markets. Even the largest European software and services firms show a limited degree of internationalization in exports and foreign direct investment. For instance, over 80 percent of SD-Scicon's revenues come from domestic sales in the United Kingdom, and 96 percent of Finsiel's sales are in Italy.

This chapter seeks to shed light on the reasons for this type of industrial structure, on international specialization and competitive performance, on the ways that the European software industry organizes its innovative process, and on the strategies followed by European software firms. A full understanding of the current structure and position of the European software industry must take into account the dynamics of competition in the world software industry, the working of vertical linkages, and the role of organizational and institutional factors. Weak European performance in packaged software and European specialization in custom software are related to the weakness of the European computer industry, early entry and market preemption by American packaged software producers, the fragmentation of regional demand among different domestic markets, and the lack of extensive interactions between European universities and industry.

The absence of a competitive European computer hardware industry has impeded the birth and performance of local producers of system software and packaged software. As we discuss later, European computer firms have been relatively unsuccessful in the past thirty years. As a consequence, during the 1970s and 1980s would be European entrants in systems software and packaged software could not benefit from cooperation and interaction with technologically advanced and commercially successful European hardware producers, and were not able to interact closely with American hardware producers that were operating at the technological frontier. For example, British firms usually gained access to specifications of new hardware products one or two years later than American software houses (Ashworth 1985).

This situation has been worsened by early entry into Europe and market preemption by the successful American system and packaged software firms such as Microsoft and Lotus. These firms benefited from continuous interactions and cooperation with highly competitive hardware manufacturers in the United States (such as the early cooperation between Microsoft and IBM in the development of DOS) and therefore could rapidly adapt their products to state-of-the-art hardware technologies. They also made major R&D investments in new standard software packages because they had a potentially large internal market. Successful American software houses entered all the European countries simultaneously, deterring entry by European firms and in the meantime reaching a certain overall threshold of sales in Europe. Their link with American hardware manufactures also gave American packaged software firms access to hardware producers' extensive sales networks.

European firms focused on relatively small national markets. The fragmentation of the European markets is due to many historical, cultural, linguistic, fiscal, and legal differences, a full explanation of which is beyond the scope of this work. These differences have reduced the opportunities for economies of scale and scope that are so important for commercially successful software packages. They have favored the

Table 7-2. Market share of independent vendors in the European software industry, 1987 and 1989 (percentage)

	Europe		Germany		U.K.		France		Italy	
	1987	1989	1987	1989	1987	1989	1987	1989	1987	1989
Market leader	2.2	1.9	5.6	3.37	5.1	3.44	5.0	5.46	9.7	13.33
Top five	7.6	6.4	12.0	7.52	19.0	12.95	17.0	16.79	17.0	27.31
Top ten	12.0	10.24	18.5	11.12	29.0	20.85	28.0	25.25	24.0	33.64
Top fifteen	16.0	13.24	23.0	13.72	34.0	25.14	34.0	31.26	29.0	38.27

Source: Elaboration on data from IDC 1988 and 1990.

development of a European industry composed of small and medium-sized firms that offer customized software and services, system integration, and hardware resale. The absence of a strong European hardware industry has favored the diffusion of standard software packages designed for American computers.

With the partial exception of Germany, the European software industry also has suffered from weak links between industry and university. In the United States, many innovative firms have emerged from university research programs; although the interactions between industry and academia vary, in general, European universities have contributed less to the local software industry than U.S. universities have in America. Even in the United Kingdom, which has an outstanding tradition of academic research in computer science, communication between industry and university has produced few products or spin-offs. The only European university spin-off that has gained a leading world position in packaged software is Germany's Software AG. As a consequence, EEC technology policy and a few national programs are now promoting cooperation between industry and university. (The EEC, or European Economic Community, became the European Union (EU) in 1994.)

Finally, previous national policies in Europe have focused mainly on computer hardware and on building a few "national champions." (National champions are large domestic firms—often created by mergers of several firms—that receive state support through direct subsidies and preferential government procurement contracts.) Only recently have some European countries and the EEC launched policies aimed at software. The regional software industry is hampered by weak legal (patent and copyright) protection in most European countries, which increases transaction costs and contributes to national specialization in customized software and services (see chapter 10 for an evaluation of the various effects of different property rights regimes).

The following sections in this chapter discuss the evolution of the European computer industry (one major factor responsible for the current status of the European software industry); the main market segmentations; the role of universities in R&D and production of skilled software developers; firms' strategies; the differences among European national markets; and the major features of European public policy.

THE EVOLUTION OF THE EUROPEAN COMPUTER INDUSTRY

One factor that has hindered the development of a successful European packaged software industry is the weakness of the European computer industry, with the partial exception of Germany. This unsatisfactory performance dates back only to the 1960s; before the late 1950s European scientific and technical capabilities in the information technology sector were in fact nearly as strong as those of American firms. The United Kingdom provides the most striking example of early entry, followed by rapid decline, in the computer industry. The United Kingdom has an advanced scientific tradition in computer science that dates back to the 1930s and was strengthened by the military alliance with the United States during World War II. During the war the British mathematician Alan Turing worked for the British Ministry of Defense on decryption of German secret communication codes. Soon after the war, Cambridge and Manchester Universities made considerable contributions to basic and applied research in computer science and to the development of the first British computers.

In 1948 Manchester University developed a prototype computer—the Manchester Mark 1—and in 1949 Cambridge University developed the EDSAC (electronic delay storage automatic computer) under the direction of Maurice Wilkes, who in 1951 invented the concept of microprogramming. Some British companies such as Marconi, General Electric Co. (GEC), EMI, and Ferranti entered the industry during the late 1950s and the 1960s. As these companies encountered problems they gradually withdrew from the industry, leaving ICL the only large computer firm in Britain. In 1990 ICL was taken over by Fujitsu. Since the late 1980s many British software firms have been taken over by foreign firms: Istel by AT&T (United States) in 1988, SD-Scicon by Electronic Data Systems (EDS) (United States) in 1991, Hoskyns by Cap Gemini (France) in 1990, and Logica by Santa Cruz Operations (United States) in 1992. As a consequence of these changes in ownership, few British firms maintain an international position in software services (see chapter 8 for a more detailed discussion).

As in the United Kingdom, in France the first steps in the new computer industry were taken for scientific and military purposes. The first French electronic computer was developed in 1953 by Société d'Electroniques et d'Automatisme (SEA) for the French Ministère des Armes. Unlike U.K. universities, however, French universities had few research programs in computer science. The leading French firm, Bull, entered the computer business only in the late 1950s. In 1958 Bull launched the Gamma 3 ET computer to compete with the IBM 650 mainframe; but Bull was unable to match the technological or commercial expertise of American firms, and in 1964 General Electric took control of the firm. In 1970 G.E. sold its share in Bull to Honeywell, and in 1975 Honeywell-Bull and Compagnie International pour l'Informatique (CII) merged into a single company: CII-Honeywell-Bull. The French government acquired a majority stake in CII-Honeywell-Bull, but the company was unsuccessful during the late 1970s and the 1980s. After Honeywell withdrew in 1990, the French government acquired complete control of Groupe Bull. Since 1991, Bull has increased its commitment to software and services, especially in Unix applications.

The case of Germany is quite different. During the 1930s and 1940s Germany accumulated significant scientific competence and technical know-how in the field of electronics, magnetism, and the theory of computer languages. After the war, the German scientist Konrad Zuse established a company specializing in computers for scientific applications. Universities and "bridging institutions" that played a major role in the birth of the German computer industry included Berlin University, the Max Planck Institute at Göttingen University, the Munich Institute of Technology, and the Institute for Practical Mathematics at Darmstadt. In 1964 the German firm Zuse was sold to Brown Boveri (Switzerland) and in 1971 to Siemens, which became the leading computer hardware firm in Germany. In 1989 with the takeover of Nixdorf (the other main German computer firm), Siemens acquired a diversified expertise in computers and software. Siemens-Nixdorf has become a major European producer of software.[1]

Other European countries entered the computer industry on a smaller scale. In 1958 Philips started its activities in computers with the acquisition of Electrologica, but in 1990, after a long period of unsuccessful performance, the firm abandoned the computer business. Olivetti entered the computer business relatively early (1959) with the ELEA 9003. Financial problems arising from its acquisition of the American typewriter producer Underwood forced Olivetti to enter a joint venture with General Electric (1964) and to leave the computer industry altogether in 1968. At the end of the 1970s Olivetti re-entered the computer industry and recently has devoted substantial resources to software and services.

MAIN MARKET SEGMENTS AND TYPES OF FIRMS

We analyze the European software industry by separating software products into two broad classes: packaged software and custom software and services. *Software packages* include programs that are developed to perform either cross-sector functions (such as scientific and engineering calculations) or sector-specific functions (in the financial sector and retailing, for example). According to the International Data Corporation (IDC 1990), software packages include the following subclasses of products: system software (operating systems and utilities), programming languages, application tools (such as computer-aided software engineering [CASE] tools), and application solutions. *Custom software and services* include software systems developed for medium-sized customers (so-called turnkey systems) and large customers (system integration services that are offered through long-term contracts), professional services (customized software, consulting, professional training, and maintenance), facilities management (at the customer EDP [electronic data processing] center), and EDP services (such as problem solving, transaction processing, and on-line information services).

The European market for software packages is expected to grow more rapidly than that for custom software and services. IDC estimates show that in 1992 the packaged software market was 35.4 percent of total traded software and services, but the share of packaged software has increased more rapidly than services since that time (EEC 1993). Within the packaged software market, the market for application solutions is expected to increase more rapidly than the market for system software (14 percent in the period 1991–96 versus 7 percent). Within the computer services market, the most dynamic segments are system integration (19 percent projected growth rate in the period 1991–96), facilities management (22 percent growth) and turnkey systems (12 percent). Professional services and EDP services, which were internationally the only types of computer services marketed in the 1960s, are not expected to grow.

Because data on firms and the organization of innovative processes in the European software industry are not widely available to the public, we conducted two surveys on the innovative activities of software firms in Europe. The survey respondents provided information on written questionnaires and in direct interviews. The surveys included questions on the competitive performance of firms, the types of innovations undertaken, the sources of technological change and the organization of the innovative process, the type of skills needed and the technological strategies followed.

Survey A: The first survey was conducted in 1990 through direct interviews with project managers of fifty-one firms located in Italy, the United Kingdom, France, and Germany (Malerba and Torrisi 1992; Torrisi 1994). The geographic coverage of

European countries was not balanced: twenty-five firms were Italian, seventeen were British, three were French, and one was German.

Survey B: The second field analysis was conducted between 1992 and 1993 as part of the EEC research project "Research and Technology Management in Enterprises: Issues for Community Policy" (Malerba and Torrisi 1993). Project managers from sixty-five firms in nine countries (Germany, France, the United Kingdom, Italy, Netherlands, Spain, Belgium, Portugal, and Greece) were interviewed. The geographic distribution of firms was more balanced than in Survey A. The database included six German firms, four French firms, six British firms, seventeen Italian firms, three Dutch firms, eleven Spanish firms, three Belgian firms, six Portuguese firms, and nine Greek firms. The firms interviewed were classified according to size: there were forty-four small firms (fewer than 500 employees), sixteen large firms (more than 500 employees), and 5 not classified.

In both surveys firms were also classified as follows:

- *Hardware producers:* There were eight in Survey A and twelve in Survey B.
- *Independent software houses:* These offer either "cross-industry" packages (for "horizontal" markets such as electronic spreadsheets and text and image processing) and industry-specific or "vertical" packages (such as packages for client portfolio management in the banking sector, for logistics in industry, and for transportation and retailing). There were twenty-four in Survey A and twenty in Survey B.
- *Suppliers of professional services and system integration services:* These include a variety of firms. Traditional suppliers of EDP (electronic data processing) services offer data elaborations and on-line access to databases, to timesharing services, or to application tools. Suppliers of professional services may also offer facility management (at the customer site), training, and consulting services. A relatively new category of professional service suppliers is *system integrators and turnkey systems suppliers,* which integrate software from different suppliers (such as accounting and payroll systems) for specific customers. System integrators and turnkey systems suppliers also offer in-house customized software, training, and consultancy services. Hardware and software distributors, including original equipment manufacturers (OEMs) and value-added retailers (VARs), also may offer professional services and resell hardware and software packages by adding custom software and services.[2] There were nineteen of these firms in Survey A and thirty-three in Survey B.
- *Users* were not directly interviewed in Survey A or Survey B. Many large users, however, produce a large amount of software in-house (especially applications software, custom software, and services). According to *Datamation* estimates, externally obtained software accounted for about 2 percent of the total information technology expenses of American firms in 1978 and about 10 percent in 1982 (OECD 1985). More recently, a British research survey of 1,354 users confirmed the importance of nontraded, internally developed software. The share of nontraded software within total software expenditures varies among hardware classes: it is large for minicomputers (27 percent of users' total software budget) and mainframes (24 percent) and smaller for microcomputers (15 percent) (Brady-Quintas 1991). Users have also codeveloped soft-

ware packages with software firms that have then been launched on the market. This codevelopment has been helped by the introduction of new techniques for software production that have facilitated the development of applications by users (ibid.).

Firms in Survey B were grouped into two classes, according to the country of activity: (1) Leading countries (leaders): Germany, France, the United Kingdom, Italy, the Netherlands, and Belgium, all characterized by high income per capita and high levels of technological capability; and (2) Follower countries (followers): Spain, Portugal, and Greece, characterized by low income per capita and comparatively low levels of technological capability.

The significance of differences among responses given by different groups of firms was subject to a chi-square test, and the tables show the values of the chi-square statistic that support rejection of the null hypothesis (no significant difference among groups) at the 5 percent significance level.

SKILLS IN EUROPE

Shortages of advanced skills have been a serious obstacle to the growth and competitiveness of European software firms. Unlike hardware, software production is a labor-intensive activity that more closely resembles a craft than an industry. As a consequence, productivity growth in software has been lower than in hardware, and the share of firms' budgets devoted to software has increased. Productivity in software may be improved by the use of new development tools, such as fourth-generation languages, object-oriented languages, and computer-aided software engineering (CASE) tools. But the diffusion of new development techniques among software developers has been slow. The adoption of new programming languages and other tools often requires modification of programs developed with the old tools and creates compatibility problems. Indeed, many widespread programming languages (such as Basic and Fortran) are improved versions of products introduced during the 1960s.

In Europe, the increased demand for software development skills reflects the need to improve the quality of software products, to increase the productivity of programmers, and to reduce software maintenance costs. Table 7-3 shows the results of a survey of newspaper advertisements in the United Kingdom for 1988–89 (*Computer Weekly* 1990, 342). The first column shows the demand for three categories of skills: programming languages, database management systems, and operating systems. For each of these categories, we provide the distribution of total demand for languages and systems.

The increasing demand for skills has been associated with major changes in skills requirements. The second column shows the percentage increase in share of advertisements for each type of skill between 1988 and 1989. The survey indicates a shift from skills related to mainframes to skills related to minicomputers and personal computers. There is also an increasing demand for skills in the management of backlogs of applications and standardized (packaged) solutions on new operating systems (for example, IBM AS/400 and Unix). Demand for skills in customized applications on old proprietary systems (such as IBM MVS and System 38, and Dec Vax VMS) declined during this period. The most requested software language and development

Table 7-3. Information technology skills required in the U.K. market, 1988–89

	% of jobs advertised requiring a particular skill	% change from 1988 to 1989
Programming languages		
Cobol	37.4	−7.0
Fourth-generation language	8.9	50.0
RPG3	7.6	−6.1
PL/1	5.2	26.5
C	5.1	−9.8
Basic	5.1	−0.8
RPG2	3.5	2.7
Quickbuild	2.9	11.9
Powerhouse	2.7	47.2
Assembler	2.1	7.2
Database management systems		
DB2	5.8	74.7
IDMS	5.8	3.1
Oracle	5.1	32.0
Adabas	3.2	52.7
DL1	3.2	−3.0
IMS	2.4	7.1
Ingres	2.1	76.2
dBase	2.1	27.7
DMS	0.5	−14.6
IDS	0.3	70.1
Operating systems		
IBM AS/400	6.8	279.2
IBM MVS	6.0	−12.1
ICL VME	5.9	7.5
IBM System 38	5.9	−21.8
Unix	4.7	7.5
Pick	3.8	13.9
DEC VAX VMS	3.7	−10.6
IBM System 36	2.0	−30.2
MS-DOS	1.8	−5.3
IBM DOS/VSE	0.5	−32.0

Source: Computer Weekly 1990, 342.

expertise is in fourth-generation languages (4GL) and database management systems (DBMSs) (including relational DBMSs like DB2, Oracle, Ingres, and Adabas) while there is a decrease in demand for skills in traditional programming languages (such as Cobol, Basic, and RPG (Report Program Generator)). Moreover, the *Computer Weekly* survey shows a high demand for skills in structured design methodologies, which reflects the need to overcome problems of low productivity and high maintenance costs. With respect to the professional profile of the personnel required, the survey shows the increasing importance of systems engineers (or analysts): their wages grew 11.6 percent between 1988 and 1989, those of system programmers grew 6.8 percent, and analysts/programmers 8 percent. This trend is corroborated by other surveys in the United States and Japan.

In addition to changing their skills requirements, European firms are confronted with the need to integrate and manage a variety of different skills. The results from Survey B illustrate the different skills that are important for the innovative activities of European software firms. Firms consider systems engineering to be the most relevant area of competence; the second most important is computing (analytical and programming skills). Experience with applications, services, and project management is also considered important by the interviewed firms.[3] Skills in marketing and sales are considered somewhat relevant. More generic proficiencies (for example, in mathematics) are considered less relevant. Interestingly, there are no sharp differences in the responses from different countries, except for experience with applications and services (which are considered more important by firms in the leading countries than by those in the follower countries). There are differences, however, between the responses of hardware manufacturers and those of specialized software firms. Electronics engineering and marketing skills are quite important for the software-related innovative activities of hardware manufacturers. These firms recognize that the integration of competencies in electronics engineering, computer science, system engineering, and marketing critically affects innovative performance (see Table 7-4).[4]

The most serious skills shortage identified by European firms is in management, systems engineering, and applications and services (Table 7-5). Their responses suggest that the leading countries suffer from a lack of skilled personnel more than the follower countries. The gap between leaders and followers is particularly large in applications capabilities and systems engineering skills. As one would expect, hardware manufacturers perceive bottlenecks in the labor market to be less problematic than software firms do, perhaps in part because hardware manufacturers invest fairly heavily in on-the-job training. But even large firms have shortages of personnel with project management and systems engineering skills. There are significant differences in the responses of packaged software producers and services suppliers with respect to the lack of systems engineers (considered not important by packaged software producers) and project managers (considered not important by services suppliers) (see Table 7-5).

Table 7-4. Value of internal competencies to European information technology firms (average scores)

	Math.	Comp.	Syst.	Eng.	Appl.	Mktg.	Comm.	Mgmt.
Europe	2.3	4.4	4.6	2.5	4.2	3.6	3.4	4.1
Leaders	2.2	4.4	4.6	2.6	4.4	3.7	3.7	4.1
Followers	2.4	4.5	4.7	2.4	3.9	3.5	3.0	4.1
Chi square[a]	0.42	0.40	—	4.66	0.61	0.41	4.30	0.91
Hardware	2.2	4.5	4.8	3.6	3.9	4.0	3.5	3.8
Packaged software	2.6	4.6	4.8	2.3	4.3	3.6	3.6	4.5
Services	2.2	4.4	4.6	2.4	4.3	3.6	3.4	4.1
Chi square[b]	3.35	4.29	—	5.14	5.28	2.05	0.78	6.64

Source: Malerba and Torrisi 1993.

Abbreviations: Math. = mathematics; Comp. = computing; Syst. = software system engineers; Eng. = electronics engineers; Appl. = experience with applications and services; Mktg. = marketing; Comm. = distribution and sales; Mgmt. = project management.

[a] Chi square = 2 degrees of freedom (d.f.); 5 percent probability point = 5.99
[b] Chi square = 4 d.f.; 5 percent probability point = 9.49
Scores: from 1 (not relevant) to 5 (very relevant).

Table 7-5. Relevance of bottlenecks in competencies to European information technology firms (average scores)

	Math.	Comp.	Syst.	Eng.	Appl.	Mktg.	Comm.	Mgmt.
Europe	1.5	2.0	3.0	1.9	3.3	3.0	3.1	3.8
Leaders	1.5	1.9	2.7	1.8	2.9	2.9	3.0	3.6
Followers	1.4	2.1	3.4	2.0	3.8	3.1	3.1	3.9
Chi square[a]	1.77	1.64	2.13	0.36	3.52	1.87	3.57	3.43
Hardware	1.6	2.4	3.0	2.7	2.7	2.2	1.8	3.4
Packaged software	1.3	1.4	2.6	1.6	3.2	3.1	3.4	4.2
Services	1.5	2.2	3.2	1.8	3.5	3.2	3.3	3.6
Chi square[b]	11.55	10.30	3.67	13.03	3.97	8.04	1.91	3.25

Source: Malerba and Torrisi 1993.

Abbreviations: Math. = mathematics; Comp. = computing; Syst. – software system engineers; Eng. = electronics engineers; Appl. = experience with applications and services; Mktg. = marketing; Comm. = distribution and sales; Mgmt. = project management.

[a]Chi square = 2 degrees of freedom (d.f.); 5 percent probability point = 5.99

[b]Chi square = 4 d.f.; 5 percent probability point = 9.49

Scores: from 1 (not relevant) to 5 (very relevant).

Finally, among European software firms the hiring and internal training of personnel are important factors in the innovative activities of firms (see Table 7-6). This is consistent with the labor-intensive character of this industry and the importance of tacit, person-embodied knowledge in software innovation. Differences among firms are apparent here as well. Training on the job is important in the software industry because the skills required are often very specialized (for example, image processing) and may not be taught in the university system. Skills shortages in software development are exacerbated somewhat by the stronger orientation of much European higher

Table 7-6. Importance of technology-related activities to European information technology firms (average scores)

	Basic	Appl.	NPrd.	NProc.	PDes.	PEng.	ProcEng.	Mon.	Lic.	Train.
Europe	1.8	3.8	4.2	3.4	3.3	3.9	4.1	3.6	3.0	4.0
Leaders	1.9	4.0	4.3	3.7	3.4	3.9	4.3	3.6	3.2	4.1
Followers	1.5	3.5	4.0	3.0	3.1	3.9	3.7	3.5	2.7	4.0
Chi square[a]	2.02	2.61	1.73	3.86	1.07	7.94	7.92	1.22	0.93	0.72
Hardware	2.5	3.9	4.2	3.3	4.2	3.7	3.8	3.3	3.4	3.5
Packaged software	1.7	3.8	4.4	3.5	2.9	3.9	4.3	3.5	2.5	4.0
Services	1.6	3.8	4.1	3.5	3.2	4.0	4.0	3.7	3.0	4.2
Chi square[b]	4.23	0.71	3.88	0.28	3.29	2.26	6.74	0.41	1.95	3.38

Source: Malerba and Torrisi 1993.

Abbreviations: Basic = Basic research; Appl. = Applied research; NPrd. = New product development; NProc. = New process development; PDes. = Product design; PEng. = Product engineering (improvement); ProcEng. = Process engineering and quality assurance; Mon. = Monitoring sources of scientific and technical information; Lic. = Licensing; Train. = Training in the use and application of new technologies.

[a]Chi square = 2 degrees of freedom (d.f.); 5 percent probability point = 5.99

[b]Chi square = 4 degrees of freedom (d.f.); 5 percent probability point = 9.49

Scores: from 1 (not relevant) to 5 (very relevant).

education toward pure science than toward applied engineering (Irvine, Martin, and Isard 1991). Other problems in skills training are related to the scope of specialization. The software industry requires multidisciplinary education (information technology skills combined with business and language capabilities), which is not widely available in the current European educational system (Norton 1991).

THE ROLE OF UNIVERSITIES

The different educational systems of the European countries have affected the supply of applied skills to European software firms. German firms report less serious bottlenecks in the supply of systems engineers than French and Italian firms. These differences in perceptions are consistent with the diverse structure of the national educational systems in Europe. The German educational system is oriented toward applied science and technical training and the German Technische Hochschulen (technical high schools) have played an important role in the provision of technical expertise and the diffusion of technical information to small and medium-sized firms. Our survey shows, however, that German firms have difficulty finding employees with advanced management and marketing skills.

The European universities are important in the generation of new basic and applied knowledge but not in the development of new software products. They have few direct links with the software industry, as shown by the irrelevance of consulting and university spin-offs in the survey results for both leading and following countries (Table 7-7). This situation contrasts with that of the United States, where several firms have been founded by academics and a number of languages and software packages have resulted from the interactions between industry and university.

The role of European universities in basic and applied research can be assessed by examining cooperation between industry and university within the EEC's ESPRIT

Table 7-7. The university role in European software development (average scores)

	Basic	Appl.	Train.	Cons.	Pack.	Firm
Europe	3.2	3.4	2.3	2.2	1.6	1.9
Leaders	3.1	3.4	2.5	2.3	1.8	1.9
Followers	3.3	3.3	2.2	2.1	1.4	1.9
Chi square[a]	1.05	0.18	2.65	0.88	1.11	0.13
Hardware	3.1	3.3	2.5	2.6	1.7	2.1
Packaged software	3.4	3.7	2.0	1.7	1.8	1.9
Services	3.2	3.3	2.6	2.5	1.6	1.9
Chi square[b]	5.44	7.95	1.62	7.70	0.93	7.05

Source: Malerba and Torrisi 1993.

Abbreviations: Basic = Basic and general knowledge relevant to the firm; Appl. = Specific applied knowledge; Train. = Training; Cons. = Consulting; Pack. = New software packages; Firm = New firms.

[a] Chi square = 2 degrees of freedom (d.f.); 5 percent probability point = 5.99

[b] Chi square = 4 degrees of freedom (d.f.); 5 percent probability point = 9.49

Scores: from 1 (not relevant) to 5 (very relevant).

(European Strategic Program for Research and Development in Information Technologies) program. (The first ESPRIT initiatives were undertaken in 1984; the program is discussed in more detail later in this chapter.) Table 7-8 shows the number of ESPRIT projects in software technology that involve universities and "bridging" institutions. (Bridging institutions are organizations whose aim is the diffusion of scientific and technical knowledge to business enterprises—for instance, through consulting and training.) The British universities are the most active, followed by the German, Italian, and French. France and Italy have more bridging institutions than the United Kingdom and Germany. This may reflect the fact that in Germany, as noted above, universities have a tradition of applied research and engineering. The application-oriented approach of German universities helped foster direct interactions with industry, reducing the need for bridging institutions. In the United Kingdom, university budget constraints and national policies (such as the Alvey Program, which is described in detail in Chapter 8 in this volume) have stimulated cooperation between universities and industry and the creation of informal networks of researchers, giving British universities a larger presence in ESPRIT projects. In Italy, in contrast, weak university-industry relations are partially counterbalanced by the bridging institutions. There are, finally, very few cases in which universities or research centers play the role of the coordinator within the ESPRIT research networks (see Table 7-8). This may reflect a general lack of organizational skills within these scientific institutions or their limited political influence within the regional program.

STRATEGY, ORGANIZATION AND INNOVATION AT THE FIRM LEVEL

Changing Patterns of Specialization

The increasing relevance of software and services in information technology has forced the major European hardware producers—Siemens-Nixdorf, Olivetti, and

Table 7-8. ESPRIT software projects that involved universities and bridging institutions

	Germany	France	United Kingdom	Italy	Bel- gium	Nether- lands	Greece	Spain	Portugal	Ireland	Total
Universities	25	9	33	12	9	10	2	2	1	5	108
of which:											
Coordinator	1		2			1				1	5
Partner	22	6	30	12	7	9	2	2	1	2	93
Subcontractor	2	3	1		2					2	10
Bridging institutions	2	13	5	11	0	0	2	0	1	1	35
of which:											
Coordinator	1			3							4
Partner	1	10	5	8			2		1	1	28
Subcontractor		3									3
Total[a]	27	22	38	23	9	10	4	2	2	6	143

Source: Calculations using Commission of the European Communities data (EEC 1990).

[a]The total number of projects in the table is larger than the real number of projects because some institutions were involved in more than one project.

Bull—to focus their core activities and strategies on software and services in order to maintain a satisfactory performance in the information technology industry. All of these companies have undertaken major restructuring and reorganization.

For the great majority of European firms that specialize in custom software, professional services, information system consultancy, development, and training (Cap Gemini, Sema Group, Logica, and SD-Scicon), the declining importance of the custom software and services market has forced them to refocus their business activities on faster-growing market segments such as packaged software. For a firm in professional services, however, the cost of switching to packaged software can be very high: The development and marketing of packaged software more closely resembles manufacturing than professional services. The distribution of packaged software is based on the sales networks of computer firms, value-added retailers (VARs), large distributors, and computer shops. In contrast, professional services are more customer-oriented and rely on individualized marketing strategies rather than those associated with mass marketing.

The Barriers to Entry into Different Firm Groups

Survey A highlighted the difficulties for European firms of switching from custom to packaged software (see Table 7-9). Fifty-one European software firms identified the major barriers to entry into their most relevant market segment:[5] A lack of in-depth knowledge of users' needs (generally acquired through long-term relationships with customers) and reputation are major barriers to entry into all the market segments considered in the survey. Reputation is particularly important for entry into system software and services market. But marketing and large distribution networks and financial resources are most important for entry into packaged software.

Hardware firms had more difficulty than software firms gaining access to information about users' needs.[6] For this reason hardware firms frequently enter the European software industry through cooperative agreements with users or with firms that specialize in software.

Table 7-9. Entry barriers for different types of European software producers (average scores)

Firm type	Finances	Network	Users	Tecskil	Image	Culture
Hardware and software	3.86	4.00	4.57	4.10	4.00	2.80
Software and services	2.83	3.25	3.64	3.20	3.68	2.69
System software and utilities	1.50	2.00	3.50	5.00	4.00	4.00
Packaged software	3.50	3.36	3.73	3.00	3.45	3.50
Services (EDP, consulting, training)	2.23	3.36	3.73	3.14	4.36	2.50
Technical services (software development tools, expert systems)	3.50	3.25	3.25	3.00	2.25	1.00

Source: Malerba and Torrisi 1992.

Abbreviations: Finances = Financial resources; Network = Marketing and sales network; Users = Knowledge of users' environment; Tecskil = Technological skills and capabilities; Image = Image/reputation; Culture = Corporate culture.

Scores: from 1 (not relevant) to 5 (very relevant).

High costs are one reason European suppliers of custom software and professional services find it difficult to move into packaged software or to package their customized software for multi-client markets. More external use of new development techniques, such as fourth-generation languages and object-oriented languages, however, could make it easier for software firms to diversify. Object-oriented languages in particular may expand reusability of software modules (objects) for different uses, which would also lower firms' costs and make entry easier for European firms as well as for their American and Japanese competitors. The shift from customized to packaged software is not only a technical matter, however; firms also must overcome organizational, marketing, and managerial obstacles.

Increasing Firm Size and Internationalization

The increasing commitment in software by the major European and American hardware producers and by new big new international players such as EDS, TRW, Andersen Consulting, and Computer Sciences has forced European independent software firms to increase their size, leading to a number of mergers and acquisitions and a higher level of market concentration since the mid-1980s.

European firms also have attempted to increase their exports. Within the sample of sixty-five firms in Survey B, the Italian and Greek firms are the least internationalized (with percentages of export sales lower than 10 percent), while the German firms are the most internationalized (with more than 50 percent of revenues coming from abroad). The high level of internationalization of British firms (about 40 percent) reflects the inclusion of large multinational firms, such as IBM and Reuters.

The main motive for international mergers and acquisitions that have taken place in the European software industry seems to be to reach the size necessary to internationalize successfully. British and French firms have begun to set up international linkages with suppliers, other software firms, and users. The French firm Cap Gemini has shown a particularly high propensity to grow internationally through acquisitions. In 1991 Cap Gemini acquired 34 percent of the German Debis GEI (a Daimler-Benz subsidiary), in 1990 the British firm Hoskyns, and in 1992 the Swedish firm Programmator and Volmac of Norway. Some large British firms have also grown through mergers and acquisitions. In 1988 the Cap Group merged with the French Sema Metra (to form Sema Group) and Scicon with System Designers (to form SD-Scicon).[7] Success in the domestic market may improve a firm's prospects of success internationally; several software firms have entered foreign markets after reaching a "critical size" in their domestic market (for example, Reuters in the United Kingdom with packaged banking and financial services software). Although concentration (the share of output by the largest producers) in the European software industry is likely to continue to grow, the level of concentration should remain lower than in the European computer hardware industry, where the number of suppliers is declining very rapidly.

Some European firms active in custom software have moved into new and dynamic segments of the services market, focusing on system integration and facilities management; the United Kingdom's Hoskyns diversified into facility management and SD-Scicon into system integration. There are only a few cases in Europe of growth driven by economies of scale and scope. For example, Cap Gemini is able to exploit these economies in knowledge, organization, and methodology of production. More so than its European competitors, Cap Gemini has shown a great ability to coordinate an international network of subsidiaries that reuse a stock of common knowledge for diverse markets and customers.

Organization

Different types of European software firms organize their innovative activities very differently. Several software houses and suppliers of standard packages organize their R&D primarily around products and markets (58 percent of surveyed firms); service firms and system integrators organize R&D around projects (45 percent of surveyed firms). In most of the smallest firms, R&D is organized around projects, whereas larger firms are mainly organized around products and markets. Several firms claim that their whole organization relies heavily on informal communications. Many firms rely on internal transfer of personnel and multidisciplinary development teams, both of which foster close working relationships among different functions within the firm, which in turn appear to support innovative performance in this industry. Finally, most software firms have a chief technical officer responsible for all technology-related activities.

Competitive Factors

Long-term relationships with users are a major competitive factor for European software firms (see results from Survey B in Table 7-10). This factor is more important for service vendors than for vendors of packaged software. Financial resources, proprietary technology, and consolidation of firms' positions in market niches are also important sources of competitive advantage. Diversification is less important than interactions with users and consolidation in specific market niches. Even the most

Table 7-10. Relevance of competitive factors for European software firms (average scores)

	Tech.	Fin.	Niche	Div.	Users	HW mfrs.
Europe	3.8	3.6	3.6	3.1	4.0	3.1
Leaders	3.6	3.7	3.6	2.9	4.2	2.9
Followers	4.1	3.3	3.4	3.1	3.7	3.3
Chi square[a]	2.53	3.85	0.50	1.21	7.89	3.22
Hardware	3.9	3.2	3.3	2.6	4.0	3.0
Packaged software	4.3	3.8	3.5	3.3	3.8	3.2
Services	3.6	3.6	3.7	3.0	4.2	3.1
Chi square[b]	6.89	6.79	2.46	4.58	5.74	1.11

Source: Malerba and Torrisi 1993.

Abbreviations: Tech. = In-house technology development; Fin. = Financial resources; Niche = Consolidation in a market niche; Div. = diversification; Users = Consolidated user interactions; HW mfrs. = Consolidated relationships with hardware manufacturers.

[a] Chi square = 2 degrees of freedom (d.f.); 5 percent probability point = 5.99

[b] Chi square = 4 degrees of freedom (d.f.); 5 percent probability point = 9.49

Scores: from 1 (not relevant) to 5 (very relevant).

internationalized firms are not highly diversified, reflecting the constraints of present patterns of specialization by European firms. These internationalized European firms focus more heavily on technology developed in-house than do the less internationalized firms. This tendency may reflect internationalized firms' strategy of locating internal R&D activities in countries that have a comparative advantage in these activities.

The Acquisition of Technical Knowledge and the Sources of Innovation

European software firms acquire knowledge through a variety of channels, as Survey A and Survey B show.[8] Respondents to Survey B reported that customers are the major source of knowledge and ideas that lead to innovation in European software firms. Competitors are another relatively important stimulus, particularly for hardware firms and packaged software vendors (see Table 7-11). The most important external channel for the acquisition of technical knowledge, however, is the hiring and (external) training of personnel. Informal communication with other firms also is relatively important, and codified knowledge (such as publications, meetings, and licensing) is relatively unimportant. The respondent firms assign little importance to joint R&D as a channel of knowledge acquisition, although there are significant differences among regions and firms. Firms in Germany, France, Italy, the United Kingdom, the Netherlands, and Belgium, as well as hardware firms, assign importance to joint R&D.

Technological Innovation

The competitive performance of European software firms in packaged software is much weaker than their performance in custom software and services in specific market niches. Their focus on custom software and services, however, has not been associated with lack of change in the products offered by European firms. Only a

Table 7-11. Main stimuli of innovative activity by European software firms (average scores)

	Supp.	Cust.	Comp.	Dept.	Govt.	Univ.	Swhs.	Cons.	Assn.
Europe	2.6	4.0	3.2	2.8	1.8	2.2	2.6	2.3	1.8
Leaders	2.5	4.1	3.2	3.0	1.8	2.5	2.5	2.3	1.5
Followers	2.8	4.0	3.0	2.5	1.7	1.8	2.9	2.4	2.0
Chi square[a]	1.24	0.42	0.22	1.12	1.70	4.31	1.91	1.76	2.90
Hardware	3.0	4.2	4.1	2.9	1.7	2.2	3.0	2.4	1.9
Packaged software	2.3	3.9	3.1	3.0	1.5	1.9	1.9	2.3	1.9
Services	2.5	3.9	2.8	2.6	1.9	2.3	2.9	2.3	1.7
Chi square[b]	2.48	2.77	4.31	0.51	2.99	3.28	8.81	2.24	2.58

Abbreviations: Supp. = Suppliers of components; Cust. = Customers; Comp. = Competitors; Dept. = Other parts of the corporation; Govt. = Government laboratories; Univ. = Universities; Swhs = Software houses; Cons. = Consultancy firms; Assn. = Industry associations.
[a] Chi square = 2 degrees of freedom (d.f.); 5 percent probability point = 5.99
[b] Chi square = 4 degrees of freedom (d.f.); 5 percent probability point = 9.49
Scores: 1 (not relevant) to 5 (very relevant).

few firms in Survey B (around one-fourth of the total sample of sixty-five firms) did not change their products in the period 1989–92 (that is, their new products account for less than 25 percent of total sales). For almost half of the sixty-five firms surveyed, new or incrementally modified products in the period 1989–92 constitute over 75 percent of total sales. One-fourth of the sixty-five firms derive over 75 percent of their sales from totally new products.

This high rate of product innovation is consistent with the higher percentage of R&D expenditures devoted to that activity than to in-house process innovation and acquisition of new tools.[9] But process engineering and quality assurance also are relevant for the competitiveness of firms, especially for firms active in Germany, France, the United Kingdom, Italy, the Netherlands, and Belgium. Finally, the majority of European software firms in Survey B devote less than 5 percent of their R&D to basic research.

In summary, the organization of innovative activities and strategies of European firms is consistent with the specialization of the European software industry in custom software and services. Interactions with users and customers are major sources of innovative ideas and feedback. In order to increase their size and internationalization many medium-sized and large European software firms are changing their focus from local niches to the larger regional European market.

EUROPEAN NATIONAL MARKETS

The dynamic interplay of national institutions and industrial policies, and national demand structure and domestic supply, has caused important differences among European software national markets to emerge.

Germany is the largest software and services market in Europe and has a number of firms that are competitive in both packaged and custom software. In 1992 the size of the market was $14.8 billion, according to IDC estimates (see Table 7-12). Pack-

Table 7-12. Western Europe's largest national software and services markets, 1992

Market	Software and services ($ billion)[a]	Share (%)	Packaged software ($ billion)	Share (%)	Professional services ($ billion)	Share (%)
Germany	14.76	22.0	4.9	22.0	7.4	23.0
France	11.1	17.0	3.7	15.0	6.2	19.0
United Kingdom	9.8	16.0	3.7	18.0	3.7	15.0
Italy	8.6	13.0	3.7	14.0	3.7	13.0
Spain	2.5	3.8	1.2	5.0	1.2	3.0
Other	18.45	28	6.15	26	7.38	26
Western Europe	65.19	100	23.37	100	29.52	100

Source: European Information Technology Observatory, using IDC data (EEC 1993).

[a]Total software and services market includes package software and professional, processing and network services. Values are expressed in billions of dollars at 1991 constant exchange rates.

[b]The values of the packaged software and professional services columns do not add to the total value of software and services (column 1) because the professional services figures do not include those for processing and network services.

Table 7-13.   The structure of domestic demand for software in European countries, 1990 (percentage)

	Manufacturing	Banking	Finance and insurance	Marketing and distribution	Government	Other	Total
Europe	25	13	11	8	10	33	100
Germany	25	12	12	8	9	34	100
France	24	13	12	8	11	32	100
United Kingdom	23	14	13	8	11	31	100
Italy	31	16	4	8	6	35	100

Source: Authors' calculations using IDC-Eurocast 1990 data.

aged software is the fastest-growing market segment, with a 20 percent yearly rate of growth during the early 1990s and a 33 percent share of the total German software market. German domestic demand is greatest in manufacturing, followed by banking and finance (see Table 7-13).

The large domestic market for packaged software and the presence of a comparatively strong national computer industry have favored the development of large firms specialized in these products, such as Software AG and SAP. As in other European economies, many small German firms are also present in the market. The largest German software firm is Datev, with revenues of $285 million in 1989 (mainly in processing services). Only three of the top ten software firms are foreign firms: Computer Associates (U.S.), SCS (a German firm taken over by Cap Gemini of France in 1990), and Microsoft (U.S.). As in other countries, a large number of acquisitions and mergers have recently taken place in Germany's software industry.

Software AG is one of the most interesting examples of German packaged software producers. It was founded in 1969 by academic researchers. In 1971 it entered the market for DBMS (database management systems) for IBM 370 mainframes with a new product, Adabas. More than 30 percent of its revenues now come from foreign markets. Software AG is present in several markets (Europe, the United States, South America, and Australia) through a network of subsidiaries. The international growth of the firm has been internal, rather than through acquisitions: the complexity of the firm's products and its aim to supply complementary services (training, consulting, and technical support) has required its direct presence in foreign markets. The main market segments served by Software AG are banks, other financial institutions, and insurance companies (which account for 35 percent of total sales), government (25 percent), and services (15 percent). Software AG has adapted to the competitive pressure from relational database suppliers (for example, Relational Technology and Oracle) by developing a relational version of Adabas. And the wide use of the Unix operating system and fourth-generation languages (such as SQL) has forced Software AG to further modify its products to remain competitive.

France is the second largest European market. Packaged software represents one-third of the total domestic market, a share that matches its share of the German market (33.3 percent). Unlike Germany, however, France has a leading position in the European service sector and some of the largest European multinationals. Manufacturing, banking, and public administration all represent significant shares of domestic software demand (see Table 7-13). In reaction to the pressure of foreign competition, French software firms recently have tried to strengthen their financial and organizational structures and are diversifying internationally through acquisitions. The French-British Sema Group took a majority share in the German ADV-Orga; Cap Gemini Sogeti has acquired a major stake in the British market by buying a controlling share of Hoskyns and has in addition diversified into packaged software and facilities management. Finally, the information systems departments of some large French user firms have left their parent companies and become independent providers of computer services and software.

The leading French software firm, Cap Gemini, is also the largest European software producer and is a typical example of a service supplier. It offers professional services, system integration, and turnkey systems. The company's main market segments are industry, finance and banking, distribution and services, and telecommunications. In 1989 each of these four segments accounted for 20 percent of the firm's total revenues. Government, on the contrary, accounted for 15 percent of total revenues. More recently, Cap Gemini has begun to diversify into general corporate consulting (*Datamation,* 15 June 1990). Since the second half of the 1980s Cap Gemini has grown through international acquisitions in several European countries and in the United States. This strategy has allowed Cap Gemini to increase its foreign sales: 38 percent of its sales come from other European countries and 19 percent from the United States.

In the *United Kingdom,* the third largest market after France and Germany, foreign firms have a large presence. Although packaged software represents a larger share of the total domestic software and services market than in Germany and France (37.8 percent), software services and system integration are increasingly important. Unlike other major European countries, the United Kingdom also is host to many foreign multinational software producers. In 1989 only three of the top ten companies selling in the United Kingdom were domestic enterprises: Thorn EMI Software (which left the software business in 1991); SD-Scicon (acquired by EDS in 1991); and Logica (acquired by Santa Cruz). In 1992 Datasolve, Software Sciences, Centrefile, and Sema Group (France/United Kingdom) are the only domestic firms among the largest ten. In this market the average firm size and the concentration ratios are low.

Two of the largest firms are the British-French Sema Group and SD-Scicon (now controlled by EDS), both of which specialize in custom software and services. Sema does 90 percent of its $374 million in sales in system engineering and system integration, while 10 percent is in facilities management. In 1989 the Sema Group had the following breakdown of sales: banking and finance, 24 percent; manufacturing, 21 percent; defense and aerospace, 15 percent; nonfinancial services, 10 percent; energy, 8 percent; transportation, 8 percent; government, 8 percent; telecommunications, 6 percent (*Datamation,* 15 June 1990). Before the takeover by EDS almost 90 percent of its SD-Scicon's sales were in services. SD-Scicon serves vertical markets: public administration and defense, finance and credit, and industry, and has a limited presence outside Europe. It is now investing in the development of products for facilities management (plant maintenance and manufacturing applications) and telecommunications (for a more detailed discussion see chapter 8).

Italy's software industry is very fragmented, with around 4,000 small and medium-sized firms (Assinform 1992). Given the small size of the market and the presence of one large firm, Finsiel, with over 13 percent of the Italian market, the concentration of firms is quite high compared with that in other European countries. In 1992 packaged software represented about 43 percent of the total market (according to IDC estimates), although no domestic firms specialize in packaged software. There are many fewer foreign owners of software firms than in the United Kingdom. Most Italian firms focus on particular market niches and have links with noninnovative and unskilled user firms, which provide little incentive for software firms to innovate but are quite loyal to their software suppliers. A large number of Italian software firms have spun off from large industrial firms and banks, and many of them are among the largest twenty-five independent software firms in Italy: Enidata, Cerved, Lombardia Informatica (a spin-off of the Lombardy regional government), Datamont, and SIME (a spin-off of Montedison), Pirelli Informatica, Italcad (Alenia) and Data Management (Credito Italiano). Other software firms have been created as joint ventures between computer firms and large customers (such as Intesa, an IBM-Fiat initiative).

Finsiel, the Italian market leader, specializes in services and custom software for the central and local governments (which constitute about two-thirds of Finsiel's revenues) and has no presence in foreign markets. Finsiel also supplies large systems to central and local public governments and to some large companies. Recently, the firm has tried to diversify through agreements with other companies, such as its joint venture with Logica in 1993. The structure of Italian domestic demand for software is dominated by manufacturing and banking. The combined financial, distribution and government segments of the domestic market are much smaller than those of the other large European countries (see Table 7-13).

Several of the markets of southern Europe (Spain, Portugal, and Greece) are still very small and underdeveloped. For example, in 1992 the Spanish software and services market was $2.5 billion, which is 3.8 percent of the total market in Western Europe (see Table 7-12). Software packages had a 48 percent share of the total market in 1992; the remainder of the market consisted of customized software and services. In the area of Madrid, software supply is dominated by small and medium-sized firms. Almost half of these firms employ fewer than fifty employees and develop customized software applications for small firms and professionals. The remaining firms employ between 50 and 250 employees. Medium-sized firms commercialize and adapt standard software developed abroad and specialize in the development of customized software.

PUBLIC POLICIES

European public policy toward the software industry has gone through several stages. The sequence of these stages reflects the evolution of software technology, the position of the European industry in international competition, and the specific histories and institutions of the European countries. It is possible to identify four major stages of European public policy.

The first stage covers the period from the beginning of the industry in the late 1960s to the late 1970s. During this period software was considered to be closely linked to hardware, and no government policies focused explicitly on software. During the second period, in the early 1980s, software was included in broad European national policies toward information technology. These policies were national, however, and reflected the institutional and historical specificities of the individual European countries. In the late 1980s, the emergence of a truly European approach to technology policy moved the policies for the software industry from a national to an international dimension. During the fourth stage (the 1990s), the increasing relevance of applications and the growing role of users in software development has shifted the focus of European policies from precompetitive, generic R&D support for national information technology producers to applications, diffusion, education, and interfirm cooperation. These different stages are briefly described in the following pages.

The Hardware-Driven National Policies of the Early Days of the Industry

During the first stage, the software industry was influenced by major programs of the European countries aimed at supporting their domestic hardware industries. Programs in France, West Germany, and the United Kingdom sought to foster technological innovation and the international competitiveness of the domestic industries.

The British government and several British bridging institutions were instrumental in the development of computers, primarily for military applications. The Ministry of Defense, the Royal Society, and the Telecommunications Research Establishment (TRE) gave financial and technical support to Manchester University's Digital Machine Project (MADM). Moreover, the automatic computing engine (ACE) was developed at the National Physical Laboratory with technical support from the British Post Office laboratories.[10]

France provides an example of a mission-oriented policy. The French government has given large financial support to industrial R&D in the electronics sector since the early days of the industry. In 1963 about 60 percent of R&D expenditures in the French electronics industry were financed by public programs. A coherent framework for public intervention in the computer sector, however, started only in the second half of the 1960s with the first "Plan Calcul" (1967–71) to support a French "national champion," Compagnie International pour l'Informatique (CII). The second and the third versions of the Plan Calcul (1971–75 and 1976–80) also strongly supported French national champions.

The German government followed the French example in undertaking programs aimed at computers. In the late 1960s Germany launched the first Data Processing Program (1967–69), followed by a second (1969–75) and a third (1976–79). Germany's programs differed in two important ways from the French, however. Germany's programs sought to stimulate the development of competence in computing at the university level. Second, in addition to supporting its national champion, Siemens, the third Data Processing Program gave extensive financial support to a second national firm that specialized in the new business areas of software and services, Nixdorf.

Unfortunately, these European policies largely failed to improve the performance of the domestic computer firms. They tried to pick the "winners" by focusing on a few large domestic firms, or national champions. In addition, most R&D projects aimed at catching up to U.S. firms in technologies in which the gap was very difficult to fill (for example, mainframes). And they placed little emphasis on the diffusion of information technology and skills, which would have stimulated both the domestic information technology providers and the users. Moreover, policies have paid little attention to fostering new startups or to cooperation between industry and university.

Information Technology Policies of the Early 1980s

In the early 1980s several European countries launched a set of national policies and programs aimed at information technologies. In contrast to the programs of the 1960s, these included extensive support for software development. Still, though, they were heavily influenced by the main institutional and historical features of the various European countries within which they were organized

In 1983 France launched a mission-oriented program to create an electronic *filiere* (a sort of interindustry network or value chain) (the Plan pour la Filiere Electronique, PAFE). It targeted several connected electronic sectors with the aim of improving the competitiveness of the French electronics industry. Software was part of various programs addressed to microelectronics, telecommunications, professional and military electronics, and consumer electronics. Like earlier French programs, the approach was centralized and subject to strong bureaucratic control. Its goal was to restructure the national industry and establish national champions in each major branch of the electronics industry.

During this period, West Germany also launched a program to support information technologies, including software (the Informationstechnik Program, 1984–88) This program reflected the institutional and historical features of German public policy: decentralization in the implementation of policies, major attention to diffusion, and emphasis on education and human capital. As mentioned before, the national education system is oriented toward applied science and technical training and the German technical diplomas give students an excellent technical background. As a result, cooperation among industry and universities has been strong. With the support of local government, Germany universities also play an active role in the diffusion of new technologies among small firms that perform information services and consulting.

In the United Kingdom the Alvey Program (1983–88) sought to give the country a leading position in software technology "within five years," in the face of declining performance by U.K. producers of hardware (see chapter 8 in this book). It promoted interfirm collaboration, precompetitive research, and university involvement. Software-specific programs included those to develop "intelligent knowledge-based systems" and "man-machine interfaces." This was a typical example of national mission-oriented technology policy. Despite its ambitious goals, the Alvey Program failed to produce new leading software products. Its national perspective also may have reduced British firms' incentives to set up strategic international alliances rather than only domestic ones. But in the view of some observers, the Alvey Program did stimulate cooperation between industry and university and contributed to the accumulation of national competencies and the diffusion of methodologies that are useful for the management of information technologies.[11]

All of these national policies largely failed to improve the competitive performance of European software firms, as is evident from the almost total absence of European firms in the standard packaged software market and the major European presence of the leading American software houses. The only exception to this characterization may be German policies, which focused on the development of human capital and advanced skills in software and supported industry-university collaboration. Germany now has a relatively large packaged software industry.

European Policies in the Second Half of the 1980s

The unsatisfactory performance of the European industry and the lack of a truly European market led to the launch of various regional EEC policies. In response to pressure from the main European electronics firms, in 1984 the EEC initiated the European Strategic Program for Research and Development in Information Technologies (ESPRIT I, 1984–88), together with other programs related to information technologies applications in areas such as medical science, transportation, public administration, education, and advanced communication technology. In 1987 the perceived need to integrate European R&D policies led to the creation of the Framework Program, a general policy scheme aimed at coordinating different EEC policy activities. It is the main instrument for EEC policy in the field of R&D. The First Framework Program (1984–87), was followed by the Second Framework Program (1987–91) and the Third Framework Program (1990–94) (see Table 7-14). A Fourth Framework Program was launched in 1994 for the period 1994–98. Within the Framework Program, ESPRIT is the largest recipient of research funds. The Fourth Framework Program includes a fourth ESPRIT program.

ESPRIT I had a budget of 1.5 billion ECUs ($1.85 billion at a 1991 constant exchange rate), 50 percent funded by the EEC and the rest by the participants; 19 percent of its total budget went to software. In 1988 ESPRIT II was launched, with

Table 7-14. The EEC's Framework Program, 1990–94

Focal areas	Funds (million ECUs)[a]	Share of total budget (%)
Enabling technologies		
1. Information and communication technologies, including:	2,221	38.9
—Information technology (ESPRIT III)	1,353	
—Communication technology	489	
—Telematics systems of general interest	380	
2. Industrial and materials technologies	888	15.6
Management and natural resources		
3. Environment	518	9.1
4. Life sciences and technology	741	13.0
5. Energy	814	14.3
Management and intellectual resources		
6. Human capital and mobility	518	9.1
Total	5,700	100

Source: EEC 1990.

[a]Figures given are EEC contributions, which usually cover up to 50 percent of total research costs. Figures are given in European currency units (ECUs).

a budget of 3.2 billion ECUs ($3.9 billion), 50 percent funded directly by the EEC. Information processing (computing) received 32 percent of the total EEC funds, and information technology applications 36 percent (OECD 1989b) (see Figure 7-1). Overall, information and communication technologies accounted for around 4.5 billion ECUs ($5.5 billion) between 1987 and 1994.

Some of the primary features of ESPRIT I (1984–88) and II (1988–92) were: (1) a large share of precompetitive R&D projects in ESPRIT I (approximately 65 percent of the total number of projects) and a shift to market-oriented application-specific projects in ESPRIT II (approximately 50 percent of the total number of projects); (2) interfirm cooperation; (3) user involvement, particularly in the transition from ESPRIT I to ESPRIT II; (4) support for cooperation among firms of different European countries; and (5) intellectual property rights rules that gave all participants in a project (including universities) proprietary control over the results of the project.

In 1991 the Commission of the European Union issued a directive about software copyright that has been adopted by many countries. According to Survey B, a large share of software firms located in Europe believe that European copyright provides good protection from imitation and an incentive to innovate (34 percent of total firms) rather than insufficient appropriability (22 percent). In contrast, almost half the firms (46 percent) believe their national copyright legislation is insufficient to protect innovators. In Europe, however, there is still great uncertainty about national copyright legislation. In fact, some European countries have been slow to adopt EEC recommendations on the protection of software as intellectual property. For instance, in Italy a law for software was passed only at the end of 1992. Moreover, significant differences still exist among countries. France grants twenty-five years' protection rather than the fifty years' protection granted by most of the countries that signed the 1988 Bern Convention for the Protection of Literary and Artistic Property. In Germany the German Supreme Court has ruled that computer programs must have a comparatively high degree of originality to receive protection (National Research Council 1991).[12]

In the second half of the 1980s another large European R&D program was launched: Eureka. Eureka is promoted by France as a European response to the American Strategic Defense Initiative, which is widely expected to yield important

Figure 7-1. ESPRIT program, 1987–94. *Source:* EEC 1992b.

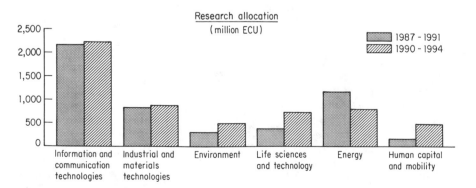

technological "spillovers" for U.S. firms in information technology and software. Eureka provides no direct R&D support; instead firms must ask their governments for funds under the program umbrella or rely on their own corporate financial resources. Between 1985 and 1992, Eureka provided eighty-three information technology projects (14.3 percent of the total number) with 2.1 million ECUs ($2.6 billion) (22.4 percent of their total costs) (see Figure 7-2). Eureka aims to increase the international competitiveness of European industry by fostering international collaboration in the development of new products and new processes. Its "bottom-up" approach implies that the initiative for collaboration should come from firms and universities.

The Principal Results of EEC Programs

What results have programs such as ESPRIT and Eureka obtained? First, they have created networks of innovators among firms and institutions that previously had few international links. In several cases, of course, the lasting networks of communication and interaction are those that emerged among the subgroups within the official network sponsored by the EEC. These subgroups are usually composed of technologically progressive firms already operating at the frontier. Several of these subgroups have cooperated on other projects as well. For instance, Siemens, Bull, and Olivetti

Figure 7-2. Eureka projects, 1985–91. *Source:* Negri and Zecchini 1992.

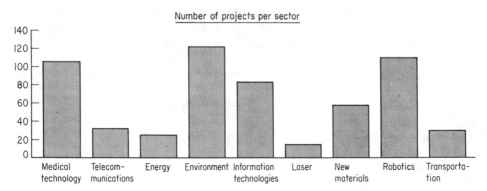

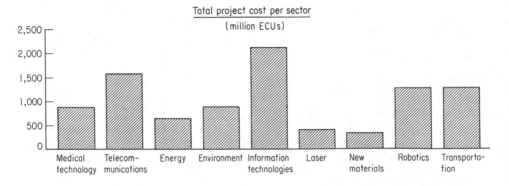

have been jointly involved in several ESPRIT and Eureka projects and have negotiated many bilateral and trilateral agreements outside the EEC umbrella. ICL also has
participated in several EEC projects with Bull and Siemens and has formed a joint
R&D laboratory in the field of artificial intelligence. Second, EEC programs have
increased the amount and degree of internationalization in the research activities of
several small and medium-sized firms. Third, they have allowed the opening of technology windows at the state-of-the-art frontier for small and medium-sized firms.
Fourth, they have led to the creation of some European standards (for example, in
software development methodologies). Finally, they have generated the successful
development of some new technologies and products.

Some major results in standards and products can be identified. In the field of
standards, the portable common tool environment (PCTE) is one of the main results
of ESPRIT I. The project to develop the PCTE started in 1984 with the participation
of Bull, ICL, Siemens, Nixdorf, and General Electric. It developed an open European standard interface for the creation of an integrated software development environment in computer-aided software engineering (CASE) tools. The PCTE standard
has been adopted by European and American vendors. Another project, the open
microprocessor system initiative (OMI), aims to bring the "open system" concept to
the level of a microprocessor chip and its associated software.

Research in advanced business and home system peripherals in the ISA project
(Integrated Systems Architecture) led to the development of ANSAware, a system
that enables users to link heterogeneous hardware and software in a distributed system and that can work with every operating system and within local and wide area
networks (LANs and WANs). ANSAware has been widely adopted in Europe and
by NASA for the Astrophysics Data System (ADS). Multimedia products (video,
voice, sound, and graphics) are another area of EEC sponsorship of collaborations
among firms: The Domesday project became important commercially when Philips
and its partners developed an interactive system on compact disk for the consumer
electronics market (CD-Interactive); and the Multiworks project (Olivetti, Bull,
Acorn, SGS Thomson, Philips, STC, and others) developed multimedia integrated
office workstations. These results were exploited later by Acorn Computers through
a joint venture with Apple and VLSI Technology, which led to the ARM 610, a
RISC processor used in Apple's pen-based pocket computer, Newton. Finally, in
computer integrated manufacturing and engineering, the DIAS (Distributed Intelligent Actuator and Sensors) project to create connections among sensors and computing and control elements led to the development of three prototypes, which have
been installed in several plants.

Three key projects within the Eureka Program merit mention. The first is EAST,
which designed an integrated project support environment (IPSE) that can support all
phases of software development based on the European developed standard interface
PCTE. It will result in a commercial product with a publicly available interface, at a
total cost of ECU 60 million through September 1992. The EAST project, which
was completed in late 1993, involved SFGL (France), Nokia (Finland), Datamat
(Italy), and other European information technology firms. A second project is ESF
(European Software Factory), which seeks to improve software production and to
introduce standard interfaces, and will deliver new process methodologies and tools.

All the major European software firms (Cap Gemini Sogeti, Cap Group, Sema Metra, and Softlab, as well as universities and research centers) are involved in ESF. The third one is Prometheus, started in 1986, which aims to develop new solutions to reduce traffic congestion by developing such features as a computerized system to give drivers help, vehicle-to-vehicle communications, and mobile communications technologies.

Mission-Oriented Policies and Diffusion-Oriented Policies in the 1990s

During the 1990s, a division of labor in technology policies seems to have emerged between the EEC and the individual European countries: The EEC now focuses more on major programs of international cooperation and mobility of the mission-oriented type, while the single European countries focus on diffusion policies. This structure is designed to increase the general level of competence of firms in state-of-the-art technologies, the adoption of European standards, the support for more application-oriented and more vertical (user-producer) cooperation, the supply of advanced skills, and the incentives to diffuse new technologies.

EEC policies

The EEC launched the third Framework Program (1990–94) and ESPRIT III (1991–94) in the early 1990s. The total budget for the third Framework Program was 5.7 billion ECUs ($7.01 billion). Within the third Framework Program, ESPRIT III (information technologies) had a budget of 2.2 billion ECUs ($2.7 billion), which is about 38 percent of the total budget. EEC support covers up to 50 percent of the total R&D costs of each project. Two key features of these programs are noteworthy. First, by emphasizing horizontal generic projects, their aim is to create a truly European regional market and increase the basic proficiency of European firms in state-of-the-art technologies. The programs focus on the development of European standards and on increasing investments in human capital (through, for example, COM-ETT (European Community Program in Education and Training for Technology) and DELTA (Development of European Learning through Technological Advance)). Second, ESPRIT III intensified its focus on cooperative R&D projects to produce applications and products that are near commercialization and enlist the participation of potential users. Within these projects, software is an important technology, particularly in the areas of standards, communication, and user interfaces.

Country policies

Individual European economies have launched a large number of diffusion-oriented programs that affect the software industry. Examples include Sweden's Jamtland Technology Diffusion Project, which seeks to foster awareness and information about information technologies and the development of advanced capabilities in the field; the United Kingdom's Open System Technology Transfer Program, which promotes the use of open systems; and Germany's Micro System Technology Program, which focuses on information technology diffusion, investments in human capital, and open systems.

All of these programs have focused mainly on small and medium-sized firms and on both the demand and the supply sides of the diffusion process by improving firms' information about new technologies and increasing their incentives to adopt them (see OECD 1989b and Arnold and Guy 1991).

What are the main effects of the evolution of the European information technology policies for European competitiveness? In software European firms have some opportunities and space to catch up to the world leaders in the field. The EEC policies have shown an increasing awareness of these opportunities and have taken advantage of them. The cooperation of European firms within many EEC projects has made it possible for them to share techniques of software production and will likely stimulate some of them to restructure some of their production activities and increase quality control. Firm cooperation through EEC projects also gives momentum to independent interfirm collaboration.

Despite the increasing emphasis on software technology, few new European software products have resulted from EEC projects; the focus on precompetitive technology-driven research (in the Framework Program) and competitive user-driven research (by Eureka) and an insufficient coordination of the overlaps between these two lines of research activity has hampered the production of commercial results. In addition, there are still few European firms with the technical and managerial expertise to capture the knowledge generated in these R&D activities. However, the effect of these positive externalities on commercial performance should be assessed in the long run; in the short and medium run one may expect an increase of firm competencies, which will eventually result in the development of new products. The more recent EEC programs have put more emphasis on marketing and service competencies and interactions with users. Indeed, Esprit II and III took a more market-oriented approach than Esprit I, and their expected results should concern mainly products.

CONCLUSIONS: WHAT DOES THE FUTURE HOLD FOR THE EUROPEAN SOFTWARE INDUSTRY?

This chapter has shown that the European software industry is highly fragmented, exhibits a limited degree of internationalization, and specializes in custom software and services. The main reasons for this general pattern of structure, specialization, and performance are the weak links between industry and universities, the absence of a highly competitive and technologically advanced European computer industry, the early entry and market-preemption strategies of the leading American systems and packaged software producers, the fragmentation of the European market, and the diverse demand structure in each country. The dynamic interaction and the coevolution of local firms, domestic customers, and specific institutional features (such as university and government policies) generated different types of national software industries: Germany has specialized in package software; France has some of the few large European multinationals that specialize in services; the United Kingdom has a substantial presence of American multinationals, and Italy has several small firms and a large enterprise serving the protected market of public procurement.

Two aspects of the innovative activity of European software firms may explain this pattern of specialization. First, European software firms place great importance on close links with users, who are a major competitive factor and an important stimulus to innovation. Although interactions with users are an important feature of software production worldwide, in Europe these close relationships have led firms to specialize in custom software and explain their weak internal capabilities in packaged software. Second, European software firms do not typically have strong direct links with universities. European universities are a source of general, basic knowledge, but do not take part in the development of software products. In contrast with the United States, where a number of software packages have been developed by academic researchers, university spin-offs are not a significant source of innovation for the European software industry. EEC programs such as ESPRIT, and national programs (such as the United Kingdom's Alvey), have tried to overcome this weakness by increasing the cooperation between industry and university, mainly through the creation of networks of informal, personal contacts among researchers.

The development of a more homogeneous regional market in Europe will be advanced by the increasing importance of packaged software within the market for software. The same thing is happening in the United States and Japan. The diffusion of European standards (fostered in part by the various EEC policies discussed in this chapter) will help make European demand more homogeneous, as will new regulations governing public procurement if they are applied consistently in all EEC countries.

The acceptance of European standards will also cause major changes in the structure and specialization of the European industry. In order to compete internationally with large American companies, especially in packaged software, European firms must reach a "critical size" and expand their presence in international markets. This seems to be the main object of international mergers and acquisitions that are taking place in Europe in the software industry. Through these and others strategic maneuvers, French and British firms such as Cap Gemini and Sema Group have begun to establish international links with suppliers, other software firms, and users.

Despite the increasing relevance of packaged software, however, custom software and services activities are still important for the competitiveness of the European software industry. As a consequence, close relationships with users, personal contacts, skills in marketing, and high quality maintenance will remain strategic competitive factors for European firms. The integration of the European market, the increasing relevance of standards (fostered in part by EEC programs) and the growing relevance of packaged software also will introduce new threats for existing European software firms, by creating additional incentives for outside firms to enter the market or to expand in Europe. New competitors (European as well as foreign) from downstream industries may enter the industry, following the example of other firms in the United States (such as McDonnell Douglas, EDS, and Arthur Andersen) and in Europe (Enidata, Pirelli Informatica, and Reuters). Existing American hardware and software firms also may strengthen their productive and marketing activities in Europe to exploit the expected economies of scale and scope related to the "Europeanization" of the various markets. Finally, the existing European hardware and software firms (such as Siemens, Olivetti, and Bull) have also made large investments in software and services.

Although in the near future the number of firms in the European software industry will remain high, all of these trends will likely increase market concentration in the industry, as many small and medium-sized local firms leave, new large American software players and some big European users enter the market, and established American leaders and a few successful European software firms continue to grow.

NOTES

1. In 1991 Siemens reported revenues of $964.4 million from software, significantly larger than those reported by Olivetti ($630.8 million) in 1991 (*Datamation,* 1 July 1992).

2. Increasing competition by hardware firms and system integrators has reduced the market share of VARs.

3. The responses of those interviewed may have been biased toward project management because of the professional position of the respondents.

4. The relatively minor importance of project management skills is difficult to explain.

5. Hardware and software firms' responses refer to system software. The values for the entry barriers for software firms were obtained by averaging the scores given in the four different market segments: system software, standard packages, software services, and tools.

6. This was true for both the American and the European hardware manufacturers in our survey.

7. As mentioned before, in 1991 EDS acquired SD-Scicon (Predicasts 1988–91; IDC-Eurocast 1988; *Datamation* 15 June 1988; Assinform 1992.

8. For a deeper discussion of external sources of innovations based on data from Survey A, see Torrisi 1994b and Malerba and Torrisi 1992.

9. Note that in our survey the adoption of new software production tools from outside and in-house development of new tools cannot be distinguished.

10. Flamm (1988) gives a rich historical reconstruction of the European position in the early stages of the computer industry.

11. Our discussion reaches conclusions that differ somewhat from those of Grindley in this book (see chapter 8). Our two positions are not wholly contradictory, however, because Grindley focuses his discussion more on the lack of commercial results obtained by the Alvey Program. On the Alvey Program see Georghiou et al. 1991.

12. For a more detailed discussion of intellectual property rights in Europe, see chapter 10 in this volume.

REFERENCES

Arnold, E., and K. Guy. 1991. "Diffusion Policies of IT: The Way Forward." Meeting of the OECD/ICCP Expert Group on the Economic Implications of Information Technologies. Summary paper. Paris: OECD. 7–8 November.

Ashworth, J. 1985. "The Crisis Facing the U.K. Information Technology Industry." *Information Technology and Public Policy* 3, no. 2: 95–101.

Assinform. 1992. *Rapporto sulla situazione informatica in Italia* (Report on the information industry in Italy). Milan: Assinform.

Brady, T., and P. Quintas. 1991. "Computer Software: The IT Constraint?" In C. Freeman, M. Sharp, and W. Walker, eds., *Technology and the Future of Europe.* London: Pinter.

Computer Weekly. 1990. "Computer Weekly Guide to Resources." Special issue. Computer Weekly Publications, Sutton (England).

Datamation. 1992. "The Datamation Top 100." 15 June.

EEC (European Economic Community). 1990. *EC Research Funding.* 3d ed. Brussels: Commission of the European Communities, Directorate General XIII, Telecommunications, Information Industries, and Innovation.

———. 1991. *L'industrie Européene de l'electronique et de l'informatique* (The European electronics and information industry). Brussels: EEC. March.

————. 1992a. *ESPRIT Synopses*. Brussels: Commission of the European Communities, Directorate General XIII, Telecommunications, Information Industries, and Innovation.

———— 1992b. *ESPRIT Results and Progress 1992/92*. Brussels: Commission of the European Communities, Directorate General XIII, Telecommunications, Information Industries, and Innovation.

————. 1993. *European Information Technology Observatory 1993*. Frankfurt: EITO and IDC.

Flamm, K. 1988. *Creating the Computer*. Washington, D.C.: Brookings Institution.

Georghiou, L., K. Guy, P. Quintas, M. Hobday, H. Cameron, and T. Ray. 1991. *Evaluation of the Alvey Programme for Advanced Information Technology*. London: Her Majesty's Stationery Office.

IDC. 1988. *Software and Services Marketplace: Western Europe*. Paris: Eurocast Software Service, IDC-Europe.

————. 1990. *European Software and Services.: Review & Forecast*. Paris: IDC European Research Centre. August.

Irvine, J., B. Martin, and P. Isard. 1990. *Investing in the Future: An International Comparison of Government Funding of Academic and Related Research*. Aldershot, Eng.: Edward Elgar.

Mackintosh, I. 1986. *Sunrise Europe: The Dynamics of Information Technology*. Oxford, Eng.: Blackwell.

Malerba, F., and S. Torrisi. 1992. "Internal Capabilities and External Networks in Innovative Activities: Evidence from the Software Industry." *Economics of Innovation and New Technology* 2: 49–71.

————. 1993. "Software." Research and Technology Management in Enterprises: Issues for Community Policy, Sectoral Report, Monitor—Strategic Analysis in Science and Technology (SAST) Activity. Project no. 8, Brussels.

Malerba, F., S. Torrisi, and N. von Tunzelmann. 1991. "Electronic Computers." In C. Freeman, M. Sharp, and W. Walker, eds., *Technology and the Future of Europe*. London: Pinter.

National Research Council. 1991. *Intellectual Property Issues in Software*. Washington, D.C.: National Academy Press.

Negri, L., and C. Zecchini. 1992. *Eureka: Partecipazione Italiana* (Eureka: Italian participation). Rome: CNR (National Research Council).

Norton, H. 1991. *Informatics in Europe*. Manchester, Eng.: NCC Blackwell.

OECD (Organization for Economic Cooperation and Development). 1985. *Software: An Emerging Industry*. ICCP Series, no. 9, Paris: OECD.

————. 1986. *La politique d'innovation en France* (The politics of innovation in France). Paris: OECD.

————. 1989a. *The Internationalization of Software and Computer Services*. ICCP Series, no. 17. Paris: OECD.

————. 1989b. *Major R&D Programmes for Information Technology*. Paris: OECD.

————. 1991a. *La genie logiciel: Un defi pour l'action gouvernamentale* (Software engineering: A challenge for government action). Paris: OECD.

————. 1991b. *Reviews of National Science and Technology Policy: Italy*. Paris: OECD.

————. 1992a. *From Higher Education to Employment*. Paris: OECD.

————. 1992b. *Information Technology Outlook*. Paris: OECD.

Predicasts. 1988–91. *F&S Index of Corporate Change*. Cleveland, Ohio: Predicasts, Inc.

Torrisi, S. 1994. "The Organisation of Innovative Activities in European Software Firms." Ph.D. diss. Science Policy Research Unit, University of Sussex.

8

The Future of the Software Industry in the United Kingdom: The Limitations of Independent Production

Peter Grindley

The independent computer services industry provides software, consulting, and processing services for computer users. As in other countries, the industry in the United Kingdom emerged in the late 1960s, when the growing use of computers provided a demand for software that could not be met by computer manufacturers or users. By the early 1980s it had earned the right to be called a distinct industry. By 1994 the total U.K. software and services market had risen to more than $12 billion, around half of which was supplied by independents. This represented about 15 percent of the $83 billion Western European market and 4 percent of the worldwide market of about $325 billion. The U.K. software market alone was about $7 billion, or 4 percent of the total world software market of about $170 billion.

The hope in the United Kingdom during the 1980s was that computer services could become a major national industry, leading the world in software production. Business and government alike saw an opportunity to exploit software skills despite the United Kingdom's weak position in computer manufacturing. The U.K. computer industry had been in decline for decades: Of the many U.K. firms that had helped pioneer the early development of the computer, only ICL remained, and it relied on Japanese hardware. It was thought that concentrating on software could tap the United Kingdom's strong tradition in computing and take advantage of its reputedly well-developed software skills. Government policymakers hoped to stem the country's growing trade deficit in information technology (IT) by stimulating the development of the software industry. Programs such as Alvey and the European Community's ESPRIT initiative aimed to develop advanced software technology and establish high-value-added "software factories," which would develop software on a formal "assembly line" process. These programs were in turn linked to broader educational and training programs aimed at improving the supply of software skills.

This goal of building a strong national industry has proved elusive. The industry has remained oriented around custom services for the domestic market and is not a major exporter. Although custom development, consulting, and processing services are still relatively healthy, further growth is limited by the rate of growth of the economy as a whole. Significantly, U.K. firms have almost no position in packaged software, the fastest growing segment of the global software industry and the one most open to international competition (because it is most easily traded). This segment in the United Kingdom is dominated by imports, mainly from the United States. Packages are profiting from the shift to personal computers (PCs) and other microprocessor-based systems, which demand lower-cost standard software. As computer systems become more standardized, packages are replacing more types of custom software. Meanwhile, traditional systems vendors throughout the world continue to put increasing emphasis on software as a source of revenue and to expand their efforts in systems integration and personalized services.[1] These longer-term effects threaten the custom sector, which after decades of steady growth suffered its first recession in the early 1990s. Yet there has been little change in the independents' basic business strategy. Most firms are still not far from their roots in the "cottage industry" model of contract development. Focused on local markets they have made little attempt to compete in global markets. The industry has acquired characteristics of some other British service industries: successful at home but tied to the performance of the domestic economy, weak in traded sectors, and potentially vulnerable to competition from abroad.

Government policies have had little impact on this situation. Collaborative R&D programs, including Alvey and ESPRIT, have attempted to help build up the industry by strengthening capabilities in software engineering. Although these have apparently changed industry attitudes (for example, toward industry-academic collaboration), the programs have had little tangible effect. The United Kingdom is far from becoming a world center for software design. Training and educational efforts have increased the general awareness of computer use and the level of available skills. But, as the recession in the industry in 1990–92 showed, this does not ensure that the skills will be employed. Procurement policies in the defense industry and public service corporations have yielded few spillovers for the commercial industry's performance.

The problems in the United Kingdom highlight the difficulties facing an isolated software industry. Links between the development of hardware and software technologies seem to be sufficiently important that in key market segments a strong national software industry cannot easily exist independently of a strong national hardware industry. Links to other software developers are also becoming more important with the rise of large software corporations and open systems. As a custom service provider, the U.K. industry prospers along with general growth in the use of computers, but in standardized packaged software, where competition is more intense, the U.K. industry's inability to keep abreast of developments in hardware and software is a major disadvantage. Compare this with the U.S. situation, where packaged software suppliers have close contacts with computer and semiconductor developers and with a large community of software developers.

Although the Japanese experience (see chapters 5 and 6 in this volume) suggests that a strong national hardware industry may be a necessary, but not sufficient, condition for the emergence of a competitive national software industry, the lack of a strong U.K. computer manufacturing base has hampered the U.K. software firms. Operating systems software is directly related to computer development. As discussed below, applications software may also benefit from close contacts with hardware and other software developers that can provide early access to new designs. Alliances with software suppliers are now important elements of many computer manufacturers' strategies. Software firms in the United Kingdom and other European nations do not have strong links with manufacturers and as a result gain access to new technology only after it is released on the world market, perhaps a year later than competitors in the United States (see Ashworth 1985). There may be ways to offset these problems by building closer links with foreign manufacturers and software firms and by putting stronger emphasis on user-oriented systems. However, few firms have done this successfully, other than some banking specialists and the U.K. computer company ICL.

STRUCTURE OF THE INDUSTRY

The Development of the U.K. Computer Industry

The tradition of computer science R&D in the United Kingdom goes back to the origins of the electronic computer, if not even further back to Babbage's "analytical engine" of the nineteenth century. Both the United Kingdom and the United States contributed to the development of the first computers. One of the earliest electronic calculating machines was "Colossus," developed at Bletchley Park in the United Kingdom during World War II for code breaking. Colossus may have predated ENIAC (the electronic numerical integrator and computer, developed at about the same time at the University of Pennsylvania in the United States), though ENIAC is usually reckoned the first computer. There were numerous U.K. research projects immediately after the war, at Manchester, Cambridge, and London (Birkbeck) Universities and the National Physical Laboratory. EDSAC, developed in 1949 at Cambridge and Manchester, was the first practical stored program computer (using paper tape and teletype input) and was probably the first system recognizable as a modern computer. Each of these academic projects eventually became the basis for commercially produced computers in the United Kingdom, with the involvement of British firms such as Ferranti, English Electric, Leo, EMI, and British Tabulator Machines (later ICT) (Kelly 1987).

Despite this early role in developing and manufacturing computers, U.K. universities and industry proved to be more adept at the science of computing than at business exploitation. The Colossus machine, for example, which was designed for code breaking, was never adapted to more mundane tasks, and some aspects of it are still classified. After the war, the universities were very active in developing the first computers, and developed machines for military and scientific use; yet it was Lyons, a chain of tea shops, that first exploited the potential for business machines with its Leo computer in 1952 (Gregory 1971).

The U.K. computer industry grew during the 1950s, but by the 1960s large U.S. firms had begun to dominate the world market. Among other problems, the

U.K. firms were too small to finance the huge development costs needed for a new computer. Another problem, which would figure prominently in the software industry later, was the remoteness of U.K. computer firms from many critical developments in electronics. They also did not have the stimulus of the huge U.S. market, particularly in the corporate sector. The introduction of the IBM 360 system in the mid-1960s, the first integrated circuit (IC)–based machine and one aimed at the business market, brought these pressures on the industry to a head. With the encouragement of Prime Minister Harold Wilson's government, firms began a merger process, which by 1968 left only one major national firm, ICL (see Figure 8-1). The merger process was to some extent forced on the companies and did not rationalize the individual organizations, which continued to operate as fragmented divisions. Partly for this reason the economies of scale sought by managers and policymakers did not materialize, especially in the development of new computers. ICL, along with most other European computer manufacturers, lagged behind U.S. competitors, and performance continued to decline.

This long-term decline was reversed only in the mid-1980s, when ICL made major strategic changes. It began sourcing components for its computers from Fujitsu and assumed the role of systems integrator, bringing together hardware and software focused on user-oriented systems. This combination of strategies, formalized in a corporate restructuring in 1990, has been successful for ICL and may provide a model of the use of integration, international links, and applications-oriented development for U.K. software firms. After coming close to oblivion in the early 1980s, the firm (now 80 percent owned by Fujitsu) is now one of the best performers in the industry (Metropolis et al. 1980; Campbell and Kelly 1989).

The U.K. computer industry's development has influenced software firms in several ways. First, computer development has focused on scientific and military markets rather than on business systems. Military development has been crucial to

Figure 8-1. Concentration of the U.K. computer industry, 1945–95. Computer interests only; formation year in parentheses; merger year in italics. *Source:* Author.

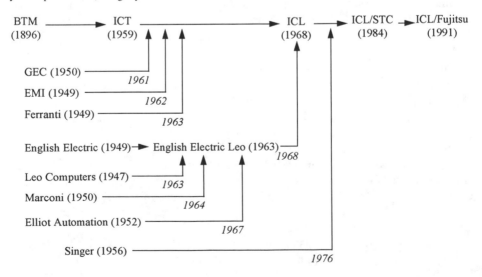

the industry on both sides of the Atlantic, but it is interesting to compare the initial U.K. effort in code breaking, which was not applied to commercial systems and remained secret, with the U.S. effort, used for calculating ballistics tables and quickly exploited by start-up firms after the war. Second, its remoteness from the technological centers of microelectronics development weakened the industry, except in dedicated military systems supported by specialized U.K. semiconductor development. Third, government industrial policies have tended to be "corporatist" and supply-side oriented, aimed at the needs of large firms and seeking to retain a world-class IT industry for the supply of hardware rather than the use of computers. This has continued, even though the remaining large U.K. computer firm became successful only after it took a user-oriented approach and opened itself to foreign technology.

Software and Services

The beginnings of the independent software and services industry were apparent in the United Kingdom by the late 1960s. Software houses and consultants began to provide contract programming and systems analysis for users with insufficient in-house expertise. So-called bureau services also appeared, providing centralized processing services, time-sharing services, and facilities management. Initially the industry was very small; about 2,500–3,000 people were employed in independent software firms in 1970, with revenues of £7.5–10 million, approximately the same number as were employed in software development groups in user companies and computer manufacturers (Foy 1971). The U.S. industry was already larger, though still small relative to total software production. The total U.S. market for software in 1970 was about $5 billion, of which in-house development amounted to $4.3 billion and contract services to $650 million. Some packaged software had also appeared in the United States; independents supplied $50 million and manufacturers $20 million. Software worth about $300 million also was provided by the manufacturers and "bundled" with the price of their computers (Fisher, McKie, and Mancke 1987).

The U.K. industry was given a major boost by IBM's unbundling of software and hardware in 1969, which triggered rapid growth in independent software and services firms. Figure 8.2, depicting the growth of the software and services industry during the 1977–94 period, shows revenues (in local currency) for traded software and services from independents and computer manufacturers. The total market in 1994 (excluding support services) was about £7 billion ($10.3 billion), of which packaged sales accounted for about £3.1 billion and custom software and consultancy about £2.7 billion. Processing and other services (excluding hardware support services) accounted for about £1 billion. Total industry revenues grew during the 1970s and 1980s at average annual rates of 15–25 percent.

Market structure

Table 8-1 shows the total market in information technology for the United Kingdom and Western Europe in 1994, including hardware as well as software and services. To put the U.K. software and services market in context, in 1994 it accounted for 56 percent of the total U.K. IT market. Total software (packaged software, IT consulting, and custom software) amounted to $7.1 billion, or 32 percent of total IT

Table 8-1. Total information technology markets: United Kingdom and Europe, 1993–94

	United Kingdom					Total Europe				
	Revenues 1993 ($ million)	Revenues 1994 ($ million)	Share 1994 (%)	Growth 1993–94 (%)	Projected AGR 1994–99 (%)[a]	Revenues 1993 ($ million)	Revenues 1994 ($ million)	Share 1994 (%)	Growth 1993–94 (%)	Projected AGR 1994–99 (%)[a]
Hardware										
Multi-user	3,093	3,055	31	–1	1.9	18,393	17,842	33	–3	1.3
Single user	5,142	5,557	56	8	6.7	29,438	31,656	58	8	7.3
Datacomms	1,252	1,391	14	11	1.6	4,558	5,281	10	16	2.4
Total hardware	9,487	10,003	100	5	4.5	52,389	54,779	100	5	4.9
Software and services										
Packaged software										
Systems/utilities	1,196	1,243	10	4	3.3	6,356	6,618	8	4	4.8
Applications tools	1,062	1,124	9	6	4.9	7,283	7,971	10	9	10.6
Applications solutions	2,163	2,298	18	6	5.3	11,065	11,976	15	8	8.7
Subtotal	4,421	4,665	37	6	4.7	24,704	26,565	32	8	8.3
Professional services										
IT consulting	636	701	6	10	5.1	5,617	5,979	7	6	6.9
Custom software	1,485	1,771	14	19	4.1	10,498	11,068	13	5	4.2

Systems/network implement.	269	293	2	9	5.1	4,223	4,468	5	6	5.4
Education/training	358	398	3	11	4.7	4,167	4,516	5	8	8.1
Facilities management	549	850	7	55	9.6	2,252	2,833	3	26	11.8
Subtotal	3,297	4,013	32	22	5.6	26,757	28,864	35	8	6.3
Processing services										
Problem solving	261	259	2	−1	−1.7	3,048	3,053	4	0	0.1
Transactions processing	941	950	8	1	1.0	7,078	7,256	9	3	2.5
Network services	375	417	3	11	7.8	2,009	2,225	3	11	10.4
Subtotal	1,577	1,626	13	3	2.3	12,135	12,534	15	3	3.3
Support services[b]	2,209	2,203	18	0	0.5	14,862	14,570	18	−2	0.4
Total software and services	11,504	12,507	100	9	3.9	78,458	82,533	100	5	5.4
Total information technology	20,991	22,510	100	7	4.2	130,847	137,312	100	5	5.2
Share total IT										
Hardware	9,487	10,003	44	5	4.5	52,389	54,779	40	5	4.9
Software[c]	6,542	7,137	32	9	4.6	40,819	43,612	32	7	7.1
Other services	4,962	5,370	24	8	3.1	37,639	38,921	28	3	3.6

Source: International Data Corporation.

[a] Compound annual percentage growth rate; IDC estimates.

[b] Hardware maintenance and other support services.

[c] Packaged software, IT consulting, custom software.

revenues; services, including professional services other than software development, processing services, and support services, accounted for 24 percent.

Packaged software accounted for 37 percent of total software and services, at $4.7 billion. Applications solutions accounted for about half the packaged software market, with revenues of $2.3 billion, with the rest of the packaged software market roughly evenly divided between systems/utilities and applications tools, with about $1.1 billion each. The software categories are:

- Systems/utilities: the basic control over the operations of the computer. These include operating systems, file managers, network controllers, sort and merge utilities, and language compilers.
- Applications tools: generalized support systems to be used as part of specific applications. These include database management systems, computer-aided software engineering (CASE) tools, and fourth-generation languages (4GLs).
- Applications solutions: solutions specific to an end use. These are the bulk of what a user normally thinks of as software. They may be for (1) general functions, such as accounting systems, payroll, CAD/CAM, graphics, word processing, and spreadsheets, or (2) specific functions, such as banking systems, foreign exchange transactions insurance, retailing systems, electronic funds transfer at point of sales (EFTPOS) systems, manufacturing materials planning, airline reservations systems, and computer games.

Professional services accounted for another 32 percent of total software and services, at $4.0 billion. Within this segment, IT consulting, which typically performs systems analysis and overall project management functions, accounted for 7 percent of total software and services. Custom software development accounted for 14 percent of the total. Custom systems are typically large, specialized applications, such as in banking operations, airline reservations, defense, or government services. Packaged products have gradually taken over the more standardized systems. There is a wide range of custom software houses, ranging from one-person operations to large integrators offering a complete set of capabilities. At one end are the archetypal "body shops," providing professionals to work on contract; at the other are large organizations able to produce major software systems to given specifications. The boundaries between "body shops," custom services, and consulting are not clearly defined: Some self-styled custom houses and consultancies provide contract personnel, and some custom houses provide systems analysis and project management. There is a great deal of subcontracting to small firms within projects controlled by larger consultants or integrators. Systems and network implementation, which includes delegated staff (such as data entry clerks, word processor operators, or computer operators, as well as some more skilled systems personnel), accounted for 2 percent of the market. Education and training, and facilities management, together accounted for a further 10 percent of the market.

Processing services accounted for 13 percent of industry revenues. Processing services are usually considered to be quite separate from the software segments of the IT industry, but these firms now often offer more complete services as systems integrators (Ashe et al. 1986; Grindley 1988; *Datamation*, 1 July 1993). The remaining 18 percent of the software and services market in 1994 consisted of hardware maintenance and support services.

In 1994 packaged software constituted a higher share of the U.K. market (37 percent) than it did for Western Europe (32 percent) as a whole. Within the U.K. software market (packages, IT consulting, custom software), packages accounted for 65 percent of the total $7.1 billion, and in Europe for 61 percent of the total $43.6 billion. For Europe excluding the United Kingdom, the share of packaged software was 60 percent. Processing services accounted for a lower share of the software and services industry in the United Kingdom (13 percent) than in Europe as a whole (15 percent), although the gap was small.

Growth rates of the different segments of the U.K. market have generally been high. Packaged software sales grew at an average rate of 21 percent over the period 1980–94 (in local currency), professional services at 19 percent and processing services at 9 percent (using data shown in Figure 8-2). From 1980 to 1994, packages increased from 29 percent to 45 percent of the total U.K. software and services market (excluding support services), professional services from 30 percent to 39 percent, while processing services have decreased from 41 percent to 16 percent. There was clearly a large shift in the market in favor of software and professional services, though given the huge changes worldwide in the computer industry during this period, including the introduction of the PC, the ratio between the size of the packaged software market and the professional services (primarily custom systems development) market remained remarkably constant. This suggests that although the packaged software market as a whole grew faster than professional services, the increased use of PCs and workstations, which overwhelmingly use packaged software, has not

Figure 8-2. Growth of U.K. software and services, 1977–94. *Source:* National Computing Centre 1977, IDC 1980–94.

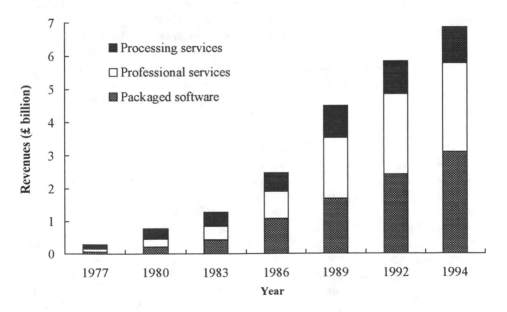

yet had a decisive impact on the structure of the U.K. software and services industry. Higher volumes in these segments of the packaged software market may have been offset by falling prices, moderating the revenue growth. We return to this issue below.

To some extent these high growth rates mask a more important aspect of long-term performance: the variability in growth rates between segments. Packaged software growth rates have been fairly uniform from year to year. They were especially high during the 1980s, but have fallen gradually, as might be expected in a maturing market, and as prices in the newer segments continue to fall. Thus packaged software revenues grew at rates of 17 percent per year during 1989–92 but only 6 percent during 1993–94. The International Data Corporation (IDC) estimates that growth rates for the second half of the 1990s will be about 5 percent per year.

In contrast, the performance of the professional services market has been more volatile. Growth rates of professional services fell significantly during 1990–92 because of reductions in demand for systems integration, custom applications, and consulting in response to the downturn in the U.K. economy at that time. Although professional services as a whole continued to grow during this period, some segments declined. There were significant numbers of layoffs and downsizing by firms in 1991 (CSA 1991). Professional services grew at an average 13 percent annual rate during 1989–92, which is low by historical standards. There was a recovery in performance after 1992, with growth of 10 percent in IT consulting and 19 percent in custom software in 1994. Total growth in processing services in 1994 was especially high because of the high growth in facilities management (22 percent), as firms shifted away from in-house management of their data processing facilities. Projections for growth of professional services for the second half of the 1990s are about 5 percent, about the same as for packaged software.

Processing services have proved relatively immune to recession, as firms seeking to cut overhead have switched to contracting out their data processing. Although processing services' share of the industry revenues has gradually fallen, they have remained an area of steady long-term growth and profitability.

Rates of growth in Europe during the 1980s and early 1990s were similar to those of the United Kingdom. The European software and services market went into recession about a year later than the U.K. market in the early 1990s, so that by 1994 its growth was still lower than in the United Kingdom. The European market is expected to grow somewhat faster than the U.K. market for the second half of the 1990s. Packaged software is expected to grow at about 8 percent per year, and professional services at about 6 percent.

The 1989 market shares held by providers of software are shown in Table 8-2. The U.K. market for packaged software is divided roughly equally between hardware manufacturers and independent software producers. However, the two different kinds of producer tend to focus on different types of software. Computer manufacturers still account for most of the sales of operating systems and utilities packages, which are designed specifically to work with their computers, although this is now less true for PC systems. Revenues from applications tools are split roughly equally between manufacturers and independents; independents, however, account for the bulk of revenues from applications solutions. Most of the professional services segment (81 percent) is provided by independents, with hardware manufacturers accounting for

Table 8-2.   U.K. software and services market by provider, 1983–89

	Revenue ($ million)			Share (%)		
	1983	1986	1989	1983	1986	1989
Packaged software						
Hardware manufacturers	361	1,003	1,423	19	23	19
Independents	298	822	1,367	15	19	18
Subtotal	659	1,825	2,790	34	41	38
Professional services						
Hardware manufacturers	85	190	398	4	4	5
Independents	450	955	1,751	23	22	24
Subtotal	535	1,145	2,149	28	26	29
Training	96	252	498	5	6	7
Facilities management	10	100	392	1	2	5
Processing services	635	1,098	1,602	33	25	22
Total	1,935	4,420	7,431	100	100	100

Source: International Data Corporation.

only 19 percent of total revenues. Packages are sold through various kinds of distributors, and their sales revenues are not included in the revenues of the independent software houses in the professional services segment. One group of independents, the value-added retailers (VARs), often combine these functions, putting together systems of hardware and customized and packaged software to meet specific customer requirements. The importance of these firms has declined, as hardware manufacturers and consulting firms have expanded their activities as systems integrators.

Table 8-3 shows the market for packaged software for 1989–92, by hardware system type, compared with corresponding sales of hardware systems. Multi-user systems, consisting of large-scale (mainframes), medium-scale (minicomputers), and small-scale (local area networks) systems together accounted for only 42 percent of the hardware market in 1992 but for 85 percent of the packaged software market. Single-user systems (PCs and workstations) accounted for 58 percent of the hardware market but only 15 percent of the packaged software market. This partly reflects the lower unit cost of PC software packages but also the fact that minicomputer and mainframe software still serve a much larger installed base in the United Kingdom.

As PCs and workstations continue to expand their share of the hardware market, the single-user segment, and possibly the small-scale (network) segment, should increase their share of the software market. However, a comparison of growth rates by hardware segment shows that it may be some time before this takes effect. As a group, multi-user systems sales were falling by about 8 percent a year during the period, but software revenues for this group were growing at about 19 percent a year. Single-user systems were growing at 4 percent a year, but packaged software sales were growing at only about 2 percent. Single-user systems represented an increasing share of the hardware market (going from a 45 percent to 58 percent share) but a declining share of the packaged software market (going from a 22 percent to 15 percent share). This phenomenon is presumably influenced by the falling price of single-user software and the rising price of software for large-and medium-scale systems. Once the installed base of single-user systems (and networks) is high enough,

Table 8-3.   U.K. packaged software market by hardware type, 1989–92

	Revenues ($ million)				Share (%)				Growth rate (%)[a]
	1989	1990	1991	1992	1989	1990	1991	1992	1989–92
Hardware									
Large scale	1,578	1,457	1,251	1,139	18	15	14	14	−10.3
Medium scale	1,665	1,609	1,428	1,283	19	17	16	16	−8.3
Small scale	1,153	1,286	1,041	1,025	13	13	11	12	−3.8
PC/workstations	4,256	5,299	5,337	4,808	49	55	59	58	4.1
Total systems hardware[b]	8,652	9,651	9,058	8,255	100	100	100	100	−1.6
Packaged software[c]									
Large scale	578	822	831	921	21	23	21	21	16.8
Medium scale	921	1,355	1,420	1,574	33	37	36	36	19.6
Small scale	670	990	1,050	1,164	24	27	27	27	20.2
Single user	622	466	597	662	22	13	15	15	2.1
Total packaged software[b]	2,791	3,633	3,898	4,320	100	100	100	100	15.7
Services									
Professional services	3,039	3,576	3,849	4,336	30	31	32	33	12.6
Processing services	1,602	1,517	1,635	1,781	16	13	13	13	3.6
Support services[d]	2,603	2,663	2,749	2,772	26	23	23	21	2.1
Total software and services[d]	10,035	11,389	2,131	13,209	100	100	100	100	9.6

Source: International Data Corporation.

[a] Compound annual percentage growth rate.

[b] Totals not directly comparable with 1993–94 series because of exchange rate adjustments.

[c] Category breakdown within packaged software not available for 1992; assumed 1991 in-group ratio.

[d] Support services for 1989 estimated (using 1990 share of total IT).

and software prices stabilize, we would expect the relative sizes of the software segments to reflect this. In the meantime, it highlights the extent to which the U.K. software and services industry is still linked to the traditional pattern of the hardware market, via the installed base. This may help explain the stability of the relative sizes of the packaged and custom software markets, noted above.

Traded software is only part of the total production of software, which also includes software development by users and the large amount of embedded software developed for electronic capital goods, such as telecommunications and defense systems, by manufacturers of these products and their subcontractors. Some indication of the total U.K. production of software is given in Table 8-4. In 1984, traded

Table 8-4.   Total U.K. software production, 1984

	Value ($ billion)	Share (%)
Traded software	1.4	24
In-house data processing	2.5	42
Electronic capital goods	2.0	34
Total	5.9	100

Source: NCC, industry estimates; in Grindley 1988.

software accounted for only one quarter of all U.K. software. This share has undoubtedly risen since then, with increased use of PCs and continued growth in the share of packages rather than custom software. In addition, U.K. production of electronic capital goods has probably declined in relative terms, resulting in a drop in the share of embedded software within the total U.K. market.

Industry employment

The U.K. software industry originated with individuals and small firms contracting to provide software development to users that formerly had relied on computer manufacturers or their own data processing departments. The bulk of the software side of the industry is still made up of small, loosely organized firms, but a few large corporations have gradually emerged in both software and processing services. But many large software firms are also organized informally and make wide use of subcontracting. Data on industry structure are scarce, but the size distribution for the member firms of the Computer Services Association (CSA), shown in Figure 8-3, gives some indication of the overall structure of the industry. CSA membership is biased toward larger firms. Its 333 member firms represent software and services revenues of £3.7 billion ($6.0 billion), which account for about 60 percent of the total U.K. market and a higher percentage of custom services and processing services. CSA member firms employed 64,000 individuals in 1991, implying total employment in the U.K. software and services industry of around 110,000 (CSA 1991). Assuming that the firms that are not CSA members are mostly small firms, small firms (1–50 employees) accounted for roughly 40 percent of employment in the sector, medium-sized firms (50–500 employees) accounted for 20 percent, and large firms (more than 500 employees), accounted for 40 percent of total employment. Firms with more than 2,000 employees alone accounted for 20 percent of total employment. Processing services tend to be performed by large firms and accounted for about 50 percent of the employment of large firms. Of the largest member firms, seven employed more than 2,000 individuals, and twelve employed 1,000–2,000 individuals. The largest members of the CSA (independents and subsidiaries of other corporations), are listed in Table 8-5.

Figure 8-3. Distribution of U.K. software firms (CSA members) by size, 1991. *Source·* CSA 1991.

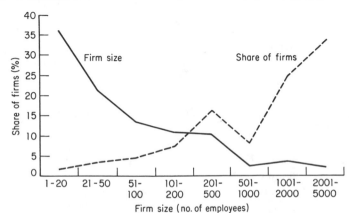

Table 8-5.   Major U.K. computer services firms (CSA members), 1991

	Firm type	Ownership
Group 1: (2,000–5,000 employees)		
Hoskyns	Software	U.S.
IBM (U.K.)	Bureau[a]	U.S.
ICL Services	Software, Bureau	Japan
Logica	Software	U.K.
SD-Scicon	Software, Bureau	U.S.
Sema	Software	U.K./France
Group 2: (1,000–2,000 employees)		
ACT Logsys	Software	U.S.
Andersen Consulting	Software	U.S.
BIS	Software	U.S.
BT Customer Systems	Software, Bureau	U.K.
Centrefile	Bureau	U.K.
Data Sciences	Software	U.K.
EASAMS	Bureau	U.K.
EDS (U.K.)	Bureau	U.S.
Ferranti Computer Systems	Bureau	U.K.
Granada Computer Services	Bureau	U.K.
Oracle (U.K.)	Software	U.S.
PA Consulting	Software	U.K.

Source: CSA (1991)

[a] Bureau services firms provide centralized processing, time sharing, and facilities management.

Foreign dominance

One of the more startling features of the U.K. industry is the high number of the larger firms that are now foreign-owned. The top forty independent firms by sales in 1992 are listed in Table 8-6; eight of the top ten firms in the table were foreign-owned, mainly by U.S. firms, and twelve of the top twenty were foreign-owned. Table 8-7, which shows the revenue shares of foreign-owned firms, shows that foreign-owned firms accounted for 83 percent of the sales revenues of the top ten and for 69 percent of the sales of the top 20. Remarkably, foreign-owned firms accounted for 63 percent of the revenue of the top forty independent U.K. software firms.

Foreign ownership grew significantly between 1986 and 1992. Table 8-8 shows changes in the membership of the top twenty independent software and services firms (excluding hardware manufacturers and general consulting firms) since 1986. Nine of the top ten firms were U.K.-owned in 1986, but by 1992 five of those had been taken over by foreign firms. Of the four that remained U.K.-owned, two, Datasolve and Software Sciences, merged to form Data Sciences in a management buyout from Thorn-EMI in 1991. In the wake of foreign acquisition of Hoskyns and SD-Scicon in 1990 and 1991 respectively, Logica remained the only major independent U.K. systems integrator that was U.K.-owned. The other major remaining U.K.-owned firm in 1995 was Centrefile, a bureau owned by National Westminster Bank. The Sema Group is jointly controlled by U.K. and French interests, with the French the major shareholders.

Table 8-6. Top 40 U.K. independent software and services vendors, 1991

Firms 1–20	$ million	Owner	Firms 21–40	$ million	Owner
Hoskyns	273	France	McDonnell Douglas	66	U.S.
AT&T Istel	255	U.S.	PA Consulting	60	U.K.
Sema Group	254	France/U.K.	Computer Sciences	60	U.S.
SD-Scicon	229	U.S.	KPMG	59	U.S.
Andersen Consulting	202	U.S.	Misys	59	U.K.
BIS Group	202	U.S.	Centrefile	56	U.K.
Logica	195	U.K.	ITNet	50	U.K.
Microsoft	195	U.S.	Lotus	48	U.S.
Oracle (U.K.)	181	U.S.	Fraser Williams	45	U.K.
Data Sciences	172	U.K.	Admiral Computing	44	U.K.
ACT Group	152	U.K.	Touche Ross	44	U.S.
EDS (U.K.)	125	U.S.	Capita Group	43	U.K.
BT Customer Systems	123	U.K.	Sherwood Computer	39	U.K.
EASAMS	116	U.K.	Data Logic	38	U.K.
Computer Associates	102	U.S.	FI Group	37	U.K.
PE International	98	U.K.	Kalamazoo	35	U.K.
Price Waterhouse	88	U.S.	Comshare	27	U.S.
Coopers & Lybrand	88	U.S.	Ernst & Young	25	U.S.
CMG	68	U.K.	LBMS	24	U.K.
Computer People	66	U.K.	EDP	23	U.K.

Source: International Data Corporation.

These figures do not include the management consultancy arms of large U.S.-based accounting firms that have entered the U.K. market with a spectrum of services including advice, hardware purchasing, systems analysis, custom software writing, training, and third party software sales. Andersen Consulting, for example, had 1986 U.K. revenues of £24 million, putting it among the top independents. Its 1991 European IT revenues of $881 million placed it behind only Cap Gemini of France and Finsiel of Italy among the independents.

A portion of this foreign ownership reflects the general merger and acquisition activity of the late 1980s, which led to a number of management buyouts of software subsidiaries of large corporations. Additional impetus for these takeovers by foreign firms, however, came from the poor performance of many of the firms in 1990 and 1991 and the desire by foreign firms to ensure market access in specialized software

Table 8-7. Foreign ownership among the top 40 U.K. computer services firms, 1991

	Foreign owned	Revenues ($ million)		Foreign revenue (%)
		Total	Foreign	
Top 10	8	2,158	1,791	83
Top 20	12	3,184	2,194	69
Top 30	16	3,701	2,427	66
Top 40	19	4,036	2,523	63

Source: International Data Corporation.

Table 8-8. Ownership changes in the top 20 U.K. computer services firms, 1986–92

	Main type	Revenue 1986 (£ million)	Ownership, 1986	Ownership change, 1986–92
EDS	Bureau	72	U.S.	—
Hoskyns	Software	62	Independent (U.K.)	Cap Gemini (France) 1990
Istel	Software	60	Independent (U.K.)	AT&T (U.S.) 1988
Logica	Software	48	Independent (U.K.)	—
Datasolve	Bureau	47	Thorn-EMI (U.K.)	Data Sciences (U.K.) 1991[a]
Scicon	Bureau	44	BP (U.K.)	SD-Scicon (U.K.) 1988; EDS (U.S.) 1991
CAP	Software	43	Independent (U.K.)	Sema (U.K./France) 1988
Centrefile	Bureau	40	NWB (U.K.)	—
Software Sciences	Software	35	Thorn-EMI (U.K.)	Data Sciences (U.K.) 1991[a]
Systems Designers	Software	31	Independent (U.K.)	SD-Scicon (U.K.) 1988; EDS (U.S.) 1991
Compower	Bureau	30	British Coal (U.K.)	—
Data Logic	Software	24	Independent (U.K.)	Raytheon (U.S.) 1990
CMG	Bureau	24	Independent (U.K.)	—
BIS	Software	23	Independent (U.K.)	NYNEX (U.S.) 1986
Kalamazoo	Software	22	Independent (U.K.)	—
Comshare	Bureau	19	U.S.	—
Pactel	Software	16	PA Group (U.K.)	—
Computer Sciences	Bureau	15	U.S.	—
CCF	Software	13	Independent (U.K.)	—
P-E	Software	13	Ensign (U.K.)	—

Source: Datalink, March 30, 1987; Dun and Bradstreet Newsletter (various issues),1992.

[a] Datasolve and Software Sciences merged to form Data Sciences in a management buyout from Thorn-EMI.

market segments. The acquisitions spree among the larger systems integrators now seems to have been completed. According to the Sema Group president, most of the remaining independent software firms are "body shops" with little marketing expertise (*Datamation*, 1 July 1992).

Balance of trade

About 50 percent of the software sold in the United Kingdom is produced domestically, mainly in the custom business. U.S. firms have always occupied a strong position in the U.K. software market, but their market share is increasing with the growth in packaged software sales. Of the applications packages sold in the United Kingdom about 70 percent are of U.S. origin. Examples include all the well-known PC applications packages such as Lotus 1-2-3, Excel, WordPerfect, Word, and dBase, and leading mainframe applications packages, such as MSA General Ledger, Mark V database management, and IBM's Material Requirements Planning System (MRPS). Almost all operating systems are of U.S. or Japanese origin, supplied by the computer manufacturers or, for PCs, by independents such as Microsoft and Novell.

No more than 7 percent of U.K. software output is exported (ACARD 1986). Foreign sales are hard to measure, because those reported by U.K. firms may include earnings of overseas subsidiaries, U.K. staff working for overseas subsidiaries, and sales to associated companies. U.K.-produced packages sold extensively in foreign markets are rare. Apart from ICL operating systems, there are a few internationally known packages in banking and finance, such as BIS's Midas, Metier's Artemis, and CCF's Super Xtas. Among the top twenty independents only BIS, CCF, Kalamazoo, and Comshare are known for packages.

TRENDS IN THE U.K. SOFTWARE INDUSTRY

The U.K. software industry has had difficulty responding to several long-term trends that are affecting the global software industry. It has remained generally successful as a developer of custom systems for the domestic market, and the spate of takeovers in this area consolidating market access indicates the importance attached to the segment by global firms. In other areas such as PC packages and the latest developments in network systems, U.K. firms have almost no presence in either global or domestic markets. In these areas the United Kingdom is largely an observer and consumer of new products rather than a producer. This is not solely a British problem: the dominance of the U.S. computer hardware and software industries is equally apparent in the rest of Europe. Moreover, some British firms have responded to the challenge: The case of ICL, though not primarily a software producer, is discussed below.

Maturity of Custom Software and Consulting Services

Although the custom area has grown more slowly than packages, until the early 1990s it was still growing remarkably quickly. From 1980 through 1985, it grew at nearly 20 percent per year in real terms. This growth rate gradually slowed, falling to 11 percent by 1989, and the segment exhibited its first employment declines in the second half of 1990. Output continued to fall in 1991 and 1992. Employment among CSA member firms (in all areas) fell by 2 percent between 1990 and 1991, from 64,600 to 63,600, a figure that underestimates the reduction because it includes the increases in the number of CSA member firms during the period (CSA 1991). The demand for software was so great during the 1980s that the industry was thought to be recession-proof, with constant shortages of skilled personnel and excess demand. Labor shortages were one reason for the independent industry's appearance in the first place; the independents provided a flexible way to supply skills in a rapidly changing market and allowed individual contractors to capture a greater share of rents. By 1988, however, demand had slackened in the less sophisticated product segments, as employment markets in nonspecialized areas softened. Demand nevertheless remained strong in newer, more sophisticated areas, such as specialized defense and other systems, networks (linking existing systems in preparation for the European single market), and other systems integration (Grindley 1988). During 1990–92, however, even these specialized markets showed slow growth. Users postponed large software projects, and the custom houses suffered losses. Staff were reduced for the first time in many of the firms' histories. The industry recovered during 1993–94 and is predicted to continue growing at a moderate pace. The recession shows, however, that the U.K. custom applications and consulting area, as it has existed since the 1970s, has become a mature service business tied to the performance of the economy as a whole.

Expansion of Packaged Software

The maturation of the custom software market has occurred in part because of the inroads made by packaged software into areas long thought to require custom solutions. This trend, of course, is only the latest manifestation of a displacement process that has been under way throughout the industry's history; IT has progressively standardized functions that once needed specialized software.[2] Although this process continually reduces the need for one type of customized software, until the early 1990s it supported growth in the market for computers and demand for custom applications. This may still be true for major "strategic" systems, but the new high-growth markets for software in the PC and workstation segments are those for packages, both because of the size of the market and the pressure for low-cost solutions. Even many users of major systems prefer an off-the-shelf package that allows for system upgrades over an expensive custom solution that has a high initial cost and high maintenance costs, which may quadruple the initial investment (Lientz and Swanson 1980).

As a result many applications that once were served by custom systems are now available as inexpensive packages. A CAD/CAM system that in the mid-1980s would have cost several hundred thousand pounds using a dedicated minicomputer might typically be available in the mid-1990s as a workstation package costing perhaps thirty thousand pounds. The same is happening in desktop publishing, graphics, data retrieval, multi-media, and many other areas. This process has contributed to the reversal of the long-standing excess demand for U.K. custom software, which became apparent in the downturn of the early 1990s. The beneficiaries of this transfer of demand tend to be foreign producers.

Changing Types of Custom Software

Demand for custom software, however, will not disappear. Cheaper hardware also creates new demands for custom software. But the type of custom software needed is likely to differ from that of the past. The types of software for which demand has become strong are specialized areas such as communications and the design of networks for specific user applications. The need for customized integration of systems based on standard packages and hardware also should support growth. So far the U.K. custom software houses have been quick to adapt to new areas of demand. The growth of systems consulting at the expense of contract programming represents part of a broader shift in the role of software firms toward a systems integrator role. Whether this can make up for declines in demand for traditional applications is not clear; recent experience suggests that it cannot.

Systems Integration and Links to Manufacturers

The success of the efforts by major software houses in the United Kingdom to meet the growing demand for systems integration will be critically affected by the entry of the manufacturers into this role. At one level their entry reflects the increasing importance put on software and services by the manufacturers, which has been under way since the 1980s. As hardware prices have fallen, software and services account for a larger share of revenues and are a key to earnings growth. Software is also an important way to differentiate products. As recently as the late 1980s, this strategy consisted of ensuring that specific applications were available for one's machines, and some manufacturers developed strengths in particular areas (for example, manufacturing, retailing, or scientific systems). There was a partial "rebundling" of software as manufacturers integrated forward into applications.

More recently, effort at such differentiation has been extended to broader strategies that treat software as a business in its own right, as well as a means to ensure a market for the manufacturers' hardware. Rebundling has been superseded by more informal, flexible integration, often through alliances with other manufacturers and software producers. Manufacturers want to ensure that independently produced software packages (operating systems and applications) are available for their machines and will perform efficiently with their particular computer architectures. Collaboration with independent software developers tends to be of two kinds: close alliances at the systems level aimed at specific developments (for example, IBM's collaboration with Microsoft on the PC-DOS and OS/2 operating systems) and looser collaboration on applications, such as providing system specifications and marketing help and arranging joint distribution (for example, IBM encouraged software developers, such as Lotus, WordStar, and Ashton-Tate, to provide the applications that helped establish the PC).[3] An example of manufacturing integration is Hewlett-Packard's production of laser printers, which relies on externally developed software font control systems and standard printer languages (such as Apple and Microsoft's TrueType), H-P's proprietary Page Control Language, and a hardware laser printer engine bought in from Canon.

Collaboration with manufacturers, formal and informal, is only one of several ways to develop software systems. It nevertheless gives software developers advantages, both directly and indirectly, in keeping up with the technological frontier. Because adoption by a computer manufacturer is still a crucial seal of approval for a new software package, U.K. and other European software firms, which lack an indigenous computer industry, are at a disadvantage. Potential U.K. package developers do not get early access to design specifications that would enable them to develop software for new generations of hardware before they appear on the market, putting them at a permanent disadvantage. This problem applies most strongly to packages, especially packaged operating systems and mass market applications, which need to be at the frontier to compete. Even in the areas in which local user knowledge is more critical, such as custom systems, U.K. independent producers are under pressure/the computer manufacturers act more as systems integrators, they directly or indirectly offer complete systems solutions. At the same time, the U.K. independents are being challenged by the entry of processing service firms such as EDS and consultants such as Andersen Consulting into integrator roles.

One U.K. company that has succeeded as an integrator is ICL. Although it remains a computer manufacturer, ICL also designs systems that combine externally supplied equipment, mainly from its parent company, Fujitsu, with its own hardware elements and a diverse array of internally developed software for systems and applications. Collaboration between ICL and Fujitsu began with an agreement in 1981, in which ICL retained responsibility for system architecture and design but relied on components from Fujitsu. ICL's position relies on its strengths in developing user-oriented applications and services and its ability to combine these with broad systems design. Although ICL has been a major advocate of open systems, the firm recognizes the continued importance of software and hardware links:

> Yet paradoxically in the commodity-like computer market of the 1980s and 1990s, in which the user has become less and less concerned with the physical realization of information systems (IS) products, success in the business will depend crucially on access to the best emerging technology. ICL is not large enough to develop this all by itself and so has gained long-term access to the best semiconductor technologies from Fujitsu, and to communications technology from STC [ICL's parent corporation during 1984–91]. (Campbell and Kelly 1989, 355)[4]

Links to Major Packaged Software Producers

Much of what has been said about links to U.S. hardware manufacturers applies to links with major software developers. An important recent trend in the software industry is the consolidation of the market across product lines. The large software producers now rival the manufacturers in their ability to influence market development. This is most evident in PC software, the market for which, following mergers in the 1990s, is now dominated by four producers (Microsoft, Novell/WordPerfect, Lotus, and Aldus/Adobe), who offer all-encompassing applications combining many features within a single system.[5] Major packages now tend to encompass tools such as grammar checking, presentation assistance, and drawing features, which once were provided only by specialized, stand-alone programs.

Consolidation among product lines in packaged applications software influences the type of software a new independent producer can offer and the route taken to establish it on the market. Applications that may once have been provided by small producers are now covered by the major packages, and new applications need to be compatible with an existing package with an established installed base. This raises barriers to entry in certain segments. In order to establish a new software product, a small producer must be aware of the software development plans of the major firms. It is difficult for British firms to keep abreast of developments in the software market because of its domination by firms headquartered in the United States. British firms may consider focusing on user-oriented applications, as other firms in Western Europe have done (see chapter 7), and relying on formal or informal links with international software corporations to establish a package in the market and keep up with the technology. Although British software producers often collaborate with other software producers on individual projects, these tend to be custom systems for domestic customers. There is little evidence of attempts by U.K. software firms to develop links with packaged software producers, especially producers based outside the United Kingdom.

Open Systems

A key change in the computer industry since the mid-1980s has been the rise of open systems, which allow software to run on hardware from different manufacturers and equipment to be interconnected in networks. Standards are defined by the operating system and the computer architecture: for example, for the PC by Microsoft's DOS operating system and Intel's x86 chip architecture; for larger systems by Unix and the X/Open architecture. Although its implications can be considered only briefly here, the rise of open systems is of crucial strategic importance to the IT industry and is part of the major restructuring now under way within the industry.[6]

Among other effects, open systems mean that hardware and software development become more independent of each other. For software producers, the "platform independence" of software should mean that software development need not be deeply concerned with the characteristics of the particular equipment on which it runs. It simplifies some of the technical aspects of systems integration and allows systems developers more freedom to concentrate on user applications. As a result, the importance of links to manufacturers may decline in the future. For example, applications mght not have to be fundamentally redesigned if, each time improvements in hardware performance increase the speed at which an application runs, the interface is unaffected. Nevertheless, even in a "commoditized" hardware industry developers need access to the most advanced technology to retain their competitive edge.

As the growth of open systems makes it easier for U.K. and other European firms to compete in global software markets, they may be able to exploit their skills in user-oriented applications development, based on familiarity with markets and user needs. They will still need to retain close links to technological advances and to the creators of the de facto standards. In this respect, it is interesting that ICL led early efforts, starting with the establishment of the X/Open group with other European computer manufacturers in 1984, to introduce open systems and the use of the Unix operating system as a counterweight to IBM's market power. U.K. systems developers also have benefited from European Commission (EC) rules favoring Unix-based systems, but it is probably too soon to know whether open systems will create other opportunities in package markets.

U.K. GOVERNMENT POLICY FOR SOFTWARE

Policy Aims

British policymakers became increasingly concerned during the early 1980s about the decline in their nation's performance in IT. A number of studies pointed out that the United Kingdom was becoming uncompetitive in most aspects of IT and took the view that although the U.K. computer hardware industry was unlikely to regain a leading position, the software industry could still become a major force (Alvey 1982; OECD 1984; ACARD 1986; DTI 1987). Another motive for action was the prospect of large and increasing trade deficits in IT. The deficit in 1983 was £928 million for IT as a whole and was expected to reach £9 billion by 1990. Of this projected amount, software alone accounted for £2 billion. The result of this consensus was a series of new efforts in R&D and education, some of which also utilized longstanding IT development programs for defense needs. The most significant of the research initiatives in the software area was the Alvey program, running from 1983 to 1988, which combined funding from defense, industry, education, and research in a single program aimed specifically at building U.K. capability in software development. This section discusses U.K. policy initiatives in software development, education and defense, starting with the Alvey program.

The Alvey Program

The Alvey program was a collaborative R&D program in software technology with participation by industry, government, and academia. The program was named for Sir John Alvey, former head of R&D at British Telecom, who had chaired the Committee on the Future of IT in the United Kingdom, which had recommended the joint program in its 1984 report. The focus was on precompetitive R&D, to strengthen the technology base and create a software industry able to compete in domestic and export markets. Program supporters believed that the United Kingdom could regain a leadership position by concentrating on software alone and need not be handicapped by its poor performance in computer manufacturing. The optimistic goal in 1983 was to achieve a world leadership role "within five years" (Alvey 1984).

The program was given political urgency and shocked into existence by the Japanese Fifth-Generation (5G) Program in computer architecture, which was started in 1981. British industry managers and officials feared that it would lead to Japanese dominance of the computer industry (Keliher 1990). Alvey was approved in 1982 and ran from 1983 to 1988; plans for a second five-year program were scrapped in 1988. Alvey was modeled on 5G, both in its subject matter and in its stress on precompetitive collaborative research (Gaines 1984). The program was planned to cost £350 million ($550 million) over five years, of which £200 million was contributed by the government and £150 million by industry. Funding for industrial projects carried out within the firms, which involved two or three members each (firms and academic institutions), was split equally between the government and the firms involved. There were also a large number of smaller academic projects that involved "industrial uncles" (collaborators and advisers) that were 100 percent government-funded. Participation was limited to U.K. companies, with few exceptions. Government funding was shared by the defense, industry, and education ministries (see Table 8-9).[7] Alvey involved no new funding; instead, in contrast with previous government R&D support, funding for existing programs was coordinated under a single program.

Alvey was organized into five areas:

- Very large scale integration (VLSI): Design, manufacturing, and testing of integrated circuits, development of chip architectures, and CAD techniques.
- Software engineering (SE): Development of formalized methods of specifying and generating software, leading to automatic software production, including integrated project support environments (IPSEs) and tools, reusable software, formal methods, and reliability and testing.

Table 8-9. Government sponsorship of the Alvey program
(£ million)[a]

Department	Plan	Actual
Ministry of Defense	40	37
Science and Engineering Research Council (SERC)	50	64
Department of Trade and Industry (DTI)	110	110
Total	200	211

Source: Guy et al. 1991.

[a] Final figures.

- Intelligent knowledge-based systems (IKBS): Development of expert systems and artificial intelligence (AI) techniques.
- Man-machine interface (MMI): Overcoming human problems of computer input and output, ergonomics, and speech and graphics processing.
- Large-scale demonstrators: Development of demonstration systems for software engineering and other techniques.

The project costs, number of projects, and average project size are given in Table 8-10. Although software engineering did not receive the largest single share of funding, it was the key discipline; it embodied the main objectives of the program and was central to success in other areas. It was concerned with systems design aids (workbenches) and automatic code generation from high-level specifications. Design aids consisted of support environments (IPSEs) within which to design a system, as well as computer-based tools such as code generators, reusable code, and quality and reliability testing. The specification area was concerned with advanced tools that were based on untried techniques. These included formal methods (mathematical procedures for creating and verifying code from formal specifications), reliability testing, and IKBS tools. The bulk of the funds (56 percent) within software engineering were dedicated to developing support environments. The four largest software engineering projects sought to develop IPSEs and accounted for 45 percent of the software engineering budget (Grindley 1988).

The mix of projects within Alvey reflected the interests of the funding bodies. The Ministry of Defense was concerned with VLSI (in the United Kingdom a technology mainly used in defense products), the Department of Trade and Industry (DTI) with the larger projects in software engineering and large demonstrators (support environments and tools) that seemed to have commercial promise, and the Science and Engineering Research Council (SERC) with the academically oriented programs (formal methods and artificial intelligence). The relative size of these activities within the program was influenced by each group's monetary contribution (Alvey 1987; NAO 1988; Guy et al. 1991).

One hundred and twenty-seven organizations participated in Alvey; many of these were academic institutions; most involved large projects and large firms. The top five Alvey projects received 61 percent of the government funding, and the top ten received 81 percent. As Table 8-10 indicates, Alvey's academic projects were much smaller. In software engineering, which sponsored 103 projects, the single largest project accounted for 20 percent of the funds and the top five for 50 percent. A few large firms were involved in many Alvey projects. The six most active firms (General Electric, ICL, Plessey, British Telecom, STC, and Ferranti) accounted for over £76 million, or 36 percent, of government funding and 53 percent of the "participations" (see Table 8-11). The leading Alvey participants were not software houses but capital goods manufacturers. These firms had long-standing ties to U.K. government R&D and procurement programs and had resources to contribute their required share of project costs (Keliher 1990). Their predominance also reflected their activity in the defense-oriented VLSI program, which was dominated by these top six firms. However, these firms also were prominent in the other Alvey research areas. Software houses such as Software Sciences, Logica, SDL, and CAP were active on a smaller scale, mainly in software engineering and IKBS.

Table 8-10. Alvey projects and expenditures

Project group	Expenditure (£ million)[a]					Number of projects				Avg. project expenditure (£ mil.)		
	Industry	Uncle	Total	%	Alvey	Industry	Uncle	Total	%	Industry	Uncle	Total
VLSI	143.8	1.9	145.7	39	73.8	61	21	82	26	2.36	0.09	1.78
Software engineering	48.4	5.1	53.5	14	29.3	35	31	66	21	1.38	0.16	0.81
IKBS (expert systems)	51.4	4.5	55.9	15	30.2	55	46	101	32	0.93	0.10	0.55
Man-machine interface	44.6	1.5	46.1	12	23.8	40	15	55	18	1.12	0.10	0.84
Large demonstrators	41.0		41.0	11	20.5	7		7	2	5.86		5.86
Nonproject	33.4		33.4	9	33.4							
Total	362.6	13.0	375.6	100	211.0	198	113	311	100	1.83	0.12	1.21

Source: NAO 1988; Alvey 1987.

[a] 1988 figures.

Table 8-11.   Major industrial participants in the Alvey program[a]

Firm	Project participations	Government funding (£ million)
General Electric	66	23
ICL	37	15
Plessey	39	10
British Telecom	31	9
STC/STL	31	9
Ferranti	18	9
Racal	9	4
Software Sciences	7	3
Logica	16	2
Systems Designers (SDL)	10	2
British Aerospace	7	2
CAP	2	1
Hewlett-Packard	2	1
Total Alvey	425	210

Source: Guy et al. 1991.

[a] Firms receiving over £1 million funding; final figures.

The tangible results of the Alvey program were disappointing. Aimed at providing a technological base for British firms' penetration of world markets in the 1990s, few of the projects had much market impact. Of the two hundred industrial projects only ten had generated marketable products by 1987 (NAO 1988). These ten projects were predominantly defense applications drawn from the VLSI program. Software engineering, the centerpiece of the program and the one most intended to lead to exploitation, produced no marketable output at all.

Other analysts, however, have emphasized Alvey's intangible benefits: changing industrial attitudes toward collaboration and influencing future policies. Perhaps the most important attitude change has been a shift in favor of collaboration between participating firms and with academic institutions. Collaboration has become a virtual byword of business strategy in the 1990s, but at the start of the Alvey program it was less well appreciated, and many participants noted that it made a change in their approach. There was also an increased awareness of new techniques in the industry and greater belief in the value of links between academia and business.

The attitude changes induced by Alvey are important, but they were never the main goal of the program, and some almost certainly would have occurred without Alvey. In addition, Alvey's lack of demonstrable results gave fuel to critics of corporatist industrial policy, especially within a government that during the 1980s placed greater emphasis on small business.[8] Its lack of tangible results made the continuation of Alvey hard to justify, and it was abandoned after its first five years. More modest U.K. efforts continue as part of ESPRIT and other EC programs.

Many of Alvey's problems reflected the way it was devised and organized. It was justified "from the top down" on political grounds by the threat of foreign competition and the desire to "regain lost leadership," without much detailed analysis of the problems of the industry or what it realistically was capable of achieving.[9] Alvey was modeled on the 5G program, even though this Japanese program focused on basic research rather than marketable products (Pollack 1992). Alvey was managed by a small "umbrella" directorate composed mainly of government administrators rather than industry personnel.[10] The directorate succeeded in getting a portfolio of projects together and under way remarkably quickly, within fourteen months. But the structure of the program meant that project selection and evaluation, advisory committees notwithstanding, was largely an administrative exercise rather than anything that was carefully coordinated with program strategy. This probably contributed to the bias toward large firms, which were better able put together appropriate projects.

Alvey's structure also contained a basic contradiction. Its "precompetitive" design masked a serious tension between generic research and the demand by the government sponsors for demonstrable results and commercial impact. Collaboration was expected to end before marketable products were produced; participants would then use the research results to develop marketable products outside the program, in many cases competing with one another in commercialization. In the event, participating firms were willing to collaborate on generic research but were less willing to share key technologies that might be commercialized by competitors. Except in VLSI, which was aimed at existing defense markets, it is hardly surprising that Alvey concentrated on generic software engineering in areas that were unlikely to convey an immediate competitive advantage, and in fact did not lead to deliverable output.

More fundamentally, the failure of Alvey may indicate the difficulty of trying build a software industry based on "technology push." Program managers took it as an article of faith that formalizing the development process would support the rapid growth of a new industry. The software engineering program's choice of projects may have been too heavily influenced by large capital goods producers and academic specialists. This led to projects that emphasized the control and automation of the software writing process, on the one hand, and esoteric AI techniques and formal methods, on the other. The original policy committee lacked significant representation by users or small producers. The resulting "technology-push" approach reflected the views of a narrow segment of the industry, despite its original aims of broad exploitation of software.

The SE program's stress on automated factories was also inconsistent with the changing demands on project management resulting from the growth of packaged software, which required user-oriented systems development. The "factory model" has been shown to be effective in a narrow set of circumstances, particularly in organizing large numbers of analysts and programmers in the production of closely specified, often custom, systems (Cusumano 1989). In these cases, such as the development of large-scale computer operating systems, consistency rather than originality is critical. Where development depends more on the generation of new ideas and new ways of organizing tasks, as in most applications areas, a less formal approach with scope for individual responsibility may be more effective. Moreover, even the Japanese "factories" have focused mainly on methods of organizing people rather than on automating the production process.

In addition, Alvey's exclusion of foreign-based firms prevented access to valuable inputs and markets in what is now a global industry. The United Kingdom represents about 4 percent of the world software market and only about 2 percent of world production; it is unrealistic to expect to create an internationally competitive industry in such a small market. Another indication of the program's inattention to the needs and capabilities of the U.K. software industry were the problems created within Alvey by major skills shortages in software engineering. These affected half the projects, causing delays and many project cancellations. In the area of IKBS (expert systems) it was estimated that *all* the available expertise in the United Kingdom was involved in Alvey projects (NAO 1988).

Alvey influenced the design of other IT support programs in the European Community and elsewhere. The EC's ESPRIT program was strongly influenced by Alvey. It was also aimed at software and covered virtually the same areas as Alvey, including advanced microelectronics, software engineering, and artificial intelligence, with applications efforts in office automation and computer integrated manufacturing. It ran in two five-year phases, from 1984 to 1989 and 1988 to 1993, budgeted at ECU 1.5 billion and ECU 3.2 billion ($1.25 billion and $2.75 billion) respectively. It was organized as a series of precompetitive collaborative R&D projects carried out on-site at members' premises, with 50 percent EC funding, under the administration of an "umbrella" directorate. About half the Phase I projects were from industry, half from academia; Phase II put more stress on applications (Nasko 1983; Nelson 1987). ESPRIT has itself produced few marketable products, though it has completed its second five-year phase. Commentators have stressed the benefits of more openness toward cooperation and diffusion within the fragmented European industry.[11] ESPRIT has in turn become the model for a number of other European programs with strong software elements, including AIM, BRITE, Eureka, and RACE.[12] There have also been a series of similar programs in other technologies.[13] In this sense the Alvey program has been highly influential on policy and helped set the agenda for government-backed research programs for over a decade.

Education and Training

A consistent concern of government and industry has been the shortage of skilled software development personnel, which has been a problem for most of the history of the software industry. The original Alvey committee argued that skills shortages restricted the industry's ability to expand, and it recommended that education and training programs in software engineering be part of the program (Alvey 1982). The need for increased education and "in-service" training in software, as well as other areas of IT, has been noted in many other policy studies, including those of the Advisory Council on Applied R&D (ACARD) in 1979 and 1986, the Finniston Committee on the Engineering Profession in 1980, and the Select Committee on Science and Technology in 1984 (ACARD 1979, 1986; House of Commons 1980, 1984). The situation has not improved since. The Bide Committee, studying the successor to Alvey in 1986, reported that Alvey had not solved the skills problem (Bide 1986). The National Computer Centre reported in 1986 that 25 percent of software suppliers stated they were "crippled" by lack of staff, and the most frequent problem reported by industry representatives to the Warren Committee on the U.K. information technolgies industry (which focused on software) in 1988 was lack of training (NAO 1988; House of Commons 1988). The consensus has been that responsibility for the shortage lies both with educational policy and with industry.

Government funding of higher education has attempted to increase the supply of graduates in engineering and technology with skills in IT. The IT in Higher Education (ITHE) initiative, which began in 1982, increased IT student places at universities and colleges. The Engineering and Technology Program (ETP), initiated in 1985, also increased student places in IT subjects. These programs raised the number of graduates in mathematics and computer science from 4,200 in 1982 to 7,200 in 1990, and in electronic and electrical engineering from 2,700 to 4,600.

A number of government initiatives have promoted IT in other areas of education (see Table 8-12). Some of these schemes are aimed at technology training in general but have included large elements of IT and software, while others have been aimed specifically at IT and software. Several schemes have encouraged more widespread use of computers. Early schemes such as the Micros in Education Program (MEP) focused on the introduction of PCs in primary and secondary schools. Later schemes, such as the establishment of the City Technology Colleges, provide specific training in IT for sixteen and seventeen year olds. Postgraduate education programs have established partnerships between industry and colleges in the employment and training of technology graduates, including IT and software. The main ones are the Teaching Company Scheme (TCS), the Integrated Graduate Development Scheme, and the Cooperation Awards in Science and Engineering (CASE). Finally, a number of continuing education programs have been established. The Manpower Services Commission (MSC) has schemes (associated with unemployment programs) such as the Training Opportunities Program (TOPS) and Opentech for adult and youth training that include IT training, mainly at the technician level. Other schemes such as Interactive Video provide training for individuals working full time. The Alvey program proposed to include research studentships and training, and to monitor IT skills needs, but these steps were not approved by the government. Some monitoring functions were later set up by the DTI and the Confederation of British Industry (CBI).

Simply increasing the numbers of software engineering graduates may not by itself reduce the supply shortages, at least in the short run. The skills most needed by industry are highly specialized and are in especially short supply in new fields that may not have established training courses, such as communications networks and graphics. There are fewer shortages in standard software programming skills and even some unemployment. In other words, the supply of general skills may be adequate, but supply does not match demand in some specialized areas. The problem is not one of sheer numbers but of the types of training required. The skills that are in short supply are those that combine business understanding and technical ability. This suggests an opportunity for broadening educational syllabuses, but many such skills may be best learned on the job. Industry needs to be involved in the training process, and this view has motivated the education-industry collaboration in many of the programs named above. These schemes have received positive evaluations, especially the postgraduate programs.

A large part of the skills problem lies with the industry itself and its low rate of training. The U.K. software industry itself invests very little in training, the level having been described as "pitifully low" by international standards.[14] Many IT firms have admitted that they have a responsibility for on-the-job training and could do more (House of Commons 1988). They support less of this than they would like because of the difficulties of retaining trained employees. Shortages of personnel and

Table 8-12. Representative U.K. education policy programs in IT areas, 1974–88

Type	Title	Starting date	Sponsor	Description
Schools	Micros in Schools Scheme	1980	DTI	Aid for purchase of PCs; 6,500 installed
	Micros in Education Program (MEP)	1980	DTI	Aid for development and teacher training
	Support for Educational Software	1985	DTI	Support for purchase of software
	Mini-Enterprise Scheme	1986	DTI	Mini-companies in schools
16 year-olds	Information Technology Centers (ITECS)	1981	DTI/MSC	IT training; 175 centers (1986); 6,000/yr.
	City Technology Colleges	1988	DES	Government/industry sponsored colleges
Higher education	IT in Higher Education (ITHE)	1982	DES	Increase IT student places in higher education
	CNC Machine Tools in Further Education	1983	DTI/DES	Bought U.K. CNC machine tools (engineers)
	Engineering and Technology Program (ETP)	1985	DES	Increase technology student places
	Polycad Scheme	1986	DTI/UGC	Grants for CAD equipment; 94 colleges
Postgraduate	Teaching Company Scheme (TCS)	1974	ITI/SERC	Industry/academic partnerships
	Integrated Graduate Development Scheme	1979	SERC	College/business collaboration in training
	Cooperation Awards in Science and Engineering (CASE)	1980	SERC	Industry and univ. supervised research grants
Continuing education	Microelectronics Application Program (MAP)	1978	DTI	College course grants (microelectronics)
	Training Opportunities Program (TOPS)	1981	MSC	Adult technology training; various levels
	Opentech	1982	MSC	Open learning for technicians and supervisors
	Interactive Video	1985	DTI	Grants for distance learning

Source: NAO 1988.

225

the active market for independent contractors has made it easy for workers to switch jobs (reported attempts by some firms to retain graduates via employment contracts have usually proved unsuccessful). The downturn in the early 1990s in the job market for software engineers suggests that firms should have focused more on the long term in training investment. But the ability of a firm to adopt a farsighted policy depends on the business environment in which it finds itself, and for the software houses this has always been unpredictable. Firms' employment and training policies reflect their overall business strategies, which stress flexibility and low levels of commitment. The elements of "market failure" in this problem suggest some scope for greater use of the long-term joint programs between education and industry as an effective way of combining theoretical and practical training and as a mechanism to retain trainees with their sponsoring firms for longer periods.

A further difficulty in the U.K. software skills supply has been that what university education and research delivers has not necessarily met industry needs. The weak links between British universities and industry that hampered industrial exploitation of the original university-developed computers continues in the 1990s in software techniques. Computer science as an academic subject is often oriented more to software theory than to the practicalities of creating systems. Computer science in the United Kingdom grew up in mathematics and statistics departments of the universities rather than in engineering departments, and the academic departments have tended to concentrate on theoretical concepts such as formal proofs and mathematical methods rather than on developing usable software. The emphasis on formal methods and artificial intelligence techniques in the Alvey academic projects are examples of this. Industry has argued that college researchers are too academically oriented; they assert, only half in jest, that "the trouble with computer science departments is that no one writes programs."

There are some recent signs of change in this orientation. Computer science in the 1990s is an independent academic department at many universities that are able to determine their own direction. Moreover, as educational policy has required universities and colleges to be more self-financing, colleges have been forced to seek industrial sponsors for teaching and research. As a result, many academic researchers in computer science have become more sensitive to the needs of industry. Nevertheless, this embryonic partnership is still in its early stages and bears little resemblance as yet to the interaction between business and academia that exists in the United States (see chapters 2 and 3 in this volume).

Defense and Government Procurement

The defense industry remains internationally competitive, and the United Kingdom is the third largest global exporter of weapons. The industry is characterized by close collaboration among the Ministry of Defense, defense firms, and various research laboratories in sponsoring R&D and planning weapons procurement. Defense represents over half of U.K. government–supported R&D. This collaboration has heavily influenced the direction taken by high-technology industries, leading many firms to emphasize defense products rather than commercial areas.[15] This has not, however, always been beneficial to overall U.K. economic performance. There has been little technological spillover into civilian markets, and defense contractors have often been unable or unwilling to branch out into other sectors. Military R&D and procurement have proven especially influential in the development of segments of the IT industry, which has always been a major contributor to defense systems.

In the initial development of the computer industry, U.K. defense and other agencies were an important factor, as they were in the United States. However, unlike in the United States, few major commercial computer products resulted from this relationship. One reason for this lack of spillover was (and is) the tendency of many British firms to regard many of the nondefense markets as too small or too competitive for them to succeed in. Defense-oriented firms such as Ferranti, General Electric, and Marconi were active in building early computers but had little impact on business markets and eventually merged their commercial computer subsidiaries into ICL in the 1960s. In contrast, most U.S. computer manufacturers have seen the business market as their main target. They have developed major military systems and have exploited military technology where possible, but their largest markets have always been in business areas.

The separation of defense markets has continued to the present day. The U.K. Ministry of Defense has not attempted to sponsor "dual use" technologies (technologies that may be used for both military and civilian purposes), or to assist in the conversion of defense industries to civil production.[16] Beginning in the 1980s, however, the Ministry of Defense attempted to transfer technologies from military to civilian use, and British defense firms also have sought civilian markets for defense-oriented software and other IT products. British defense firms, in their primary market, also have tried to find civilian uses for developed defense technology. British Aerospace, for example, has investigated possibilities to adapt "fly-by-wire" systems to control high-speed trains. Ferranti and Sema, the software company, have sought civil applications of the Ada software language developed for U.S. military systems and have applied this successfully to the development of control systems for nuclear power stations (*Financial Times*, 13 July 1990). GE-Marconi sought to develop civilian applications in command-and-control systems for air traffic management, industrial simulators, road traffic monitoring, and highway safety, but these were abandoned in favor of remaining focused on military markets in 1991.

In general the U.K. software industry reveals very few examples of economically successful spillovers from military to civilian products. It has been said that the difficulties are "not primarily technical. . . . but reflect a cultural gap between companies' marketing other activities for the defense and civil markets."[17] Even in areas of potential spillover, MoD procurement has favored a small number of incumbent producers specializing in defense markets and has done little to promote private innovation or to change the structure of the IT industry.[18] Equally, there are important differences between military and civilian technologies. Many military computers, for example, require guaranteed fault-free software, operating in real time, responding to military events as they happen. Although reliability is also important in civil software, developers and users have not been willing to pay for this level of quality, and developers are more concerned with user-oriented applications.

Thus, although defense continues to provide a large volume of business for the U.K. software industry, it is a niche market with few spillovers into other areas. Much of the defense market consists of embedded software for defense systems produced by or for capital equipment manufacturers. Some independent software vendors, such as specialized subsidiaries of SD-Scicon and Sema-CAP, concentrate on defense systems. Among the key capabilities of the software firms are relationships with the government and the defense industry that have been built up over long periods. Although the client-producer relationship may provide useful lessons for other sectors, the technology, the type of systems, and the customer relationships associated with defense markets are so specialized that they have not proved to be applicable to commercial markets.

Other U.K. government departments also purchase large quantities of software, but extensive use of computers by the U.K. government began in earnest only in the early 1980s. The first major government-inspired system was the computerization of vehicle licenses by the Driver Vehicle Licensing Centre (DVLC) in 1978. The software for the DVLC was developed in-house. Although it eventually succeeded, the development task was such a traumatic experience that large projects since then have drawn heavily on outside management and contractors. Other projects include the computerization of Pay-As-You-Earn (PAYE) tax by Inland Revenue during 1986–90, at a cost of £650 million, and of local office supplementary benefits by the Department of Health and Social Security (DHSS), which began in the late 1980s and is scheduled not to be completed until early in the twenty-first century, at a projected cost of some £2.3 billion. But like defense contracts, these large public software procurement programs have yielded few direct spillovers into commercial sectors. The government has lagged behind the business world in the introduction of computer systems, and any spillovers generally have flowed in the other direction, from business to government. In addition, the modest software-related research sponsored by the main public procurers of software is focused on specific departmental requirements (Dyerson and Roper 1991a, 1991b).

Industry managers and policymakers have long encouraged the British government to use its purchasing power to support the domestic IT industry, or at least to "level the playing field" with foreign competitors (House of Commons 1988). As a practical matter, however, the government's scope for doing this is limited. Since the mid-1980s, rules for government procurement of software and hardware have required competitive tendering and acceptance of the lowest compliant bid, mediated by the Central Computer and Telecommunications Agency (CCTA); similar rules apply in defense. These policies place greater competitive pressure on domestic hardware manufacturers and standard software suppliers than on custom software producers, who may successfully develop a competitive position based on familiarity with domestic requirements.

Recent historical experience also suggests that U.K. procurement is not likely to provide a solid basis for developing new markets. The use of procurement for industrial policy has a poor history in the United Kingdom, frequently resulting in the development by "national champions" of expensive domestic products with few export markets. One example is System X, the U.K. telecommunications switch developed from 1977 to 1986, which included large amounts of software. The System X development program exceeded its original budget, fell behind schedule, and when finally introduced in 1986 was several years behind international competitors. It failed in export markets (Grindley 1987).[19] A broadly parallel case is the airborne Nimrod early warning defense radar system, which also depended heavily on software. After costly delays, development was abandoned in favor of the U.S. AWACS (airborne warning and control system) in the mid-1980s.

OPTIONS FOR THE INDUSTRY

Work Organization

The U.K. industry can be characterized broadly as consisting of a large number of small firms together with a few large corporations; each group accounts for about 40 percent of industry employment. Only 20 percent of employment is in medium-sized firms. Processing services account for around half the employment in the large firm segment, so that half the overall employment in software development appears to be in small firms. In software the large firms' main advantage is their capacity to handle major projects and their access to certain markets. These marketing strengths motivated the many acquisitions among the large software houses during the 1980s.

This structure partly reflects differences among the types of software being produced and differences in the organization of product development for different software markets. Large systems, such as operating systems for capital goods manufacturers and major processing systems for government departments, require large investments and extensive project management. These large custom systems are the preserve of the large firms. For other types of systems, where individual creativity and responsiveness to market needs are more important, smaller firms working with a less highly structured work organization may be more effective. In addition, much of the development effort for large systems in the United Kingdom is subcontracted to smaller firms and individuals. Subcontracting provides flexibility to the prime contractor in staffing but also matches the preferences of many independent software developers, who stress flexible organization rather than strictly defined roles (Freedman and Greenbaum 1984). Individuals have less formal working conditions and often are able to extract higher rents for their skills. This is the basis for the "cottage industry" of small, loosely organized firms and outsourcing by much of the U.K. software industry.

The structure reflects different approaches to systems development, formal and informal. The problem is that new software, even for large systems, depends on individual creativity and does not seem to be amenable to the usual methods of large-scale organization. Large projects often choke up as more people are involved. To avoid this, organizations must decide whether to aim for more formality so as to manage projects more closely, or less structure so as to allow more creativity and individual responsibility. Most of the U.K. industry has followed the informal route. A few areas, epitomized by the "large projects" approach of Alvey, have adopted a formalized factory process and often have attempted to use software technology to organize and automate development.

Developing software is an unpredictable process. Software is often seen as a critical obstacle holding up the development of IT systems, and software productivity has rarely advanced as rapidly as that of hardware.[20] This phenomenon is known as the "software bottleneck." Yet the bottleneck characterization, which puts all the blame on software, may be misleading. Weaknesses in overall project definition or management often show up only in the software stage. Comparisons of "rates of progress" in hardware and software also draw a false analogy between two different processes. Developing new software involves a balance among technical possibilities, applications requirements, and various organizational and communications problems. In contrast, improving hardware performance is primarily a technological question.[21] The Alvey program, for example, attacked the software bottleneck directly by automating software development, adopting too literal a view of the problem. The main problems for new systems are at the specification stage, where what they need to do and how they should be structured is decided. Automating the production of software may do little to improve the effectiveness of overall product and project definition.

For most user-oriented packaged applications software, with poorly defined initial requirements, fast-changing technology, and broad-based needs, formal methods are unlikely to be effective. The bulk of new products are untried applications, whose success requires that they reconcile user needs, hardware capabilities, and software techniques. This task calls for breadth rather than specialization, informal rather than rigid control, and integration of different knowledge bases rather than rapid generation of new code. Although reliability is important, the main challenge is to develop systems that meet new needs. Since these are the kinds of applications that hold the greatest promise for the U.K. software industry, its informal organization may not in itself be a weakness.[22]

Formal methods for software development are likely to be most useful for a narrow range of systems with well-defined rules that do not involve identifying new needs or applying new technology and by their nature do not interact with an outside environment; examples include chess systems and purely technical systems (Land and Somogyi 1986). The "software factories" of Japanese computer firms such as Hitachi and Toshiba apply structured project management to the development of computer operating systems (Cusumano 1989; Doe 1992). These are large, standardized systems with well-defined parameters; consistency and project control are especially important. Japanese software factories are not simple production lines; they approach production organization and management with imagination rather than automation. Thus attempts to develop "automation" technologies for software development appear to have been irrelevant to the needs of the most rapidly expanding U.K. and global software markets. In Alvey's case the focus on automation reflected the dominant role within the program of large, defense-oriented firms.

Links to Hardware Development

A serious disadvantage for U.K. software producers is the lack of a domestic computer and electronics industry. The only major British computer company, ICL, uses foreign hardware. There are some PC producers, such as Apricot (also foreign-owned) and Amstrad, but these only perform final assembly in the U.K. of systems mainly manufactured abroad. In 1992 the small British firm Meiko developed a supercomputer based on the Inmos transputer. Interestingly, this development was made possible by the close links between Meiko and Inmos, the only remaining U.K. nondefense semiconductor manufacturer.

As the U.K. computer industry declined, so did the production of packaged operating system software. As the new global computer industry emerged, based on

PCs and small systems, a new U.K. packaged software industry, to serve the new segments, has not been able to establish itself, in either operating or applications systems. U.S. software firms have had a first-mover advantage in these new markets, working closely with the first PC developers. Also, competition in these software markets is different from that in traditional software markets. Product success depends on the development of constantly improved generations of software in step with rapid improvements in hardware performance, centered in the United States. In this dynamic, U.K. software developers have so far not found a way to keep close to developments. Their choices are to either improve their links to hardware developers or focus on user-oriented applications for which being at the technological frontier is less important. The problems of remoteness from hardware developments are only partially alleviated by the rise of open systems (systems in which hardware can run any one of several operating systems and their applications).

Links between software and hardware development are crucial in two ways. The architecture of widely adopted computers has obviously driven the market for the operating systems and utilities that run the computers. Operating software for large and mid-range systems is supplied by the manufacturers themselves. PC and workstation operating software is mainly developed by independents and designed for a given microprocessor architecture. Manufacturers may form alliances with independent vendors to ensure that software systems are compatible with their products (as IBM and Microsoft did for the development of the DOS and OS/2 operating systems). Also, independent vendors may supply utilities, add-ins (boards that combine hardware and software), and network software. Various versions of the Unix operating system are now being developed by both independents and manufacturers, optimized for different machines.

Because of the importance of proximity to new technological developments, applications developers also benefit from links with computer and semiconductor manufacturers. Both software and hardware firms benefit from interaction during the development of new computer and chip designs. Manufacturers are eager to ensure a supply of software for the new machines, which is especially important in efforts to establish a design as a de facto standard. Companies such as IBM, Intel, Apple, and Sun Microsystems provide the specifications of new systems to selected software producers before launch so that software is available when the machines are released.[23] They provide information, involve key software developers in prelaunch testing, and may have joint marketing agreements and other support. Large custom systems may require close cooperation between hardware and software suppliers, such as in the data networks included in the U.K.'s DVLC computerization. Links to hardware developers may become less critical with the rise in open systems but will still remain important, especially where software needs to be optimized to run efficiently on a specific architecture. The result is that the leading edges of hardware and software development move together.

For the most part, strong links between hardware and software firms are a U.S. phenomenon and most of the examples involve U.S. firms. U.K. and other European producers are left at a disadvantage. In theory, there is no reason why geographic proximity or common nationality should be a prerequisite for advance knowledge of new hardware specifications. U.S. computer firms could, for example, commission software from foreign development groups in the United Kingdom or elsewhere. In practice, however, the close ties needed to keep fully abreast of competitive developments cannot be preserved without frequent interactions over a range of issues, which are hard to organize between firms on different continents, in different time zones, and with different organizational cultures. Software firms in the United Kingdom are unlikely to take part in prerelease testing of new U.S. hardware or software and usually have access to a new technology only after it is released on the market. This limited access need not affect the domestic custom software business but may exclude British firms from international markets in packaged software.[24]

Paradoxically, Japan's microcomputer software industry, in which a strong hardware industry has failed to support the growth of a vibrant software industry, may illustrate a similar point (see also chapter 6). The lack of standardization among Japan's microcomputer platforms has stunted the growth of a large domestic packaged software market. Although software producers in this case have been able to stay close to developments in hardware from individual manufacturers, the market is fragmented between different architectures, and each segment has been too small to support a competitive software industry. The influence of the hardware industry on the growth of a national software industry thus is strong.

Can the U.K. software industry become more competitive without a strong domestic or European computer industry? Several steps could lead to a healthier industry. Government policy could encourage closer ties with foreign manufacturers. The potential for using hardware links to improve competitiveness is highlighted by ICL. As a systems integrator, it is closely associated with Fujitsu, yet it operates independently. In 1992 it was one of the few U.K. IT firms to remain profitable, while all the software houses were suffering losses and cutting staff. Many of the larger independents such as Hoskyns, SD-Scicon, and Logica have moved toward the integration role, but have not gone as far as forming close relationships with specific companies. Software firms could also consider links with other software corporations and stress user relations, as discussed below.

Links among Software Developers

Links among software developers provide another important way of keeping abreast of the market. Open systems do this by making operating systems the critical interface between applications software and a variety of hardware; applications then do not rely on a particular hardware configuration. Thus, it is also important for software developers to establish links with operating systems developers, and applications may also need to be compatible with major "keystone" applications systems. For example, in some applications software markets, major producers such as Microsoft and Lotus now define the dominant product designs and standards; any new applications system must be compatible with their products, and advance knowledge of changes in their products will give other applications producers a competitive advantage. Such links also provide marketing advantages, as they do for hardware.

These advantages are generally less available to a U.K. firm, far from the U.S. market. To change this, British firms may need to form links with established software producers, and public policy might do more to support this. Because the leading U.S. software producers are abreast of hardware developments and help define the interface between hardware and software, stronger links between them and U.K.

software firms would also provide an indirect vehicle for remaining close to advances in hardware technology.

User-Oriented Software Development

Handicapped by its lack of proximity to computer and semiconductor manufacturers, the U.K. software industry has followed an evolutionary path that differs from that of U.S. industry. U.S. hardware and software industries recognize their joint interests in ensuring that advances in software are up to date with hardware developments and that new hardware is supported by software. Several of the fastest growing software markets have been closely linked to new hardware introductions, such as the software applications needed to establish the PC in the early 1980s and those needed for RISC chips in the 1990s (see chapter 4). In developing its strong service and custom software orientation, the U.K. software industry at times has seemed to weaken its remaining links with hardware developers. In stressing the "professional" nature of the industry and its consultancy aspects, the U.K. industry has made little effort to develop mass-market packaged software products.

Although the weak links between the U.K. software industry and hardware developers are a significant disadvantage, they might be offset by greater attention to the user relationships that are so crucial to software development. Stronger user-producer links in the United Kingdom could create the software expertise on which to develop package markets and might provide a basis for alliances with manufacturers and software corporations. Despite the limits imposed by the small size of the U.K. software market, there are some sectors in which British firms could develop special knowledge, just as French and German software firms have done (see chapter 7). The major international successes in U.K.-produced packaged software have been based on close links with users in banking and finance and in project control and distribution systems.

Another advantage associated with this "user-orientation" that redounds to the benefit of the entire economy is that this strategy will encourage diffusion of IT, as suppliers of software and services work closely with users to solve problems and improve performance. By accelerating U.K. adoption and improving the productivity of the U.K. installed base, this strategy could improve overall U.K. economic performance. Unfortunately, many earlier initiatives almost entirely ignored this possibility, by emphasizing technologies of interest to large producers of custom or embedded software rather than trying to meet the needs of the enormous pool of current and potential users.

CONCLUSION

Software production in the United Kingdom has followed a different path of development than its U.S. counterpart, albeit one that has some resemblance to that of other European economies. As the number of U.K. computer manufacturers declined, software producers weakened or broke their links with domestic computer firms and developed an independent service industry, concentrating on custom software and other services. Although the industry has continued to grow with the increase in computer usage, its focus on custom software and services has left the United Kingdom out of step with the world market, which is increasingly turning to packaged software. The United Kingdom imports a very high proportion of its domestically consumed packaged software, and as much as half the software bought in the United Kingdom is of foreign (mainly U.S.) origin. The trade deficit in software is large, with scant prospect of change. The problem is likely to become more severe because the custom business may itself be threatened in the long run. The huge increase in the market for software that has resulted from the dramatic fall in the cost of computing power means that mass-produced packages are likely to encroach on many markets now served by custom software. Yet the industry is still geared to the production of expensive specialized software systems from an era of equally expensive mainframes.

The interdependence of hardware and software development remains a serious handicap for the U.K. software industry. The demand for software, measured in terms of volume, type of systems, or the mix between custom and packaged software, is changing rapidly, as new computer systems replace old mainframe equipment. U.K. software producers are not responding proactively to these changes but instead are continuing in their current path. Their distance from the centers of computer and software development in the United States and Japan makes it hard to keep up with changing demand for software and advances in hardware technology. Since the mid-1980s the computer industry has changed dramatically, with the huge rise in computer power and reduction in cost, the spread of PCs and workstations, the increase in open standards, and the use of computer networks. U.K. firms have been involved only peripherally in these changes and seem likely to take almost no part in incipient developments in multi-media, personal data communications, and integrated information services unless their behavior changes significantly.

Against this background it is possible to make some observations about strategy and policy. With current strategies the U.K. industry will likely continue to enjoy moderate success in custom software and services, facilitating the wider use of information technolgies in the United Kingdom. But the industry's prospects as a major supplier of global software are not promising, and the domestic custom market itself may be threatened in the long run. The changes listed above, such as the introduction of open systems, provide opportunities for U.K. firms. If the industry can strengthen its position in packaged software, it might expand beyond the domestic market and reduce the inroads now being made by imported packages in the custom systems market. This will require the development and marketing of user-oriented systems, a task that in turn will demand closer relations with users, together with greater use of alliances with manufacturers and software corporations, most likely foreign.

U.K. government industrial policy has so far been largely ineffective in changing the industry. The Alvey program focused on improving the production of existing types of software, particularly for large-scale systems. But Alvey was fraught with contradictions. It aimed to create a U.K. industry that could compete in international markets, yet it ignored demand trends by concentrating on software supply technologies. Successful software firms focus on the opposite strategy of stressing new uses for computers rather than seeking to improve the performance of old ones. Software efficiency, for example, may be of little consequence when hardware performance is improving so quickly. Moreover, the Alvey program's approach to improving software production technology failed to represent a spectrum of interests, opting instead for greater formalism. This too countered the trend in the global software industry toward more flexible organization and less formal means of developing systems. Software development in many sectors is moving away from "top-down development," which emphasizes the early-stage definition of requirements, toward greater involvement of users in defining and introducing systems. A third contradiction is that although greater reliability and project control are always welcome, and may be important, they are not especially marketable commodities. They tend to be most important for specialized custom systems, which are likely to be developed domestically in any case and rarely are traded internationally.

A key policy area that needs to be addressed is education and training. Although shortages of skilled personnel in IT remain, and raising the level of IT skills will benefit the industry and the economy as a whole, current unemployment levels in the industry suggest that education alone cannot ensure its health. The most severe remaining shortages are in the specialized skills associated with the most recent growth areas, which change constantly. Private firms are best positioned to recognize and respond to these changes and must assume more responsibility for in-service training, as well as for the retention of skilled personnel. Otherwise, policies to increase the numbers of graduates in computer science and engineering will have little effect on the long-term prospects for the U.K. software industry.

NOTES

Research for this article was supported by the Alfred P. Sloan Foundation through the Consortium on Competitiveness and Cooperation. Thanks go to Yasunori Baba, Tom Cottrell, Franco Malerba, Ronnie McBryde, Robert Merges, Mel Slater, Edward Steinmueller, Rob Stevens, Peter Swann, Salvatore Torrisi, and others for helpful discussions and comments, and in particular to David Mowery for editorial advice. Responsibility for opinions and any remaining errors in the paper lies with the author.

1. This includes IBM (which in 1992 received 18 percent of its revenues from software and 10 percent from services) and other computer manufacturers such as DEC, Unisys, and ICL (*Datamation*, 15 June 1990; 1 July 1992). For twenty-nine firms identified as leading hardware companies in 1992 (including PC manufacturers), computer sales accounted for only 40 percent of their combined revenues, the remaining revenues coming from software, maintenance, services, and peripherals (*Datamation*, 15 June 1993).

2. The first compilers allowed users to write programs without knowing machine code; preprogrammed utilities allowed developers to concentrate on user applications; compatible operating systems (such as the IBM 360) freed programmers from the details of individual machines; high-level languages allowed nonspecialists to write programs; worksheets and word processors allowed nonprogrammers to use computers; and so on.

3. An example of the interdependence of hardware and software development is the need for software to take advantage of the speed of Apple's Power Macintosh, which uses the PowerPC chip, introduced in March 1994. The machine's success depends on the availability of software, and Apple encouraged suppliers to produce fast versions of applications.

4. The role of the systems integrator is described by ICL as follows: "With the new products in the 1980s, computer manufacturers expanded from being suppliers of hardware and software to becoming true systems builders. ICL responded with new products-knowledge engineering, financial services, retail systems, management information systems, and decision

support systems. The new businesses are close to the spirit of professional services and distinguish the true information systems (IS) firms from suppliers of 'boxes.' Today ICL sees itself not as being primarily a hardware manufacturer, but as a creator and distributor of complex information systems and professional services. This is an appropriate stance for the 1990s" (Campbell and Kelly 1989, 356).

5. For example, there are now only three main word processing main packages (WordPerfect, Microsoft Word, and Lotus AmiPro), three spreadsheets (Lotus 1-2-3, Microsoft Excel, and Novell/Borland Quattro Pro), two database producers (Borland with dBase and Paradox, Microsoft with FoxPro and Access), one main network system (Novell NetWare), and two or three main operating systems producers (Microsoft MS-DOS and Windows, IBM OS/2, and Apple).

6. For further discussion of the impact of open systems on the computer industry see Grindley 1990 and 1995).

7. The Alvey committee originally sought 90–100 percent government support, which the Japanese government provided for the companies involved in 5G. In Britain, the government's provision of 50 percent funding, which has become the norm in collaborative programs, was reportedly insisted on by Margaret Thatcher, the prime minister at the time (Keliher 1990). This was in line with most Japanese precompetitive collaborative ventures other than 5G (Fransman 1990).

8. For public relations purposes the Department of Trade and Industry was renamed the Department of Enterprise in 1987.

9. These have been familiar themes of U.K. technology policy, evident in programs from Concorde and Advanced Gas-Cooled Reactors to System X and advanced materials (Henderson 1986; Grindley 1987).

10. The program at first sought a business leader to head the program but was unable to find one. It was eventually led by a career civil servant (Keliher 1990).

11. There were, however, political constraints on ESPRIT, which as an EC program was required to include participation from all the member states. This implies that performance comparisons between it and Alvey should not be drawn too closely (Mowery and Rosenberg 1989).

12. Representative programs are Advanced Informatics for Medicine (AIM), Basic Research in Industrial Technologies (BRITE), the European Strategic Program for Research and Development in Information Technologies (ESPRIT), European Research Technology Program (Eureka), and R&D in Advanced Communications for Europe (RACE).

13. There have been approximately forty EC collaborative R&D programs in various technological areas (Watkins 1991a, 1991b; Blau 1992), as well as collaborative programs in the United States, such as the National Center for Manufacturing Sciences (NCMS) and the Semiconductor Manufacturing Technology Corporation (Sematech) (Grindley, Mowery, and Silverman 1994).

14. This is part of a broader problem in the United Kingdom. According to a report by the U.K. Federation of Recruitment and Employment Services, U.S. businesses spend 3 percent of revenues on training in all areas, U.K. businesses only 0.15 percent (*Guardian,* 24 July 1987).

15. For example, the British semiconductor industry has consolidated and largely withdrawn from commercial markets. With the exception of Inmos, it now produces only defense-related components.

16. "British industry is perfectly capable of determining its own product ranges without government assistance," according to Alan Clarke, minister of defense procurement (*Financial Times,* 12 July 1990). Even so, defense research laboratories such as the Royal Signals and Radar Establishment (RSRE) have sought to find licensees to exploit technology and to exchange scientists with industry. The MoD and a group of 200 private sector firms, called Defense Technology Enterprises, began an initiative in 1985 to attempt to hunt out ideas from

MoD laboratories for civilian use (*Financial Times,* 9 June 1987). Since 1990 all MoD defense laboratories have been coordinated within the Defense Research Agency, as part of the U.K. policy of using agency status to introduce market principles to government institutions, giving them more autonomy, developing customer/supplier relationships in procurement and allowing them to take on outside business.

17. The statement comes from a joint DTI/MoD report on the potential civil benefit from military R&D (*Financial Times,* 12 July 1990). William Gosling, former technical director of Plessey, stated: "Basic military research carries across very easily to civil sector, but it is more difficult to transfer the techniques for the development and manufacture of military products." For example, civilian aircraft radar systems are "cooperative," with airliners fitted with transponders to identify themselves; military radar is "noncooperative," with aircraft not revealing their presence (*Financial Times,* 13 July 1990).

18. Mowery and Rosenberg (1993) point out that this is an important area of contrast between U.S. and Western European postwar defense procurement policies.

19. The cost was especially high because the delay meant that British Telecom (then government-owned) had to install interim equipment until System X was ready.

20. Improvements in electronic hardware have followed "Moore's Law," which says that performance and cost measures double every year and a half, a relationship that has held true for over two decades. In contrast, improvements in software productivity, where they can be quantified, have amounted to only a few percent a year (Brooks 1987). However, Moore's Law may soon reach its technological limits (Holden 1993). See also chapter 2 of this volume.

21. Some software concepts (such as distributed processing and computer networks) have waited years until hardware advances have made them economically feasible, yet there has been no talk of a "hardware bottleneck."

22. For a discussion of possible methods of improving software development productivity see Brooks 1987.

23. For example, to take full advantage of the new "open systems" RISC (reduced-instruction-set computing) chips, such as the IBM/Apple/Motorola PowerPC chip used in the Apple Power Mac, software writers have been encouraged to rewrite applications originally optimized for the Intel x86 and Motorola 680x0 architectures (used in the PC and Macintosh).

24. Support for the view that the dynamic performance of the software industry is linked to the size of the adjacent hardware industry is given in Swann 1993. Using U.S. data, Swann finds that the *rates of entry* of software and peripherals firms in a geographic region are positively correlated with the size-weighted number of computer manufacturing firms (i.e., hardware, components, and systems) in the same regional cluster. However, the growth rates of (existing) software and peripherals firms are uncorrelated with the same measure of manufacturing size (effectively the estimated employment).

REFERENCES

ACARD. 1979. *Technological Change: Threats and Opportunities for the U.K.* London: Her Majesty's Stationery Office.
———. 1986. *Software: A Vital Key to U.K. Competitiveness.* London: Her Majesty's Stationery Office.
Alvey. 1982. *Report of the Alvey Committee: A Program for Advanced Technology.* London: Her Majesty's Stationery Office.
———. 1984. *Software Engineering Strategy.* London: Department of Trade and Industry.
———. 1987. *Alvey Program Annual Report 1987.* London: IEE for Alvey Directorate.
Ashe, G., P. Jowett, and J. McGee   1986. *The Software Industry in the U.K.* Project Report, Centre for Business Strategy, London Business School.

Ashworth, J. 1985. "The Crisis Facing the U.K. Information Technology Industry." *Information Technology and Public Policy* 3, no. 2: 95–101.

Bide Committee. 1986. *Information Technology: A Plan for Concerted Action.* London: Her Majesty's Stationery Office.

Blau, J. 1992. "Europe Stumbling in Semiconductor Race." *Research, Technology and Management* (March–April): 3–4.

Brooks, F. 1987. "No Silver Bullet: Essence and Accidents of Software Engineering." *Computer* (April): 10–19.

Campbell, A., and T. Kelly. 1989. *ICL: A Business and Technological History.* Oxford: Clarendon Press.

Computer Services Association (CSA). 1991. *Annual Report 1991.* London: CSA.

Cusumano, M. 1989. *Japanese Software Factories.* New York: Oxford University Press.

Department of Trade and Industry (DTI). 1987. *Computing Services Industry 1986–1996: A Decade of Opportunity.* London: DTI.

Doe, P. 1992. "Here's the Truth about Japan's Software Factories." *Electronic Business* (June): 65–68.

Dyerson, R., and M. Roper. 1991a. "Building Competencies: The Computerization of PAYE." In B. Williams, ed., *IT in Accounting: The Impact of Information Technology.* London: Chapman and Hall.

———. 1991b. "When Expertise Becomes Know-How: Managing IT in Financial Services." *Business Strategy Review* 2, no. 2: 55–74.

Fisher, F., J. McKie, and R. Mancke. 1983. *IBM and the U.S. Data Processing Industry.* New York: Praeger.

Foy, N. 1971. "Government Strategy for Computer Software and Services." In E. Moonan, ed., *British Computers and Industrial Innovation.* Oxford: Oxford University Press.

Fransman, M. 1990. *The Market and Beyond: Cooperation and Competition in IT in the Japanese System.* New York: Cambridge University Press.

Freedman, J., and J. Greenbaum, J. 1984. "Wanted: Renaissance People." ICON Working Papers 4, Bristol University, Bristol, England.

Gaines, B. 1984. "Perspectives on Fifth Generation Computing." *Oxford Surveys in Information Technology,* 1–30.

Gregory, A. 1971. "The Need for Computer Education." In E. Moonan, ed., *British Computers and Industrial Innovation.* Oxford: Oxford University Press.

Grindley, P. 1987, "System X: The Failure of Procurement." Working Paper no. 29, Centre for Business Strategy, London Business School.

———. 1988. *The U.K. Software Industry: A Survey of the Industry and Evaluation of Government Policy.* Report Series, Centre for Business Strategy, London Business School.

———. 1990. "Winning Standards Contests: Using Product Standards in Business Strategy." *Business Strategy Review* 1, no. 1: 71–84.

———. 1995. "Open Computer Systems: A Standards Revolution." In P. Grindley, *Standards Strategy and Policy: Cases and Stories.* Oxford: Oxford University Press.

Grindley, P., D. Mowery, and B. Silverman. 1994. "Sematech and Collaborative Research: Lessons in the Design of High-Technology Consortia." *Journal of Policy Analysis and Management* 13: 723–58.

Guy, K., L. Georghiou, et al. 1991. *Evaluation of the Alvey Program for Advanced Information Technology.* London: Her Majesty's Stationery Office.

Henderson, D. 1986. "Concordes, AGRs and Technology: Problems of Government Policy." Paris: Organization for Economic Cooperation and Development.

Holden, D. 1993. "Statute of Limitations on Moore's Law?" *Electronic News,* 5 April, 3.

House of Commons. 1980. *Report on the Engineering Profession (Finniston Committee).* Cmnd 7794. London: Her Majesty's Stationery Office.

————. 1984. *Report by the Select Committee on Science and Technology*. House of Commons Papers. London: Her Majesty's Stationery Office.

————. 1988. *Information Technology: First Report*. House of Commons Paper 25–II. London: Her Majesty's Stationery Office.

Keliher, L. 1990. "Core Executive Decision Making on High Technology Issues: The Case of the Alvey Report." *Public Administration* 68, no 1: 61–82.

Kelly, T. 1987. *The British Computer Industry*. Beckenham, Eng.: Croom Helm.

Land, F., and E. Somogyi. 1986. "Software Engineering: The Relation between a System and Its Environment." *Journal of Information Technology* 1, no. 1: 14–21.

Lehman, M. 1981. "The Environment of Program Development and Maintenance." In A. Wasserman, ed., *Software Development Environments*. New York: Computer Society Press.

Lientz, J., and B. Swanson, B. 1980. *Software Maintenance Management*. New York: Addison Wesley.

Metropolis, N., J. Howlett, and G. Rota, .1980. *A History of Computing in the 20th Century*. New York: Academic Press.

Mowery, D., and N. Rosenberg. 1989. *Technology and the Pursuit of Economic Growth*. Cambridge, Eng.: Cambridge University Press.

————. 1993. "Does Airbus Industrie Yield Lessons for EC Collaborative Research Programs?" In M. Humbert, ed., *European Industry and Globalization*. London: Frances Pinter.

Nasko, H. 1983. "European Common Market." *IEEE Spectrum* (November): 72.

National Audit Office (NAO). 1988. *DTI: The Alvey Program for Advanced Information Technology*. London: Her Majesty's Stationery Office.

Nelson, R. 1987. "Government Policies towards the Microelectronics Industry." In Richard Langlois, ed., *Government Policy in Technology*. Oxford: Oxford University Press.

Organization for Economic Cooperation and Development (OECD). 1984. *Software: An Emerging Industry,* Paris: OECD.

Pollack, A. 1992. " 'Fifth Generation' Became Japan's Lost Generation." *New York Times*, 5 June, C1.

Swann, P. 1993. "Can High Technology Services Prosper If High Technology Manufacturing Doesn't?" Working Paper no. 143, Centre for Business Strategy, London Business School.

Watkins, T. 1991a. "A Technological Communications Costs Model of R&D Consortia as Public Policy." *Research Policy* 20, no. 1: 87–107.

————. 1991b. "The EC and Institutions of Cooperative Industrial R&D." Harvard University. Duplicated.

9

Institutional Structure and Innovation in the Emerging Russian Software Industry

Valery Katkalo and David C. Mowery

Previous chapters note that the unique characteristics of software have given rise to significant differences between the development of the software industry and that of other high-technology industries in the industrial economies. But these chapters also demonstrate the importance of national influences on industry evolution. In the case of Russia, the evolution of the software industry cannot be divorced from the institutional and political context. A discussion of the Russian software industry must therefore include some consideration of the late-twentieth-century changes in Russia's economic and political systems.

In its early years (1960–85) the Russian software industry was especially vulnerable to the constraints imposed by the highly centralized Soviet innovation system in its dependence on intellectual property protection, user-producer interactions, human resources, and a broad hardware base. The pervasiveness of the Soviet military-industrial complex prevented extensive use of military R&D as a source of civilian software innovation. Only in the early 1990s did organizational and technological changes enable the Russian software industry to respond to an emerging business environment that was beginning to resemble those of other advanced industrial societies.

This chapter's discussion is organized chronologically. The following section provides a brief overview of the software industry's evolution under the Soviet economic system. Next we examine changes in the Russian market for software after perestroika and subsequent reforms. We then discuss the Russian software industry's new institutional structure and conclude with the outlook for the Russian software industry.

THE EMERGENCE OF THE SOFTWARE INDUSTRY UNDER THE SOVIET ECONOMIC SYSTEM, 1960–85

Before 1985, the Russian software industry had passed through two stages. By the 1960s programs for computer technology development had been defined, but the Soviet microelectronics industry began only in 1962, in Zelenograd (near Moscow). Eight research centers and related experimental factories were established in this location over the next ten years.[1] The delayed development of the Soviet software industry, a central theme of this chapter, reflected the backward state of Soviet computer hardware during much of this period. Mass-produced computers of two types, the United System (ES) and Riad models, appeared only in the early 1970s. The institutional framework for Soviet software activities also was established at that time.

The Early Years of the Soviet Software Industry

The period before the 1970s consisted of two phases. During the 1940s and 1950s, Soviet computer technology advanced rapidly drawing mainly on military programs.[2] A substantial gap between advances in U.S. and Soviet computer technologies began to appear after the mid-1950s, as U.S. firms entered the commercial development of computers, quickly expanding their markets, defining standard architectures, and expanding production. The rapid pace of these commercial developments, especially the widespread adoption of computers, was not matched in the Soviet computer industry.[3]

During the 1960s, Soviet civilian computer industry policies were guided by the socialist concept of the "information society" (Judy 1986; Staar 1988, 11–18). The "information society" concept was based on two principles: support for the growth of the "command economy" and reliance on copying Western hardware designs. Under the first principle the highest priority was assigned to the needs of the institutions of the centrally planned economy and the military-industrial complex, which demanded industrial, military, and data processing applications. As we note below, the second principle proved to have severe long-term limitations in the absence of supportive changes in other policies and institutions.

These priorities omitted any significant role for higher eduation. Although the Soviet and Russian scientific academies initially had a role in the emerging computer industry, their independence from the Soviet university system reduced the role of universities in the developing software industry. This situation was exacerbated by the decision, in the early Brezhnev years, to strip the USSR Academy of Sciences of its role as chief computer designer, which forced it to give up many of its research and production facilities. By the end of the 1960s, two federal ministries closely connected with the Soviet military, Minradioprom and Minpribor, had become the dominant Soviet computer designers and manufacturers. Although the Council of Ministers established a State Committee for Science and Technology (GKNT) in 1965 to coordinate computer and other key technology programs, it remained relatively weak and was restricted to monitoring plan assignments.

The desire of government policymakers to reduce both R&D costs and uncertainty in the development of new computers, coupled with failures in the domestic development of computer hardware (such as the Ural and Minsk series) influenced the decision to choose imitation over innovation as the key approach for developing the Soviet computer industry. Minradioprom controlled efforts by the Council for Mutual Economic Assistance (CMEA) to develop mainframe computers based on IBM technology, and Minpribor did likewise for CMEA's program to develop mini-computers based on DEC designs. A large inventory of software originally written for these computers was made available at low cost. State agencies bought a few copies of such software legally (then copied them illegally) and distributed them to the users of related hardware (enterprises and organizations). Pirating of software designs was also not uncommon. This approach to developing a domestic computer industry yielded significant near-term progress, but its long-term viability was questionable. In the absence of other radical reforms in the structure of the industry and economy, a simplistic imitation strategy could not provide a viable "catch-up" vehicle, in contrast to the technology import strategies of Japan and other Asian economies during this period.

By the end of the 1960s, Soviet progress in software was modest and highly localized among industries and ministries. Much of the systems software effort focused on compiler development for ALGOL-60 and Fortran. Applications software was developed for defense uses, scientific and technical computing, and the management of complex transportation networks (such as rail and air traffic control). The small number and specialized needs of users slowed the development of Soviet computer applications. The population of experienced programmers in the USSR remained small, and there was a particularly critical shortage of modern systems programmers who had worked on large software systems. The most successful examples of systems software were some systems for managing databases and multitask monitors for computers with architectures IBM-360/370 and DEC PDP-11.

Organization of the Soviet Software Industry

In the early 1970s, high-level recognition of the importance of computer technologies for Soviet economic and national security gave a new impetus to programs supporting the Soviet software industry. The 9th Five-Year Plan (FYP), announced in 1971, set out to create a computer network to link organizations at every level of the economy. Subsequent party congresses endorsed this concept, without specifying the date by which it should be implemented. Senior Soviet officials viewed computers as a natural ally of central planning, supporting economic modernization and increasing enterprise productivity. Consistent with this emphasis, software development efforts focused on automated control and management systems (ASUs),[4] and in the early 1970s two series of computers (Riad and ASVT—created by Minradioprom and Minpribor respectively) became available for civilian industrial applications.

Rapidly growing demand for software increased the importance of university computer science training programs. To help meet the need for programmers and software engineers, universities in Moscow, Leningrad, Novosibirsk, and Voroneh (all in the Russian republic) established special faculties of "applied mathematics" in the early 1970s. A number of other computer-oriented higher education institutes were also established in Moscow at this time. With the exception of a few elite schools, however, computers were still unknown in secondary and higher education.

Soviet software producers during this period can be divided into four groups:

(1) computer centers of the Academy of Sciences, local governments, and other institutions; (2) programming organizations of ministries, including those related to the military; (3) groups of programmers at enterprises, Scientific and Production Associations (NPO), and research institutes of various industries; and (4) groups of programmers at academic institutes and universities, supported mainly by industry contracts. The bulk of the effort of the first three of these groups was on in-house software development and production for their own requirements, generally associated with their specific computer hardware installations. The necessary legal or economic (that is, intellectual property or venture capital) framework to support specialized software companies simply did not exist. Prices for application software were low and rarely exceeded 10 percent of the total cost (hardware plus software) of systems (Zotov 1991, 41).

In many Western industrial economies at this time, software development and diffusion were beginning to assume a "horizontal" structure, with specialized providers and computer manufacturers selling packaged software to users in many sectors. But the vertical structure of the Soviet ministry system worked against software standardization and diffusion. User-producer interactions were restricted to those attainable within a single ministry or enterprise, which meant that the potential economies of scale associated with supplying standard software to a broader market were largely precluded.

The Soviet economic system concentrated software development activities in several official organizations and bureaus (both regional and sectoral) and distributed programs through them. In many ministries, however, especially in the sectors related to the military, these organizations were closed to nonaffiliated users, resulting in duplication of programmers' efforts. The most important of these software development organizations, established in 1974, was the NPO Tsentrprogramm (central system of programs) organization in the city of Kalinin (now Tver) near Moscow. This organization undertook the development of some software for the ES family of computer systems (United Nations 1988, 42), but its primary task was the distribution of management systems (ASU) software. In the mid-1980s this NPO was reported to be a distributor of software for more than 3,000 enterprises and organizations (Vorobieva and Popsuev 1986, 747).

Because software development requires intensive interaction between the producer and a broad cross-section of customers, centralized development and distribution of programs by a small number of autonomous organizations was inefficient at best. Centralized development of software focused on creating programs to meet projected demand for certain software categories and gave little or no attention to the functional performance or compatibility with specific user needs (see ibid.; Morozov and Popsuev 1986, 1,074; Romanovskii and Cherkasskii 1988, 929). Meanwhile, a large "shadow economy" in trading software products emerged, which was much more flexible in meeting the needs of computer users and partly replaced the official distribution system (see ibid., 927; Kozyrev and Sokolov 1987).

Constraints on Soviet Software Innovation

In addition to problems associated with industry and market structure, the security, legal, and hardware environment constrained Soviet software innovation. First, the priority given to military applications undermined innovation for civilian applications. As is well known, a large share of Soviet R&D activity was concentrated in the defense industry, and this was true of software development as well (see *Tribuna NTR* 1990, 8). The Soviet military could assert control over all essential findings in computer-related research, including those developed outside the defense sector, and was not obliged to give anything to civilian industries (ibid.; Kuznetsov and Shirokov 1989, 17–19). Much of the software work at the Academy of Sciences and universities, for example, was carried out on military contracts, and its dissemination was tightly controlled. Secrecy in this and other militarized high-technology sectors obstructed technology transfer within the MIC and severely restricted the international contacts of Soviet programmers.[5]

Second, the Soviet system of intellectual property protection (IPP) provided no incentives for programmers to develop original software, market their products, or support and enhance these products.[6] The final owner of inventions in all cases was the state, and the inventor, who was given an inventor's certificate, could officially receive no more than Rb20,000 (at the official exchange rate of the time, slightly more than $12,000). Intellectual property was viewed as being in the public domain, and copying of software was legal and rampant. The IPP system supported the official focus on imitation rather than innovation: Western computer programs were extensively copied and applied to Soviet "clones" of IBM and DEC mainframe and minicomputers. But piracy of Western software imposed significant costs; Western commercial applications software often proved unsuitable for the special needs of Soviet computers. The absence of copyright protection, as well as the inefficient domestic software distribution system, led users to write their own software, resulting in a world without standards and with incompatible, unsupported programs.

The underdeveloped state of the Soviet computer industry imposed a third serious limitation on expansion of the Soviet software industry, a small domestic market. From 1965 to 1983, the output of the U.S. computer hardware industry amounted to $358 billion, while the USSR produced about Rb22 billion ($13 billion, at the official exchange rate), less than 5 percent of the value of the U.S. industry alone (Judy 1986, 358–59). Imports of computers from all CMEA countries in 1984 amounted to less than 20 percent of domestic production.

The main obstacle to the development of the Soviet computer hardware industry, as the director of the Institute of Informatics pointed out in the 1980s, was not the design of the computer, but the organization of its production (see Tate and Hebditch 1987, 43; also Kassel 1986, 3). Innovation in computers and software, as in many other industries, was hampered by the highly bureaucratic Soviet innovation system and by the monopolistic structure of the overall economy, which reduced incentives to develop new products or improve existing products. A lack of coordination among producers of computer hardware and software, which reflected the "vertical" allocation of resources mentioned above, further reduced innovative performance. And because Soviet electronic components manufacturing was so underdeveloped, even copies of good Western designs often were of low quality.

One of the paradoxes of Soviet computer development is that although the hardware and software development programs relied on state-controlled enterprises, these organizations were slow to adopt computers. By 1984, according to some estimates, only 7.5 percent of the USSR's industrial enterprises—3,300 out of 44,000—and only one-third of the large plants (those with at least 500 employees) had mainframe computers (Seligman 1985, 33). Soviet managers of monopolistic enterprises had little incentive to invest in improvements in information technology and hence no incentive to support the development of computer networks at the enterprise level (Seligman 1985). The lack of incentives to adopt computer technology further reduced any motivation for the user-producer interactions that figured so prominently in the development of the computer hardware and software industries of other industrial economies during this period.

The development of Soviet mainframe and minicomputer software, including CAD/CAM software, was slowed by a shortage of computers and the deficiencies of the available machines; but the situation with PC hardware and software was worse still. Even after PCs were widely available in the West, Soviet officials asserted that the Soviet Union did not need them. The strategic choice had already been made to develop large computer centers, and PCs threatened the collectivist ideology and governance structure of Soviet society. As a result, according to Velikhov (1984), vice president of the Academy of Sciences, by the early 1980s only a few dozen PCs were produced annually in the USSR. Very little Soviet software was available for them: the only applications software developed for the Agat (the dominant Soviet PC, a clone of the Apple II) supported information-processing operations.

An additional problem for software development stemmed from the limitations of the classic Soviet approach to high-technology industrial development through large, centralized "national programs." This approach had been successful in several industries (such as the space program) but did not work in the software industry, where decentralized efforts have significant advantages (see Selin 1986, 8; U.S. Central Intelligence Agency 1987, 11). The reliance on custom, agency-specific software further reduced the potential effectiveness of a large-scale national program in software development.

In May 1984 it was officially reported that while the planned annual value of software production was between Rb2,500 million and Rb3,000 million (at official exchange rates, $1.5–3 billion), the actual value of annual production was Rb10–15 million ($6–9 million; U.S. software consumption in 1985, according to the data in chapter 1, amounted to $16.5 billion).[7] Despite the worldwide acknowledgement of Soviet programmers' high potential, based on their successes in fundamental research in mathematics and computer science, the unsupportive intellectual property rights system and thin hardware base frustrated the realization of this potential. Both Soviet and Western experts agreed that the quality of software produced in the USSR was very low (Romanovskii and Cherkasskii 1988; Wellman 1989). No Soviet computer language was used internationally, and few were used widely even within the USSR. Fortran, Cobol, PL/1, and APL—all high-level computer languages expressed in English—were used most extensively. But much industrial programming was done in assembly language or even machine code, because of the limited memory capabilities of Soviet hardware. These practices limited the development of applications software, just as they had in the United States in the early 1950s (see chapter 3), because users found it extremely difficult to adapt code from one computer architecture to another. Moreover, the available code contained numerous errors, which were difficult to find and to fix. Even the successful innovative efforts (such as Shkol'nitsa [Schoolgirl] educational software) did not lead to successful commercialization.

Based as it was on central planning and technological "followership" (worse yet, "followership" without the complementary institutional and economic policies to exploit the spillovers associated with being a follower), the Russian software industry in the mid-1980s was primitive, in both organization and output.[8] Development of a viable software industry required significant change in the scale and structure of demand for software, as well as the introduction of market-based incentives for software producers. The recent political and economic reforms in Russia have begun to create these conditions and have altered the profile of the national software industry.

REFORM, THE RUSSIAN COMPUTER INDUSTRY, AND SOFTWARE DEMAND

The year 1985 began a new era in the evolution of the nation's computer-related industries. Mikhail Gorbachev and his supporters played a key role in this process. In January 1985 the Politburo approved a "nationwide program of creation, development of production, and effective use of computer technology and automated systems [for] the year 2000" (*Isvestiia* 1985).[9] For the first time the information sector was awarded a top priority in public policy.

Like many other ambitious decisions made in the first years of perestroika, however, these guidelines for the computer industries were not well supported by complementary policies and reforms. In the case of software, both research funding and expenditures for personnel training remained low. In the late 1980s, Soviet "outlays for software did not exceed 1.5 percent to 2 percent of overall outlays for computer hardware" (Vladov 1988, 4), a sharp contrast with the corresponding figure for the United States, where in 1990, sales of software and services accounted for 50 percent of total computer sales revenues (see chapter 2). According to some Soviet estimates, there were no more than a dozen highly skilled professionals among the country's 500,000 programmers at the time (Aivazyan et al. 1989, 726). The USSR State Committee for Computer Technology and Informatics (GKVTI), was created in March 1986 to coordinate all computer-related activities. But its institutional powers conflicted with the interests of powerful manufacturing ministries, and the organization became just another bureaucracy in the Soviet computer industry.[10] Nevertheless, steps were taken at this time to modestly improve copyright protection, in conjunction with attempts to open up the economy internationally.

Evolution of the Computer Hardware Base

A large, diversified, and dynamic user community, as well as an extensive hardware base, were necessary preconditions for more rapid growth in the Soviet software industry. Since the mid-1980s, changes in the Russian economy have strengthened both of these important factors. Demand and the installed base of computer hardware have grown, but the growth has been confined largely to PCs and workstations and a far smaller number of supercomputers (Riabov 1991). The role of minicomputers and small mainframes thus has diminished somewhat. Table 9-1 shows how these changes in demand have influenced the output mix of the Russian computer industry.

The most rapidly growing segment of the Russian computer hardware market is

Table 9-1. Change in output of computers and related items, 1991–93
(percentage change)

Activity	First half of 1992 as compared with first half of 1991	First half of 1993 as compared with first half of 1992
Assembly		
PCs		
by state enterprises	− 20	+ 10
by joint ventures	+ 25	+ 5
by distributors[a]	[b]	+ 100
minicomputers	− 35	− 60
large computers	− 65	− 60
Production		
diskettes	+ 45	+ 10
monitors	+ 5	+ 10

Source: ComputerWorld Moscow. 1993, no. 34, 26.

[a] Assembly of PCs by distributors reflects the shift in activities from sales of imported PCs to assembly of imported PC components.

[b] Insignificant.

dominated by IBM-compatible machines: in 1994, 98 percent of Russian desktop computer installations were IBM-PC architecture machines.[11] Soviet ministries traditionally preferred to deal with IBM, and today IBM PCs and clones are well known in the Russian market. Western export controls prevented extensive Russian imports of Apple desktop computers until 1991, and the initial marketing and distribution campaign of Apple Computer in Russia failed. As a result, in 1992 the overall population of Apple Macintosh machines was estimated to be only 3,000–6,000, and their share of sales in early 1994 was only about 6 percent.

At first, Russian PC imports were dominated by older, relatively inexpensive machines. Only in August 1993 did the market share of 80486 machines for the first time exceed that of machines based on the 80286 microprocessor. The 80386-based PC became the 1993 market leader, with a 50 percent market share, a sharp increase from its 1992 market share of 10 percent (*ComputerWorld Moscow* 1993, no. 35, 38; *Softmarket* 1993, no. 4, 3). Although PC purchasers now give greater weight to quality and brand name (rather than low price alone),[12] the PC market is likely to remain sharply divided: on the one hand, high-quality machines are needed by such customers as commercial banks, for which the cost of computer mistakes have become high; on the other hand, many less prosperous users require inexpensive machines, mainly for office management. The prices of PCs in Russia have not declined in parallel with international trends, which reflects continuing high domestic inflation, rapidly growing demand, and bottlenecks in the nation's distribution system.[13]

Since 1985, the relative importance of the three major sources of supply of computer hardware—state enterprises, private firms (including joint ventures), and imports—has changed. During perestroika, efforts by state enterprises to increase computer production were unsuccessful, because the prevailing technocratic approach to the development of information technologies avoided comprehensive reform.[14] As a result, the state enterprises were ill-prepared for market liberalization. During 1989–92, the Soviet state computer industry suffered a deep crisis: the workforce at

Table 9-2.   Computer hardware and software enterprises on the territory of the
former USSR, 1992

Region	Producers of computers and spare parts			Producers of software
	I[a]	II[b]	PCs	
Russia	124	119	26	62
Ukraine and Moldavia	23	54	8	10
Caucasus republics	16	30	22	8
Baltic republics and Belorussia	9	11	4	2
Middle Asia republics	3			5
Total	175	214	60	87

Source: Electronnaya Promyshlennost 1992, Vol. 1; *Electroteckhnicheskaya Promyshlennost i Priborostroenie* 1992, Vol. 1.

[a] I. Enterprises of the Ministry of Electronic Equipment and Instrument-Making Industry (Minpribor).
[b] II. Enterprises of the Ministry of Electronic Industry (Minelectronprom).

the large plants decreased by 15–20 percent (*ComputerWorld Moscow* 1993, no. 34, 27), with the biggest reductions occurring among producers of non-PC machines. Most of the Soviet computer-related industrial sector was located in the Russian Federation (see Table 9-2), so this decline is not attributable solely to the disintegration of the USSR. Instead, it reflects the drop in military contracts, large imports of Western hardware, and the financial problems of many of the state enterprises that purchased computer equipment.[15]

Of the ten or fifteen state-owned computer manufacturing plants that have survived, most now concentrate on PC assembly and have formed contractual relations with foreign companies or new Russian businesses. The "Kvant" plant in Zelenograd began licensed production of IBM PS/1 systems in 1993. The plant also manufactures 386- and 486-based PC clones in a joint venture with the private Russian company IVK, which has invested $10 million in the project.[16] But the Kvant plant in 1994 planned to produce only 50,000 PCs, well below its capacity of 700,000 machines.

The private firms that now play an important role in the Russian computer industry are a diverse group. In Moscow alone there were more than a thousand small so-called screwdriver firms in 1993, the majority of which did not have large production facilities: only the thirty or forty leaders in this group have ten or more employees (*Softmarket* 1993, no. 3, 2). Reliable sources suggest that there are approximately 5,000 Russian workers directly engaged in PC assembly (Shershulsky 1993). All experts agree that Russia's computer industry remains highly concentrated: 20 percent of the workers produce 80 percent of all Russian-made PC computers, and eight or ten private firms (all located in Moscow), together with branches of major Western computer companies, dominate the domestic computer market.[17] Nevertheless, these levels of producer concentration are significantly higher than those observed in most Western industrial economies.

In 1992–93, combined production of PCs by Russian state-owned enterprises, joint ventures, and distributor-assemblers grew (see Table 9-1), but the most rapid growth by far was in the output of distributor-assemblers. During this period, imports (mainly from Asia) of cheap PC components and parts, relatively cheap labor, and huge domestic demand made the assembly of PCs in Russia an attractive business, providing a 15 percent return on investment rather than the 8 percent return (due to high customs fees and taxes) on the import of PCs (Rudenko et al. 1994, 32). A large share (as high as 70 percent) of imported components are of low quality, however, and computer-assembly firms routinely ignore final testing of the machines:[18] nearly 80 percent of new Russian-assembled PCs need to be repaired (*Softmarket* 1993, no. 17, 6). Nonetheless, these inexpensive parts and practices allow Russian firms to charge low prices.

Despite growth in domestic PC assembly operations, the total output of the Russian computer industry remains modest: in 1993 it accounted for 30–35 percent of the national market and included very few advanced machines (*Delovoy Mir*, 31 January 1994, 11). The future Russian computer market will continue to be dominated by imported technology and brand-name machines. Before the early 1990s, Russian computer imports were limited by Western restrictions on high-technology Western exports to the Eastern bloc, shortages of hard currency, and the lack of a distribution infrastructure. In the mid-1990s computer imports are dominated by technologically advanced PCs. Many Western computer producers now have direct distribution relationships with one of the major Russian firms in Moscow and/or St. Petersburg. A small number of Russian computer users have begun to apply computers to much more complex commercial uses (bank automation, multiuser networks, and the like), which require new computer systems because so much of the installed base has become obsolete. The resulting "second wave of Russian computerization" (Rudenko et al. 1994) will rely on imports.

At the beginning of 1994 there were 1.5–2.5 million PCs in Russia (Rudenko et al. 1994, 30). Although this was a large increase over the estimated number of PCs in use in 1985 (200,000 machines) or even 1990 (500,000), serious shortages remain (*Update USSR*, Feb.–March 1986, 4; *ComputerWorld*, 11 June 1990, 123). This installed base also includes a large number of outdated and low-quality machines, which cannot operate many of the standard packaged software programs developed by Western firms for PCs with at least an 80386 microprocessor.[19]

Profile of the Software User Population

The rapid increase in the installed base of Russian computers has been paralleled by substantial changes in the software user community. New economic institutions—commercial banks, exchanges, and trading and other entrepreneurial firms—have replaced the military and industrial enterprises as the main customers. As users have become more numerous, the range of uses for desktop computers has become more diverse. In the state enterprises computers often were regarded as simply an investment in an inflation hedge; PCs also were a source of prestige, even if they were never used. In contrast, private business entities, lacking subsidies from the federal budget, buy PCs only if the equipment is vital for their business. These different attitudes toward computer technologies mean that the main customers for accounting software are entrepreneurial firms and privatized enterprises; state-owned entities are still not interested in automating their operations (*Kommersant Daily*, 11 June 1993, 5). As Figure 9-1 shows, state enterprises still spend far less per employee on information systems than private enterprises do.

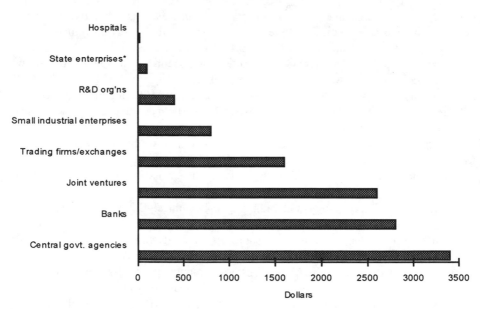

Figure 9-1. Russian expenditures on information technology per employee, 1992. *In some sectors, this figure is higher. *Source:* Shershulsky 1993, 27.

The shifts in demand for software were linked to the economic reforms of the early 1990s, including the rise of new businesses and the establishment of joint ventures with Western companies. The Russian experience in new software enterprises resembled those of other "latecomer" countries (see Schware 1989), in its emphasis on specialized financial applications and russification of Western packaged software. The peculiarities of the Russian accounting system (such as payroll and fixed asset management) and the rapid expansion of entrepreneurial activities have made custom and packaged accounting applications software the most popular types of software since the late 1980s. Accounting programs currently account for 20 percent of the Russian software market (*Kommersant Daily,* 4 June 1993, 5). Local and Western designs, which have occupied different market niches, now are coming to resemble each other more closely, because of the "marketization" of the Russian economy, the spread of Western accounting standards, and the need for multilanguage and multicurrency programs.

The demand for Western software is constrained by several factors, most of which are illustrated by the case of banking software. In the 1990s commercial banks are among the leading consumers in the Russian software market because of their need for software to support quick payments, which are vital for competition in the industry. But the idiosyncratic Russian national bank accounting system and the instability of Russian banking legislation prevent mass introduction of standard Western programs. The narrow array of financial services offered by Russian banks further limits the advantages of using Western software designed for a broader spectrum of services (*Softmarket* 1993, no. 20, 9). According to a 1993 poll of the main Moscow and St. Petersburg banks, Western software accounted for only 10 percent and 6 percent respectively of the software used by these institutions (Tsuprikov 1994, 56).

The structure of computer hardware in Russian businesses also influences software demand. The majority of Russian banks cannot afford systems that require the advanced hardware extensively utilized by their Western counterparts. Instead, Russian banks demand applications that can ease the routine work of bank clerks (*Kommersant Daily*, 25 February 1993, 4). The price of advanced hardware and software deters other Russian customers, who prefer to use IBM-compatible PCs in business operations where most non-Russian enterprises use workstations. This is one reason for the slow diffusion of Sun workstations in Russia (only 700 of which were sold in 1993), when the main users of these powerful machines were the KamAZ auto plant and the Sukhoi avionics R&D lab (*Kommersant Daily*, 15 June 1993, 1). Some advanced computer technologies can be found among Russian branches of foreign firms, large government agencies, embassies, and companies with a mixed form of ownership, which need the equipment for solving large scientific or production tasks.

In contrast to financial services, other Western programs are much more important than the products of local firms in other market segments. Spreadsheet applications are dominated by the products of Lotus Development, Borland, Computer Associates, and Microsoft. Autodesk is a virtual monopolist in the market for CAD software with its AutoCAD (*Kommersant Daily*, 12 February 1993, 8), and Novell dominates the rapidly growing market for network software. Although such products were first sold in Russia only in 1991, by 1993 there were roughly 10,000 installed networks. The lifting of Western export controls on networking hardware and software will support the sales of new versions of Novell's NetWare product. Russian demand for advanced Western software is restricted not only by financial and political factors but also by the level of development of business management practices. This factor explains the limited utilization of "project management" systems: in 1992 only 1,000 such packages were sold in Russia (*Kommersant* 1993, no. 10, 29).

The division of labor in software development between in-house production and outsourcing in Russia's software industry is affected by several factors. Although more and more institutions seek external sources for software, suppliers of standard and custom programs for business-specific applications are scarce. Thus, banks, which seek independence from control by the Russian Central Bank and wish to offer new financial products, are actively developing in-house applications programs for financial and information management. In an environment of regulatory uncertainty and change, in-house development also enables Russian banks to protect details of their internal operations and cash flows from the scrutiny of government regulators.

The amount of outsourced software equals the amount developed in-house at the main Moscow and St. Petersburg commercial banks. While 80 percent of thirty-four St. Petersburg banks were developing software in-house, only 18 percent of these banks sold their products on the open market (Tsuprikov 1994, 60). Software designed by a single bank nevertheless may be adopted by other members of its banking group. It is likely that, as was the case in Japan and other industrial economies, Russian banks will eventually serve as sources of specialized, "spin-off" software firms.

Large industrial enterprises looking for CAD software and automated systems, Russian designs of which rarely are competitive with Western software, search for outside sources among domestic and foreign firms but generally direct their demand to foreign suppliers. In 1993, for example, the Cherepovetsk metallurgical plant placed a DM40 million order for a new CAD system with Siemens (with a minor role in the development and application of this system to be played by a St. Petersburg software supplier) (*Kommersant Daily,* 30 July 1993, 1).

With limited capital resources, new state and nonstate enterprises and organizations seeking software must look for programs that are already available or easily modified for their needs, rather than investing in long-term development projects for new software products. This pressure has produced a "market-driven" approach to software development by specialized Russian vendors; programmers focus more on the creation of products with an assured market rather than on developing radically new concepts.

The absence of standards in the Russian software market and/or poor distribution of information mean that fragmentation of demand remains a serious problem. The small domestic markets for standard, Russian-produced software makes it difficult for Russian firms to exploit scale economies, and pricing of software products is arbitrary to the point of chaos (chapter 5 makes a similar point in its discussion of software pricing in Japan's domestic market). And the Russian population that regularly uses computers remains small and consists mainly of users who live in major cities and work in prosperous firms and organizations.

The spread of computer knowledge across the country is modest, and little educational software is available. The development of educational software suffered even more than management or industrial software because there was no market for it. In 1985, however, educational computing in Russia began receiving a great deal of attention—a fifteen-year plan was developed for the introduction of computers into the country's secondary and higher educational institutions and to combat the tremendous problem of computer illiteracy (see Aivazyan et al. 1989, 725–30). But by 1988 only 2,000 out of 60,000 Russian secondary schools had PCs (Ershov 1990). And the severe financial pressures on all aspects of Russian public spending will likely limit the spread of computer hardware in public education.

The major Russian producer of educational software, the Scientific Center of Educational Software, located in Moscow, successfully developed thirty packaged programs, but its ability to continue this ambitious development agenda has been limited by the small software acquisition budgets of most Russian public schools (Zubchenko 1991). The small number of hardware installations in Russian schools and the lack of expertise by users also limits interactions between producers and users. The rapid expansion in business demand that has resulted from the market reforms, combined with stronger intellectual property protection (see below), has led the Russian software developers to concentrate on commercial software development at the expense of educational software (Fedotov 1991).

The circumstances surrounding software development for higher education are not much different. In Russian university economics departments, for example, several hundred applications programs were in use in 1990, but the vast majority of these (90–95 percent) were outdated (Aronovich et al. 1990, 361). The rapid diffusion of PCs in Russia has affected only a small number of the leading universities, and even in these institutions the installed base is not standardized on any single architecture. Although Western firms such as Sun Microsystems, Microsoft, and DEC have established software development centers at leading Russian universities, these centers will have little influence in the remainder of Russia's large higher education system.

Intellectual Property Protection

The rapid growth of the Russian software market, along with market reforms and Russia's growing links with the world economy, has made protection of intellectual property an important issue throughout the Russian economy. Nowhere has this issue been more significant than in the software industry. With the opening of Russia's economy in the late 1980s, software piracy grew rapidly. Even some advanced CAD packages, export of which to the Soviet Union had been prohibited by formal controls, found their way into Soviet factories (Burrows 1990, 16). According to independent experts in the early 1990s, roughly 95 percent of Russian software had been illegally copied (Savelieva 1992). Indeed, the Russian government gave software copying its backhanded encouragement during the late 1980s and early 1990s by employing programmers to rewrite popular application interfaces for use by Russian-speaking users.

Faced with a large market opportunity and little formal protection of their intellectual property, U.S. and other foreign firms found ways to capitalize on unauthorized copying of their products. Microsoft distributed its products in Russia through joint ventures and used these licensing agreements to protect the company's copyrights. Ashton-Tate, having discovered that five different versions of its Framework integrated software were in widespread use in republics of the former USSR, tracked down the authors of the best of these adaptations and signed them to a marketing agreement.[20] Western firms also have attracted users to their "authorized" software by providing an array of financial and service incentives to users (Nikolaev 1991; Ivanova 1991). After-sale contracts with the designer of software (for example, for subsequent modifications of the product) now are vital for large Russian users of software. In late 1993, Borland, Microsoft, and Symantec also began site-licensing multiple installations of their products in Russia.

With the acceleration of political and economic reform during the late 1980s, the absence and/or nonenforcement of intellectual property rights imposed the greatest costs on Russian software developers. Allowed for the first time to sell their products independently, Russian software producers were unprotected in both national and international software markets. The absence of intellectual property regulations damaged trade in the domestic software market, undercut trends toward standardization, and thereby slowed the development of the Russian software industry. Customers understood that the purchase of one copy of a product was sufficient to support extensive copying of it inside their firms (*Softmarket* 1993, no. 3, 3). Software piracy also created serious incompatibility problems within government and business entities that were using different (pirated) versions of allegedly standard software.

In recent years, both official and unofficial attempts to introduce legal protection for software-related intellectual property have been undertaken. The most important was the establishment in 1992 of the Association of Software Suppliers (ASS), which united more than forty major national software firms and Western companies doing business in Russia. Although the courts occasionally enforced prohibitions on illegal software practices in the early 1990s (*Kommersant* 1992, no. 41), only in October 1992 did legal protection of software for computer and databases come into effect.

This law prohibited *trade* in illegally copied software immediately upon its passage, but illegal copying of software for private use was prohibited only beginning January 1, 1994. ASS experts considered the law to correspond with the norms of May 1992 EEC directives on legal protection of computer software and related laws of the United States and Japan (Podshibikhin and Vitaliev 1993). In a January 1993 poll of professionals in Moscow, 60 percent agreed with the law, 5 percent opposed it, and the remainder were unsure (Malkov 1993). As has been the case in other economies, during the first three months after the passage of the law sales of legal software increased 300–400 percent (although the ASS estimated that sales only doubled).[21]

Although the new intellectual property regulations have been in place for only a short time, they have had a positive effects on business practices in the Russian software industry. The number of official registrations of software products is increasing rapidly. As of early October 1993 only twenty-seven programs and one agreement on software licensing had been registered; by the end of 1993 forecasts projected nearly five hundred other applications for product registrations and no fewer than one hundred registered licensing agreements. Registrations are helpful in infringement cases and provide a basis for seeking tax benefits for patent and licensing expenses. Nonetheless, many Russian software firms (most of them small enterprises) were unable to pay the nearly Rb300,000 (at the time of the law's passage, approximately $300) associated with patenting their products.

The strengthening of intellectual property protection complements two other trends that have supported growth in the domestic software market. New computer installations began to grow rapidly, and businesses began to *use* the PCs that had originally been acquired mainly for prestige. In addition, users began to demand greater levels of producer support and product quality from suppliers of computer hardware and software. Both of these developments strengthened the market for legally protected, higher-quality, packaged applications and operating system software for desktop computers. Although these changes appeared relatively slowly and often contradicted one another, their cumulative effect has been to transform the Russian software industry, improving its level of product quality and creating new institutions in the industry.

STRUCTURAL CHANGE IN THE RUSSIAN SOFTWARE INDUSTRY IN THE ERA OF MARKET REFORM

Institutional restructuring was vital for the growth of the industry. During the 1980s, much was done to improve Russian software productivity by developing software modules that could be used by noncomputer specialists and encouraging the use of standard interfaces, automatic testing, graphic images, "artificial intelligence," and natural languages (Authens 1990). But the main obstacle to increasing low levels of productivity was the fact that programmers were scattered among unrelated organizations, working in isolation from each other, and spending a great deal of time overcoming compatibility problems (Vladov 1988).

Some of these problems have been addressed by the dramatic transformation in the software industry's structure since the late 1980s. The industry restructuring was a response to the destruction of the old economic institutions and the lack of new state-controlled entities to replace them, as well as the end of CMEA's joint efforts in computer technology. The dissolution of the Soviet Union in 1991 inflicted surprisingly little harm on the Russian software industry, since the majority of the USSR's computer industry enterprises and organizations were located in the Russian republic (sixty-two out of the total of eighty-seven; see Table 9-2).

In recent years the number of Russian software firms has increased; ASS experts estimated in 1993 that there were 2,000–3,000 firms devoting at least a portion of their efforts to software development.[22] But the painful financial transition to a market economy and the delayed introduction of intellectual property protection have prevented the industry from blossoming. In 1992, total sales of software in Russia were estimated to be only $8 million; domestic designs constituted 10–15 percent of this amount, and Microsoft products accounted for more than 50 percent of sales (ibid.; Latypov 1993, 26). As Figure 9-2 shows, sales of software continued to grow (with some seasonal fluctuation) through 1993, and by the fourth quarter of that year had increased sixteenfold above the first quarter of 1992. Software development and marketing now constitute the primary business activities for 200–300 Russian firms, a group that includes 70–80 entities that are dealers for Western software companies. The Russian software industry remains very geographically concentrated, with centers in Moscow, St. Petersburg, and a few other cities around Moscow, on the Volga River and in the Urals region.[23]

Despite its still-modest level of output, the Russian software industry now differs sharply from that of the Soviet period. Structural change is most apparent in the state sector, in the industry's private small business sector, and in the widespread international joint ventures.

Figure 9-2. Software sales in the Russian market, 1992 and 1993 (First quarter of 1992 = 100). *Source: ComputerWorld Moscow* 1993, no. 35, p. 27.

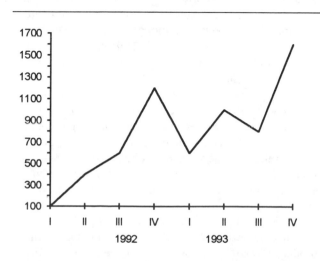

Changes in the State Sector

Until the late 1980s, the Soviet response to software shortages resembled earlier attempts at economic reform, consisting largely of the creation of new institutions with little or no change in the ownership system. Having been excluded from developments in Soviet computing since the mid-1960s, the Academy of Sciences was given a new mandate to support the computer industry in 1983 and restructured its computer development programs. This reorganization greatly increased the Russian Academy of Sciences' control over much of the research effort in computer technology, largely at the expense of state-controlled industrial enterprises (Kassel 1986, vi). The key role in the new academic network was played by the newly created Institute of Informatics Problems (IPIAN), which employed around 900 computer specialists in its Moscow office and three other facilities across the country and supported a great deal of work on PC software. Two other new bodies in the academy— the Institute of Programming and the Scientific Technical Institute of Informatics and Computer Science of the Academy of Pedagogical Sciences (formed in 1985 and 1986 respectively)—focused on the development of educational software.

Although the re-entry by academic research institutes into software research and development was a positive step, problems remained. Academic programmers and developers reaped few financial rewards from software innovation and often were unable to pursue new lines of research. The links between fundamental research and commercialization remained very weak. During the most recent (post-1991) era of market reform, the research institutes in the academy and in industrial ministries have suffered severe reductions in state funding, which has reduced their long-term research activities. The programmers who remain at the institutes and universities are working either on military contracts or on software applications currently in demand.

Except in a few major enterprises, the state-controlled industrial software developers have performed poorly. At the end of 1992, the directories of the Minpribor and Radiotekhprom groups indicated that these historically important developers of software retained only twenty-nine software-producing organizations with rather weak potential. Because of their historic concentration on custom software, most state-owned entities did not enjoy economies of scale in the software business and had problems marketing their products. Among the state-owned enterprises, the largest software operations were at NPO Volga and NPO Parma, which reported 1992 sales of only Rb8.2 million and 5.8 million respectively. Many others reported output of Rb1 million and less (*Biznes-karta-93* 1993).

Privatization frequently has divided these enterprises with modern computer installations into five or ten small business entities, one of which became the owner of buildings and PCs (amounting to 90 percent of the value of the enterprise's fixed assets), typically operated by the management of the former organization. Programmers remain employed in the other new small enterprises, which lease hardware from its new owner. The damaging consequences of this form of privatization have been exacerbated by the outflow of researchers and engineers from the state sector of the Russian software industry.

The low salaries of Russian programmers at state entities, combined with opportunities for additional income through personal contracts and the absence of copyright protection, have produced in a tremendous brain drain from the Russian computer industry to the West.[24] This migration may result in Russia's loss of an entire generation of talent.[25] Sun Microsystems has developed one novel response to this issue by signing several contracts with the Moscow SPARC Center (a joint stock company founded mainly by the Institute of Precision Mechanics and Computer Technologies within the Russian Academy of Sciences). These contracts, which support work on new compiler techniques, have permitted more than a hundred programmers to remain in this institute under the leadership of Dr. Babain (the developer of the supercomputer "Elbrus" used for Soviet space and nuclear projects).

Other programmers have sought opportunities outside the state sector, in new entrepreneurial firms and international joint ventures, both of which offer salaries (and hardware availability) unmatched by the state-owned enterprises. Unfortunately, the attractions of these alternatives have broken up promising research groups at academic and industrial entities, without compensating improvement in the quality of development activities in the new private entities.

New Entrepreneurial Firms

Entrepreneurial activities in the Russian software industry began only in the second stage of perestroika, when economic decentralization became an essential part of its policies. Beginning in 1987, cooperatives and other types of nonstate firms were allowed to operate in the Russian software industry. But their efforts often were frustrated by the overall business environment of the early market reform era.

Origins and business strategies

Immediately after their legal recognition, many R&D cooperatives were established. Between 1988 and 1991 the number of such cooperatives jumped sevenfold (from 1,129 to 7,870; see Table 9-3). One-third of this population consisted of software developers, although many of the cooperatives in this and other sectors were inactive. Among the active cooperatives, software cooperatives employed less than 30 percent of the workforce in Russian R&D cooperatives but generated around 40 percent of total cooperative revenues by 1990, a higher share than in either of the two other areas in which R&D cooperatives were active. Interestingly, software cooperatives' share of the total number of R&D cooperatives and of cooperatives' employment declined during 1988–90, while their share of revenues was more stable.

Software cooperatives were small firms: the average number of workers in 1988–90 was around twenty, below the average for all cooperatives (see Table 9-3). In the early 1990s most Russian software firms were small businesses, including the industry leaders: more than one-third of ASS member firms had fewer than twenty employees (calculated from the 1993 directory of ASS members). However, they were well equipped with hardware, having 0.85 PCs for each employee, which is higher than the ratio for all ASS members (ibid.). Each of the largest Russian nonstate software firms (for example, ParaGraph, which is not a cooperative) employed an average of roughly two hundred professionals.

In many cases software firms were formed by groups of programmers from research institutes and universities who maintained close contacts with these institutions. The director of an academic research institute often serves as chairman of a software cooperative affiliated with the institute, providing substantial administrative

Table 9-3. R&D cooperatives in Russia, 1988–90

Activity	Active cooperatives		Employees		Revenue from sales	
	Total	%	Thousands	%	Million rubles	%
Research						
1988	280	24.8	7.0	26.3	29.1	30.3
1989	1,996	32.0	72.1	38.3	771.5	34.1
1990	2,583	33.2	66.6	34.6	1,029.8	3.1
Design, development, and adoption of R&D in industry						
1988	451	40.0	11.9	44.7	30.2	31.5
1989	2,122	33.9	67.8	36.0	528.5	23.4
1990	2,650	34.0	75.7	39.4	800.2	25.7
Software development						
1988	398	35.2	7.7	29.0	36.6	38.2
1989	2,132	34.1	48.4	25.7	962.3	42.5
1990	2,554	32.8	50.2	26.0	1,285.5	1.2
Total						
1988	1,129	100	26.6	100	95.9	100
1989	6,250	100	188.3	100	2,262.3	100
1990	7,787	100	192.5	100	3,115.5	100
1991[a]	7,870		200.0		3,012	

Source: *Delovoy Mir* (Business world), 19 March 1993, 11.
[a] Estimate.

support to the cooperative in dealing with the state bureaucracy and facilitating free access to the institute's computer hardware by the cooperative's members.

In the late 1980s another legal form of small business in the Russian software industry were Centers of Scientific and Technical Activities of Youth (TsNTTMs), established by the Young Communists League (Komsomol). These organizations received legal and political protection for their business operations and enjoyed better investment and tax incentives than cooperatives. By 1989, roughly five hundred TsNTTMs had been established in the former USSR; especially in the major cities; most were involved in computer-related activities, including software development and marketing.

The cooperatives and TsNTTMs, as well as the subsequently established joint ventures and private firms, changed the economic foundations of the Russian software industry. These new business entities did not rely on subsidies from the state budget or contracts with the ministerial hierarchies but contracted independently and directly with software users. Because of the very limited demand from private computer users for software, software cooperatives marketed nearly all their products to state and nonstate institutions (in St. Petersburg 96 percent, in the region 99.9 percent).

Their very success, however, unleashed a political backlash against cooperatives. Amendments to the Law on Cooperatives in the USSR and other political pressures, as well as the poorly defined property rights for cooperative firms, forced many of the entrepreneurs of the "first wave" of cooperatives to turn in the early

1990s to different legal forms of business: joint stock companies, partnerships, and the like. In 1994 only one ASS member remained a cooperative; it was the only entity registered before 1989.

Financial constraints influenced the business strategies of the software cooperatives. Venture capital financing, a key element of high-technology entrepreneurship in other industrial economies, did not exist in the former USSR. Although a venture capital fund—the Russian Innovation Concern—was established in December 1990, its operations were limited by (1) the very primitive state of the stock exchange in Russia (especially for nonfinancial firms); (2) the dominance of short-term (no more than one year) loans with high annual interest rates at commercial banks (more than 200 percent in mid-1993), which made it difficult for cooperatives to finance extensive market research or large software projects (Vasiliev 1992); and (3) the low profitability of the software business, which reflected weak protection for intellectual property and a relatively small number of users, most of whom had limited technical skills (Vitaliev 1993).

These factors, along with ruble nonconvertibility and growing inflation, drove many small software firms to seek contractual relationships with foreign hardware and software companies. Their need for modern computer hardware was a further incentive to form alliances with Western firms.

Another organizational response to undeveloped external capital markets has been the creation of diversified firms with "internal capital markets" that resemble those of some U.S. conglomerates of the 1960s and 1970s (for a detailed discussion of this phenomenon see Williamson 1985). Through diversification of their activities, many of which involved trading or export of commodities, such firms increased their ruble cash flow and accumulated hard currency reserves to finance high-technology product development, manufacturing, and marketing activities. The St. Petersburg joint stock company DEKA includes computer assembly through a joint venture, retail and lumber trading operations, as well as software projects and fundamental research in scientific instruments (the traditional profile of DEKA's parent organization, NPO Nauchnye Pribory), is one of the best examples of this structure.[26]

This highly diversified internal structure is quite typical of contemporary Russian software firms, which might more accurately be labeled "computer firms." In a 1992 poll, 75 percent of 120 Moscow software firms reported also selling hardware, in many cases having diversified into this activity after their establishment (*Finansovay Gazeta* 1992, no. 27, 9). For example, one major firm in the Russian computer business, Steepler, was organized in 1990 by twelve young mathematicians to sell their own software designs. By 1992, as a dealer of Hewlett-Packard and Rank Xerox computers and office equipment, only 2 percent of the firm's $15 million in annual sales were derived from software (*Kommersant Daily,* 4 December 1992, 4).

The absence of a domestic distribution infrastructure and attractive product design, as well as inexperience in advertising or after-sales support, hampers the competitiveness of Russian producers in their domestic market. According to ASS estimates, development accounts for 80 percent of the costs of developing software products for the domestic market; in Western software firms, by contrast, development costs account for 20 percent, and marketing and product support (including software maintenance) 80 percent, of development costs.

The development of a stronger domestic software industry requires that Russian software users become better-informed consumers. Russian software firms are investing more heavily in the identification of specific users needs and in the instruction of the population in software-related topics (through seminars and exhibitions, for example). Ninety-two percent of Moscow software firms were reported to be supporting these activities in 1992.[27]

Product development priorities

During their first years of operation, software cooperatives developed custom applications software, worked on russification of Western software, and provided consulting on the use of these products. The strong demand for virtually any software meant that they did not have to invest in creating innovative products: many cooperatives had a one- to two-year order backlog. Many enterprises also faced a familiar problem in organizing their innovative efforts—an imbalance between programming and management skills. The former were often brilliant, but the latter usually were very weak. The limited availability of management education programs meant that nearly all software cooperatives lacked any business or product development plans (*Forbes*, 20 April 1989).

The innovative activities of Russian software firms since 1990 have been influenced by several new factors. First, increases in software prices have lagged behind the growth of the dollar/ruble exchange rate, which has made imported software highly competitive with domestically produced programs. Western firms' Russian pricing of their products suggests that many are pursuing aggressive market penetration strategies. In 1992 the costs of software production jumped fifteenfold, but price competition from the major Western software firms prevented Russian enterprises from raising prices for software more than fivefold (*Kommersant Daily*, 11 December 1992, 10). In the same period, the attempts of many small Russian firms to find lower-cost sources of software increased imports of cheap, low-quality products, intensifying competitive pressure on Russian software firms. Russian firms also compete fiercely on price among themselves, further reducing profit margins.

These financial pressures mean that rapid development of commercial software products at low cost is essential to survival. The greatest opportunities for such products are in applications. The focus on applications means in turn that firms that want to survive in the software business must either produce novel designs or significant modifications of widely used standard products. The latter is easiest for antivirus applications, such as the 167 versions of the "Aidstest" product developed during the period 1989–93 and sold by the Moscow firm Dialogue-Nauka.

As in Western Europe and Japan, in the face of strong competition from imports of standard software, Russian firms have focused their innovative efforts on products that meet market needs and niches that are unique to the Russian market. In many cases, these niches are created by unique aspects of the domestic business and language environment. Thus, accounting and other financial applications, text editing packages, and language training programs are the best-selling Russian designs (along with russifications of the more complicated Western applications). Producers of these items are among the few firms (all from Moscow) that enjoy the advantages of large-scale operations.

In May 1993 monthly sales of the text editor Lexicon (a product of the firm Microinform) reached 6,900 copies, and the product of the 1C company, "1C: Accounting" (the number two seller), reached 2,700 copies. Because of the large scale of its parent firm's operations, the price for the latter program was Rb24,000—half as much as one of its competitor's products (*Kommersant Daily,* 4 June 1993, 5, and 11 June 1993, 5). The rise of ParaGraph, an industry leader and a supplier of hand-writing recognition software to the Apple Newton (Ignatius 1994), was based on its russification of Western software for fonts and typefaces. Having sold several thousand copies of its "Russian Word" product, ParaGraph established itself as the leading source of the russified version of the Microsoft Word wordprocessing software in Russia. Other successful Russian software firms often compete with Western rivals in specific product areas. For example, in 1993 Lexicon held 33 percent of the Russian market for text editors for IBM-compatible PCs (more than the combined share of Microsoft Word and WordPerfect) (*Kommersant Daily,* 27 October 1993, Supplement, 1).

Another unique aspect of the Russian operating environment for software is the great heterogeneity of business operations: accounting and other applications often are very firm-specific. The market for Russian accounting applications software has been influenced by general and sector-specific legislative changes, changes in payment terms and practices, and differences in the educational level of users. The result is a proliferation of custom and "semi-custom" versions of accounting software—in Moscow alone around six hundred firms produce accounting applications. Standard versions of spreadsheet programs, such as Excel, Quattro Pro, and Lotus 1-2-3, are popular in Russia, but do not dominate the Russian market as completely as they do in most Western desktop software markets.

Russian programmers cannot compete with Western colleagues in the areas of operating systems and databases, which require less "localization" but whose development and marketing need large groups of programmers and extensive product support (as chapter 1 notes, this is true as well of European and Japanese software firms competing with U.S. suppliers). Russian software firms have done fairly well, however, in computer games and entertainment programs, which require far less product support. The game "Tetris," developed in 1985 by A. Pazhitnov of the USSR Academy of Sciences, is still the best-known Russian software export (see Savell 1990b). The leader in this segment of the Russian software business today is the specialized Moscow firm Nikita (producer of such best sellers as "Perestroika" and "Defense of the [Russian] White House"), which are distributed to international markets through Israeli and Swiss firms (*Kommersant Daily,* 1 October 1993, 11). Among the other Russian software designs that have been licensed for sale abroad are language-related products (dictionaries, translators, and spell-checking systems) from Steepler and Bit Software.

The long-term strategy of Russian programmers for entering the world software market is linked with their activities in so-called vertical markets, highly specialized applications markets with a few hundred customers each. These markets can be served by relatively small firms that lack global distribution and marketing operations (Pachikov 1993). They also are attractive to the many Russian software firms that have strong basic research capacities and little marketing expertise.

Two trends have caused the innovation activities of Russian software firms to change direction. On the one hand, russification of Western software became less attractive after many imported software products were russified (Microsoft did this with Windows, and Symantec russified its most popular products). On the other hand, the growing complexity of Russian users' needs and the rapidly expanding domestic market in desktop software created greater opportunities for Russian software firms in such areas as optical character recognition programs, protection of database information, communication systems (such as bank telecommunications), and multimedia.

In a very short span of time, intensified international competition and segmentation of the Russian software market, along with the above-mentioned financial problems, forced Russian software firms to begin paying more attention to mass marketing their designs. Rivalry in the most competitive segments of the domestic software market focuses increasingly on expanding markets for the "core" software products that dominate a firm's sales (similar to the role of Netware in Novell's product line) by expanding the array of closely related products for specific applications. For example, the 1C company expanded the capabilities of its widely sold accounting program through a strategy that resembles those of U.S. and Western European software firms. 1C acquired a small producer of a promising application to sell under its own name (as its "Salary" product) and signed agreements with other firms to combine several programs into a single multifunction product (*Business Moscow News,* 9 February 1994, 8).

The new entrepreneurial firms are the most promising entities in the emerging Russian software industry. Their ability to combine entrepreneurial know-how with high-quality programming skills and academic research has allowed them to build up strong positions in a number of market niches. A combination of strong technical skills, external opportunities, and internal financial distress has paradoxically made Russian academic and research institutions very important incubators and sources for these entrepreneurial spin-off software firms. The most serious competition for new firms comes not from the Russian state entities (industry or the academy) but from international software companies.

Because domestic and foreign designs still occupy different niches in the Russian software market, this competition does not always assume the form of competition among products in the market. Instead, an important form of competition between domestic Russian and foreign software firms involves competition for the skills of Russian programmers. Beginning in the late 1980s, national and foreign software entities entered into a number of bilateral contracts or agreements with Russian software researchers, institutions, and enterprises. Most of these began as joint ventures of one form or another.

International Joint Ventures

Foreign investment through joint ventures has been allowed in the former USSR since 1987, and software joint ventures were among the first. The well-known joint ventures in the industry by the firms Dialogue and Microinform were the twenty-first and sixtieth such ventures to be registered. In 1990 the number of registered computer-related joint ventures increased rapidly, 192 having been registered in that year alone. Many of the early joint ventures, including those in software, were transitional vehicles to support rapid market access or other short-term goals.

The international joint ventures of the late 1980s focused primarily on the computer hardware market in Russia, which was characterized by strong demand for PCs, insufficient supplies, and price differentials between Western and Russian hardware. The "computer-related" joint ventures reported in official statistics thus included among their activities both computer hardware trading or assembly of PCs from imported components and the development of new hardware and software products. A good example of this type of activity is the Dialogue joint venture, which during the first two years of operations assembled and sold 7,000 PCs in the former USSR. The Dialogue joint venture also exported applications software worth more than $600,000 (Druzenko 1990).[28] In the early 1990s, declining profits and increased rivalry in computer hardware trading led many firms to exit this activity, and new joint ventures (such as that involving Microinform) focused more exclusively on software development and marketing, supported by capital originally generated from computer hardware trading.[29]

The formation of joint ventures in Russia also was affected by changes in laws that in the late 1980s had provided substantial tax privileges to the founders of joint ventures. In the early 1990s, these statutes were revised to provide tax advantages to firms with more than 30 percent foreign capital participation, registered as joint stock companies and partnerships. These changes reduced the purely tax-based advantages associated with joint ventures.

But other factors continued to provide incentives for Western firms to enter software joint ventures. Some of these were based on the complementary assets controlled by the Russian partners in these undertakings (Teece 1986). Russian programmers "know how to make the best use of limited resources, which is why they are writing excellent code" (Keefe 1990b, 95). The cost of their labor was much lower than that of Western programmers. The products developed by Russian programmers within a joint venture also might be exported and sold for hard currency, drawing on the international marketing and distribution networks of the Western partner firms. Some promising joint ventures linked Western firms with Russian state-owned entities, but the majority of successful software joint ventures appear to have linked Western firms with Russian nonstate businesses.

This was true of the cooperative Infograph, which was founded in 1988 by a group of former scholars from the Building Ministry's research institute. In January 1989, Infograph and Autodesk established the successful joint venture "Parallel."[30] A software cooperative headed by S. Pachikov at the Central Economics and Mathematics Institute (TsEMI) went through a similar evolution: members of this cooperative joined the joint venture ParaGraph, headed by Pachikov, which is partly owned by the U.S. firm Matrix (which provided 50 percent of the initial capital), TsEMI, and the Academy of National Economy (which each provided 25 percent of the seed capital).

Such new joint ventures provided Russian programmers with unique opportunities for innovative activity. They offered strong salary incentives to programmers and use of the best computer hardware; they were able to sell computer hardware and software together; and they built their own distribution channels. Perhaps most novel was the fact that for virtually the first time in the Russian software industry, the developers of software found themselves working in close contact with customers, allowing for significant improvements in products.[31]

Nonetheless, most Russian joint ventures concentrated on russification and modification of Western software rather than the development of new products, and they supported the flow of Western software into the promising Russian market. In other cases, their international distribution and marketing channels were used by foreign software firms for the export of new products developed by their Russian joint venture partners. Autodesk, the foreign cofounder of the Parallel joint venture, exported three new CAD programs developed by their Russian partner (see Dyson 1991, 36). A number of software joint ventures were divided into specialized entities, each dedicated to a specific market niche. Specialization provides greater opportunities for close supplier-user interactions in the development, support, and maintenance of software. These close relationships are essential for Russian software developers faced with competition from illegally copied software, which is rarely supported by its sellers.

Since 1992, Western software firms have been shifting their Russian entry strategy from forming joint ventures to establishing wholly owned subsidiaries. The introduction of copyright protection has improved the ability of non-Russian firms to penetrate and profit from Russian software markets without local partners. In addition, a 1992 law gave tax benefits to Russian subsidiaries of foreign firms and contributed to the opening of many branches and representative offices of Western software firms in Moscow in 1993. These entities usually hire local programmers and sell their designs in the West, which costs them 25–50 percent less than employing Russian emigré software engineers in the West (Shershulsky 1992, 8). In 1993 exports of Russian software products and licenses for Russian designs (both of branches of foreign companies and of national firms) were estimated to be $25–30 million (Pachikov 1993), which exceeded legal domestic software sales but still was only one-tenth the level of software exports from India.

Despite the fact that joint ventures no longer are the most popular form of business arrangement between Russian software firms and their Western counterparts (because of the improvements in the intellectual property rights environment and the above-mentioned reduction in the tax advantages of joint ventures), contracts with Western companies remain important to the improvement of Russian software firms' innovative activities. Many of these projects provide the infrastructure to bring software products developed by Russian programmers to international markets. In other cases, foreign hardware manufacturers provide a platform for Russian-developed programs that is unavailable in Russia (for example, the handwriting recognition software for the Newton, developed by ParaGraph). In still other cases, Russian software developers can reduce the development costs for software that will be sold almost entirely in foreign markets (such as multimedia products, many of which are now designed in Russia for Western markets).

CONCLUSION

The correlation between Russia's market reforms and the emergence of the domestic software industry is clear. Since the late 1980s, the Russian software industry has benefited from a more favorable business environment, growth in the size, standardization, and quality of the Russian computer hardware base, the reduced influence of the military-industrial complex, stronger intellectual property protection, and the legalization of private business. These and other reforms have laid the groundwork for updating and intensifying the interactions between software producers and users.

Although their overall effects on the Russian software industry have been positive, changes in the regulatory and economic environment often emerged in a halting and contradictory fashion. The size of Russia's installed base of computers remains modest and is concentrated on PCs. Even within PCs, less technically sophisticated machines dominate the market and installed base.[32] The market reforms of the early 1990s produced a substantial reorganization of the software industry: cooperatives and joint ventures declined in importance, and the state-controlled entities are no longer an important force in software. But the private firms that have become the main domestic contributors to progress in the Russian software industry cannot yet replace academic and industrial state entities in conducting long-range research, supporting training of scientists and engineers, or developing the complex software for national projects in aerospace or nuclear plant operations (Authens 1990). The innovative activities of Russian programmers are rather narrow and usually focus on applications software, much of which is intended for microcomputers. This reflects the growth of demand by an economically independent population of PC users, and the limited availability of other types of computer hardware.[33] This market focus, of course, is not unique to Russia's software industry, as a cursory glance at the market data in chapter 1 reveals. The most attractive entry opportunities in the global software industry are those that draw on domestic firms' deep familiarity with unique user needs. This knowledge and these opportunities typically are greatest in custom software and in standard applications software.

All three sources of investment in the Russian software industry—the state, private funds, and foreign capital—have limited funds to devote to the industry. Public funding is scarcely sufficient to support academic research institutes, which may survive only as centers specializing in fundamental software development (contracts with Western firms, like that with Sun Microsystems, are another possible avenue for the financial support of such institutes). In general, the Russian software industry needs new public policies that will strengthen the publicly funded research and training infrastructure that has been shown to be necessary in the software industries of other economies. The private sector is no more ready or willing to provide this support, especially for infrastructure investment, than they are in other industrial economies.

The small and fragmented Russian software market discourages the exploitation of scale economies within most Russian software companies (Lazareva 1994). Because of competition and financial pressures, even the relatively successful software firms have pursued the development and marketing of programs with guaranteed demand, rather than far-reaching innovative strategies. Commercial banks, which are among the only potential sponsors of software R&D projects, rely largely on in-house development efforts. Although their in-house expertise is likely to spawn spin-off firms eventually, as they did in Japan (see chapter 5), financial institutions are not extensively supporting the efforts of independent software vendors. Successful commercialization, rather than radical innovation, has become imperative for the survival of many Russian software firms (both state and private), thus forcing these entities to emphasize the production and distribution of already proven domestic and foreign designs.

The pressures for incremental innovation, of course, are hardly unique to the Russian software industry—in this respect, it resembles those of other industrial economies. Nevertheless, given the shortage of venture and other sources of capital, there is some basis for concern that the innovative capabilities of Russian software developers may be applied mainly to the development of new products for non-Russian firms. Although the software industry is hardly capital-intensive by comparison with other high-technology industries, their needs for investment funds will continue to constrain the innovative strategies of Russian software firms for some time to come.

Foreign (mainly U.S.) software companies have provided Russian programmers new opportunities to pursue product development in Russia. Since the late 1980s, many of these firms have negotiated contracts with Russian software-producing entities, enhancing competition for human capital in the Russian software industry. Many domestic Russian software producers, especially those in packaged applications software, face stiff competition in the product and labor markets and must develop or greatly strengthen their marketing capabilities. The "second wave" of Russian computerization will expand users' demand for new applications, which Western software firms may be better prepared to meet. Nonetheless, the idiosyncratic structure of software demand, the possibilities for upgrading the Russian installed base to include more large systems with greater requirements for custom software, and the strength of Russian universities and research institutes all should preserve opportunities for entry by entpreneurial Russian firms into software development and production. Moreover, the expansion of Russia's domestic market will eventually provide a stronger "launching platform" for Russian software firms to compete in international markets.

A few Russian firms have developed successful software products (most are customized applications) in several niches in both the domestic and international markets. The main challenge facing Russian software firms is to redirect their innovative efforts from russifications and Russian-specific applications to products for the international market. Market reform and the education of a larger domestic user market will influence the pace of these changes within Russia. Any redirection of Russian software firms' innovative efforts nonetheless will be complicated by their limited capital resources and strong competition from Western firms. Consolidation of the national software business through mergers and acquisitions and more informal efforts is likely in the near future, as well as expanded formation of international alliances by the surviving Russian software firms. Because independent development will be difficult in a nation that has only begun to make the transition to an information-based economy, international alliances will remain essential.

NOTES

The research for this chapter was supported by the Alfred P. Sloan Foundation, the Consortium on Competitiveness and Cooperation, and the U.S. Air Force Office of Scientific Research. The chapter benefited from the comments of other contributors to this volume.

1. In 1993 this unique research and production center, often referred to as the Russian Silicon Valley, employed approximately 32,000 researchers and other workers in computer-related industries (*Delovoy Mir* (Business world), 17 July 1993, 5).

2. See Goodman and McHenry 1986, 338–39; and Aivazyan et al. 1989, 726.

3. For a detailed look at the Soviet computer industry see: United Nations 1988, 21–29; Tate and Hebditch 1987, 50; and Judy and Clough 1989.

4. The ASU spectrum runs from the simple monitoring of small production processes to a grand national automated data system for planning and controlling the USSR economy. The latter resulted in the world's largest application of computers to management, known as OGAS. However, ASUs were not a remedy for the Soviet economy, whose inefficiency was primarily due to systemic, organizational failures.

5. The first chance for Soviet programmers to meet openly with international vendors and development experts came only in July 1990 at the PC World Forum in Moscow. The first Russian language international journal for programmers, *Mir PC* (PC world), began publication in 1988.

6. For a detailed examination of the origins and practices of the Soviet system of international property protection, see Martens 1982.

7. Wellman 1989, 114–15. By comparison, Dataquest reported that U.S. software sales reached $16 billion in 1986 (Judy 1986, 359).

8. Some experts doubt that it even fit the definition of a "software industry" (see Judy and Clough 1990, 226). The same authors argue that "up until the mid 1980s, the Soviet software industry was best described as a loose collection of user groups that struggled through uncertain links to provide themselves with the most able software" (ibid., 291).

9. At this time, M. Gorbachev, then one of the CPSU Central Committee secretaries, was already managing Politburo meetings.

10. GKVTI was succesful mainly in putting obstacles in the way of small nonstate businesses in the software industry by applying its price controls to software.

11. Top managers of IBM are reported to consider Russia "the most promising country from the viewpoint of the computer business" (*Delovye Liudi*, September 1992, 26). During 1993 and early 1994, the staff of IBM-Russia increased from 70 to 160 persons while in all other countries IBM imposed massive layoffs (*Kommersant*, 22 February 1994, 9).

12. According to a January 1994 poll, 47 percent of 120 Russian firms and organizations polled were willing to buy expensive, high-quality, and brand-name computers (only 19 percent would have done so in mid-1993). Fifty-three percent of polled firms mentioned reliability (44 percent in mid-1993), 26 percent complex calculation tasks (20 percent in 1983), and 10 percent prestige (3 percent in 1983) as reasons for their response (*Kommersant Daily*, 11 March 1994, 11).

13. The effects of the price war in the international computer markets reached Russia only in late 1994.

14. For detailed discussion, see Katkalo 1992; Tate and Hebditch 1987, 50; Judy and Clough 1990, 294.

15. Domestic economic problems began to threaten the priority of the defense sector even before perestroika (Weickhardt 1988). But only in 1989 did the first National Program for defense industry conversion promote using defense sector capabilities to increase the output of computers by 2.1 times and PCs by 3.8 times during 1990–95. In the absence of financial support or broader reform of the economic system, the first results of conversion were quite destructive for high-technology enterprises, since military R&D and procurement were severely cut. During 1992, military purchases of Russian-made military microelectronics products fell tenfold (*Delovoy Mir*, 17 July 1993, 5).

16. *Kommersant Daily*, 17 December 1993. Ten million dollars is the minimum investment considered sufficient to enter domestic assembly of PCs for the Russian market (ibid.).

17. *Kommersant Daily*, 5 February 1993, 8. Large Russian computer firms (Eksimer, NTTs Kami, and others) had annual sales of only 15,000–20,000 PCs in 1993 (mainly assembled domestically) (*Softmarket* 1993, no. 17, 7; *Kommersant Daily*, 9 February 1994, 9).

18. Recent official tests of the products of major Russian PC assembly firms revealed that

PCs that claim to have identical features in fact may differ by a factor of 2–3 in productivity (*Kommersant Daily,* 2 July 1993).

19. At the end of 1993, the share of i386 and i486 machines was 36 percent within the total installed base and 53 percent among computers used by Russian programmers (*Pachikov* 1993).

20. Ashton-Tate reportedly supported a copyright obtained by S. Barilov and M. Figurin of the St. Petersburg Institute of Information, alhough their development of a "russified" version was not authorized by the U.S. firm (Brandel 1990, 1).

21. For example, in Italy and Spain, after copyright protection was extended to software, sales of software increased 200–300 percent (*Kommersant Daily,* 29 October 1992, 5).

22. Interview with A. Feniov, executive director, ASS, March 1993.

23. Not surprisingly, the winners of a recent open competition for the best accounting applications software were all from Moscow (*Kommersant* 1993, no. 14, 28).

24. In the summer of 1993, an employment advertisement from the St. Petersburg Youth Employment Agency listed a vacant position for a chief engineer-programmer at a state enterprise with a monthly salary of Rb30,000 (roughly $30); a private firm on the same list of vacant jobs advertised an opening for a secretary at the same compensation (*Smena,* 7 July 1993, 3).

U.S. firms are widely estimated to pay programmers average salaries that are roughly ten times those paid to Russian programmers, a differential that provides strong incentives for U.S. firms to use Russian programming talent (Shershulsky 1992, 8).

25. See Rutherford 1991. Not surprisingly, programmers form the largest group—15–20 percent of the total—of emigrating Russian scientists (*Izvestia,* 15 February 1994, 7).

26. Interview with Dr. B. Komev, vice president, DEKA, June 1992.

27. *Finansovay Gazeta* 1992, no. 27, 9. In 1993, approximately fifteen specialized exhibitions and competitions among designs took place in the area of accounting software alone in Russia (*Kommersant Daily,* 4 February 1994).

28. The participants in the Dialogue joint venture were the U.S. firm Management Partnership International and a team of Russian state-owned institutions: KamAZ auto company, Moscow State University, the association Vneshtekhnika, the Calculation Center of the USSR Academy of Sciences, and the USSR National Exhibition of Economic Achievements.

29. Microinform formed a joint venture with the Central Research Institute of Applied Computer Systems (of the USSR Academy of Sciences) and the Hungarian telecommunications company Telefon Djar.

30. During its first two years in operation, Parallel achieved revenues of nearly $650,000 (Dyson 1991, 36).

31. In the early 1990s, some joint ventures were reported to generate up to 25 percent of their revenues from such contacts with customers (*Kommersant* 1992, no. 11, 9).

32. Despite progress in this field, Russia remains a poorly computerized country. In early 1994 it was reported that there were only three computers for every one hundred workers in Russia (*Kommersant Daily,* 1 February 1994, 3).

33. For example, only in 1993 were the first legal imports of supercomputers for industrial purposes negotiated with the German producer Parsytec. This transaction may open the way for the Russian development of software for solving complicated mathematical tasks (*Kommersant Daily,* 7 May 1993, 8).

REFERENCES

Aivazyan, S. A., et al. 1989. "Ekonomicheskie Problemy Kompiuterizatsii Obschestva" (Economic problems of the computerization of society). *Ekonomika i Matematicheskie Metody* (Economics and mathematical methods) 25, no. 4: 710–38.

Authens, G. H. 1990. "Soviets Plan Their CASE against Nuke Disasters." *ComputerWorld*, 16 April, 38.

Aronovich, A. B., et al. 1990. "Napravlenya Komiuterizatsii Vysshego Ekomicheskogo Obrazovanya" (Directions for computerization in higher economic education), *Economika i Matematicheskie Metody* (Economics and mathematical methods) 26: 360–69.

Biznes-karta-93. 1993. Priborostroenie. Radiotekhnicheskaya promyshlennost (Business map 93. Electronic instrument-making industry. Radio technologies equipment industry). Moscow: ADI- MP NIK.

Brandel, W. 1990. " 'Copyright' in Russian: Right to Copy." *Computerland*. 9 February, 1, 14.

Burrows, P. 1990. "U.S. Firms Find Demand from Soviet CAD Users," *Electronic Business*, 17 September, 16.

Business Moscow News. 1994. "Konkurentsiya na Rynke Bukhgalterskikh Programm Smeschaetsya v Oblast Marketinga (Competition in the accounting software market moves into the marketing area)." 9 February, 8.

Druzenko, A. 1990. "Dialog o 'Dialoge' ": V Chiom Sekret Uspekha? (Dialogue about "Dialogue": What is the secret of success?) *We/My*, 4 July, 4.

Dyson, E. 1991. "Micro Capitalism: Eastern Europe's Computer Future," *Harvard Business Review* 69: 26–37.

Elektronnaya Promyshlennost' (Electronics industry: Industry directory). 1992. Vol. 1. Moscow: ASU Impuls.

Elektrotekhnicheskaya Promyshlennost' i Priborostroenie (Electronic equipment and instrument making industry: Industry directory). 1992. Vol. 1. Moscow: ASU-Impuls.

Ershov, A. 1990. Komputerizatsya shkoly i Matematicheskoe Obrazovanie (Computerization school and mathematics education), *Programmirovanie* (Programming) 1: 5–23.

Fedotov, Y. 1991. "Uchebnye programmy v Stikhii Rynka" (Education software and elements of the market). *Informatika i Obrazovanie* (Informatics and education) 3: 105–07.

Finansovaya Gazeta (Financial newspaper). 1992. "Chto Proiskhodit na Rynke Bukhgalterskikh Program" (What happens in the market for accounting software), no. 27, 9.

Goodman, S. E. 1979. "Software in the Soviet Union: Progress and Problems." *Advances in Computers* 18: 231–87.

Goodman, S. E., and W. K. McHenry. 1986. Computing in the USSR: Recent Progress and Policies, *Soviet Economy* 2: 327–54.

Ignatius, A. 1994. "Russian Software Firms Look Overseas." *Wall Street Journal*, 8 July, A5.

Ivanova, A. 1991. "Kupit' Programmnyi Produkt 'Oracle' Teper' Mozhno Legal'no" (It is now possible to purchase "Oracle" products legally), *Kommersant*, no. 11: 8.

Izvestiia. 1985. "V Politburo TSk KPSS" (In the Politburo of the Central Committee of the Communist Party), 19 October, 1.

Judy, R. W. 1986. "Computing in the USSR: A Comment." *Soviet Economy* 2: 355–67

Judy, R. W., and R. W. Clough. 1989. "Soviet Computers in the 1980s," *Advances in Computers* 29: 251–330.

———. 1990. "Soviet Computing in the 1980s. A Survey of the Software and Its Applications." *Advances in Computers* 30: 223–306.

Kassel, S. 1986. *A New Force in the Soviet Computer Industry: The Reorganization of the USSR Adademy of Sciences in the Computer Field*. Santa Monica, Calif.: Rand Corporation.

Katkalo, V. 1992. "Measuring Soviet Economic Growth. A Comment." *Journal of Institutional and Theoretical Economics* (March): 98–102.

Keefe, P. 1990a. "Helping the Soviets Help Themselves." *ComputerWorld*, May 28, 93–97.

———. 1990b. "Comrades, We Were Born to Code." *ComputerWorld*, 4 June, 95, 99.

————. 1990c. "Piracy Paved the Way." *ComputerWorld,* 4 June, 99.

Kozyrev, S., and S. Sokolov. 1987. "Kompiuter s Aktsentom" (Computer with an accent), *Komsomol'skaya Pravda* (Comsomol truth), 3 March, 2.

Kuznetsov, E., and F. Shirokov. 1989. "Naukoemkie Proizvodstva i Konversiya Oboronnoy Promyshlennosti" (High-tech sector and conversion of the defense industry). *Kommunist,* no. 10: 15–21.

Latypov I. 1993. "Programmy Mozhno ne tolko vorovat, no i pokupat" (Software may be stolen as well as purchased). *Delovoy Peterburg* (Business Petersburg), 1 December, 26.

Lazareva, N. 1994. "Rossiysky Soft: Vyzhivet—ne vyzhivet?" (Russian software: Will it survive or not?). *Delovoy Mir* (Business world), 10 January, 2, 11.

Malkov, L. 1993. "Proekt Zakona i Industriya Programmirovaniya" (Draft of the law and the software industry). *Delovoy Mir* (Business world), 19 February, 14.

Martens, J. A. 1982. Soviet Patents and Inventors' Certificates. *Soviet Economy in the 1980s: Problems and Prospects.* Part 1. Washington, D.C.: U.S. Government Printing Office.

Morozov, V. P., and A. N. Popsuev. 1986. "Spetsifichnost' Programmnykh Sredstv kak Produktov Truda" (Specificity of software as labor's products). *Ekonomika i Matematicheskie Metody* (Economics and mathematical methods) 22: 1073–77.

Nikolaev, V. 1991. "Borland Rasshiriaet Rubliovye Prodazhi i Obeschaet L'goty Postoiannym Pol'zovateliam" (Borland increases sales for rubles and promises benefits for permanent users of its products). *Kommersant,* 14 January, 11.

Pachikov, S. 1993. "Rossiyskie programmisty imeut shans vyiti na Zapadnye Rynki" (Russian programmers have chance to enter Western markets). *Finansovye Izvestiya* (Financial news) 58, no. IV.

Podshibikhin, L., and Vitaliev G. 1993. *Ob osobennostiakh pravovoy okhrany program dlva EVM i baz dannykh v Rossiyskoi Federatsii.* (Specifics of the legal protection of computer software and databases in the Russian Federation). Moscow: ASS.

Press, L. 1991. "Personal Computers and the World Software Market." *Communications of the ACM* 34, no. 2: 23–28.

Riabov, G. 1991. "K ispol'zovaniu super-EVM v SSSR" (Toward utilization of supercomputers in the USSR). *Programmirovanie* (Programming), no. 4: 32–33.

Romanovskii, I. V., and B. V. Cherkasskii. 1988. "Organizatsionno-Ekonomicheskie Aspekty Rasprostraneniya Programmnogo Obespecheniya" (Organizational and economic aspects of software diffusion). *Ekonomika i Matematicheskie Metody* (Economics and mathematical methods) 24, no. 5: 925–33.

Rudenko, V., et al. 1994. "Vtoraya Volna Kompiuterizatsii v Rossii?" (Second wave of Russia's computerization?). *Kommersant,* no. 3: 30–32.

Rutherford, A. 1991. "Soviet Union Fears Brain Drain as Scientists Take Work Abroad." *Wall Street Journal,* 3 May, A10.

Savell, L. 1990a. "Software Copyright: Two Views." *ComputerWorld,* 16 July, 95, 96.

————. 1990b. "The Tetris Case." *ComputerWorld,* 16 July, 96.

Savelieva, I. 1992. "Rossia: pravovaya okhrana program stanovitsa realnostyu" (Russia: Legal protection of software becomes a reality). *Delovye Liudi* (November): 66–67.

Schware, R. 1989. *The World Software Industrv and Software Engineering.* Washington, D.C.: World Bank.

Seligman, D. 1985. "The Great Soviet Computer Screw-Up." *Fortune,* 8 July, 32–36.

Selin, I. 1986. "Communications and Computers in the USSR: Successes and Failures." *Signal* (December): 8.

Shershulsky, V. 1992. "Skolko 'stoyat' inzhenery—kompiuterschiki i programmisty" (How much do computer engineers and programmers "cost"?) *ComputerWorld Moscow,* no. 7: 1, 8.

————. 1993. "Rossyiskaya electronnaya promyshlennost': leto 1993 goda" (Russian electronic industry: Summer 1993). *ComputerWorld Moscow*, no. 34: 1; no. 35; no. 36.

Smith, H. 1990. "The Russian Character." *New York Times Magazine*, October 28.

Staar, R. F., ed. 1988. *The Future Information Revolution in the USSR*. New York: Crane Russak Co.

Statistics Bureau of Leningrad. 1990. *O Razvitii Seti Kooperativov v Leningrade i Leningradskoy Oblasti v 1 Kvartale 1990 goda* (On the development of a network of cooperatives in Leningrad and Leningrad Region in the 1st Quarter of 1990). Leningrad: Statistics Bureau of Leningrad.

Tate, P., and D. Hebditch. 1987. "Opening Moves." *Datamation*, 15 March, 43–56.

Teece, D. J. 1986. "Profiting from Technological Innovation." *Research Policy* 15, no. 6.

Tribuna NTR (Tribune of scientific and technological revolution). 1990, nos. 13–14, 8.

Tsuprikov, S. 1994. "Itogui Avtomatizatsii Bankov Rossii" (Results of Russian banks' automation). *ComputerWorld Moscow*, no. 7: 56–61.

United Nations. 1988. *Data Goods and Data Services in the Socialist Countries of Eastern Europe*. New York: United Nations.

Vasiliev, A. 1992. "Sovetskiy Rynok Programmnykh Produktov" (The Russian software market). *ComputerWorld Moscow*, no. 6, 10.

Velikhov, E. P. 1984. "Personal'nye EVM—Segodniashniya Practika i Perspectivy" (Personal computers—today's practice and perspectives). *Vestnik Akademii Nauk SSSR* (Herald of the USSR Academy of Sciences), no. 2: 3–8.

Vitaliev, G. 1993. "K Tsivilizovannomu Rynku Programmnykh Produktov" (Toward the civilized software market). *Delovoy Mir* (Business world), 12 February, 14.

Vladov, F. 1988. "The Intricacies of Information Networks." *NTR: Problemv i Resheniya* (Scientific and technical revolution: Problems and solutions), no. 15: 1–4.

Vorobieva, R. A., and A. N. Popsuev. 1986. "Prognozirovanie Sprosa na Pakety Prikladnykh Program" (Forecasting of demand for application software packages). *Ekonomika i Matematicheskie Metody* (Economics and mathematical methods) 22, no. 4: 747–50.

U.S. Central Intelligence Agency. 1987. *The USSR Confronts the Information Revolution: A Conference Report*. SOV-87–10029. Washington, D.C.: Directorate of Intelligence.

Weickhardt, G. G. 1986. "The Soviet Military-Industrial Complex and Economic Reform." *Soviet Economy* 2: 193–220.

Wellman, D. A. 1989. *A Chip in the Curtain*. Washington, D.C.: National Defense University Press.

Williamson, O. E. 1985. *The Economic Institutions of Capitalism*. New York: Free Press.

Zotov, A. 1991. "Iz Plena Dikosti" (From the captivity of wildness), *Delovye Liudi* (Business in the USSR). July-August: 40–42.

Zubchenko, A. 1991. "NTsPSO—sovremennaya industria programmnykh pedagogicheskikh sredstv" (Scientific Center of Educational Software—the Contemporary Industry of Educational Software). *Informatika i Obrozovanie* (Informatics and education), no. 5: 27–30.

10

A Comparative Look at Property Rights and the Software Industry

Robert P. Merges

The growing importance of intellectual property rights affects many industries. The questions raised by strengthening rights, and the increase in enforcement actions this brings, are not restricted to any industry in particular. But the questions seem especially acute in some industries—those in which the policies sought to be furthered by strengthening rights are most in doubt. For a variety of reasons, the software industry is one of these.

There is one well-known reason why intellectual property policy affects the software industry so much: because of the nature of software, firms cannot appropriate much of the benefit of product innovation without some form of legal protection.[1] Even with relatively strong legal protection, outright piracy still skims off several billion dollars in revenues in the United States alone.[2]

But there is another reason why those concerned with the development of the software industry must worry about current intellectual property trends. Intellectual property may exert a subtle but important influence on entry into the industry and industry structure. If so, then to the extent that entry and industry structure affect the pace of innovation, intellectual property may in fact play a significant role in determining whether the industry will remain as vital and innovative as it has been so far. In addition, because software, like most goods, emanates from firms located in many nations, national intellectual property policy toward this industry will affect its success vis-à-vis its international rivals.

I begin with a brief description of what is known about the software industry, including the nature of the three major software markets, the United States, Europe, and Japan. Next I consider how past and current intellectual property rules—what I call "intellectual property policy"—may have played a role in the formation of industries with distinctive characteristics in each of the three major markets. Then I consider some possible future effects of current trends in intellectual property protection, most notably the emerging scope of copyright protection and the beginnings of patent protection for software. Finally, I discuss industry prospects under a moderately strong regime of intellectual property rights.

AN OVERVIEW OF THE INDUSTRY

The Structure of the U.S. Software Industry

The software industry is a bit amorphous; it covers everything from computer game cartridges to advanced telecommunications switching programs. Nevertheless, it is possible to outline the industry's major features.

Best estimates are that the U.S. industry totaled about $25 billion in revenues in 1988 and about $42 billion in 1991.[3] Fast growth is expected to propel the industry to the $100 billion level in annual revenues by 1995.[4]

It is generally recognized that the industry has two main segments: prepackaged software, sold "off the shelf" as a commodity product; and "custom programming services," in which the software is created specially (or adapted) for a particular client. Although estimates of the relative size of the two segments vary, it is thought that prepackaged software accounts for approximately 70 percent of industry reve nues at present. However, the elusive nature of the industry yields some very different estimates.[5]

Average firm size in the U.S. software industry is also difficult to estimate. The most recent survey, however, provides some rough indications.[6] In general, firms in the industry are small. Of the survey's 466 respondents, 18 percent had 5 or fewer employees; 20 percent had 6–15; 21 percent had 16–30; 21 percent had 31–99, and 16 percent had more than 100 employees (Massachusetts Computer Software Council 1991, Question 1). Thus fully 38 percent of the firms had 15 or fewer employees, and about half (49 percent) had 30 or fewer. Commentators have generally remarked on the small firm size in the industry.[7]

It is difficult to obtain data on average firm size in the two main segments of the industry, custom software and prepackaged software. However, the survey data just mentioned do provide some suggestions along these lines. Respondents were asked to classify their products into two broad categories, vertical market and horizontal market software. Vertical market software is sold to a specific industry—for example, bookstores, car dealerships, or hospitals. Horizontal market software is designed for a general application such as word processing or financial spreadsheets and thus is sold in many industries. In general, vertical market software tends to be more customized while horizontal software is by definition prepackaged. Using this admittedly rough guideline, the survey response data show that firms producing vertical market software products are slightly larger than those producing horizontal market software. In other words, it appears that firms in the custom software segment of the industry are slightly larger, on average. This is what one would expect given the need for more custom service and user input.[8]

In comparing profitability across industry segments, again only indirect data are available. But a comparison of price-to-earnings ratios for publicly traded firms in the two segments shows that the stock market anticipates more growth in the prepackaged software market. Average price-to-earnings (P/E) ratios for publicly traded firms in this segment are 18.7; for firms in the custom programming services segment, the average P/E is 15.2 (Massachusetts Computer Software Council 1991, C120).[9] Thus at least the stock market believes prepackaged software has a rosier future.

A Comparative Look at Europe and Japan

The European and Japanese software industries, though roughly comparable in size, are quite different from the U.S. industry. Europe's total market is conservatively estimated at $48 billion in 1991; while the most recent figures for Japan show a $42 billion market (see *Economist* 1992, 82; Japanese Information Service Industry Association 1994, 40; chapter 6 in this volume). Size apart, the main difference between these markets and the U.S. market is that custom programming still dominates. Estimates are that the custom programming segment was 90 percent of the Japanese industry and 46 percent of the European industry in the mid-1980s (U.S. Congress, Office of Technology Assessment, 1987, 163, 166).[10] While the custom segment has been shrinking in Europe, it has not shrunk by much in Japan; according to one recent estimate it is still 85 percent of the industry there (Cottrell 1994).[11]

While sales of prepackaged software constitute 54 percent of the European market, much of this revenue apparently goes to U.S.-based firms. Of the software firms located in Europe, the largest and most prominent are in the custom service segment of the industry. If the data reported earlier are accurate, this means that European software firms are on average slightly larger than their U.S. counterparts. Indeed, a 1992 news article corroborates this. The article reports that small firms can still contribute in the prepackaged segment of the market: "But in the fast-growing software services business, economies of scale matter. To win contracts to manage entire computer systems from multinationals, service companies must be global too. They must also be capable of assuming the big financial risk involved in signing such long-term, fixed-price contracts and of dealing with a wide range of technologies.[12]

This is not to say that European firms are not interested in pursuing the prepackaged software market; it is just that so far, the high-visibility firms in Europe have tended to specialize in custom services.

The Japanese industry is also closely associated with custom software. Most notably, the much-publicized Japanese "software factories" (in which large numbers of programmers churn out code in a highly structured programming environment) are designed to produce high-quality custom software.[13] Whether one believes in the software factory model or not, it does demonstrate the extent to which the Japanese industry concentrates on custom programming.

To summarize, it is clear that the software industry is large and growing; that it has two main segments, prepackaged and custom; and that the United States leads in the prepackaged segment of the market, followed by Europe, with Japan a distant third.

OVERVIEW OF THE LEGAL REGIMES

More detailed accounts of the development of the software industry in the three major regions under discussion here (such as those in the other chapters of this book) consider a wide array of factors: the strength of the pre-existing electronics and computer hardware industries; the adequacy of university-level training in computer science; government policies, from procurement to subsidies to scientific grant-making; and many more. Thus one must be careful in trying to identify the influence of one particular factor. Yet that is what I attempt here, when I ask: how has the intellectual property regime affected the development of the software industry in these major markets? As we shall see, the answer must be incomplete unless one considers the converse question—how has the industry affected the legal regime?

To begin, it is helpful to sketch the basics of the legal regime in each area. As general background, keep in mind that copyright for the most part protects only the literal expression of software code. "Look and feel" copyright protects the more generalized features of a program's user interface or operation, such as the menu structure, screen icons, and the like. Patent law, however, protects the general inventive concept specified in patent claims, such as a method for performing some software function or operation.

Japan

It is well known that Japan has followed an industrial development strategy that at least in part emphasizes domestic diffusion and adoption of new technology (Ergas 1987). One component of the Japanese strategy is relatively weak intellectual property protection (Ordover 1991, 43). The software industry is a good example of these features of Japan's domestic technology policy.

The 1985 amendment to the Copyright Law finally extended copyright protection to software.[14] It specifically excludes programming languages and the structure and flow of information in the program from coverage. One account lists several of the law's major features:

> The protection of interfaces is of major importance in computer programs, and they are not protected under the 1985 amendment. . . . [t]he . . . law permits upgrading to the extent necessary to use a program more efficiently. However, the legal distinction between lawful upgrading and prohibited adaptations is unclear. . . . [r]everse engineering is generally a permissible or encouraged method of development in an industry. However, the Copyright Law does not specifically provide for this to be authorized use. If the law is literally interpreted, it would prohibit such reproduction and adaptation. (Welch and Anderson 1991, 287)

Although there have been few cases, the lack of protection for interfaces appears to mean that Japan does not protect the broad features of software design that have been the focus of the recent "look and feel" cases in the U.S. courts.[15] In this and other areas, however, there is little case law that lawyers and business planners can use for guidance. This creates a good deal of uncertainty. In addition to this uncertainty, some U.S. observers are worried about Japan's recently announced plans to adopt a provision similar to the European Directive discussed below.[16] The consensus is that Japanese copyright protection, though greatly enhanced, still carries some significant limitations.

Likewise, a number of idiosyncrasies make Japanese patent law a less tractable source of rights than U.S. patent law.[17] In general, applications are published eighteen months after filing; coverage under a single patent is narrower in Japan; courts are more likely to construe the patent narrowly; competitors can more easily ham-string efforts to obtain a patent; and remedies for infringement are less favorable. Although these factors influence protection of any invention sought to be patented in Japan, an additional hurdle faces a software inventor seeking protection there: under the Japanese Patent Office's "Standards for Examination of Computer Programs as Inventions," a program may be eligible for patent protection only if it is a work embodying a "technical idea utilizing natural laws."

To be sure, Japanese patent law does not declare that any invention containing software is per se unpatentable. To the contrary, under guidelines enacted in the 1970s, at least some software-related inventions can be patented.[18] But the examples in the guidelines mostly describe software embodied in larger industrial processes, such as machine tools; software by itself may not be covered by the current guide-lines. Japan's patent policy for software may well be revised—for example, in re-sponse to liberalized treatment for software in the United States.[19] But at present, despite some signs of change,[20] Japanese patent law provides a modest level of intel-lectual property protection for software in Japan.

Europe

European developments in the late 1980s and early 1990s made two points clear: (1) software is definitely protectable under copyright, if not also by patents; and (2) the exact scope of rights is limited to try to balance the interests of rightsholders and others. In thus recognizing but limiting rights, the Europeans appear close to the Japanese view.

The European approach to software protection is set forth clearly in one docu-ment: the Council of European Communities Directive of May 14, 1991.[21] The direc-tive bans reverse engineering in general but allows such copying when necessary to achieve "interoperability" between programs (Common Market Reporter 1991).[22] Ar-ticle 6.1 allows decompilation,[23] a key step in the reverse engineering of many pro-grams, if required to achieve the interoperability of the independently created pro-gram with other programs, provided that:

- the decompilation is performed by the licensee or another person having the right to use a copy of the program, or a person authorized on their behalf;
- the information necessary to achieve interoperability has not previously been published or made available to the person; and
- the acts are confined to the parts of the original program which are necessary to achieve interoperability.

Article 6.2 of the directive severely restricts the application of the information obtained through such decompilations, stating that such information cannot:

- be used for purposes other than the achievement of interoperability.
- be given to others, except when necessary to achieve interoperability.
- be used for any act that would infringe the copyright of the original program, especially programs substantially similar in expression to the original.

The struggle that produced this directive is as instructive in some ways as the final text. One group of companies—mainly European and Japanese—fought for permissive rules on reverse engineering. These "procompetition" forces were opposed by other firms, mostly large companies based in the United States, which argued for stronger property rights, including a prohibition on reverse engineering.[24] To the extent that these two groups of companies were representative of their respective national industries, they show that the large Japanese and European companies preferred a weaker property rights regime than did their large U.S. counterparts.

In addition to software copyright, the coverage of European patent law has expanded to a limited extent to embrace computer program-related inventions. No true software patents—that is, patents covering a computer program having no hardware elements—have yet issued, however.[25] For example, in Great Britain in 1991 a patent for a ROM-based program for calculating square roots was denied on the grounds that, despite the application's "hardware" claims, its only novelty was in the steps of the program, rendering the claim unpatentable (*BNA International Business Daily* 1991). This is consistent with other decisions of the centralized European patent processing authority, the European Patent Office (EPO). The EPO has found a number of software inventions unpatentable, including a method for automatically abstracting, storing, and retrieving a document in machine readable form, and a method of decoding phrases and obtaining a readout of events in a text processing system.[26] The board held that merely setting out the sequence of steps necessary to perform an activity in terms of functions that are carried out by conventional computer hardware elements does not make for a patentable claim.[27] On the other hand, the EPO has announced that inventions producing a "technical effect"—meaning some impact on physical items or processes, rather than on mere abstract numbers—are patentable. The EPO invoked this principle to uphold patents on such subject matter as a method for digitally processing images,[28] a method for creating computer-enhanced X ray images involving digital processing of the raw image data,[29] and a data processor network control and coordination system, which the board likened to an operating system.[30]

Although these decisions recognize the possibility that software is patentable, they are inconsistent and yield no clear guidance. They leave the general impression that the law is unsettled in this area, which can only mean a lack of effective patent protection for software in the economies of the European Community.

United States

The United States has traditionally embraced strong protection for computer software. Despite some early 1990s cases moderating the strength of copyright protection, the emergence of patent protection for software ensures that overall this strong protectionist regime will continue.

In copyright, the widely publicized "look and feel" cases in U.S. courts effectively extended copyright protection to broad structural features of programs, especially user interfaces and command menus.[31] In the late 1980s and early 1990s, however, several opinions cut back on the broad protection offered to software features.

In one such case, the Second Circuit Court of Appeals, the influential regional federal court based in New York City, held that a computer program must be carefully dissected into copyrightable and uncopyrightable components before determining infringement.[32] Moreover, the court held that only specific expressions and features of the program were copyrightable. The broader structural features—precisely those held protectable in earlier cases—were excluded.[33] Although this ruling has been followed in some recent cases, the broad-protection view still retains adherents.[34] The doctrine may stabilize over time;[35] if it does not, a Supreme Court resolution will be necessary.

A second important case was *Lotus v. Borland*,[36] in which the First Circuit held that the command structure for Lotus's famous 1-2-3 spreadsheet product was an uncopyrightable "method of operation." While the case is limited to software user interfaces, it established the important principle that copyright will not extend to these interfaces even if they become highly successful "standards."

Another significant departure from the earlier trend of stronger protection is a series of cases on reverse engineering. In one, *Atari v. Nintendo*, the court found for the copyright holder and thus dismissed the infringer's reverse engineering defense, but not without first making some general statements that suggest the need to permit reverse engineering in other cases.[37] In *Nintendo*, the plaintiff Atari was found to be an infringer because it acquired Nintendo's source code listing from the Copyright Office under false pretenses, and used the listing to check the results it obtained by reverse engineering the program code from a ROM chip. Despite the holding, however, the court made this important statement about reverse engineering:

> Reverse engineering, untainted by the purloined copy of the . . . program and necessary to understand [it], is a fair use [and thus not infringement]. An individual cannot even observe, let alone understand, the object code on Nintendo's chip without reverse engineering. Atari retrieved this object code from [Nintendo] security chips in its efforts to reverse engineer the . . . program. Atari chemically removed layers from Nintendo's chips to reveal the [program's] object code. Through microscopic examination of the "peeled" chip, Atari engineers transcribed the . . . object code into a handwritten list of ones and zeros. While these ones and zeros represent the configuration of machine readable software, the ones and zeros convey little, if any, information to the normal unaided observer. Atari then keyed this handwritten copy into a computer. The computer then "disassembled" the object code or otherwise aided the observer in understanding the program's method or functioning. This "reverse engineering" process, to the extent untainted by the [program] copy purloined from the Copyright Office, qualified as a fair use.[38]

Another court seized on this language almost immediately in upholding a reverse-engineering defense.[39]

Although these developments suggest some moderating forces, the overall trend in the United States since the mid-1980s has been strengthened legal protection for software. Subsequent cases in which courts adhered to strong copyright protection bear this out,[40] but the clearest evidence is in the law of software patents.

Patents now are being granted on pure software inventions, and software patents are beginning to be upheld by the U.S. courts in litigation.[41] A series of cases in the late 1980s and early 1990s held that a patent applicant need only cite a token hardware element to obtain patent protection for essentially software-based inventions. This development, together with the "look and feel" cases, suggest that the United States has adopted—perhaps unintentionally—a "strong protection" strategy in the international software arena.

Because it is not widely known that patent protection is now available for software in the United States, I quote from a recent article by a U.S. patent lawyer:

A significant number of technologically sophisticated companies have in fact been getting software patents and continue to do so. "Household word" companies such as IBM, Tektronix, NCR, Hitachi, Singer, Texas Instruments, Unisys, AT&T, Merrill Lynch (!), RCA, NEC, Hewlett-Packard, Wang, and Exxon have all climbed on this bandwagon. And many small, technically advanced companies have similarly acquired such patents. This increasing flow of software patents attracted the interest of a committee of the State Bar of Michigan. In September 1988 that committee published a survey that concluded:

The patentability of computer programs is now firmly established. The use of patents to protect software technology is now becoming more and more attractive, due especially to changing judicial attitudes toward patents. The survey . . . indicates that the Patent Office is now issuing a large number of patents for computer programs operating on computers in a wide variety of applications. Many of these patents are 'pure' software patents which indicate that the Patent Office is now willing to grant patents for novel and nonobvious computer programs operating on conventional, off-the-shelf computer hardware. Consequently, software developers should be made aware of this powerful form of legal protection for their computer programs so that they can factor this information in their business decision of how to protect their software technology.

Indeed, software patents are issuing in four major areas: (1) computer-controlled processes (where in fact software-related inventions have been patented for decades) . . . ; (2) business methods implemented through the use of computers; (3) the human/computer interface; and (4) computer-implemented algorithms (Bender 1991, 511).[42]

It should be noted that many of the independent programmers who work as consultants and have founded start-up software firms are opposed both to strong copyright protection and to software patents. The most visible leader of this segment of the computer science world, Richard Stallman, strongly advocates abolishing most property rights over software, on the ground that the industry has developed rapidly in a low-protection regime.[43]

In 1994, for the first time, a software patent was successfully enforced. A jury ruled that Microsoft had infringed data compression software patents held by Stac Electronics,[44] and awarded damages of $120 million to Stac.[45] According to reports in the press, Microsoft tried to license Stac, but the parties failed to reach agreement. Microsoft announced plans, pending appeal of the jury verdict, to excise the infringing code from its MS-DOS operating system software; the parties ultimately settled. The case clearly shows the potential impact of software patents in that Stac was able to force Microsoft to temporarily pull a multi-million-dollar product from the market. To some, this case serves as an example of why patents for software are so problematical (see Fisher 1994a).

To see how we arrived at the point where a patent can prevent Microsoft from selling the current version of one of its programs, we must turn back to the earliest cases in this area, which concern themselves primarily with the basic question of whether software—or "computer algorithms"—comprises patentable subject matter. Next we will consider a recent case involving software, to see how the early framework is currently applied by the Patent Office and courts in decisions on whether software-related inventions are patentable.

In the earliest major software cases, the Supreme Court struggled with whether software even qualified for patent protection. Likening computer algorithms to "laws of nature" and scientific principles, the Court was quite cautious at first; it invalidated several patents during this era, leading most in the industry to conclude that patents were not a viable form of protection.[46]

Since 1980, however, when the Court upheld a patent that recited a computer program embedded in an "otherwise statutory" (that is, patentable) invention, the cases reveal a slow thaw in the earlier attitude. This results in part from changing perceptions of the importance of intellectual property rights in general, and in part from the fact that the Supreme Court has virtually ceded jurisdiction in this area to the lower federal courts, especially the Court of Appeals for the Federal Circuit, which now handles all appeals from the Patent Office. Partly because of the pro-patent-holder attitude of the Court of Appeals for the Federal Circuit, which was created by statute only in 1982, the newer cases have been more favorable to software patents, though the "dead hand" of the 1970s cases continues to influence the reasoning of courts.

For example, an important case called *In re Iwahashi* was decided by the Federal Circuit in 1989.[47] In 1982, an inventor named Hiroyuki Iwahashi applied for a patent on a "system" for recognizing signals. The Patent Office rejected the application on the ground that it covered only a new algorithm for analyzing mathematical representations of a signal—in short, because it boiled down to a patent on a piece of software. The Federal Circuit reversed the Patent Office, essentially stating that the invention was patentable subject matter. In so doing, that court had to grapple with several issues raised in the earlier Supreme Court cases, illustrating the importance of the older cases in current analysis.

The Federal Circuit first had to decide whether Iwahashi's invention actually contained an algorithm, as that term was defined in the earlier cases. They decided that it did, which is not surprising given the lengthy mathematical formula reproduced as an "element" of each of Iwahashi's claims at the end of the patent. Second, they had to decide whether issuing the patent would effectively preempt all applications of the algorithm. This issue grew out of the consensus in earlier Supreme Court cases that granting patents on mathematical formulas might allow inventors to "lock up" computational methods that resembled other generalizable forms of knowledge long thought to be *un*patentable; the paradigmatic examples were Newton's laws of gravitation and Einstein's "$E = mc^2$." The court decided that Iwahashi's patent claims did not preempt all uses of the algorithm. This conclusion was based on the fact that Iwahashi's claims cite a piece of *hardware*—a ROM, or Read Only Memory storage device. Therefore, the court reasoned, the algorithm was not wholly preempted. Because it can be used without a ROM device, and such use would be outside the scope of the patent, the patent did not remove the algorithm from the public for all purposes. The court argued that:

> The claim as a whole certainly defines apparatus in the form of a combination of interrelated means and we cannot discern any logical reason why it should not be deemed statutory subject matter as either a machine or a manufacture as specified in 101 [of the patent code]. The fact that the apparatus operates according to an algorithm does not make it nonstatutory. We therefore hold that the claim is directed to statutory subject matter. (*In re Iwahashi* 1988, 1375)

The upshot from this and other recent cases[48] is that industry participants behave as though software is for the most part patentable, even though the courts have to work around the older cases when presented with a patent in this field.

THE EFFECT OF THE LEGAL REGIME ON INDUSTRY DEVELOPMENT

Because of the number of interrelated factors that affect the development of an industry in a given country, it is somewhat speculative to isolate any single factor as a primary cause. Nevertheless, the differing intellectual property regimes surely have played an important role in the development of the respective national software industries discussed in this book.[49] I consider the effect, if any, of the national intellectual property regime on three characteristics of the industry in each country: overall size; relative sizes of the custom services and prepackaged software segments; and industry structure—especially average firm size—for both segments. I close this section with some general thoughts about the relationship between intellectual property and the size and shape of each region's software industry.

Japan

As noted above, there is a consensus that the Japanese national strategy for technology development has been characterized by relatively weak protection of intellectual property. How has this affected the development of the Japanese software industry?

One possible effect is the size of the Japanese software industry. Although estimates vary, the Japanese industry is not as big as one might expect, given the strong Japanese presence in markets for roughly complementary goods—for example, semiconductors and some types of computers. A simple "incentive" view of the intellectual property system would explain this as a predictable consequence of a weak protection regime—weak protection of intellectual property lowers the returns to investment, reducing investment and entry into the production of software.

But when one looks into the structure of the Japanese industry, a different story begins to emerge. First, as noted earlier, the custom services segment of the Japanese industry dwarfs the prepackaged software segment; they are 85 percent and 15 percent, respectively, of the industry. Second, average firm size, though hard to measure precisely, seems quite large. To some extent this is a function of the fact that most software companies in Japan are affiliated at least informally with large Japanese companies or groups of companies—the famous *keiretsu* structure (Aoki 1990, 209). Reports in the early 1990s show that in Japan, the majority of software is developed in-house or is commissioned from independent (but affiliated) companies (Cottrell 1994). In fact, the origins of the Japanese software industry can be found in large companies, including not only the large hardware manufacturers (paralleling the U.S. experience), but also large industrial concerns such as steel companies that developed software capabilities as part of advances in process engineering (Cottrell 1994; Baba 1992a). Experts on the industry state that even today, each software firm normally supplies only one company (Baba 1992b). As other authors in this volume make clear, this is in part a reflection of the fragmented standards environment in Japan (see chapters 5 and 6 in this volume).

Once these facts are taken into account, the role of the legal regime looks different. Because many Japanese software firms are closely allied with a particular customer/patron, they do not depend on formal legal rights to protect their software. Protection of intellectual property is handled by the (largely implicit) contract between the firms. Without an arm's-length market transaction, and the attendant risks of misappropriation of intellectual property, there is less need for formal legal rights.

This suggests, of course, that industry structure caused the legal regime in Japan, rather than vice versa. To some extent, this is no doubt true. The dominance of the customized software sector made strong legal protection irrelevant. Moreover, because such protection would have restricted access by Japanese firms to the products of foreign nationals, it would have conflicted with the "technology transfer" policy fostered by the Japanese government. Weak protection allowed Japanese firms to profit from foreign ideas at lower cost. The implicit contractual protection of intellectual property was an effective appropriation mechanism for the Japanese software firm.

As many commentators are now aware, however, the legal regime that served Japan well in the past may have outlived its usefulness. Despite the heroic scale of Japanese "software factories," the inherent limits of custom programming are becoming apparent. Reinventing the wheel, or the program code for each application, is much more costly than selling off-the-shelf software. Thus even in Japan there is evidence that the prepackaged software industry will be growing significantly in the future.

This may *in part* explain the adoption of copyright protection for software in Japan in 1985.[50] Prepackaged software requires that sellers replace individual contractual transactions with market transactions. For the prepackaged segment of the industry to grow, formal legal protection for software must take the place of implicit contracts. In this sense copyright law provides an "off-the-rack" contract between buyers and sellers of intellectual property, taking the place of individually negotiated contracts. It eliminates the need for firms to negotiate directly with each other and allows for the development of a less concentrated structure. It is difficult to say categorically that Japanese policy is based on a link between the features of the property rights regime and industry structure, but it is clear that at least some Japanese policymakers have recommended changes in property rights to spur the development of the prepackaged software segment.[51]

Property rights, transaction costs, and industry structure

The Japanese software industry teaches some valuable lessons about the role of property rights in overcoming transaction costs. Without the security of a property right granted by the government, software suppliers in Japan would be loath to leave the protective contractual sphere they shared with their captive customer/patrons. But with such a right, enforceable outside the context of an individual contract (that is, a right that is "good against the world"), these firms are free to sell to other customers. Thus the establishment of the property right reduces the transaction costs of dealing with a group of widely dispersed buyers, making such transactions feasible.

This shows a transaction-based rationale for intellectual property that is related to, but in some ways distinct from, the straightforward "incentive theory." Although legal rights enhance software firms' incentive to produce more (and better) programs, they do more. Even if the same degree of appropriability can be achieved contractually, property rights permit a more flexible industry structure to emerge. They reduce transaction costs; or, more accurately, they make certain transactions feasible that otherwise would not be.[52]

This view of intellectual property rights, which might be termed the "off-the-rack-contract" view, is especially important for prepackaged software. Product attributes in this segment are general rather than specific to a particular end user. Similarly, intellectual property rights can be viewed as statutory terms of exchange that provide general transaction attributes. The nature of the rights, in other words, mirrors the nature of the market: generalized, arm's length, and standard—in a word, prepackaged.

These rights matter less in the custom software segment, where both product and transactional attributes are customized to meet the needs of the individual end user. The legal framework that governs exchanges in this market segment, primarily contract law and its closely related cousin, trade secrets, reflects this fact. Individually negotiated contracts are both much more flexible and much more expensive.

Implications of a different industry structure

Whether or not it reflects greater specification of intellectual property rules, more small software firms, many offering prepackaged software, were founded in Japan in the 1980s and early 1990s. If this trend continues, how will it affect the industry?

The experience of the software industry, and others as well, suggests that an industry that includes at least a fair number of smaller firms is more innovative than one with only a few large ones. Change in the structure of Japan's software industry thus may prefigure the development of a more competitive industry. On the other hand, if each small firm is quasi-integrated into a single large firm, becoming a "captive" supplier of software, some of the benefits of small firm size may be lost. Although suppliers of many products in Japan are not uniformly "captive"—they supply several major companies on a nonexclusive basis (Aoki 1990, 214)—this is unusual in the history of the software industry. Thus the question remains whether the innovative qualities associated with small prepackaged software firms will take root in Japan.

Europe

The European story is similar in many respects to that of Japan, with one important difference. Semi-integrated corporate groups are less common in Europe than in Japan. Thus, although custom software is the dominant sector in Europe, as in Japan, custom service and software firms are not typically associated with a single corporate group. There is a more open market for the services of the European firms.

The widespread adoption of a modest degree of copyright protection for software in most European countries early in the history of the industry helps explain the relatively dis-integrated structure of the European services sector.[53] But this modest level of protection poses an interesting problem in light of some of the preceding discussion: why did the prepackaged sector of the industry languish? If the view that "copyright protection drives market transactions" expressed above is correct, why did the prepackaged sector of the European industry grow more slowly than the custom services sector?

If an explanation is to be found, it must lie outside the content of intellectual property protection. The most plausible explanation is Europe's lack of success in the computer hardware industry (Organization for Economic Cooperation and Development 1992, 17). The European computer industry has never been at the leading edge of international competition. The industry splintered early on into a series of "national champions," each protected from competition by a national government on which it depended for an important "captive" revenue stream. This development prevented the emergence of a single standard hardware configuration manufactured by a European firm. European software developers have had to play "catch-up" as each new generation of hardware rolls off the (American) drawing boards. National government support for European hardware companies suppressed diffusion of advanced American hardware. In addition, the remoteness of European software firms from the center of hardware innovation may have hampered the software industry.[54] The slow growth of the European prepackaged software sector may be one side effect of this locational factor. This argument does not apply to Japan, which, despite a lack of hardware standards, has had a healthy hardware industry for a long time. Here the "legal-centric" explanation offered above for the slow growth of prepackaged software seems more accurate.

The United States

The U.S. Justice Department has recently recognized the role of intellectual property rights in determining industry structure. When emerging software giant Borland International sought to acquire Ashton-Tate in 1991, its chief rival in the prepackaged database software market, the Justice Department imposed a novel condition on the merger. The text of the consent decree in this case indicates the competitive importance the department attached to copyrights. The decree, to which Borland and Ashton-Tate stipulated, enjoined Borland from asserting any claim or counterclaim for copyright infringement of "the command names, menu items, menu command hierarchies, command languages, programming languages and file structures used in and recognized by Ashton-Tate's dBase family of products, standing alone and apart from other aspects of those computer programs." At the same time, the final judgment states that it does not preclude Borland from asserting its right to use these items, or "from asserting copyright protection in and copyright infringement of the computer program code (including its structure, sequence and organization) and other aspects of the user interface of Ashton-Tate's dBase family of products" (*Patent, Trademark and Copyright Journal* 1991). The decree prompted Borland to drop a lawsuit brought by Ashton-Tate (which it inherited in the merger) against a smaller database producer, Fox Software. Microsoft—one of the few software companies larger even than Borland—subsequently acquired Fox, and thus immediately entered the market for Ashton-Tate-compatible database software.

Clearly the consent decree reflected the Justice Department's awareness of the impact of intellectual property rights on industry structure, especially entry. The dBase family of software has acquired a huge and loyal following; these investments of time and money mean that users face very significant "switching costs" if they were required to learn a dBase-competitive database program. By injecting the dBase command structure into the public domain, the department sought to lower these switching costs, and thereby make entry into the industry more likely. The desired effect is a reduction in the market power of the Borland/Ashton-Tate combine.

This episode illustrates the importance of intellectual property as a competitive weapon and a determinant of industry structure. The Justice Department recognized that, as we saw earlier in the case of Japan, the availability and extent of intellectual property protection can have an impact on software industry structure. Unlike Japan, however, the problem in the United States was not that rights were too weak to induce the prepackaged segment of the industry to take off, but rather that rights might be too *strong* to permit a healthy, competitive rate of entry. In this industry and others, policymakers are beginning to see that intellectual property influences much more than R&D spending. It is a key asset with very important ramifications for industry strategy and evolution. In terms of the Schumpeterian "perennial gale," intellectual property determines the degree of legal shelter an incumbent can count on. Strong protection, like a brick wall, protects such an incumbent from the winds stirred up by potential entrants, while weak protection is more like a tent—it helps but cannot be relied on when the winds get too strong. The Justice Department in effect made Borland give up its brick structure for a tent, in exchange for more market share. The idea was not so much to encourage entry for its own sake, but to permit the kind of cumulative advance (*across* firms) that can take place only in the presence of competition (Merges and Nelson 1990, 839). In so doing, the U.S. government recognized the emergence of intellectual property in this industry as a key variable, at least as important as productive capacity or labor force advantages in a more traditional industry.[55] Recent Justice Department enforcement activities confirm the trend, especially the numerous Microsoft investigations.

The Justice Department's enforcement activities in the Ashton-Tate merger may presage other developments. Private litigants will no doubt begin to use evidence of market power as the basis for counterclaims when sued by copyright holders. These counterclaims can take two forms: conventional antitrust claims and related claims of "copyright misuse." In both cases the point of the counterclaim is that the copyright holder has market power and is using it for anticompetitive purposes. If courts uphold these counterclaims in one or more software cases, they will enhance the bargaining position of those accused of copyright infringement.[56]

THE FUTURE OF INTELLECTUAL PROPERTY POLICY

These developments will take on added significance if the embryonic trend against stronger software protection in American copyright law continues. Because the prepackaged sector of the software industry is the key source of industry growth in the near future, intellectual property policy will have a real impact. Thus the beginnings of a moderation in intellectual property policy should be of considerable interest. If current trends continue, there would be an across-the-board cutback in the property rights of software creators in the United States, leaving the United States more in line with Europe and Japan. It is of course difficult to identify the effects of such a convergence of policy across countries, but a few possibilities can be sketched out.

Some data show that in some industries weaker appropriability in general—not just weaker legal protection—may lead to *faster* technological development. In studies by Levin and Reiss, and more recently by Nelson and Wolff, econometric evidence shows that although low appropriability diminishes the incentive to engage in R&D, the enhanced spillovers can more than offset the effects of lower R&D investment.[57] In other words, the benefits to an individual firm of ready access to the results of its competitors' R&D can outweigh the effects of any difficulties faced by any individual firm capturing the rents from its own R&D. Such an industry might be characterized as one in which "cooperative piracy" prevails over a strong property rights orientation.

A recent article by a group of software engineers and designers opposed to software patents advocates weaker protection arguing that industrywide innovation will benefit:

> Soon new companies will be barred from the software arena—most major programs will require licenses for dozens of patents, and this will make them infeasible. This problem has only one solution: Software patents must be eliminated. . . . A programmer reading a patent may not believe that his program violates the patent, but a federal court may rule otherwise. It is thus now necessary to involve patent attorneys at every phase of program development. . . . However, for the inexpensive programming project, the same extra cost for dealing with the patent system is prohibitive. Individuals and small companies especially cannot afford these costs. Software patents will put an end to software entrepreneurs. . . . For example, the implementors of the widely used public domain data compression program *Compress* followed an algorithm obtained from *IEEE Computer Magazine*. They and the user community were surprised to learn later that U.S. Patent #4,558,302 had been issued to one of the authors of the article. Now [the] Unisys [co.] is demanding royalties for using this algorithm. [U]sing [this program] means risking a law suit. Most large software companies are trying to solve the problem of patents by getting patents of their own. Then they hope to cross-license with the other large companies that own most of the patents, so they will be free to go on as before. While this approach will allow companies such as Microsoft, Apple, and IBM to continue in business, it will shut new companies out of the field. A future start-up, with no patents of its own, will be forced to pay whatever price the giants choose to impose. That price might be high: Established companies have an interest in excluding future competitors. There will be little benefit to society from software patents because invention in software was already flourishing before software patents, and inventions were normally published in journals for everyone to use. (League for Programming Freedom 1990, 56)

In contrast to the arguments of those favoring stronger intellectual property protection, this view clearly links weaker protection to the historical facts of this industry's development and future innovative performance. Advocates of stronger rights carry the burden of proof on this issue, because the early system of relatively weak rights coincided with the emergence of a vital industry. It is interesting to note, however, that the current discussion of intellectual property policy focuses on the effects of policy on industry structure. The next section addresses this issue explicitly, keeping in mind the difficulty of tracing direct causal links among intellectual property regimes, industry structure, and overall industry progress.

LOWER LEGAL PROTECTION AND OPTIMAL INDUSTRY STRUCTURE

The econometric work of Levin and Reiss, Nelson and Wolff, and others shares a basic premise with the article on software patents excerpted above: changing appropriability conditions in an industry can affect industry structure and thus indirectly affect the rate of overall industry progress. Given these relationships, what is the optimal industry structure for the software industry, and what intellectual property policy will bring it about?

On the first question, the software engineers quoted above believe that having more, smaller firms is better than fewer, larger firms; they are "anti-Schumpeterians." In antitrust, this view is often associated with the great jurist Louis Brandeis; we might therefore deem these programmers "Brandeisians." On the other hand, merely because they are on the other side of this issue, the large American firms that advocate the adoption of patent protection for software (such as IBM and DEC) are not necessarily Schumpeterians. Spokespersons for these companies profess belief in a simple model whereby stronger incentives lead to more innovative software and do not tie this view to a preference for fewer, larger software firms (Clapes 1989). Of course, they wish to see their own (large) companies prosper in the growing software market. But they do not make perpetuation of firms with their companies' characteristics an explicit goal of their policy.

Will a more concentrated industry structure result from a policy of strong protection? There is some support for this in the history of other industries.[58] On the other hand, there is a logical and oft-repeated argument to the contrary. Small firms may benefit most from strong rights, because without them large incumbents would use market power to crush small entrants. This argument asserts that strong rights encourages small-firm entry. Although in general stronger intellectual property rights can be expected to encourage more inventive effort (up to a point), if those rights extend to technologies that have become standards, they will deter entry by those trying to use the standard to create compatible products that compete with those who own rights in the standard. Nevertheless, strong intellectual property rights attract investment capital to small firms, thus encouraging entry. The debate boils down to whether strong protection will deter entry more than it encourages it, perhaps only in the submarket of standard-compatible products. (One might argue that strong rights lead to *more* significant inventive activity because entrants are encouraged to explore radically new areas to escape the scope of the rights.)

It is very difficult to evaluate an argument of this sort, but empirical information (some of the armchair variety) is available. The concentration of the database software industry in the hands of a few companies, which has been duplicated in the spreadsheet market, suggests that at least at some stage of this industry's development, switching costs become so high that nonproprietary (or at least widely licensed) standards are necessary to encourage entry. Although the rents from network externalities are high, a concentrated industry with exclusive rights to sell access to the network need not fear entry. This is because the entrant's software must not only exceed the value of the incumbent's software, it must exceed it by so much as to outweigh the extra advantages of joining the incumbent's network.

Stronger protection can be expected to make entry more difficult, and in some cases it already has. This view assigns greater importance to incentives for entry than to incentives for improvement of existing products. So far, however, entry, rather than improvements by entrenched firms, has created most of the innovative products in the software industry.[59] The debate between weak and strong protectionists thus may turn on the relative merits of two competing industry structures: one in which entry is easy and more small firms can be expected, and another in which there are barriers to entry and large firms predominate. Which type of industry would we expect to innovate faster and more often?

The literature on industry structure and innovation suggests that the answer—perhaps surprisingly—is neither. Studies on this topic typically find that to achieve rapid innovation the industry should be characterized by ease of entry and the pursuit of numerous technological alternatives. To the extent that this is correlated with some average firm size, a mildly concentrated industry may be best (Kamien and Schwartz 1982, chap. 3, pp. 49–104).[60] To be sure, some related studies have found that small firms have distinct advantages over large ones: they contribute a disproportionate share of major innovations, for instance (Jewkes et al. 1958), and they perform more efficient R&D, as measured by number of patents per dollar of R&D spent.[61] Moreover, a recent book by Acs and Audretsch concludes that a *combination* of concentrated incumbents and easy small-firm entry is optimal for industrywide innovation.[62] Still, it is not at all clear—at least in the average industry—that a large number of small firms guarantees rapid innovation. But ease of entry and its corollary, pursuit of numerous technological paths, are widely recognized conditions for rapid innovation.

These findings are general ones, and often are the product of highly aggregated data. Do the software industry's unique features make these general findings irrelevant? Is the software industry one where the presence of small firms—and not just ease of entry per se—is highly correlated with industry progress?

Some observers clearly think so. Consider the following summary of comments from software pioneer Dan Bricklin, cocreator of the original VisiCalc spreadsheet program:

> Bricklin characterized the software industry as inherently cottage-based. He explained how most of the major advances in the PC industry seem to come out of small shops or out of small development teams. Some examples include WordPerfect Corp., Lotus Corp., and Software Arts. Bricklin noted that with even better tools today one programmer can do even more than he accomplished in the past. He believes that some products should be written by individuals or small groups to achieve better cohesiveness while there is still demand for large companies to handle the larger scale projects. In some cases, Bricklin notes that it is cheaper for a company to go outside and buy a software product rather than develop themselves. He believes that if the industry had the copyright protection just on the source code, it would be cheaper to buy than to make. (Bricklin 1989, 15–16)

Large software firms argue in rebuttal that because software is becoming ever more sophisticated, the costs of producing it are increasing rapidly. This higher R&D cost in turn justifies stronger intellectual property protection.[63] Some data roughly support this view; R&D as a percentage of sales appears to be increasing in the software industry.[64] Nevertheless, firms might be developing more new products, rather than the same number at higher cost. And even if the cost of each project is going up, the overall appropriability situation must be assessed before one can say that enhanced legal protection is necessary.[65] The rash of mergers that has swept the industry in recent years may also support this view.[66] If an increase in the minimum efficient scale of the U.S. software firm is afoot, it could be argued that one cause is the need for larger, more integrated research teams to tackle the problems posed by this increasingly complex technology.

This account would square well with Abernathy and Utterback's general theory of industry evolution. According to this theory, industries routinely go through an "easy entry" stage, followed by consolidation. The consolidation into a mature industry occurs after the emergence of a "dominant design" in the industry's technology (Abernathy and Utterback 1978, 1979; Utterback and Suarez 1991, 2, 6). The IBM PC and Apple Macintosh hardware, with their microprocessor and operating system "standards," could be described as the dominant designs in the industry.[67] The mergers and other indications of a shakeout in these market segments then make sense. Note that under this view, industry consolidation leads to a slowdown in the rate of technological progress, with disappointing implications for operating systems technology.

Nevertheless, the Abernathy and Utterback model may not apply to the entire software industry, or at least the industry may not have entered the consolidation phase associated with a dominant design. Small firms continue to be at the forefront of the developments in the market for *applications* programs. As one industry analyst put it, "People who say the computer industry has matured are talking about hardware. The software industry is a wide-open field, where anyone with a good idea, technical skills, and access to a computer can still strike it rich" (Sivula 1990). Others concur.[68] Computer magazines are full of product reviews for new applications programs from tiny companies. In segments of the industry other than operating systems, either the logic of the Abernathy-Utterback hypothesis does not apply, or the necessary conditions for it to apply have not yet emerged.

Even if the entire software industry follows the "dominant designs" model, this need not imply the desirability of especially strong intellectual property rights. The literature on industrywide standards, for example, does not provide clear direction for detailed policy. Some argue that operating system software produces significant "network externalities" and hence should be given weaker legal protection than that given to software in general.[69] Competitors of the firms who initiate a standard would thus be encouraged to spread the standard, permitting more end users to adopt the standard and thereby enhancing the position of all users.

Creators of standards, however, take a different view. They argue that their initial investment produced a technology so successful it has become a standard. Weakening their legal protection punishes them for their success. This argument is implicit in the stance of firms such as Lotus, which in the past argued successfully that its command structure (for example, all commands invoked with a "/" and the first letter of the command, such as "/F" for File) should be protected even though other firms wanted to adopt it as a standard.[70] The Lotus command structure has since been placed outside the domain of copyright protection, however; so others who would extend copyright to cover standard interfaces may find the law unavailing in the future.

The critical point, however, is that these standards were created when intellectual property rights were weaker. The argument that only strong rights would have created them conflicts with historical fact. In light of this, and in light of the uncertainties in the relationship among stronger intellectual property rights, industry structure, and innovation, there are grounds to reject the view that stronger rights will inevitably lead to a more innovative and prosperous industry. At the very least, we must look at the costs of those rights—especially in terms of their impact on industry structure—before concluding that they are worthwhile.

This last point holds the real key to the debate. To some extent, the "big firm vs. small firm" controversy is irrelevant. It cannot be resolved on the basis of current knowledge; and it directs attention away from the variables that correlate with innovative industries: ease of entry and multiple, rivalrous technologies. Because stronger intellectual property rights can threaten these latter conditions, this is arguably all we need to know. We need not decide which types of firms should enter and innovate—large or small—in order to know the correct course with respect to intellectual property.

CONCLUSION

In the software industries of the United States, Europe, and Japan, the software protection regime has evolved with the industry in all three regions, and to some extent the legal environment may have shaped or reinforced industry characteristics. For example, there appears to be a connection between weak copyright protection in Japan and the delayed emergence of the prepackaged segment of the Japanese software industry. Similar effects on industry structure may yet be observed in the United States, where the emergence of patent and "strong" copyright protection in recent years could reduce the rate of entry. Finally, a review of the European Software Directive, an attempt to carefully craft software protection law, illustrates the importance of reverse engineering to the competitive balance of the software industry.

Much of the analysis here, though based on empirical data, is necessarily open-ended. This stems from the difficulty of isolating one variable, such as the strength and scope of legal protection, within the rich soup of factors that determine industry structure and the rate of innovation. Nevertheless, as long as intellectual property rights exist and their policy justification is based on their stimulation of R&D investment, we must take seriously the indirect impact of this investment on related variables such as industry structure. The rate of innovation is a product of many factors besides intellectual property. If intellectual property policy affects these other factors, we may find that our policy does not work or is interacting with other industry features to cause serious unintended problems. An effective policy may have to take into account a more complex set of factors than would a policy based on a simplistic investment-stimulation model.

Intellectual property policy must take account of its effects on secondary variables such as industry structure. Indeed, policy may have to be shaped, to a limited extent at least, by the vagaries of individual industries. Software provides a test case of this dynamic, one that requires careful monitoring of the effects of any transition from weak protection to strong. At the very least, sensitivity to industry particularities—such as those detailed throughout this volume—will make for a much more realistic and responsive intellectual property policy.

NOTES

1. As is made clear below, this includes trade secret protection, especially the aspect of trade secrecy that allows parties to specify contractually what is proprietary about the goods and services they exchange. I refer to this as "establishing property by contract."

2. According to Microsoft Corp., foreign software sales by U.S. firms reached $12 billion in 1989, while losses from theft totaled an estimated $7.6 billion to $9.6 billion abroad, and $2.4 billion in the United States (see Anthes 1991b, 74).

3. See Wood 1991 (1988 figure), quoting the estimate of Input, a market consulting firm; *Economist* 1992 (1991 figure). Cf. U.S. Department of Commerce 1991, 4–74, Table 15) (survey responses show total industry revenues of respondents to be $19.7 billion). *Pacific Northwest Executive* 1990 states that industry had "anticipated" profits nationwide of $42 billion in 1989; in 1985 the western European software market was valued at $9.5 billion, 54 percent of which was derived from sales of packaged software; Green Paper 1988, 171–72, estimated that commercial software sales worldwide ranged between $30 billion and $39 billion in 1985.

4. See Wood 1991. Cf. Anthes 1991a, 4: "The global market [for prepackaged software] will reach $50 billion in 1991 and should break $100 billion by 1995, according to the Commerce Department."

5. This estimate is given directly in *Pacific Northwest Executive* 1990. Other sources concur. See Massachusetts Computer Software Council 1991, Question 55: The breakdown of revenue-generating activities is roughly as follows—"sales of proprietary software," 52 percent of all revenue for all respondents, while sales of "custom/contract software" plus "consulting/ professional services," 16 percent; which makes the latter roughly 30 percent of the total of both revenue categories); U.S. Congress, Office of Technology Assessment (1987, 162) said that contract programming comprised 20 percent of industry and was expected to shrink to 12 percent in 1990. But cf. U.S. Department of Commerce (1991, 4–74), in which a respondent survey showed opposite ratio—that is, prepackaged software constituted 30 percent of total $19.6 billion industry revenues). Note the difference between these widely quoted figures and the estimates by Edward Steinmueller elsewhere in this volume. The differences in estimates may be due in part to the effects of international trade.

6. I say "rough" because response bias is a real possibility in this survey; it was impossible to determine whether the results were accurate, given the fact that there are no other surveys to check the responses against.

7. See, for example, Haug 1991, 873 (findings from a survey of 152 software firms in Washington State): "As in U.S. industry data, the majority of these software companies are relatively small"; "average firm size . . . was approximately 28 workers."

8. Of all companies with horizontal products under development, an average of 35 percent had 15 or fewer employees, and an average of 50 percent had 30 or fewer. For vertical products, an average of 32 percent had 15 or fewer, and an average of 45 percent had 30 or fewer. Put another way, 55 percnet of companies developing vertical products had more than 30 employees, while 50 percent developing horizontal products had this many. This conclusion is corroborated by the findings of Haug (1991, 873): In Washington State, among 152 survey respondents, "average firm size was approximately 28 workers, though service companies exceeded, on average, 40 employees."

9. For each firm, the average of its high and low P/E's for 1990 was used. Then averages were obtained for each of the two industry segments. This is obviously a rough figure.

10. The most recent figures for Japan show a slight change: custom software is now thought to be 85 percent of the total industry. See Japan Information Service Industry Association 1994, 40.

11. See also Bozman 1991, 87: "Driving this U.S. move into the Japanese market is the

promise of a foothold in a packaged software market that was barely $1 billion in 1987 but could reach several times that by 1993, according to market analysts. . . . 'In Japan, they've been using [proprietary] software for so long that they've painted themselves into a corner,' said John Korondy, manager of worldwide strategic applications at Palo Alto, Calif.-based [Hewlett-Packard]. 'They've put themselves at a relative disadvantage by not being able to use off-the-shelf software.'

This may be changing: "However, the widespread acceptance of packaged applications for MS-DOS personal computers used in Japanese offices is easing the Japanese transition to packaged Unix software, U.S. software executives said" (ibid.)

See also *InformationWeek* (1991) interview with Bill Totten, founder of Asisuto, a Japanese software distribution firm:

> [Totten:] When I went [to Japan], I was the first one that ever tried to sell software packages there. Other vendors were slow getting into packages because they were so busy doing custom work.
>
> The Japanese companies that would normally build software packages or would normally distribute American software packages had so much custom business that they didn't bother building or distributing packages. That generated an even bigger demand for custom work. It's cyclical: They didn't go into packages because there were no packages.
>
> What brought about the changes?
>
> Totten: The impetus has come from people like us: the very few of us out there selling against the grain—when it was like using other people's underwear. And it was a very hard sale.
>
> It took a long time, but we've gradually built up so many good cases where people have done so much better with packages than with custom-made software that finally it's gained a reputation.

12. See the *Economist* (1992) story on acquisitions by CAP Gemini, the huge French software services firm and its head-to-head competition with American rival Electronic Data Systems.

13. See Cusumano 1991. See also Anthes 1991b, 74, reporting on Senate hearings at which Cusumano testified about production of high-quality code in Japanese software "factories."

14. Law No. 62 of 1985. See Nakajima 1988.

15. Cf. *System Science K.K. v. Toyo Sokuki K.K.* 1989: "The 'flow of processing' itself in a program is an algorithm, or in other words, a solution as provided for in Article 10 (3) (iii) of the Copyright Law, and is a portion which does *not* receive protection as a copyrightable work, it has no relevance to the creativity of the program." (emphasis added)). But see Hirakawa and Nakano 1990: "We argue that . . . most 'interface' characteristics of computer software are protected today . . . under long-accepted principles of Japanese copyright law as reflected in court cases in Japan."

16. "Japan's Barriers to Foreign IP Rights" 1993, 1847:

> [Patent Commissioner Bruce] Lehman, speaking at a seminar on "patent politics" between the United States and Japan, . . . focused on protection for computer software, and observed that more than half the software used in Japan is of foreign origin. The Japanese recognize that the competitiveness of their domestic software industry suffers because much of its product is relatively expensive and custom-designed, Lehman said. However, Japan's lack of effective intellectual property protection for foreign concerns has prevented this domestic "software crisis" from creating a large market for foreign software, he charged.

In the copyright area, Lehman continued, the greatest concern is the creation of a committee in the Cultural Affairs Agency which is considering legislation to permit both private copying of software for individual home use and reverse engineering for data exchange and interconnection between different hardware and software. Although the legislation under consideration would also prohibit tampering with copy-protected disks, the first two measures could be "bad news" for foreign software developers, Lehman said.

17. See, for example, "Japan IP Update" 1993:

The U.S. General Accounting Office (GAO) issued a report on July 13, 1993, revealing the results of a survey of over 300 U.S. companies that have filed for patents in Japan. The study showed that 39 percent of the respondents were dissatisfied with the Japanese patent system, while only 3 percent were dissatisfied with the European system. U.S companies appeared to be most dissatisfied with the length of the Japanese patent process. Typically, it takes about 6 to 7 years to obtain a Japanese patent, compared with the 19 month average in the United States. Forty-four of the survey respondents indi cated that it was more difficult to obtain a Japanese patent for "pioneering inventions," especially in light of the pre-grant opposition process, which exists for all Japanese patent filings. Twenty-one percent of the respondents also believe that the Japanese Patent Office is biased in favor of Japanese applicants. Only 6 percent, however, believed that the Japanese patent system greatly affected their business performance.

18. See Takaishi 1986, 187, which analyzes legal protection of computer software under old and recently amended Japanese Copyright Law, and Brown 1987, 170: "The trend toward greater availability of patent protection for computer programs in the United States . . . and in Europe (as represented in the new European Patent Office Guidelines) is similar to that of Japan, as evidenced by the Japanese Patent Office Guidelines issued in 1976." See also Yamamoto and Conlin 1979, 195–97, on examples from the Japanese Patent Office guidelines computerized process controls as patentable inventions.

19. Indeed, such proposed changes were discussed in the early 1990s. See *Nikkei Weekly* 1991, 3:

The Patent Agency will set new rules for establishing patents in the fields of biotechnology and computer software by April 1992, agency officials said. The new rules will give guidance to applicants filing applications for such patents, and are also aimed at increasing the protection such patents extend to inventions.

The rules will also expand the number of items which can be included in a single application, in response to foreign criticism of customary Japanese procedures of submitting piecemeal patent applications. The agency also plans to review the current 64 industrial categories of patents in the future, because these classifications are regarded as outdated. The planned changes represent the most comprehensive revision Japan has undertaken of its patent rules, and reflect the agency's desire to bring Japanese regulations in step with international patent rules.

20. See, for example, Kyodo News International 1993:

International Business Machines Corp. took legal action Monday against Kyocera Corp., demanding that the Japanese electronics concern pay some 18.7 billion yen for its patent on computer software.

In a suit filed with the Tokyo District Court, IBM claims that Kyocera is infringing on its patent on personal computer software called basic input/output system (BIOS) by using the technology in its products shipped abroad.

It is the first time IBM has filed a patent suit against a Japanese company. Kyocera denied IBM's allegation. It said it developed the software itself.

21. Council Directive 91/250. See Lucas 1991.

22. See generally "Let the Hackers Hack" 1992.

23. To decompile is to take the ready-to-run or executable form of a program and glean from it the full text of the program in its original instruction-by-instruction form. Since the original form of the program is "compiled" into the ready-to-run form, going in the opposite direction is described as "decompiling."

24. The European Committee for Interoperable Systems (ECIS) was composed of fifty software and hardware manufacturers, such as Fujitsu, Groupe Bull, Olivetti, and Amdahl. It sought to exclude interfaces from copyright protection and to allow reverse engineering of software, so that developers could develop compatible software. See Palmer and Vinje 1992; Styrcula 1991, 343. The Software Action Group for Europe (SAGE), a group vigorously opposed to allowing any form of reverse engineering, was composed of manufacturers such as IBM, Digital, Microsoft, Apple, and Lotus. Some U.S. firms were members of ECIS, however; they have now joined together to form an American counterpart called the American Committee on Interoperable Systems (ACIS). See id.

25. The benchmark for European software-related patents is that the claimed invention produce a "direct technical result"—that is, a result recognized in the traditional engineering arts (see Payraudeau 1989). Meijboom (1990, 409–20) skillfully summarizes the law of the European Patent Convention's European Patent Office, as well as national courts, in the area of computer software-related inventions. But compare IBM/Data Processor Network 1990, which said that a software control function that does not cause a change in configuration of hardware elements is nonetheless patentable.

26. The first case is Document Abstracting and Retrieving/IBM 1988, described in Betten 1989. The second case is IBM/Computer-Related Invention 1990.

27. But see IBM/Data Processor Network 1990.

28. Vicom 1987. The Technical Board of Appeal of the EPO in that case held that a "technical process" was not barred from patentability merely because a computer is used to carry it out.

29. Koch and Sterzel/Computer Program 1987.

30. IBM/Data Processor Network 1990.

31. See *Whelan Associates, Inc. v. Jaslow Dental Laboratory, Inc.*, 797 F. 2d 1222 (3d Cir. 1986), cert. denied, 479 U.S. 1031 (1987): "The copyrights of computer programs can be infringed even absent copying of the literal elements of the program." The key holding of *Whelan* is its broad reading of the difference between what is protectable and what is the unprotectable "idea" of the program:

> The line between idea and expression may be drawn with reference to the end sought to be achieved by the work in question. In other words, the purpose or function of a utilitarian work would be the work's idea, and everything that is not necessary to that purpose or function would be part of the expression of the idea. . . . Where there are various means of achieving the desired purpose, then the particular means chosen is not necessary to the purpose; hence, there is expression, not idea. (Whelan, 1236)

By defining the "idea" of a program so broadly—that is, as the program's overall purpose— the *Whelan* court directed that much of what is contained in a program is "expression" and hence protectable. For example, if the "idea" of a program is an electronic spreadsheet, then many of the general features of the spreadsheet, such as its rows-and-columns layout, its commands invocable with a single keystroke, and the like, are expression and hence will be infringed by other spreadsheets with similar features. A very abstract or high-level "idea," in other words, leads to stronger copyright protection. See, for example, *Lotus Development Corp. v. Borland Int'l, Inc.*, 788 F. Supp. 78 (D. Mass. 1992) (upholding copyrightability of just these elements; finding defendant Borland's Quattro spreadsheet an infringement of Lotus 1–2–3); *Lotus Development Corp. v. Paperback Software Int'l*, 740 F. Supp. 37 (D. Mass. 1990) (same as to defendant's competitive spreadsheet). These decisions were later reversed; see note 36, below, and the accompanying text.

32. *Computer Associates International Inc. v. Altai Inc.*, 23 U.S.P.Q. 2d 1241, 61 U.S.L.W. 2003 (2d Cir. 1992).

33. "A computer program's ultimate function or purpose is the composite result of interacting subroutines. Since each subroutine is itself a program, and thus, may be said to have its own 'idea,' *Whelan's* general formulation that a program's overall purpose equates with the program's idea is descriptively inadequate." (Ibid.)

34. See, for example, *Lotus Development Corp. v. Borland Int'l, Inc.*, 788 F. Supp. 78 (D. Mass. 1992) (refusing to concede that *Computer Assoc.'s* approach implied unprotectability of spreadsheet menus and commands).

35. Attempts at a middle ground approach have been floated, but they seem too unworkable to resolve the basic impasse. See *Gates Rubber Co. v. Bando American Inc.*, 798 F. Supp. 1499 (D. Colo. 1992): "The *Altai* test thus rejects any consideration of the *Whelan* factors, proposing not only different component elements to be examined (text and behavior) but also a different analysis of those elements (the abstractions test). However, this rather extreme alternative may be rendered unimportant if the abstractions test [that forms an integral part of the *Altai* approach] is used as a prelude to, instead of as a substitution [sic] for, the substantial similarity test identified with Whelan. It would also seem that, in light of these criticisms, the Whelan test could be reformed so as to not encompass such an inclusive definition of what is an idea."

36. 34 U.S.P.Q. 2d 1014, 1022 (1st Cir. 1995).

37. *Atari Games Corp. v. Nintendo of America Inc.*, 975 F. 2d 832, 24 U.S.P.Q. 2d 1015 (Fed. Cir. 1992).

38. Id. at 843–44.

39. *Sega Ent., Ltd. v. Accolade, Inc.*, 61 U.S.L.W. 2254 (9th Cir. 1992) (citations omitted):

> If disassembly of copyrighted object code is per se an unfair use, the owner of the copyright gains a de facto monopoly over the functional aspects of his work—aspects that were expressly denied copyright protection by Congress. In order to enjoy a lawful monopoly over the idea or functional principle underlying a work, the creator of the work must satisfy the more stringent standards imposed by the patent laws. Sega does not hold a patent on the Genesis console. Because Sega's video game programs contain unprotected aspects that cannot be examined without copying, we afford them a lower degree of protection than more traditional literary works. . . .
>
> We conclude that where disassembly is the only way to gain access to the ideas and functional elements embodied in a copyrighted computer program and where there is a legitimate reason for seeking such access, disassembly is a fair use of the copyrighted work, as a matter of law.

See generally "Let the Hackers Hack" 1992.

40. See *Lotus Development Corp. v. Borland Int'l, Inc.*, 788 F. Supp. 78 (D. Mass. 1992) (upholding copyrightability of broad features of Lotus 1-2-3 spreadsheet), *rev'd* 34 U.S.P.Q. 2d 1014 (1st Cir. 1995).

41. See Burgess 1994 (jury verdict in favor of Stac Electronics, Inc. for infringement of its data compression software patents); Fisher 1994b (same).

42. See generally Merges 1992, Chap. 2. To be sure, some think the United States has

not gone far enough in this respect. Gresser (1984, 59) criticizes American patent policy regarding software as example of a larger problem: "A central part of the problem is that US policymakers are not accustomed to thinking about new technologies as economically strategic, at least in terms of the patent law. There are no special rules under the patent system to reward inventors who develop technologies that have dramatic effects on industrial growth, particularly where the leap may be marginal, incremental, and ostensibly unexceptional. Computer and other programs are only one of many examples. . . . [M]any such modest improvements can have profound impacts on economic growth. The patent system seems out of touch with the needs of these entrepreneurs."

43. See *Patent, Trademark and Copyright Journal* 1992 (reporting proceedings of American Bar Association Annual Meeting): "Stallman . . . asserted that computer interface copyrights are 'bad for progress and for users.' Court decisions like the recent ruling in *Lotus v. Borland* that the Lotus 1-2-3 spreadsheet program is copyrightable and infringed by Borland's Quattro spreadsheet program will drive small software firms out of business, Stallman warned."

44. Although two software patents were asserted, the jury failed to specify whether one or both of the patents had been infringed.

45. See Burgess 1994; Fisher 1994b; Whit 1994. The jury also ruled that Stac had misappropriated Microsoft trade secrets and awarded Microsoft $13.6 million in damages.

46. For an excellent history of the progress and development of patent law relating to software, see Samuelson 1990.

47. 888 F. 2d 1370, 12 U.S.P.Q. 2d 1908 (Fed. Cir. 1989).

48. See In re Alappat, 33 F. 2d 1526 (Fed. Cir. 1994).

49. Others have ventured along this path before me. See Rushing and Brown 1990: "In contrast to these areas [where India gives does not give intellectual property protection], software is protected in India by copyright provisions. While one cannot prove a causal link, the general conclusion is that protection of software played a key role in the accomplishment by India of international partnerships in software development."

50. See, for example, Takaishi 1986, analyzing legal protection of computer software under pre-and post-1985 Japanese Copyright Law; Chyosakukenh (1978, 2(1) (x) (ii) (as amended)), adding "program works" to the statutory list of examples of protected works and defining "programs" as "an expression of combined instructions given to a computer so as to make it function and obtain a certain result."

51. See "Japanese Panel to Draft Guidelines" 1993, 31 (emphasis added):

> [A] subcommittee of the Industrial Structure Council, advisory panel to the Minister of International Trade and Industry, determined to draft guidelines to urge changes to the practices of software businesses *in an effort to better protect software copyrights and to encourage new domestic software development.* . . . Under prevailing Japanese practices, software is often treated as a service accompanying computer hardware and there is considerable concern that if software is continued to be treated lightly, the software industry will not become viable as an industry independent from the hardware industry.

52. Cf. Mowery 1983, 352: "In understanding the organization and evolution of industrial research, the requirements for knowledge transmission and utilization, as well as the difficulties encountered in the negotiation and enforcement of contracts, acquire an importance equal to or greater than that of the appropriability of the returns from research."

53. See Hidalgo 1993. Most important European countries had adopted copyright for software by the 1980s. Note, however, that standards for software protection differ from country to country in Europe; as Hidalgo notes, for example, "The Federal Supreme Court of Germany has imposed a high standard of originality for assessing whether a computer program

is a personal intellectual creation, to be determined on a case-by-case basis" (113). This is not true of all European countries.

54. There is now a small but persuasive literature describing a "locational" aspect to certain industries, many "high-technology" in orientation. Software is among them. See, for example, Haug 1991, 873; Rosegrant and Lampe 1992; Saxenian 1992.

55. Small firms generally fear patents as a barrier to entry because of the cost involved. This includes filing for patents, maintaining them, and litigating them. There is some evidence that these concerns are legitimate, given the experience of other industries. Vandenberg (1991) says the cost of patent litigation ranges from $100,000 to $1 million, with an average of $350,000). Cf. Mueller and Tilton (1969, 579): "The second major factor contributing to barriers is the accumulation of patents and know-how on the part of incumbent firms. Even if there were no economies of scale in R&D, a late entrant would have to undertake more R&D than an average firm of its size in order to acquire information about the technology and to invent around existing patents."

56. Several circuit courts have entertained defenses of copyright misuse. *Lasercomb Am. v. Reynolds,* 911 F. 2d 970 (4th Cir. 1990); *United Tel. Co. v. Johnson Publishing Co.,* 855 F. 2d 604, 610–12 (8th Cir. 1988); *Supermarket of Homes v. San Fernando Valley Bd. of Realtors,* 786 F. 2d 1400, 1408 (9th Cir. 1986); *F.E.L. Publications v. Catholic Bishop,* 214 U.S.P.Q. 409, 413 (7th Cir.), cert. denied, 459 U.S. 859, 103 S.Ct. 131, 74 L. Ed. 2d 113 (1982); *Edward B. Marks Music v. Colorado Magnetics,* 497 F.2d 285, 290 (10th Cir. 1974), cert. denied, 419 U.S. 1120, 95 S. Ct. 801, 42 L. Ed. 2d 819 (1975); *Broadcast Music v. Moor-Law,* 527 F. Supp. 758, 772 (D. Del. 1981), aff'd without opinion, 691 F. 2d 490 (3rd Cir. 1982); *Mitchell Bros. Film Group v. Cinema Adult Theater,* 604 F. 2d 852, 865 (5th Cir. 1979), cert. denied, 445 U.S. 917, 100 S. Ct. 1277, 63 L. Ed. 2d 601 (1980). Only one circuit has sustained the defense. *Lasercomb,* 911 F. 2d at 970. Although it has yet to apply the copyright misuse defense, the U.S. Supreme Court has given at least tacit approval of the defense. *United States v. Loew's, Inc.,* 371 U.S. 38, 83 S. Ct. 97, 9 L. Ed. 2d 11 (1962). In *Loew's,* the Court applied principles of patent misuse to a patentee's unlawful tying arrangements and held that recovery for infringement should be denied. The Court then went on to apply, with reference to the copyrights, the same antitrust restrictions on tie-in of sales. Numerous cases suggest that the purpose and policy of patent misuse apply as well to copyright. See, for example, *Sony Corp.,* 464 U.S. at 439, 104 S. Ct. at 787; *Loew's,* 371 U.S. at 44–51, 83 S. Ct. at 101–05; *United States v. Paramount Pictures,* 334 U.S. 131, 157–59, 68 S.Ct. 915, 929–30, 92 L. Ed. 1260 (1948); *Mitchell Bros.,* 604 F. 2d at 865; *Bellsouth,* 933 F. 2d at 960–61.

57. Levin and Reiss 1988, 538; see also Nelson and Wolff 1992; Mowery and Rosenberg 1991, 283–84, 293, which says that the disparate impact of intellectual property on various industries implies that it is not a panacea for competitiveness ills; also, effective diffusion strategy is inconsistent with enhanced intellectual property strategy, so there is a need to balance these concerns. On the use of spillover data to analyze R&D spending, see Levin and Reiss 1984, 175.

58. Lesser and Masson (1986) show the relationship between the establishment of intellectual property rights in seeds and the concentration of the seed industry.

59. Cf. Prusa and Schmitz 1991. The authors interpret their empirical findings as demonstrating that new firms have a comparative advantage in introducing category-opening software products (for example, the first spreadsheet, the first word processing program), while established firms have a comparative advantage in introducing improvements in existing categories. But the data show that new firms not only introduced the vast majority of category-opening products (eighteen out of twenty-one), they also introduced the majority of best-selling improvement products (ten out of seventeen). See Prusa and Schmitz 1991, 341. In addition, the authors define "established firms" as those in existence *for any length of time* before the opening of a category. This of course includes the possibility of some very young "established"

firms—so young, in fact, they may well be characterized as still in the "entry" stage for my purposes.

60. Kamien and Schwartz conclude that the main finding of empiricists testing Schumpeter's central hypothesis (that is, a link between firm size and innovation) is that a high degree of monopoly power is *un*related to disproportionately large research expenditures; in fact, the consistent finding is that an intermediate degree of industry concentration produces the highest volume of research and development spending. Kamien and Schwartz 1982, 104.

61. Markham (1974, 247) summarizes empirical tests of the Schumpeterian hypothesis showing (1) weak support for general form of the hypothesis, but (2) diminishing returns (measured by number of in patents) as the size of the R&D operation grows); Acs and Audretsch 1990 (same).

62. See Acs and Audretsch 1990 for a theoretical model of research and development competition among firms, explaining the seeming paradox from empirical studies that small firms make a disproportionate share of major innovations, while large firms tend to spend more (in absolute terms) on research and development than small firms do; model shows that in equilibrium, a large firm invests more than a smaller firm but, by choosing safer research and development projects, makes fewer major innovations. But cf. Geroski (1991, 212), whose econometric study finds little correlation between innovation and entry of small firms.

63. Lindsey Kiang, from the general counsel's Office at Digital Equipment Corp. (DEC), provided counter arguments at the same forum where Bricklin spoke. An excerpt from the summary of his views:

> Companies like DEC believe that patent protection is necessary to protect their investment in software R&D, especially when they're spending more than $1 billion a year on such work. [Kiang] believes that R&D costs will only rise as software development becomes more advanced and complex to meet the needs of customers. Kiang believes that companies like DEC will continue to feel an obligation to its investors to protect its R&D investment with patents. He believes that patent protection for software will continue to stimulate innovation and creativity. (Kiang 1989)

64. Tito (1991) quotes a research firm as having found that "average R&D spending [at software firms] has moved from 12.5 percent of sales to 14.1 percent, a 12.8 percent increase [from 1989 to 1991]." Davis and Stallman (1988) say the software industry spent a higher percentage of sales on R&D—12.4—than semiconductor and computer hardware companies; this represented a 3 percent jump over the preceding year.

65. Levin et al. (1987, 783) report results of an extensive empirical survey of research and development personnel at U.S. corporations, finding a high rate of variation between industries regarding the mix of appropriability techniques—trade secrets, market lead time, patents, etc.—thought to be important); Teece (1986) describes various means of appropriability.

66. There were 773 mergers in the information technology industry in 1988; down to 717 in 1989 (Wise 1990); see also Schwartz 1992, which describes the Ashton-Tate merger with Borland and Microsoft's acquisition of Fox Software.

67. See, for example, Verity 1992, 90: "Powerful chips and standardized software have already turned PCs into a low-margin commodity, and PCs have become the industry's biggest part."

68. Mouse hardware devices and other changes will make small firms competitive with large ones in the computer software industry (*Economist* 1990); survey results from the Massachusetts Computer Software Council (1991) indicate that at least 75 percent of software firms have fewer than 100 employees, with 49 percent having fewer than 30; 29 percent have revenues of less than $500,000, and 51 percent have revenues of less than $2 million per year. According to Simon (1989, 33): "One reason the industry appears to be thriving is that unlike

the hardware business, the price to start a software business is relatively low. Slightly more than half of the survey respondents said they spent less than $100,000 before making their first sale, and 52 percent shipped product within 12 months of launching a business."

69. This view is developed extensively by Menell (1989, 1099–1100): "[Stylistic] aspects of the interface would be protected by copyright law when the interface is introduced. But as users learn such features, . . . they become functional. . . . [T]he ideal legal regime protects the particular aspects of the interface for long enough to allow the creator to recover his or her development and marketing costs (adjusted for risk) and then to allow others access to the 'standard' so as to foster standardization and realize resulting network externalities."

70. See, for example, *Lotus Development Corp. v. Borland Int'l, Inc.*, 788 F. Supp. 78 (D. Mass. 1992) (upholding copyrightability of just these elements; finding defendant Borland's Quattro spreadsheet an infringement of Lotus 1-2-3), *rev'd* 34 U.S.P.Q. 2d 1014 (1st Cir. 1995); *Lotus Development Corp. v. Paperback Software Int'l,* 740 F. Supp. 37, 47–51 (D. Mass. 1990) (same as to another competitor's spreadsheet).

REFERENCES

Abernathy, W., and Utterback, J. M. 1978. "Patterns of Industrial Innovation." *Technology Review* (June-July).
———. 1979. "Dynamics of Innovation in Industry." In C. T. Hill, J. M. Utterback, and J. H. Holloman, eds., *Technological Innovation for a Dynamic Economy.* New York: Pergamon Press.
Acs, Z. J., and D. B. Audretsch. 1990. *Innovation and Small Firms.* Cambridge, Mass.: MIT Press.
Anthes, G. 1991a. "Feds Say Industry to Fare Well." *Computerworld,* 7 January, 4.
———. 1991b. "U.S. Software Position at Risk: Senate Hears Testimony That Taxes, Export Policies Affect U.S. Market Share." *Computerworld,* 25 November, 74.
Aoki, M. 1990. *Information, Incentives, and Bargaining in the Japanese Economy.* Cambridge, Eng.: Cambridge University Press.
Atari Games Corp. v. Nintendo of America Inc., 975 F. 2d 832, 24 U.S.P.Q. 2d 1015 (Fed. Cir. 1992).
Baba, Y. 1992a. "The Evolution of the Software Industry in Japan: Vertical Integration/Disintegration Model." Paper prepared for a meeting of the International Computer Software Industry Project, Haas School of Business, University of California, Berkeley, 24–25 April.
———. 1992b. Remarks on Behalf of the Japan National institute for Science and Technology Policy at a meeting of the International Computer Software Industry Project, Haas School of Business, University of California, Berkeley, 24–25 April.
Bender, D. 1991. "Software Patents: The View From 1991." In Practicing Law Institute, Patents, Copyrights, Trademarks, and Literary Property Course Handbook Series, *Current Developments in Computer Software Protection* 315: 511.
Betten, J. 1989. "New Decisions of the European Patent Office Concerning Patent Protection for Computer Software." *Software Protection* (September): 7.
BNA International Business Daily. 1991. "Non-patentability of Computer Programs: Gale's Application." 24 June.
Bozman, J. 1991. "Japan's Unix Market Beckons." *Computerworld,* 27 May, 87.
Bricklin, D., President of Software Garden, Inc. 1989. Comments recorded in the seminar notes of an MIT Communications Forum entitled "Software Patents: A Horrible Mistake?" 23 March.

Broadcast Music v. Moor-Law, 527 F. Supp. 758 (D. Del. 1981), aff'd without opinion, 691 F. 2d 490 (3d Cir. 1982).

Brown, J. 1987. "Recent International Trends in the Legal Protection of Computer Software." *Journal of Law and Technology* 2: 167.

Burgess, J. .1994. "Microsoft Found Guilty of Patent Infringement: Software Giant Ordered to Pay $120 Million." *Washington Post,* 24 February, D11.

Chyosakukenh (Copyright law). 1978. Law No. 48 of 1978.

Clapes, A. L. 1989. *Software, Copyright and Competition: The "Look and Feel" of the Law.* New York: Quorum Books.

Common Market Reporter (CCH). 1991. "Computer Software Protection Directive Adopted." 30 May, 1.

Computer Associates International Inc. v. Altai Inc., 23 U.S.P.Q. 2d 1241, 61 U.S.L.W. 2003 (2d Cir. 1992).

———. 1994. "Fragmented Standards and the Development of Japan's Microcomputer Software Industry." *Research Policy* 23, no. 2 (March): 143–74.

Council Directive 91/250 on the Legal Protection of Computer Programs, 1991. O.J. (L 122/43).

Cusumano, M. A. 1991. *Japan's Software Factories: A Challenge to U.S. Management.* New York: Oxford University Press.

Davis, D., and L. Stallman. 1988. "The Top R&D Spenders in the Electronics Industry." *Electronic Business* 14: 62.

Document Abstracting and Retrieving/IBM. 1988. Case No. T22/85, 10/5/88. In J. Betten, "New Decisions of the European Patent Office Concerning Patent Protection for Computer Software." *Software Protection* (September 1989): 7.

Economist. 1990. "Of Mice and Men." 25 November.

———. 1992. "Europe's Software War." 10 October, 81.

Edward B. Marks Music v. Colorado Magnetics, 497 F. 2d 185 (10th Cir. 1974), cert. denied, 419 U.S. 1120, 95 S. Ct. 801, 42 L. Ed. 2d 819 (1975).

Ergas, H. 1987. "Does Technology Matter?" In B. R. Guile and H. Brooks, eds., *Technology and Global Industry: Companies and Nations in the World Economy.* Washington, D.C.: National Academy Press.

Europe 2000—Communications & Information Technology. 1991. "Europe's Computer and IT Industry Faces the Crunch: National Champions: Too Soft for Too Long." June.

F.E.L. Publications v. Catholic Bishop, 214 U.S.P.Q. 409 (7th Cir.), cert. denied, 459 U.S. 859, 103 S. Ct. 131, 74 L. Ed. 2d 113 (1982).

Fisher, L. M. 1994a. "The Executive Computer: Will Users Be the Big Losers in Software Patent Battles?" *New York Times,* 6 May.

———. 1994b. "Microsoft Loses Case on Patent." *New York Times,* 24 February, D1.

Gates Rubber Co. v. Bando American Inc., 798 F. Supp. 1499 (D. Colo. 1992).

Geroski, P. 1991. "Entry and the Rate of Innovation." *Economics of Innovation and New Technology* 1: 203.

Green Paper on Copyright and the Challenge of Technology Copyright Issues Requiring Immediate Action. 1988. COM(88)172 final. Brussels: Commission of the European Communities.

Gresser, J. 1984. *Partners in Prosperity: Strategic Industries in the U.S. and Japan.* New York: McGraw-Hill.

Haug, P. 1991. "Regional Formation of High-Technology Service Industries: The Software Industry in Washington State." *Environment & Planning A* 23: 869.

Hidalgo, P. G. 1993. "Copyright Protection of Computer Software in the European Community: Current Protection and the Effect of the Adopted Directive." *International Law* 27: 113.

Hirakawa, O., and K. Nakano. 1990. "Copyright Protection of Computer Interfaces in Japan." *European Intellectual Property Review* 2: 46.

IBM/Computer-Related Invention. 1990. Case No. T115/85. *European Patent Office Reporter,* 107.

IBM/Data Processor Network. 1990. Case No. T06/83. *European Patent Office Reporter,* 91.

In re Alappat, 33 F. 2d 1526 (Fed. Cir. 1994).

In re Iwahashi, 888 F. 2d 1370, 12 U.S.P.Q. 2d 1908 (Fed. Cir. 1989).

InformationWeek. 1991. "Opening the Gate to Japan—A U.S. Marketer Scores Big with Packaged Software." 4 August, 34.

Japanese Information Service Industry Association. 1994. *Jyoho Sahbisu Sangyo Hakusho* (Information service industry white paper). Tokyo: Ministry of International Trade and Industry.

"Japanese Panel to Draft Guidelines for Software Protection." 1993. *Journal of Proprietary Rights* 5: 44.

"Japan IP Update." 1993. *Journal of Proprietary Rights* 5: 31.

"Japan's Barriers to Foreign IP Rights Are Symptoms of 'Disease,' Lehman." 1993. *International Trade Reporter* 10: 1847.

Jewkes, J., D. Sawers, and R. Stillerman. 1958. *The Sources of Invention.* London: Macmillan.

Kamien, M. I., and N. L. Schwartz. 1982. *Market Structure and Innovation.* Cambridge, Eng.: Cambridge University Press.

Kiang, L., General Counsel's Office at Digital Equipment Corp. (DEC). 1989. Comments recorded in the seminar notes of an MIT Communications Forum entitled "Software Patents: A Horrible Mistake?" 23 March.

Koch and Sterzel/Computer Program. 1987. Case No. T26/86. *European Patent Office Reporter,* 19.

Kyodo News International, Inc., Japan Computer Industry Scan. 1993. "IBM Files Suit against Kyocera over Computer Patent." 8 February.

Lasercomb Am. v. Reynolds, 911 F. 2d 970 (4th Cir. 1990).

Law No. 62 of 1985, "Chusakukenho, no ichibu o kaiseisuru horitsu" (Law amending in part the Copyright Law).

League for Programming Freedom. 1990. "Software Patents: Is This the Future of Programming?" *Dr. Dobb's Journal* (November): 56.

Lesser, W., and R. Masson. 1986. *An Economic Analysis of the Plant Variety Protection Act.* Washington, D.C.: American Seed Trade Association.

"Let the Hackers Hack: Allowing the Reverse Engineering of Computer Programs to Achieve Compatibility." 1992. *University of Pennsylvania Law Review* 140: 1999.

Levin, R., and P. Reiss. 1984. "Tests of a Schumpeterian Model of R&D and Market Structure." In Z. Griliches, ed., *R&D, Patents, and Productivity.* Chicago: University of Chicago Press.

———. 1988. "Cost-reducing and Demand-creating R&D with Spillovers." *Rand Journal of Economics* 19:538.

Levin, R. C., A. Klevorick, R. R. Nelson, and S. G. Winter. 1987. "Appropriating the Returns from Industrial Research and Development." *Brookings Paper on Economic Activity* 1987: 783.

Lotus Development Corp. v. Borland Int'l, Inc., 788 F. Supp. 78 (D. Mass. 1992).

Lotus Development Corp. v. Paperback Software Int'l, 740 F. Supp. 37 (D. Mass. 1990), rev'd 34 U.S.P.Q. 2d 1014, 1022 (1st Cir. 1995).

Lucas, A. 1991. "Copyright in the European Community: The Green Paper and the Proposal for a Directive Concerning Legal Protection of Computer Programs." *Columbia Journal of Transnational Law* 29: 145.

Markham, J. 1974. "Concentration: A Stimulus or Retardant to Innovation?" In H. J. Goldschmid, M. H. Mann, and J. F. Weston, eds., *Industrial Concentration: The New Learning.* Boston: Little Brown.

Massachusetts Computer Software Council, Inc. 1991. *Software Industry Business Practices Survey.*

Meijboom, A. P. 1990. "Software Protection in 'Europe 1992.' " *Rutgers Computer & Technology Law Journal* 16: 407.

Menell, P. S. 1989. "An Analysis of the Scope of Copyright Protection for Application Programs." *Stanford Law Review* 41:1045.

Merges, R. 1992. *Patent Law and Policy: Cases and Materials.* Charlottesville, Va.: Michie.

Merges, R., and R. Nelson. 1990. "On the Complex Economics of Patent Scope." Columbia Law Review 90: 839.

Mitchell Bros. Film Group v. Cinema Adult Theater, 604 F. 2d 852 (5th Cir. 1979), cert. denied, 445 U.S. 917, 100 S. Ct. 1277, 63 L. Ed. 2d 601 (1980).

Mowery, D. 1983. "The Relationship between Intrafirm and Contractual Forms of Industrial Research in American Manufacturing, 1900–1940." *Explorations in Economic History* 20: 351.

Mowery, D. C., and N. Rosenberg. 1991. *Technology and the Pursuit of Economic Growth.* Cambridge, Eng.: Cambridge University Press.

Mueller, D. C., and J. E. Tilton. 1969. "Research and Development Costs as a Barrier to Entry." *Canadian Journal of Economics* 2: 570.

Nakajima, T. 1988. "Legal Protection of Computer Programs in Japan." *Columbia Journal of Transnational Law* 27: 143.

Nelson, R., and E. Wolff. 1992. "Factors behind Cross-Industry Differences in Technical Progress." Duplicated.

Nikkei Weekly. 1991. "Patent Office to Alter Rules on Software, Biotechnology." 1 June, 3.

Ordover, J. 1991. "A Patent System for Both Diffusion and Exclusion." *Journal of Economic Perspectives* 5: 43.

Organization for Economic Cooperation and Development. 1992. *Information Technology Outlook 1992.* Paris: OECD.

Pacific Northwest Executive. 1990. "Computer Software: An Infant Industry Becomes a Regional Leader." January, 9.

Palmer, A. K., and T. C. Vinje. 1992. "The EC Directive on the Legal Protection of Computer Software: New Law Governing Software Development." *Duke Journal of Comparative and International Law* 2: 65.

Patent, Trademark and Copyright Journal (BNA). 1991. "Justice Department Consent Order on Borland/Ashton-Tate Merger." 7 November, 14.

————. 1992. "ABA Takes Stand against CAFC Practice of Vacating Invalidity Rulings as Moot." 3 September, 458.

Patent World. 1993. "A Stac of Complaints Filed against Microsoft." March, 16.

Payraudeau, C. 1989. "Recent Decisions of the EPO Technical Boards of Appeal." *International Review of Industrial Property and Copyright Law* 20: 362.

Prusa, T. J., and J. A. Schmitz. 1991. "Are New Firms an Important Source of Innovation?" *Economic Letters* 35: 339.

Rosegrant, S., and D. Lampe. 1992. *Route 128: Lessons from Boston's High-Tech Community.* New York: Basic Books.

Rosen, Richard J. 1991. "Research and Development with Asymmetric Firm Sizes." *Rand Journal of Economics* 22: 411.

Rushing, F. W., and C. G. Brown, eds. 1990. "Introduction." In *Intellectual Property Rights in Science, Technology and Economic Performance: International Comparisons.* Boulder, Colo.: Westview Press.

Samuelson, P. 1990. *"Benson* Revisited: The Case against Patent Protection for Algorithms and Other Computer Program-Related Inventions." *Emory Law Journal* 39: 1025.

Saxenian, A. 1992. "Technomiracles Revisited" (Book Review). *Science,* 23 October, 674.

Schwartz, E. 1992. "Two Heavyweights Go Toe-to-Toe." *Business Week,* 23 November.

Sega Entertainment, Ltd. v. Accolade, Inc., 61 U.S.L.W. 2254 (9th Cir. 1992).

Simon, J. 1989. "Software Firms See Blue Skies in Future." *Boston Globe,* 15 August, 33.

Sivula, C. 1990. "Mass. Miracle Goes Soft." *Datamation,* 1 August.

Styrcula, K. A. 1991. "The Adequacy of Copyright Protection for Computer Software in the European Community 1992: A Critical Analysis of the EC's Draft Directive." *Jurimetrics Journal* 31: 329.

Suarez F., and J. Utterback. 1991. "Dominant Designs and the Survival of Firms." Working Paper No. 42–91, Sloan School of Management, MIT.

Supermarket of Homes v. San Fernando Valley Board of Realtors, 786 F. 2d 1400 (9th Cir. 1986).

System Science K.K. v. Toyo Sokuki K.K. 1989 (Tokyo High Court, 20 June).

Takaishi, 1986. "The Perspectives from Japan on Software Protection." *Software Law Journal* 1: 187.

Teece, D. J. 1986. "Profiting from Technological Innovation: Implications for Integration, Collaboration, and Public Policy." *Research Policy* 15: 285.

Tito, S. 1991. "Microsoft, Borland, Symantec Increase Work Forces." *Computer Reseller News,* 21 January.

United States v. Loew's, Inc., 371 U.S. 38, 83 S. Ct. 97, 9 L. Ed. 2d 11 (1962).

United States v. Paramount Pictures, 334 U.S. 131, 68 S. Ct. 915, 92 L.Ed. 1260 (1948).

United Tel. Co. v. Johnson Publishing Co., 855 F. 2d 604 (8th Cir. 1988).

U.S. Congress, Office of Technology Assessment. 1987. *International Competition in Services: Banking, Building, Software, Know-How.* Washington, D.C.: U.S. Government Printing Office.

U.S. Department of Commerce. 1991. *1987 Census of Service Industries, Subject Series, Miscellaneous Subjects,* Vol. 4. Washington, D.C.: U.S. Government Printing Office.

Utterback, J. and F. Suarez. 1991. "Innovation, Competition, and Industry Structure." Working Paper No. 29–90, Sloan School of Management, MIT.

Vandenberg, J. D. 1991. "The Truth about Patent Litigation for Patent Owners Contemplating Suit." *Journal of the Patent & Trademark Office Society* 73: 301.

Verity, J. 1992. "Deconstructing the Computer Industry." *Business Week,* 23 November, 90.

Vicom. 1987. Case No. T208/84. *Euoropean Patent Office Reporter* 2: 74.

Welch, J., and W. Anderson. 1991. "Copyright Protection for Computer Software in Japan." *Computer/Law Journal* 11: 287.

Whelan Associates, Inc. v. Jaslow Dental Laboratory, Inc., 797 F. 2d 1222 (3d Cir. 1986), cert. denied, 479 U.S. 1031 (1987).

Whit, M. 1994. "Microsoft Must Pay $120 Million: Jury Finds Patent Violation." *Legal Intelligencer,* 25 February, 11.

Wise, R. 1990. "A Good Merger Is Getting Hard to Find." *Electronic Business* 16: 42.

Wood, P. 1991. "Software Overtaking Hardware in Importance." *Industry Surveys,* 17 October, C96.

Yamamoto, K., and D. G. Conlin. 1979. "Guidelines of the Japanese Patent Office for the Examination of an Invention Related to a Computer Program." *Patent and Trademark Review* 77: 195.

11

Conclusion

David C. Mowery

The computer software industry is a large and rapidly growing industry throughout the industrial world. It produces an enabling technology that affects manufacturing firms' commercialization of new products in a growing array of industries. The availability of software with greater flexibility and ease of use also influences the pace of adoption of information technologies and thereby affects the realization of the productivity gains associated with this technology. Indeed, the very pervasiveness of its products makes it difficult to discuss "the computer software industry" as a discrete entity. As many of the chapters in this volume explain, because software is produced by users, manufacturers of hardware, specialized providers of computer services, government agencies, and independent vendors, it is difficult to define the industry's boundaries. Like biotechnology, software is applied in a rapidly expanding number of industrial sectors and settings. Unlike biotechnology, software is created by a heterogeneous array of institutions, a point to which I will return.

But this book is about more than software; indeed, the purely technical details of advances in software are of secondary importance in most of the preceding chapters. Instead, they address the development of this "industry" in specific national and regional settings, analyzing the interactions among technology, industrial organization, and the institutional environment. Although the technological constraints and possibilities created by software technology and its hardware complements give rise to similarities in the evolution of national and regional industry complexes, institutional details matter a great deal, and condition the evolution and competitive strength of this industry in each of the geographic areas discussed. Accordingly, in this concluding chapter I discuss the common elements among the software industries described in the preceding chapters, many of which distinguish software from other postwar high-technology sectors. In doing so, however, I also examine the ways in which these common factors have operated differently in different "national innovation systems."

COMMON THEMES

A number of themes common to all of these national and regional software industries suggest how the software industry resembles and differs from other high-technology industries of the postwar era. One similarity between the software industry and other "new" postwar industries is the pervasive role of government in its development. Because of the close links between software and the computer hardware industry, seen by many postwar governments as an important component of a defense industrial base, from its inception, the software industry benefited from defense-related R&D funding and procurement. As in other postwar high-technology industries, the scale and structure of policies of the U.S. Department of Defense differed from those of other industrial governments and seem to have had stronger effects on the competitiveness of the U.S. commercial industry. The effects of defense-related R&D and procurement spending were influenced by two characteristics of these expenditures: (1) military demand for software, which accounted for a substantial share of industry revenues and required very different product characteristics than those of commercial software; and (2) defense-related R&D funding, which supported an extensive academic research enterprise. In both of these respects, U.S. defense-related expenditures in software differ from those of other postwar high-technology industries.

Other postwar governments, including those of Great Britain and the Soviet Union, were also concerned with the development of a strong computer industry for national security reasons, but supported their domestic hardware and software industries through very different channels. Their policies were less closely coupled to fundamental, "generic" research and education or to commercial firms, and they yielded fewer spillovers from defense to civilian applications.

Governments in Western Europe and Japan also began providing extensive funding for civilian software development programs in the 1980s. Thus far, however, the economic effects of these programs have been modest. Surprisingly, the defense-oriented "industrial policy" of the postwar U.S. government, which included substantial public funding of basic computer science research in universities, has been more successful in establishing a strong domestic industry than the civilian "strategic technology" programs of other governments. The record of success of Japanese government programs in the microelectronics and computer hardware industries, for example, is not matched by comparable results in Japan's software industry—indeed, the very success of Japan's hardware manufacturers seems to have undercut the growth of a Japanese "standard" software industry.

Another important arena for government policy in the software industry is intellectual property rights, discussed in chapter 10. As Romer (1993) points out, the software industry is characterized by high fixed costs and relatively "nonrivalrous" output (the information-intensive nature of software means that its exploitation by a number of parties does not degrade its quality, in contrast to use of a piece of grazing land, for example), and strong intellectual property rights create significant monopoly power. On the other hand, the history of the Russian and Japanese software industries suggests that weak or nonexistent intellectual property protection can also limit entry into the industry.

The importance of intellectual property rights in software has increased greatly since 1980, as the growth of mass markets for software has increased the value of property rights in software in Japan, the United States, and Western Europe has also begun to press against the limits of existing patent and copyright statute and interpretation. Technological advance in software often has a cumulative character: one generation of product technologies relies on the previous generation, and strong technological complementarities link different software programs. Tight protection of prior generations of art therefore may slow technological advance on a broad front (see Merges and Nelson 1990). As chapter 10 notes, this concern motivated the European Union's efforts to define acceptable forms of reverse engineering of protected software programs. Efforts to apply intellectual property rights in computer software already have impinged on competition policy, and they will likely continue to do so; the U.S. government's recent policy toward mergers in this industry and its antitrust suit against Microsoft are examples (see Zachary 1994a, 1994b, among other accounts).

The software intellectual property rights regimes that have emerged from legislative debates and court battles in Japan, the United States, and Western Europe are partly endogenous. Industry political action and legislators' perceptions of national economic interest have produced intellectual property regimes that serve the dominant economic interests within the software industries in each region—in some cases, these are independent software vendors, and in others, they may be subsidiaries of computer manufacturers or even users of software. Intellectual property rights thus need not be external influences on industry evolution, but are themselves affected by the path of industry development. The endogenous character of national or regional intellectual property rights regimes is hardly surprising. But because this endogeneity surely extends to many of the other institutional components of national innovation systems, analyses of their evolution and effects on industry must adopt a more nuanced and complex view of causes and effects. Among other things, this endogeneity means that the historical evolution of industries and national innovation systems is a path-dependent process.

Government policy has affected the role of universities in the software industry in several of the economies discussed in this volume. The role of universities as performers of software-related research and as producers of skilled personnel is an important theme in many of the chapters. The legitimation of computer science as an academic discipline in U.S. universities, for example, received a substantial boost from the funding commitments of the Advanced Research Projects Agency and the National Science Foundation during the 1960s. The response of U.S. universities to external interest (and external research support) in reorganizing their departments, creating new departments, and adding new components to existing departments of electrical engineering is not unique to computer software but has ample historical precedent (Rosenberg and Nelson 1994).

The organizational and disciplinary flexibility of U.S. universities in computer science has not been matched in many of the other economies examined in this volume. This difference is important, because university-based computer science research activities have proven to be important sources of innovations that have spawned new products and firms in the United States. In addition, university-based research has played an important indirect role, through its training of skilled personnel and the transfer of university research findings into industry through the movement of university graduates into employment in computer hardware and software firms. Throughout Western Europe and Japan, as chapters 5–8 emphasize, shortages of skilled personnel have been a serious impediment to the development of domestic software industries.

The interaction between emergent hardware and software industries is discussed in all of the book's chapters. Some segments of the traded computer software industry exhibit powerful "first mover advantages," the competitive effects of which are intensified by international flows of trade, investment, and technology. For example, first movers in the U.S. packaged software industry now dominate the Western European software market for operating systems and tools. U.S. dominance of the Western European software industry was facilitated by the lack of a competing hardware platform developed by Western European firms. Western European firms have remained strong, however, in custom software solutions and packaged applications that rely on close contacts between users and suppliers of software. A comparison of the U.S. and Western European computer software industries, then, suggests that (especially in standard software) a strong domestic hardware industry is necessary to support the growth of a strong domestic software industry. Indeed, both chapter 7 and chapter 8 reach this conclusion.

A comparison of the U.S. and Japanese software industries, however, suggests significant qualifications to this conclusion. Japan's computer industry remains strong, but its strength in computer hardware has not been translated into strength in traded software. In January 1993, Japan's Ministry of International Trade and Industry designated the software industry as a "distressed industry," qualifying software firms for subsidies to cover the costs of employee retraining or transfer to other divisions of the firms (Nakahara 1993). Japan's internationally competitive computer hardware industry spawned the development of several competing architectures in mainframes, minicomputers, and microcomputers, which has retarded the growth of a domestic packaged software industry. As chapter 6 points out, the lack of a "dominant design" in desktop computer hardware has discouraged entry by independent software firms focusing on the development of standard applications. The Japanese government's failure to reduce such fragmentation in the architectural environment is surprising, in view of the substantial powers of "administrative guidance" that its central government agencies have wielded in other high-technology industries in earlier eras. As in Western Europe, Japan's domestic software industry is strongest in the development of custom software solutions (by hardware manufacturers and independent firms) that rely on close familiarity with user needs.

If U.S. producers of hardware (for example, Compaq, Sun Microsystems, Apple) establish a strong position in Japan's domestic workstation and microcomputer market, the architectural fragmentation in these segments of the hardware environment will be reduced, benefiting independent Japanese software vendors. But the interaction between hardware and software that is implied by such a development is in fact the opposite of that originally hypothesized—the entry of foreign hardware producers in this case could support the growth of domestic producers of packaged software.

The interaction between domestic hardware and software producers that has influenced the development of the U.S., Japanese, and Western European computer software industries thus appears to vary significantly among segments of both the hardware and software industries. The economic importance of strong links between hardware and software developers also has changed over time, illustrating the path-dependent character of this industry's development. U.S. software producers almost certainly derived competitive advantages from their links with the dominant global producers of computer hardware in the early development of mainframe, minicomputer, and desktop systems. But the beneficial effects of these links now are weaker, at least in applications. The rapid development of networking software in the United States, however, may benefit from close proximity to manufactures of hardware (such as network servers) and certainly relies on close interaction with the large population of sophisticated and demanding users. The rapid growth in use of the U.S.-based Internet also suppports expansion of domestic producers of network software.

Vertical "dis-integration" of hardware and software, especially hardware and applications software, will remain common in the traded software industry. As a result, developers of many new hardware products must develop strategies to attract independent software developers to their architecture, creating "bandwagons" of software developers to exploit network externalities. The competition among RISC architectures, discussed in chapter 4, is a good example of these strategies in action. The strategies of technology commercialization followed by competitors in this environment differ in important ways from the prescriptions of classic analyses of commercialization strategy (Teece 1986; Abernathy and Utterback 1978). Among other things, their strategies must resolve the dilemma between protection and disclosure of firm-specific intellectual property.

The importance of software bandwagons increases as one moves from mainframes to microcomputers, reflecting the fact that microcomputers are sold to a large market of users who are far less sophisticated than operators of mainframe computers. As the number of users of desktop systems expands, the demand for standardized solutions to a broader array of nonstandard applications grows, and extensive libraries of standard software for a specific architecture become more important. These bandwagon effects thus far appear to be more important in microcomputers than in workstations, because workstations have yet to penetrate the less sophisticated user market (see chapter 4).

The strategic importance of software bandwagons for technology commercialization may decline somewhat if software becomes genuinely independent of hardware architectures in desktop and other systems. In microcomputers and workstations, the diffusion of which has spurred rapid growth in the standard software market, "open systems" now are becoming popular. "Open systems" architecture, which enables an operating system and its related applications to run on any one of a diverse array of hardware platforms, should weaken any requirement for links between the developers of such hardware and those developing standard software for these systems, and may reduce the burden on would-be commercializers of new hardware technologies to attract a significant following of software developers.

Nevertheless, because advances in microelectronics and computing hardware have been so rapid, new classes of computing devices (such as wireless "portable digital assistants" (PDAs) and new forms of multimedia) and applications (networking) will appear that are not compatible with any of the "dominant designs" in desktop workstations or computers (*Economist* 1994) and are not "open systems."

These new classes, especially networking, will create opportunities for software-based bandwagons and, possibly, for the development of new "standard" operating systems and applications. In effect, the growth of networks of desktop computers creates an opportunity for a challenger to unseat Microsoft as the dominant firm in operating systems, mainly by redefining the functions of operating systems software to include communication and greater multiuser capabilities. Although the firms that dominate desktop software markets will resist it, these new products will create considerable opportunities for entry by new independent software vendors and even the development of software by major hardware vendors. In the longer term, however, these hardware products themselves will likely move to an "open systems" architecture, which will erode the advantages of vertical integration by hardware vendors into the development of packaged operating system or applications software for their products.

In the early years of the industry, the production of computer software was dominated by users and producers of computer hardware. These software suppliers were gradually joined by other entities. In some economies, sophisticated users such as steel firms and financial institutions "spun off" firms that became important providers of software and services, while elsewhere, new firms were established to provide these services. If one adopts a broad definition of the software industry, including more than just traded software, it is clear that the software industries of the United States, Western Europe, and Japan all use an array of coexisting approaches to the division of labor. No single system for software development and production (such as in-house production by hardware manufacturers) dominates any of these industries; instead, new forms of the division of labor supplement previous structures (this point is emphasized in chapter 2). The relative importance of different structures of the division of labor varies in the United States, Japan, and Western Europe, but in all three areas a mix of structures exists.

This coexistence is attributable in part to the large installed base of older hardware with highly specialized applications and operating system software. As Bresnahan and Greenstein (1994) argue, the switching costs associated with abandoning older systems are high, and they often exceed the capital costs of replacement. Organizational routines and policies have literally grown up around these systems, and revising them is extraordinarily costly, especially for large "back-office" operations in commercial databases, for example. These high adjustment costs create opportunities for software sales by the original manufacturers and often sustain large internal efforts by users to develop and maintain complex programs. They also have supported demand for firms that provide both services and software, which can develop integrated solutions that use different computer platforms, operating systems, and applications software.

Another influence on the development of industry structure is the technology of software production. The "software factories" of Japan's mainframe computer manufacturers (Cusumano 1991), which have elaborated and extended some techniques originally employed by U.S. firms in large programming projects for the U.S. military, use an approach to software development and production that differs from that of many U.S. and Western European independent commercial software vendors. These software factories decompose small components of code that are produced by a large workforce of relatively unskilled software engineers. Their techniques include extensive reuse of high-quality code, which might support significant economies of scale or scope. Their exploitation by larger firms or computer manufacturers could increase the competitive advantages associated with vertical integration of software and hardware production.

But thus far, these advantages have not led to the extensive use of software-factory techniques by non-Japanese firms (other than those developing software for military applications). The factory approach appears to be best suited to the production of large custom programs for mainframe computers, and it has not significantly enhanced the international competitiveness of Japanese producers of standard software. Developers of complex packaged operating systems software (such as Microsoft) employ formal project management techniques (Smith and Cusumano 1993), but the constraints on innovation and technical advance imposed by the "productivity bottleneck" in software development have been reduced by the development of standard hardware platforms. Competitive success in the fastest-growing segment of the software industry now hinges on the rapid development of new packaged products (early versions of which often have significant defects for a large installed base of essentially identical computing platforms). Other new techniques, such as "object-oriented" programming (which enables programs to be written in modular form), also may change the organization of software production, with uncertain consequences for industry structure.

It is worth noting briefly that the importance of these user-producer links in the software industry, as well as the limited effectiveness thus far of "factory models" for software production, are likely to limit the potential for offshore production of software. (Yourdon [1992] regards such offshore software production as a threat to U.S. software industry employees.) Although European and U.S. firms have developed substantial software production operations in low-cost economies such as India, these are most effective for the creation of the many lines of code needed for large, complex, custom programs. But offshore production does not provide the proximity to users that short development cycles, rapid prototyping, and high responsiveness to user needs require. Offshore production of software thus may expand, but it will affect the segments of the software industry that are growing much more slowly than packaged software.

DO NATIONAL INNOVATION SYSTEMS MATTER
IN THE SOFTWARE INDUSTRY?

Does the "snapshot" of industry structure presented in each chapter represent a different stage of a common evolutionary path that is similar across all of these regions, or will different trajectories of industry development endure? Put somewhat differently, are industry-specific or region-specific characteristics more influential in industry evolution? The data in chapter 1 suggest some convergence, especially between the United States and Western Europe, in the structure of demand for software. As was noted earlier, first-mover advantages in some segments of the traded software industry are powerful enough, and the level of international interaction high enough, that U.S. firms are likely to dominate much of the packaged software market in all three markets. But this dominance may not extend to applications, because of strong national and regional differences in user needs. Moreover, the gradual standardization of desktop and other small-scale computer systems around a small number of dominant architectures may support greater entry by non-U.S. firms into the development of packaged applications software.

There are strong reasons to expect international differences in industry structure to endure. Among the most important, discussed above, are the international differences in the installed base of computer hardware. Because the costs of switching between fundamentally different approaches to computing services within an organization are so high (for example, moving from a centralized mainframe computer to a network of desktop machines linked through a central "server"), adoption of new architectures will occur gradually, rather than rapidly. And because much of the installed base of computers in Japan and Europe is of domestic origin, substantial country-specific niches will remain for software vendors, both independents and vertically integrated units of manufacturers. But growth in these niches will be modest at best; the appearance of new opportunities for entry depends on the development of new applications or the adoption of new hardware platforms.

A related influence that will preserve international differences is the importance of close user-producer links and interaction in software development, especially custom software for specialized applications. The market data discussed in chapter 1 illustrate the importance of these links, and the custom software and even the applications segment of the packaged software industries appear likely to provide country-specific niches for entrants and incumbents.

The development of the U.S. and Japanese software industries exhibits some of the same contrasts associated with other postwar high-technology industries: new firms are very prominent in the U.S. software industry, and established producers (especially mainframe computer manufacturers) remain far more important in Japan. National financial systems and intellectual property rights regimes clearly underlie much of the U.S.-Japanese contrast.

The Western European traded software industry, however, occupies something of a middle ground between the extremes represented by the U.S. and Japanese industries. Although there have been fewer new entrants in Western Europe than in the United States, the weakness of European computer manufacturers has prevented their software subsidiaries from developing strength in domestic markets comparable to that of the Japanese computer vendors' software subsidiaries. The emerging Russian software industry also is populated by numerous new firms, many of which are joint ventures with European and U.S. software firms.

Other "national" influences have also been extremely powerful in the industry, partly because of its low physical capital–intensity and high human capital–intensity. Thus, different domestic systems of higher education develop links with industry- and government-funded research that vary in strength and structure; those in the United States appear to be much stronger than those in Western Europe, Russia, or Japan. The structure of domestic higher education systems also affects the linkages within them between research and training of qualified scientists and engineers. These differences have had significant consequences for the development of national or regional software industries. The domestic intellectual property rights regime of the United States, which also has given greater protection to software developers than those of Russia or Japan, also has tended to favor the growth of a domestic packaged software industry. The far larger installed base of desktop computers in the United States relative to Russia or Japan has given further impetus to the growth of these firms.

The effects of national "competition policy" have yet to be felt. Postwar U.S. antitrust policy has been considerably more stringent than that of Japan or most Western European economies. Indeed, one reason for the importance of new, small firms in the postwar U.S. semiconductor and computer industries was domestic antitrust policy (Mowery 1994). During the 1980s, however, the United States relaxed its antitrust policy, especially in sectors with strong R&D and strong foreign competition, and owners of intellectual property rights benefited from a more benign judicial attitude (see chapter 10). But at least some more recent actions of the U.S. Department of Justice suggest that the competitive effects of intellectual property rights in software are being scrutinized carefully (as in the acquisition of Ashton-Tate by Borland, discussed in chapter 10). The 1994 antitrust investigation of Microsoft concluded with the negotiation of a modest consent decree that is likely to have only minor implications for the firm's future competitive position (see Zachary 1994a, b). Nevertheless, the investigation and its sequelae have influenced Microsoft's subsequent behavior. The Justice Department's 1995 opposition to Microsoft's acquisition of Intuit forced the termination of that transaction, and antitrust scrutiny of Microsoft is likely to remain intense. The theoretical basis for competition policy in the software industry is underdeveloped, to put it mildly, and the implications of these actions by U.S. antitrust authorities for the future development of the U.S. industry remain unclear. Simultaneously, the emerging EU policies toward market power and intellectual property rights seem to be moving somewhat closer to the revised policies of the U.S. government. Indeed, one of the most novel aspects of the Microsoft antitrust investigation and settlement was the close coordination between EU and U.S. Justice Department antitrust authorities (Novak 1994), in a tacit acknowledgment of the growing similarities in their enforcement philosophies.

The analysis of "national innovation systems" has made important contributions to our understanding of innovation, industry evolution, and policy, but its conclusions have been framed at a high level of aggregation. By focusing more narrowly on a single industry, the contributors to this volume have sought to clarify the technological and strategic influences that are unique to this industry as well as to highlight the institutional and policy differences among nations and regions. This should enable the reader to separate industry-specific from country-specific influences and to better understand how industry development influences, and is influenced by, institutional and policy factors. Extended to encompass additional industries, this analysis has considerable potential for revealing more about the role of national innovation systems in modern industrial evolution and competitiveness.

But this volume has made other contributions as well. As chapter 1 noted, the software industry has received surprisingly little attention, given its size, rapid growth, and apparent importance to the development of a broadening array of high-technology industries. These chapters have begun investigations that will continue into the foreseeable future, although a definitive analysis of the industry requires far more comprehensive and internationally comparable data. Like the industry itself, the stylized facts in these chapters will themselves be revised and updated, as other scholars join in the analysis. This "research bandwagon" should improve our understanding of this complex and dynamic industry.

REFERENCES

Abernathy, W. J., and J. M. Utterback. 1978."Patterns of Industrial Innovation." *Technology Review* 80 (June/July): 40–47.

Boehm, B. W., T. E. Gray, and T. Seewald.1984. "Prototyping versus Specifying: A Multiproject Experiment." *IEEE Transactions on Software Engineering* 10: 290–303.

Bresnahan, T. F., and S. Greenstein. 1994. "The Competitive Crash in Large-Scale Commercial Computing." Presented at the conference "Growth and Development: The Economics of the 21st Century," Center for Economic Policy Research, Stanford University, June 3–4.

Cusumano, M. 1991. *Japan's Software Factories.* New York: Oxford University Press.

Economist. 1994. "Computers Cut the Cord." 14 May, 71–72.

Merges, R. P., and R. R. Nelson. 1990. "On the Complex Economics of Patent Scope." *Columbia Law Review* 90:839.

Mowery, David C. 1994. *Science and Technology Policy in Interdependent Economies.* Boston: Kluwer Academic Publishers.

Nakahara, T. 1993. "The Industrial Organization and Information Structure of the Software Industry: A U.S.-Japan Comparison." Center for Economic Policy Research, Stanford University, May. Duplicated.

Nelson, R. R. 1993. *National Innovation Systems: A Comparative Analysis.* New York: Oxford University Press.

Novak, V. 1994. "Antitrust's Bingaman Talks Tough on Microsoft Case." *Wall Street Journal,* 19 July, B1.

Organization for Economic Cooperation and Development (OECD). 1985. *Software: An Emerging Industry.* Paris: OECD.

———. 1989. *The Internationalisation of Software and Computer Services.* Paris: OECD.

Romer, P. M. 1993. "Implementing a National Technology Strategy with Self-Organizing Industry Investment Boards." *Brookings Papers on Economic Activity,* 345–99.

Rosenberg, Nathan, and Richard R. Nelson. 1994. "American Universities and Technical Advance in Industry." *Research Policy* 23, 323–48.

Smith, S. A., and M. Cusumano. 1993. "Beyond the Software Factory: A Comparison of 'Classic' and PC Software Developers." Sloan School of Management Working Paper no. 3607-93, Massachusetts Institute of Technology.

Swann, P., and J. Gill. 1993. *Corporate Vision and Rapid Technological Change.* London: Routledge.

Teece, D. J. 1986. "Profiting from Technological Innovation: Implications for Integration, Collaboration, Licensing, and Public Policy." *Research Policy* 15: 285–305.

Yourdon, E. 1992. *Decline and Fall of the American Programmer.* Englewood Cliffs, N.J.: Prentice-Hall.

Zachary, G. P. 1994a. "Microsoft Aides to Be Deposed in U.S. Probe." *Wall Street Journal,* 6 June, A3.

———. 1994b. "Microsoft Will Remain Dominant Despite Pact in Antitrust Dispute." *Wall Street Journal,* 18 July, A1.

Index